PARIS, THE PROVINCES AND THE FRENCH REVOLUTION

PARIS, THE PROVINCES AND THE FRENCH REVOLUTION

ALAN FORREST

Professor of History,
University of York

A member of the Hodder Headline Group
LONDON

Distributed in the United States of America by
Oxford University Press Inc., New York

First published in Great Britain in 2004 by
Arnold, a member of the Hodder Headline Group,
338 Euston Road, London NW1 3BH

http://www.arnoldpublishers.com

Distributed in the United States of America by
Oxford University Press Inc.
198 Madison Avenue, New York, NY10016

British Library Cataloguing in Publication Data
A catalogue record for this book is available from the British Library

Library of Congress Cataloging-in-Publication Data
A catalog record for this book is available from the Library of Congress

ISBN 0 340 56434 2

1 2 3 4 5 6 7 8 9 10

Typeset in 10pt Sabon by Charon Tec Pvt. Ltd, Chennai, India
Printed and bound in Great Britain by The Bath Press, Bath

What do you think about this book? Or any other Arnold title?
Please send your comments to feedback.arnold@hodder.co.uk

Contents

The departments of France in 1790

Preface

Provincial identity was strong in *ancien régime* France, even in regions of
the country where the institutions that had given shape to that identity –
most notably the provincial assemblies and estates – had declined or had
been allowed to atrophy. In spite of the best efforts of a centralizing monarchy, the nation state was still in the process of formation, and many people
continued to see themselves as Bretons or Burgundians before they were
French, looking to their local *parlements* to dispense justice and to defend
their interests against the incursions of royal power, especially in moments
of political crisis. The rapid growth of nationalist sentiment, however, and
its incorporation after 1789 into the ideology of the French Revolution
posed a real threat to these traditional loyalties and produced a political culture in which one's identity as a Frenchman occupied a pivotal role. Paris
was now the centre of the nation and, increasingly, of the Revolution, a city
whose patriotism and civic virtue were held out as an example to others. At
the same time Paris had developed a less welcome reputation for violence
and bloodletting which many regarded with horror, especially once the
September Massacres demonstrated the inability of the national government to curb the excesses of the Paris streets or what they saw as the
overblown ambitions of its sectional militants.

   The often tangled relations between Paris and provincial France during
the French Revolution are the subject-matter of the present book. They
could never be straightforward. Much depended on the nature of local elites
and the fate of the local economy as economic privileges were abolished and
as the war – both on the Continent and in the colonies – brought contrasting threats and opportunities. Much depended, too, on the character of revolutionary politics at local level, on the strength of Jacobin activity and the
impact of local militants. Laws passed at the centre had wildly different
impacts on different regions of the country – on provincial cities and Atlantic
ports, on peasant economies of the interior, on frontier zones overrun by
soldiers or affected by heavy emigration, on areas of devout Catholicism
whose traditional religious practices were undermined, above all, perhaps,
on those regions like Brittany, the West and parts of Languedoc which found

themselves in the throes of counter-revolution and open insurrection. For that reason it is difficult to talk of the 'provinces' as if they constituted a single entity. The idea of *la province*, of a France distinct from and often opposed to, Paris, would be a nineteenth-century invention. But, like so many of France's political traditions in the nineteenth century, it had at least some roots in the French Revolution.

My purpose in writing this book is not to present a survey of the Revolution in the provinces. Rather it is to show that provincial history cannot be understood in a vacuum, and that there was continually and unavoidably tension between what local people expected and what Paris tried to impose. This is a book about the relationship between Paris and provincial France, between centre and periphery, in a period marked by ideological struggle and administrative obduracy. For its preparation I worked in the archives of a number of towns and departments, where I found the archivists, as always, unfailingly helpful. I also incurred numerous intellectual debts which it is a pleasure to acknowledge. My original interest in the subject was kindled by Richard Cobb, who despatched a generation of Oxford research students, myself included, to the archives of *la France profonde*, where we learned the important lesson that, even at the height of the Terror, there were limits to the control that Paris could exercise and even greater limits to the loyalty it could attract. His influence is clear throughout the present work. Colin Lucas, Peter Jones, Malcolm Crook, Michael Broers, Bill Scott, John Merriman, Paul Hanson, Peter McPhee and Isser Woloch have all dealt in their different ways with the interface between local culture and government centralism, and I have greatly benefited from discussions with them all. In France I presented arguments from this book at colloquia organized by Jean-Pierre Jessenne in Rouen and Jean-Clément Martin in La Roche-sur-Yon, and in England at the Early Modern History Seminar of the Institute of Historical Research, hosted by Roger Mettam. Over the years I have also had the good fortune to supervise a number of excellent graduate students, first in Manchester and more recently in York, on aspects of French provincial history and its wider cultural context. I should like to mention particularly Jonathan Dalby, Jonathan Skinner, Jill Maciak Walshaw, Dave Andress and Matt Shaw, who have all made their own distinctive contributions to French Revolutionary studies, while Godfrey Rogers and Piers Willson wrote excellent theses on provincial France in the nineteenth century. At Arnold I wish to thank those people who kept faith with this project over the years: Christopher Wheeler – now with Blackwell – who first signed up the book and provided such unstinting encouragement; and Christina Wipf Perry and Tiara Misquitta who finally coaxed the manuscript from me and who saw it through its various stages of production. My thanks are due to them all, as, of course, they are to Rosemary and Marianne for their tolerance and good humour during what has been a long-running and at times disruptive enterprise.

|1|

The Revolution and provincial France

Tensions between Paris and the provinces, between centre and periphery, have played an important role throughout French history; and as the pretensions and capacities of the state were extended, the significance of that role could only increase. They were not the creation of the French Revolution, though they were undoubtedly aggravated by some of the underlying assumptions of revolutionary politics. Provincial anger had been directed against the centre in earlier eras in a wide variety of contexts – during the Wars of Religion and the Fronde in the seventeenth century, for instance; in defence of the provincial estates and *parlements* against the policies of Louis XIV; or in the endless attacks on eighteenth-century intendants, perceived as trying to extend royal administrative authority at the expense of provincial institutions and their claims to autonomy. Provincial identity showed itself also in repeated demands for local justice, whether through the maintenance of seigneurial courts or the preference for royal justice to be administered locally rather than at Versailles. Conflicts over custom and provincial liberties took place long before 1789, just as conflicts over levels of taxation or military exactions had their origins well before the outbreak of revolution. In this context the Revolution is best seen as perpetuating a long and honourable tradition of rivalry, accusation and counter-accusation between centre and periphery which has been one of the hallmarks of modern French history.

But the Revolution did not just perpetuate existing tensions; it did much to exacerbate them and to rekindle an image of Paris as a violent, dangerous and predatory city whose ambition placed provincial rights in jeopardy. The revolutionaries were more capable of exercising central power than most previous regimes – even those regimes that had laid claims to rule absolutely could often be shown to depend on the cooperation of local elites, especially in times of war when the provincial estates were crucial to royal financial strategies.[1] In its pursuit of the ideal of citizenship, the Revolution played down local difference and denied provincial liberties that often had their roots in custom or in hard-won concessions from the king. It is not a matter of chance, therefore, that many nineteenth-century regionalists blamed the revolutionaries for undermining the prosperity of provincial France, denouncing their intransigence in pursuing a Jacobin model of centralization that gloried in conformity and emphasized the need for all Frenchmen to be equal before the law and equal in their relationship to the administrative processes of the state. For many in nineteenth-century Brittany or Provence, for those regionalists who took up the study of local dialects and peripheral languages or who helped raise popular awareness of local culture by writing the history of their regions, the Revolution had a particular responsibility for which it would not be forgiven. It was, they argued, the moment when regional identities had been allowed to die, when the centralized state had been identified with the future, with citizenship and ideological virtue, and portrayed as the guarantor of the rights of man. It was, they claimed, the revolutionaries' intolerance of regional difference which transformed the history of modern France into a relentless pursuit of centralization and standardization in which cultural diversity played little part.

There is clearly a degree of truth in these charges, in so far as the republican tradition of the nineteenth and twentieth centuries is deeply embedded in the idea and the language of the 'one and indivisible republic'. But is revolutionary history itself so pronouncedly centralist? Provinces and regional capitals, towns and even villages had their own experiences of the Revolution, demonstrating very different perspectives and priorities. If laws were promulgated centrally and for the whole nation, the ways local communities responded to them, their degree of revolutionary conviction and the prominence in local agendas of issues like religion, anti-seigneurialism and requisitions – to say nothing of popular involvement in political activity through clubs, sections and the electoral process – diverged greatly from one region of the country to another. As the proliferation of local studies of the Revolution shows (many of them published in the wake of the upsurge of enthusiasm that accompanied the bicentenary in 1989), there was no common experience of events, no single timetable of revolution that could be applied throughout France.[2] The provinces did not always follow blindly the lead set down at the centre. Indeed, such an idea ran counter to the practice of eighteenth-century France, where towns and cities were accustomed to enjoy a wide degree of autonomy, where local elites were powerful within their bailiwicks, and where they fostered economic growth and a proliferation of the arts that was often distinctive to themselves. Even villages had experience of administering their own affairs and they showed considerable institutional diversity, reflecting in part contrasting legal codes and very different systems of landholding.[3] Two centuries later, at a moment when the regions of Europe are being encouraged to reclaim their individuality within a European Union in which the legitimacy of the nation state is increasingly being brought into question, it is surely appropriate to look afresh at provincial France and its distinctive contribution to revolutionary history.

Even if the Revolution and Empire were not solely to blame for France's predilection for centralism – and most provincial spokesmen had the grace to admit that part of the responsibility must be laid at the feet of Louis XIV and absolute monarchy – it was generally agreed that the men of 1789 peddled a vision of the nation which greatly expedited the process. The Revolution, after all, deliberately rejected any notion of provincial autonomy and denounced all vestiges of 'federalism', despite the fact that in 1790 it had taken such pride, at the *Fête de la Fédération*, in the image of the regions of France coming together of their own free volition to glory in the new nation. It had, equally deliberately, obliterated the old provincial divisions from the map in an attempt to rid the country of its still emotive cultural loyalties. Yet, even in 1790, we should take care not to misconstrue that pride. The festival was seen as a new beginning, the moment which marked the start of a new era.[4] Sovereignty now lay in the French people, who had been regenerated by the Revolution, their spirits cleansed of former prejudices as they prepared to take their place in a society of free men. Regeneration implied the creation of a new man with the instincts and qualities of a citizen, a new man whose loyalty was to the sovereign people and who saw his salvation in the brotherhood that was the French nation. It followed that for many revolutionaries the very idea of regional loyalties was anathema, a concept which they equated with the maintenance of privilege and with the powerful elites of *ancien régime* society. The provinces were identified with the prestige and patrimony of the local aristocracy, their governance with noble power and provincial elites. Provincial liberties were not to be confused with the rights of man; rather liberties were regarded as local privileges, sought or purchased to advance economic prosperity and stridently defended by powerful interests and corporations in an *ancien régime* which was constructed on corporate identity. As privileges they necessarily posed a threat to the rights of citizens, to economic individualism and to the equality of all before the law, those most central tenets of 1789. From this it followed that they could have no place in the new order which the Revolution set out to create.

It was all too easy, indeed, to identify the French regions with opposition to that new order, with the stubborn defence of privilege and the status quo. It was equally easy, once war had been declared, to identify the Revolution and the nation, and to suggest that in order to be a good citizen or a true revolutionary one necessarily had to be French and identify incontrovertibly with the struggle of the French people. This was what made the position of foreigners so difficult during the Revolution; those who, though they might be resident in France and might sympathize with the revolutionary cause, were reluctant to abandon their allegiance to countries or to sovereigns beyond France's frontier.[5] Their somewhat ambivalent situation raised fundamental questions about the two central concepts of citizenship and nationhood at a time when the ideals of the Revolution were increasingly being identified as specifically French. In a slightly different way, the same questions were raised by those millions of Frenchmen whose day-to-day language was not French but Breton or Catalan or Provençal, who spoke and possibly read in patois, and who felt no reason to abandon their cultural loyalties or merge their proudly nurtured identities. They formed an important minority who tended to congregate around the periphery: German-speakers in Alsace and Lorraine; Flemings in Dunkerque and Hazebrouck; Breton-speakers in large areas of Brittany; Basques in the Soule and Labourd; Catalans in the Roussillon; Corsicans (all of whom spoke separate languages and might understand little or nothing of written French); dialect-speakers like the Occitans in much of the Midi and the South-West; and those speaking a Franco-Provençal dialect in Savoy and Dauphiné.[6] Could such people become full citizens of the Republic or fully fledged members of a French nation state? Could they be won over by a revolution that was conducted in a foreign tongue?[7] Or was it really the case, as Bertrand Barère would maintain, that the only language of the Revolution was French, while others should be regarded as suspect, ambivalent in their attitude to the *patrie*? Before 1792 the revolutionaries had been prepared to be conciliatory and pragmatic in their approach to France's linguistic minorities, to the extent that they had laws published locally in patois, and there was a 'remarkable efflorescence' of the various regional languages.[8] But in Barère's world picture there was little room for compromise. 'Federalism and superstition speak Breton,' he ranted; 'emigration and hatred of the Republic speak German; counter-revolution speaks Italian; and fanaticism speaks Basque'.[9] Indeed, we are forced to ask whether there was some degree of incompatibility between the provincial and the revolutionary, an incompatibility that would prove durable and would help to mould the identity of modern France and especially that of successive French republics.

For those suspicious of the French Revolution and all its rational, humanist antecedents, the equation of provincialism with conservative values was an obvious and comforting one. Amongst the most notable provincial families were many who, fearful of an imposed change from the centre, sought solace in the time-honoured institutions of their province or in the hard-won liberties of their local capital. It was perhaps only natural, in times of turbulence, when change emanated from Paris and was enacted in the name of the nation, that those whose principal interest lay in maintaining rather than transforming the polity should have rejected national politics in favour of a local stage, where their title, wealth or social pre-eminence guaranteed them a modicum of the respect and deference which they regarded as theirs by right. At the provincial level many of them could claim to be the natural leaders of society, their families having provided over the centuries the elites to whom others turned for government, leadership and electoral representation. They were leading landowners at a time when the ownership of land still lay at the heart of fortune and prestige, and landownership was a prerequisite of office. They dominated provincial institutions and had been destined to do so almost from the moment of their birth. They provided the magistrates on the local *parlements*, like the legal and commercial elites who, from generation to generation, had sat on the *Parlement* of Bordeaux and dominated the social life of the city.[10] Theirs were the families from which the upper clergy were drawn, whether the archbishops and bishops of provincial sees or the *abbés* who controlled the great monastic houses, assuming the role of ecclesiastical seigneurs. Where provincial estates still existed, as in Dauphiné and Provence, those same elites would occupy the key offices on bodies that were deeply rooted in the tradition and corporate order of the *ancien régime*.[11] They also filled positions on municipal councils, those closed and unrepresentative authorities which governed the largest provincial cities in the land, like the *Capitouls* of Toulouse or the *Jurade* of Bordeaux, and which carefully guarded municipal traditions and defended established liberties. In 1767, for instance, when the council of Lille staged a public celebration of the city's annexation to France by Louis XIV one hundred years earlier, it dedicated a whole day to celebrating the King's vow to preserve its ancient rights, usages and privileges.[12] At every level provincial government was more and more on the defensive, seeking to protect ancient customs and usages against innovation. None was more conservative than the provincial aristocracy, those who chose to make their mark locally rather than at court or in the king's service. Just as in other European states, whether in the German duchies or in Imperial Russia, to say nothing of the English shires, provincial France provided the old elites with reassurance and a safe haven in times of turbulence, emphasizing their traditional rights and customs, their commercial franchises and their continued freedom from centralized control. In times of stability this passed almost uncontested, since it provided a focus for local interests and offered a counterbalance to the pretensions of royal absolutism. But in a period of revolution that role lost much of its legitimacy.

Since the one thing that united the revolutionaries, at least in the early stages of the Revolution, was their loathing of privilege and their belief that all must stand equal before the law, any identification of provincial France with privilege could only be deeply damaging, building a wall of suspicion between Paris and the regions of France. This was, of course, a suspicion based on expectation, on a preconceived image of the other: for the Parisian, the provinces were only too easily represented by a rich and self-interested farmer or a noble magistrate, eager to preserve what he could of a privileged lifestyle, just as, for the Breton or Lyonnais, Paris assumed the role of capital city and seat of government, bureaucracy and centralized power. Paris might benefit from having been a centre of enlightened ideas and humanism during the later eighteenth century, but it now became identified with a process which showered them with laws and decrees, made financial demands and plunged them into war with all its attendant miseries. In these ways Paris aroused resentments and attracted envious criticism. But that Paris was largely an abstraction, a city which housed the national government and to whose prosperity that government contributed mightily, as well as a city that rapidly acquired added status, claiming to represent the Revolution and civic virtue, and which was widely suspected of benefiting from the sacrifices of others. The criticisms were of *Paris-capitale* rather than of a flesh-and-blood city where people worked, sought entertainment or engaged in politics. Many of those voicing them had never been to Paris the city, never shopped at its markets or breathed in the bustling atmosphere of the docks along the Seine or the workshops of the Faubourg Saint-Antoine. Their reaction was to Paris as a concept rather than to real-life Parisians. Much that was said was based on hearsay and rumour rather than on first-hand experience, and this may explain the lurid language that was often used to depict the characteristics of the other.

The events of the Revolution and the ways in which these events were reported would have a significant impact on these stereotypes. Once Paris had become widely identified with bloodshed and political extremism – the lynchings on 14 July, the massacres at the Champ de Mars and outside the Tuileries, the brutal prison massacres of 1792, the threats of popular violence from the more radical sections, the waves of victims of the Terror and the guillotine – they only became more lurid and more deeply ingrained in the provincial imagination. Under the Republic, in particular, Paris was often depicted as a city running with blood, a community where law and order had broken down and where the city authorities gave in to the forces of extremism and anarchy. The sections and the Paris Commune, it was widely believed, were dominated by wild and bloodthirsty anarchists intent on waging class war against the respectable citizens of the capital. And as the Jacobins came to power, these were the elements which, provincial deputies assured their electors, were now masters of the polity. In Lyon, for instance, the revolt against the Convention in the summer of 1793 was prefaced by wild rumours about the political and moral state of the capital. Paris was reduced to anarchy; Paris was terrorized by violent gangs who suppressed opinion in the Jacobin cause; bread had been dumped in the Seine as part of a plot to incite still further disruption.[13] Many provincials, it would appear, were wont to believe whatever was said about the Parisians, however implausible the claims that were made. But the propaganda was not all one-way. Parisians were equally wont to see themselves as the embodiment of the Republic, as that sovereign people born in 1789 and endowed with new rights, including, they held, the right to insurrection, to use violence to overthrow tyranny. Increasingly they saw themselves as 'the people', whose duty it was to supervise the deputies and maintain constant surveillance over those who governed in their name. In the process Paris gained a new and unique status as the capital of the Revolution, while the provinces became increasingly identified with self-interest and apathy, religious superstition and political reaction.[14] Its political outlook could appear to others as quite unbearably complacent and self-congratulatory, and almost invited a vigorously hostile response from those living beyond the city gates.

But, of course, not all the engagement between the people of Paris and provincial Frenchmen took place on the level of political rhetoric; nor yet was their mutual regard based solely on abstraction. Paris, like other major cities, had been growing rapidly during the eighteenth century, to reach a population of some 650,000 on the eve of the Revolution, more than four times the size of its nearest rival in provincial France, Lyon. This growth had been due not to reproduction – the city had a disproportionately high number of single households and young unmarried workers – but to a steady process of immigration. Often this had its origins in long-standing traditions of seasonal migration, the movement to the city during the winter months constituting an essential element in what Olwen Hufton has termed the 'economy of makeshifts' of the rural poor, a period of forced absence from their own village economy which allowed them to earn small sums of money which, in turn, would allow their families to see out the agricultural year.[15] Migrant workers were a common sight at certain seasons, trudging the highways of France towards their chosen destination – to expanding commercial cities like Marseille, Nantes or Bordeaux, cities capable of providing labouring work through the long winter months, which proved to be powerful magnets for rural labourers and artisans from across whole provinces; to local urban centres like Bourges and Moulins, offering the prospect of clerical charity or of casual jobs to the rural unemployed of their hinterland; to the towns and villages of the plain, where men from poor mountain communes might scratch a livelihood by selling their crudely made pots and pans to local people. Many were attracted by the prospect of work in the building trades, to which those from the countryside found it relatively simple to adapt: Tours, Nancy and Toulouse were all cities which saw a substantial growth and renewal during the eighteenth century.[16] More than anywhere else, however, they converged on Paris, which was not only exceptionally richly endowed with religious charities – the poor were often first attracted to the city by its reputation as a source of charitable relief – but which, as a capital city, enjoyed a level of urban growth and economic prosperity that attracted the poor from all over France and not just from a regional hinterland. With time, many of those who had come as seasonal migrants stayed on and became absorbed into the permanent population of the capital. As a result, the people of Paris – especially the working people – were being constantly renewed. If many came from the farming communities on Paris's doorstep – Picardy, Artois, Normandy and the Île-de-France – others were attracted from much further afield, from the departments of the Massif Central to the south and from Alsace and Lorraine to the east.[17] By the time of the Revolution Paris was a city of provincials.

This makes any simple distinction between Paris and the provinces, or between Parisian and provincial mentalities and outlooks, rather difficult to sustain. Not only were large sections of the city's population recent arrivals in the capital, but they also continued to live in communities and work in trades where their provincial identity was maintained. Certain city trades, indeed, appear to have been monopolized from an early date by people from a single province or region, who recruited their friends and younger brothers and thus encouraged the continuation of distinct migratory traditions. Often, too, they congregated in the same streets and *quartiers* of the capital, speaking their local patois and colonizing the local bars and wineshops. This is the world of neighbourhood and provincial identity which Richard Cobb knew so well and described in such affectionate detail. For him this localism was a vital ingredient in Parisian life, reducing the anonymity which greeted the incomer and giving Paris much of its warmth and flavour. The gilds, it is true, might be dominated by second- or third-generation Parisians, those who had had time to put down roots, make some money and establish their stake in the economy of the capital. But for many humbler trades, local identity was everything, with recruiting routinely carried out on a family basis or through village friendship networks. 'Thus,' writes Cobb, 'the Paris water-carriers nearly all came from one District of the Aveyron. The horse-dealers, like the horses, were Normans. Building labourers were Limousins … or from the Creuse. Stonemasons were Normans; *crocheteurs* and *porteurs de chaises* were from Lyon; the Savoyards specialised in the filthier trades – *décrotteurs, frotteurs, dégraisseurs*, chimney sweeps'. Many came to Paris by river, the *flotteurs* floating with their logs downstream from the Yonne. And if masculine trades were local in their recruitment, the same could also be said for the capital's female workforce, with – among others – laceworkers coming from Caen and Beauvais, laundresses from the villages of the Île-de-France, and wet-nurses from the Beauce. Many Parisians retained links with the countryside, writing occasional letters home or returning to their *pays* to visit family and friends. In periods of unemployment or dearth they could usually rustle up a country cousin to whom they could turn.[18] They were not lost or abandoned in a vast, hostile city.

Paris, indeed, should not be seen as a single whole, austere and unwelcoming, but rather as a series of neighbourhoods, communities or urban villages within the political walls of the city. These broke down the apparent anonymity of Paris to reveal a world where people went about their daily business in streets and workshops, at bar counters and market stalls, where they were themselves widely known and where the faces they encountered were often familiar. Many Parisians, especially artisans and journeymen, could be said to have lived in the streets, to have had something of a proprietorial relationship with the physical fabric of the quarters where they lived and worked. They bought and sold their goods at street corners and in bars; they roamed the streets delivering orders or meeting customers; and they enjoyed a surprisingly large degree of freedom in the ordering of their working day. The rapidity of urban growth, it is true, was changing the character of many neighbourhoods, making them less socially integrated and more exclusive, but that merely served to create a day-to-day sociability of a different kind, into which the new arrival could hope to integrate both quickly and easily. Some did, as we have seen, form their own provincial communities, based on trade and family, and continued to take pride in their local roots and customs. But not all needed or chose to do so. Parisian society was a surprisingly open one for those who wanted to belong. It was this very openness which distinguished a big city like Paris from the villages from which many of the immigrants had come. It seemed strange to many of them, an unfamiliar ambience which some took time to appreciate and which may even have created in some minds an initial impression of chaos and unstructured anonymity.[19] But once that impression had passed, Paris became transformed into a series of local communities where friendships and acquaintanceships were formed in shops and markets, in the street and the workplace, and where the mentalities of the capital – often suspicious of authority and given to ideas of conspiracy – rubbed off on each succeeding wave of provincial migrants. These mentalities, as recent research has demonstrated, were complex and intricate, and did not stem from any single identity, whether of place or social class. Rather they were a blend of family and community values, work culture and neighbourhood gossip, religion and folklore, and popular superstition. By the eve of the Revolution they were marked also by ingrained attitudes towards political authority and popular fears of police spies and undercover agents.[20]

These fears went far in shaping their collective attitudes and determining their reactions towards outsiders. Parisians were necessarily large consumers of staples like bread and cereals, and the recurrent food crises of the eighteenth century made them ever vigilant, fearful of plots and conspiracies to raise food prices and starve them into submission. Markets were obvious points of conflict as well as sources of supply, and grain merchants, like millers, provided the hate figures of popular fantasy and folklore. Since in times of crisis it was the government that took charge of the victualling operation, it was only too easy to accuse that same government, from the king and his ministers through to local agents and bands of brigands in their pay, of plotting to subvert the whole enterprise and make obscene profits out of hunger and misery. Such allegations were constantly repeated throughout the eighteenth century, fuelling popular hatred and exaggerating levels of stress and phobia. If the government did not achieve an immediate improvement in the provisioning of Paris, Parisians were wont to allege that plots, greed and even deliberate hatred by provincial grain merchants must lie behind that failure. They wanted and expected instant gratification in the form of plentiful and affordable bread, something that could be achieved only by plundering stocks in Paris's bread basin, the corn lands of Normandy and the Beauce, Picardy and the Île-de-France. They seldom got this, of course, and in the confusion that followed popular Paris was as likely to blame the people of the hinterland for holding on to their supplies as they were the king and the court nobility for plotting their starvation. The famine plot persuasion was a form of collective paranoia, reflecting Parisians' feelings of insecurity faced with shortages. By 1789 it could reasonably be regarded as a vital part of the collective mentality of the city.[21]

For many city-dwellers, feelings of insecurity were only increased by personal experience of the swathe of countryside which formed Paris's immediate backyard. The topography of the Île-de-France was hardly reassuring, the gates of Paris leading along dark, bandit-infested roads through dense woods and forests, places where the unwary were always likely to be duped of their possessions and where violence seemed endemic. Wayside inns were notorious as dens of thieves and pickpockets, army deserters and other assorted villains on the lookout for potential prey, and any journey that had to be made at dusk or after nightfall inspired fear in the most intrepid traveller. In the forests that lay to the south and east of Paris – Vincennes, Sénart, Fontainebleau – government mails were regularly waylaid, and merchants and other passers-by were systematically preyed upon, while the roads leading to the principal markets of the region, like Milly-la-Forêt, Dourdan and Etampes, all passed through dense and menacing forests where bands of footpads were known to hang out. To the north and east, the forests of Montmorency and l'Île-Adam enjoyed an even more fearsome reputation, badlands at the city's gates where escaped convicts and deserters robbed and murdered local people and those travelling to and from the capital. In places the Seine itself assumed a sinister reputation as a favoured dumping ground for the bodies of murder victims. In short, the hinterland of Paris inspired a certain fear in the city's inhabitants. The forests of the Île-de-France, scene of so many royal hunting parties during the *ancien régime*, now became the haunt of an underclass that preyed upon Paris and its insecurity, while those further down the Seine, in the hinterland of Rouen, won notoriety as strongholds of the bands of *chauffeurs* who famously tortured and burned the feet of their victims to force them to hand over their possessions. During the revolutionary years, and especially under the Directory, this reputation for violence steadily worsened, the number of violent crimes and highway murders showing a particularly alarming increase, just as the ending of seigneurial privilege had led to a proliferation of wolves to the north of the capital.[22] For many Parisians their strongest image of the countryside was of what lay at their doorstep, and the villages and hamlets beyond the *barrières* did little to raise their confidence. Similarly, those who lived in Paris's shadow were always ready to believe the worst they heard of the excesses of the capital. It was an instance where immediacy bred fear and distrust.

These everyday contacts unavoidably altered the stereotypes of public discourse and official language. In the main they accentuated existing impressions of disorder and violence, lawlessness and favoured treatment. They added new detail to a pre-existing picture, new contours to what had always been a tense and somewhat uneasy relationship. People allowed themselves to be swayed by their own experiences and by those of their friends, by the rumours and stories they heard and the dramatic disclosures of police reports and the popular press. In the countryside they listened, as they had always listened, to those they trusted to tell them the latest news, whether mayors and deputies, who told the official story, or others – pedlars and soldiers, *curés* and innkeepers, blacksmiths and rural tradesmen, or simply those who had been elsewhere or had returned home from market in a nearby town. The government had no monopoly of news or of representation, even in the darkest depths of *la France profonde*, and there was no reason for people to turn to the official voice of government. Indeed, some republican leaders, in their attempt to get their message across to country people in regions like Alsace and Corsica, found it prudent to swallow their pride and compose their speeches in patois.[23] They did well to do so if they were to convince country-dwellers that they had common interests as Frenchmen and that they spoke with a common voice, for few in rural areas were naturally inclined to trust the state or to appreciate the tenor of its decrees, especially when it seemed to favour Paris so blatantly in matters of pricing and provisioning. For many in the granary belt of the Paris Basin, this would always remain the prime issue. Paris seemed to be granted economic privileges that were denied to others, sending out sectional *commissaries* into the villages of the Île-de-France to demand and, where necessary, seize requisitions for the city. The grain merchants of Paris did not only have the money to buy up supplies from countrymen who themselves feared dearth and high prices later in the year, but they had the backing of the police, the club network and the *armées révolutionnaires* recruited from the more radical Paris sections. They also had political logic on their side, a logic which the government itself was prone to expound. In the words of the *Commission des Subsistances* in October 1793, 'in one day without food Paris can annihilate the Republic through the shockwaves and the general upheaval which it communicates to the rest of France'.[24] However great the sufferings of others, it seemed that it simply was not an option that Paris should be allowed to go hungry.

The subordination of provincial interests to those of the capital merely served to widen the gulf between Paris and the provinces, demonstrating what many had always feared, that Paris was treated differently from other cities and that its people enjoyed a higher status in the affairs of the nation. Provincial France was alive to snubs and insults, for already that other concept of the provincial existed in people's minds, the concept of a collective entity that was *la province* – not in the sense of historic provinces with their honoured traditions, but in its more pejorative sense, a collective term for all the simple, innocent, ill-informed people who had the misfortune to live beyond the *octroi* gates of the capital. That usage already existed, of course: images of the provincial aroused laughter, mocking or sympathetic according to circumstance, in literature and in the theatres along the Paris boulevards. Here *la province* conjured up unflattering pictures of boredom and lethargy, weariness and hibernation; it was a place bereft of conversation and culture, a place where the pace of life was unnaturally slow, the sort of place one might go to die. It was removed from the court, from the Palais Royal, from Enlightenment and high society; in short, it was the other, a world cut off from civilization, bereft of Paris.[25] By placing so much emphasis on national unity and praising the moral qualities of the capital, the Revolution contributed to this sense of abandonment and deprivation, accentuating the impression of distance between the cradle of the Republic that was Paris and the distant, undifferentiated mass that formed *la province*.

Notes

1 A good example of this is provided by the frontier province of Picardy during the sixteenth century; see David Potter, *War and Government in the French Provinces. Picardy, 1470–1560* (Cambridge, 1993).

2 Michel Vovelle, *La découverte de la politique. Géopolitique de la Révolution Française* (Paris, 1992); for an overview of the activity of the bicentenary in the French provinces, see Vovelle (ed.), *Recherches sur la Révolution* (Paris, 1991), pp. 283–324.

3 Peter Jones, *Liberty and Locality in Revolutionary France. Six Villages Compared, 1760–1820* (Cambridge, 2003), pp. 48–84.

4 Mona Ozouf, *La fête révolutionnaire* (Paris, 1976), p. 44.

5 Michael Rapport, *Nationality and Citizenship in Revolutionary France: the Treatment of Foreigners, 1789–99* (Oxford, 2000), p. 332; for a more linguistic treatment of the subject, see Sophie Wahnich, *L'impossible citoyen: l'étranger dans le discours de la Révolution Française* (Paris, 1997), especially pp. 56–81.

6 Emmanuel Le Roy Ladurie, *Histoire de France des régions. La périphérie française, des origines à nos jours* (Paris, 2001), p. 17.

7 Martyn Lyons, 'Politics and patois: the linguistic policy of the French Revolution', *Australian Journal of French Studies* 18 (1981), p. 264.

8 David A. Bell, *The Cult of the Nation in France. Inventing Nationalism, 1680–1800* (Cambridge, MA, 2001), p. 173.

9 Michel de Certeau, Dominique Julia and Jacques Revel, *Une politique de la langue: la Révolution* (Paris, 1975), p. 288.

10 William Doyle, *The Parlement of Bordeaux and the End of the Old Regime, 1771–1790* (London, 1974), p. 23.

11 Michael Kwass, *Privilege and the Politics of Taxation in Eighteenth-century France* (Cambridge, 2000), p. 259.

12 Gail Bossenga, *The Politics of Privilege: Old Regime and Revolution in Lille* (Cambridge, 1991), p. 2.

13 W. D. Edmonds, *Jacobinism and the Revolt of Lyon, 1789–1793* (Oxford, 1990), pp. 224–5.

14 Raymonde Monnier, 'L'image de Paris de 1789 à 1794: Paris capitale de la Révolution', in Michel Vovelle (ed.), *L'image de la Révolution Française* (4 vols, Paris, 1989), vol. 1, pp. 73–82.

15 Olwen Hufton, *The Poor of Eighteenth-century France, 1750–1789* (Oxford, 1974), p. 69.

16 Philippe Ariès, *Histoire des populations françaises et de leurs attitudes devant la vie depuis le 18e siècle* (Paris, 1971), pp. 275–8.

17 Jeffrey Kaplow, 'Sur la population flottante de Paris à la fin de l'Ancien Régime', *Annales Historiques de la Révolution Française* 187 (1967), pp. 1–14.

18 Richard Cobb, *The Police and the People: French Popular Protest, 1789–1820* (Oxford, 1970), pp. 228–30.

19 David Garrioch, *Neighbourhood and Community in Paris, 1740–1790* (Cambridge, 1986), especially p. 257.

20 Arlette Farge, *La vie fragile: violence, pouvoirs et solidarités à Paris au dix-huitième siècle* (Paris, 1986), *passim*; David Andress, *Massacre at the Champ de Mars: Popular Dissent and Political Culture in the French Revolution* (London, 2000), pp. 25–6.

21 Steven L. Kaplan, 'The Famine Plot Persuasion in Eighteenth-Century France', *Transactions of the American Philosophical Society* 72 (1982), pp. 66–72.

22 Richard Cobb, *Paris and its Provinces, 1792–1802* (Oxford, 1975), pp. 42–6.

23 Jill Maciak, 'Learning to Love the Republic: Jacobin Propaganda and the Peasantry of the Haute-Garonne', *European Review of History* 6 (1999), pp. 173–4.

24 Quoted in Richard Cobb, *Paris and its Provinces*, p. 88.

25 Alain Corbin, 'Paris-province', in Pierre Nora (ed.), *Les lieux de mémoire* (Paris, 1992), part 3, *Les France*, vol. 1, *Conflits et partage*, pp. 777–84.

$\big|\,2\,\big|$

Centralization and diversity in the eighteenth century

Eighteenth-century Paris had all the attributes of a genuine metropolis. It was the second largest city in Europe (behind London) and it was by far the most populous in France, its 650,000 inhabitants dwarfing such major provincial centres as Lyon (with a population of 150,000), Marseille and Bordeaux (with around 100,000 each). Indeed, by the time of the Revolution, Paris was home to as many people as the nine largest provincial cities combined.[1] It was a capital city on a European scale, widely visited by both provincial Frenchmen and foreigners, and was admired by contemporaries for its architecture, taste and elegant lifestyle. It was visibly prosperous, without much sign of industrial or manufacturing activity: this was a city of aristocrats and rentiers, lawyers and office-holders who were not afraid to flaunt their prosperity, to impress through wealth and property-ownership. The new dynasties of commercial bourgeois were already in the making, while powerful gilds both regulated and protected trade.[2] Its reputation was further enhanced as a centre of intellectual progress, as the 'Ville des Lumières', attracting writers and journalists, eager to share the experience of living in the unquestioned capital of the Republic of Letters and contributing to the cultural and moral project of the Enlightenment.[3] Paris at the end of the *ancien régime* was a vibrant, confident capital which claimed to represent the most advanced civilized values of the day and which, in consequence, inspired both admiration and a certain jealousy throughout provincial France.

Of course there was another Paris, a city of docks and markets, immigrant workers and beggars, rent rooms and overcrowded tenements, which was already being seen as a source of danger and violence.[4] The streets of the old central area, as many visitors noted, were surprisingly cramped and insanitary. 'The streets are very narrow,' remarked Arthur Young, 'and many of them crowded, nine-tenths dirty, and all without foot pavements. Walking, which in London is so pleasant and so clean that ladies do it every day, is here a toil and a fatigue to a man, and an impossibility to a well-dressed woman'.[5] Whole neighbourhoods were given over to *garnis*, rooms rented out by the month or by the day, and cheap lodging houses where migrant workers could find some sort of shelter, however insalubrious. This was the Paris of the poor, of those seasonal workers who had left the misery of their native province to seek employment and to claim their share of the city's imagined opulence until the onset of the new agricultural year. Their whole existence was precarious, as they were hired by the day to work in the docks or on one of the capital's many building sites. For others, still more marginal to the life of the city, subsistence depended upon begging or charity; they came in their droves in periods of dearth because of the capital's many monasteries, convents and clerical foundations, which held out the promise of alms and succour that would have been unthinkable in the countryside. But fear was never far removed, whether fear of sickness or injury, or fear of losing the job or the lodging which alone offered some insurance against penury.

This was a community that feared for its own future and inevitably spread fear amongst others. Popular Paris was constantly prey to rumour and allegations of plots and conspiracies, most notably provoking fear of dearth and starvation. Rumours spread easily in a world of bars and workshops, stalls and street markets, a world where neither the state nor any other single authority could claim a monopoly of information or public credence. In the eighteenth-century city there were many people to whom the destitute might turn for news and perhaps a glimmer of hope – men who had recently arrived from the countryside and brought news of the harvest, soldiers who had seen the world, innkeepers who had overheard secret conversations, stallholders who had inside information about food deliveries – providing news which official channels might seek to hide. Paris was repeatedly swept by rumours, whether of the death of the king, the poisoning of the baby prince, or the kidnapping of the children of the poor. Opinion was rarely unanimous as conflicting tales were passed from mouth to mouth. Alchemy mingled with superstition and social antagonisms in a world where popular opinion was formed and manipulated by outsiders and Paris was besieged with stories that were at once plausible and unverifiable.[6] Such stories were the more easily believed when they concerned the rich and powerful, who had, it was alleged, every interest in keeping the popular masses repressed, while the potential enemies lurking in the city were legion. Aristocrats, wholesale merchants, speculators, hoarders, spies working for the authorities or for the police, all might have an interest in oppressing the people, and rumours about their supposed machinations were readily believed. Paris, like any other city where the poor were dependent on the supply of cheap bread, feared shortage and the violence which that could unleash, and was vulnerable to rumours of plots to starve it to submission, what Steven Kaplan has called the 'famine plot persuasion'.[7]

For new immigrants Paris could seem an unwelcoming place, a city where the stranger found himself alone and abandoned, and where traditional rules of hospitality no longer applied. Life in a *garni* could be depressingly lonely, which added a further challenge to the daily struggle for survival which so many migrant workers faced. As Louis-Sébastien Mercier rightly observed, it took far more than a letter of introduction for the newcomer to be accepted in Paris or shown any degree of human warmth;[8] in the main, he would remain an outsider, an *étranger*, someone who was not known, whose morals and character could not be vouched for, and this had important consequences in times of hardship. Eighteenth-century Paris was an intensely policed city, where order was maintained by constant surveillance interspersed with moments of repression, and at such moments it was on the floating population of the *garnis* – perceived as restless, without fixed abode or any obvious stake in society, and naturally predisposed to crime and disorder – that policing was focused. The *commissaires de police*, like all police forces, looked for criminal activity where they expected to find it, and they had their spies and agents in the community, generally drawn from those on whom they could apply the greatest pressure. Most notably these included innkeepers and bartenders, who needed to come to the police for a licence to pursue their business; prostitutes, who risked arrest at any moment; and *logeurs*, those who made a living by providing rooms for passing strangers or newly arrived provincials. Undeclared *garnis* could be closed down and their owners arrested; while those running lodging houses were obliged by law to make available to the police the names of all those who stayed on their premises. Provincials in the capital found it difficult to hide.

Close policing should not, however, be taken to indicate that the authorities in the later eighteenth century were expecting trouble; rather it was a means of keeping the streets safe and discouraging beggars and others who were deemed to present a threat to public order.[9] Though Paris had the reputation of being somewhat volatile and its crowd given to riot and noisy protest, in 1788 few would have forecast the turmoil that was to come. The city had expanded steadily throughout the previous century, throwing up new suburbs and building elegant boulevards that would be the envy of Europe. Its size impressed as much as its elegance, and it left an indelible mark on travellers who approached it for the first time. 'On leaving Villejuif,' wrote Rétif de la Bretonne, 'we came upon an immense mass of buildings crowned by a cloud of steam. I asked my father what it was. "It's Paris", he said, "it's a great city, you can't see all of it from here!"'[10] Part of that greatness lay in its capacity to lure people from all over France, whereas provincial cities rarely had more than a regional catchment – Rennes and Nantes from rural Brittany, or Marseille from Provence and the Rhone valley. Even Bordeaux at the height of the Atlantic boom lacked a truly national appeal, recruiting essentially from a rural South-West that stretched from Gascony and the Pyrenees to the Charentes and Poitou, as well as parts of the western and southern Massif.[11] But Paris's catchment was not geographically defined in the same way. A study of the male population of the capital during the Revolution, based on the *cartes de civisme* issued by the revolutionary sections, shows that the people of Paris were overwhelmingly of provincial origin, with northern France, from Normandy to Belfort, providing the most substantial contingent. In all, nearly 72 per cent of the sample had been born elsewhere, 65 per cent of them moving to Paris as adolescents or young adults between the ages of fifteen and thirty-five.[12] Paris, it is clear, held out the promise of betterment, for some the chance of social promotion and rapid enrichment, for others the possibility of escaping from poverty, enjoying some independence or experiencing leisure and fun. They came from all social classes and from every corner of the country, the ambitious and pleasure-seeking, the poor and the desperate, lured by the image of the capital to forsake their native provinces and seek their fortunes. They came to work, to enter government service and to study. 'Poverty has forced him to abandon his property and withdraw to Paris to try to provide for his family,' wrote the *subdélégué* of Saint-Flour in 1768.[13] But they also came to spend, for just as Paris was a centre of commerce and learning, so it boasted opportunities for consumption of luxury that dazzled wealthy provincials.

Elegance and good taste lay at the heart of the image which the very name of Paris evoked among contemporaries. This could, of course, lead to disappointment when they first saw the city. Jean-Jacques Rousseau frankly admitted that he found it deceptive, and that when first he visited Paris he had suffered deep disillusionment. 'How greatly the appearance of Paris contradicted the idea I had of it!' he wrote in the *Confessions*. 'I had imagined a city that was as beautiful as it was large, with the most imposing appearance, where there were only superb streets and palaces of marble and gold'.[14] Like Dick Whittington's London, the real thing could only disappoint, such was the sublime image which many provincial Frenchmen had in their heads, and Rousseau admitted that he could never quite sublimate his feeling of disgust at the misery and squalor of large parts of the city. But the image of riches and elegance was one that would not go away. To many contemporaries Paris remained the undisputed capital of lavish consumption and exquisite taste. In his *Tableau de Paris*, published during the 1780s, Mercier could write of the 'limitless grandeur' of Paris and 'its monstrous wealth, its scandalous luxury. Paris sucks up money and people; it devours the other cities, like a beast looking for something to swallow'.[15] If Paris acted as a magnet for those wishing to exert power and influence, it also attracted visitors from all over France by holding out the promise of pleasure, the prospect of consumption and gratification.

There was a sense in which eighteenth-century Paris might appear to have grown at the expense of provincial France, draining the provinces of their most talented and entrepreneurial sons. But why was Paris able to exercise this pull? How far did it owe its special position to its status as a capital city during a period when government was claiming more and more central authority and when provincial liberties were increasingly being eroded?

At first glance this might seem a promising hypothesis. The last century of Bourbon rule was a period when the state, in order to maintain peace and public order in its increasingly complex and heavily populated kingdom, laid claim to new powers of administration and law-enforcement, spent increasing sums of money and employed growing numbers of staff in its ministries. Backed by the philosophy of absolutist writers like Loyseau and Bossuet, it preached a doctrine of state power, and presented the monarchy as the only body that was above the political turmoil and thus capable of dispensing justice equitably. Persuading others to agree was, of course, a gradual process; but it was the Bourbons' ambition, from the time of Louis XIV, to extend what Jay Smith has termed 'the Sovereign's gaze', something that could be achieved only at the expense of the old nobility and what remained of provincial autonomy. 'The administrative state's emergence as an independent category of ontology,' says Smith, 'and its permanent inscription within the modality of royal service' complicated the king's relations with his nobles and undermined the traditional influence of provincial power-brokers.[16] It also led to greater centralization of administrative power, as ministries began to be centralized in single buildings and the number of functionaries, especially in finance and the *Service de la Ferme*, rose sharply. *Hôtels* that had begun their existence as aristocratic town houses were now converted into offices for government departments.[17] The result was a shift in the balance of power between the main provincial centres and the capital, once again to the disadvantage of the provinces, and a boost to the economy of the double capital that was Paris and Versailles.

And yet there is reason for us to exercise caution, for Paris did not grow at a disproportionate rate during the eighteenth century, as it had done previously. Between 1650 and 1790, Paris grew from around 450,000 to 690,000 inhabitants, or an increase of 44 per cent, which was only slightly higher than the population growth of France as a whole (around 40 per cent).[18] In part, no doubt, this was due to the rapid growth of the Atlantic economy, which produced a golden age for the west-coast cities of Nantes and Bordeaux. In part, too, it reflected the lack of industrial and commercial concentration on the capital. But it may also lead us to reflect on the limited impact of the process of centralization in the administrative sphere. Indeed, there is a strong case for thinking that, while the Bourbons wished to impose uniformity of thought and belief on France, they were far less interested in ideas of centralization.[19] Paris by the eve of the Revolution was still, of course, the dominant urban force in the French economy, but in the course of the century it had encountered obstacles that had checked its unbridled expansion. It had failed in its attempts to expand its frontiers to incorporate its immediate hinterland. And the final installation of the court at Versailles, while concentrating executive power in the Île-de-France, had subtly distanced Paris from royal government and decision-making. This had important implications both for the city's demographic growth and for its aspirations to national dominance. As Bernard Lepetit remarks, if the king had remained at the Louvre, the overwhelming majority of courtiers and those working in the royal administration would have been Parisian.[20]

That clearly did not happen. Indeed, if the monarchy was aiming to increase centralized control during the eighteenth century, the old provincial institutions of government remained remarkably robust. This may seem rather surprising, given the confusing and overlapping jurisdictions of *ancien régime* France and the contrasting structures of royal administration, justice, trade and religion. But it should not surprise, since the claims to royal absolutism made by Louis XIV and his successors were no more than claims, and they were often bitterly contested by the provincial bodies they sought to displace. Royal initiatives might seek to effect change across a whole gamut of activity, from government to social structure and economic investment, but these initiatives could not be taken discreetly; they involved the levying of new taxes and the imposition of new royal officials, neither of which was popular in the provinces. The old elites felt themselves threatened by royal ambitions, and they responded vigorously to centralizing measures which they regarded as yet more evidence of royal usurpation, often taking refuge in claims to provincial autonomy. Of course the monarchy did its best to conceal its intentions, playing down the loss of autonomy which its reforms would involve, and there are numerous instances where the king ostentatiously declared his respect and admiration for provincial liberties and usages and promised to respect existing municipal autonomy. In Lille, Louis XIV was forced to agree not to create new magistrates or sell judicial offices before he could gain any concessions from the local authority;[21] and he famously attended a Te Deum in the Collégiale Saint-Pierre where he swore the ancient oath of the counts of Flanders.[22] In the provinces, and especially in those regions with a strong tradition of particularism, the extension of the royal imperium could never be achieved easily, and the need for compromise was recognized by both sides. Royal authority could be and was extended during the eighteenth century, often by offering employment to the very men whose autonomy was under threat. But it could not be extended indefinitely. In particular the monarch had to show respect for local privileges if he was not to encounter a fierce and corrosive undercurrent of rebellion fuelled by accusations of royal tyranny.[23]

But it was not only the elites who felt threatened, since any move to centralize authority, to remove power and influence from the localities, also raised issues of loyalty and identity. How far did eighteenth-century Frenchmen identify with the monarchy and with centralized authority, with a nascent nation state? Or did they assume more localized identities, with their province or *bailliage*, or even with their immediate town or parish? Did they welcome the process of state-building or did they see it as an assault on their traditional liberties or a threat to their regional cultures? There is no simple answer that can be applied indiscriminately across the whole country, since there was no single mentality that can be defined as provincial. For some, identification with the nation presented more of a challenge than for others – for those, for instance, whose territories had only recently been annexed and who could not share in a long tradition of Frenchness, as in Alsace or Corsica, French only since the 1760s. Language, too, might play an important role in the construction of identity. Where local people spoke their own patois, as in much of the South, or where their day-to-day dealings were conducted in an entirely different language – Breton, Flemish, Basque or Catalan – provincialism could be an especially vexed issue, and one that would have important ramifications during the Revolution. Things were very different in these provinces – often far distant from Paris and somewhat peripheral to the *hexagone* – from those which had the longest history of integration into the monarchy and which did not question their allegiance to France, like Champagne, Touraine, or the Île-de-France itself.

The loss of provincial autonomy is often equated with the growth, not only of the state and the powers it could assert, but of the nation and national sentiment. Once again, as David Bell has explained, nationalism was not the creation of the French Revolution, however much it came to be identified with it later. Rather the idea of the nation was a construct based on humanistic philosophy that took shape throughout eighteenth century. Ideas of nation and *patrie* were deployed in a variety of different contexts – to help mobilize the population in wartime, to take pride in the cult of great men of past centuries that so characterized the last decades of the *ancien régime*, and even to inform discussions of the nature of the constitution. As the century wore on, so the range of meanings attached to the nation widened and it assumed strong emotional and cultural significance. In Bell's words, 'the nation was coming to signify not merely a particular group of people living on a particular territory, but an intense political and spiritual union of like-minded citizens – a union that manifestly remained to be built, and whose construction stood logically prior to all other political tasks'.[24] This was the cultural background to the world in which the revolutionaries grew up and matured, a culture steeped in Rousseau and Enlightenment thought. It certainly informed many of their republican ideas and helps to explain their insistence on the indivisibility of the French people. But it was not a revolutionary creation. It existed, powerfully, in the France of Louis XV and Louis XVI.

It was only during the Revolution, however, that the concept of 'nation' would acquire a clear moral quality – that of defending the people against monarchical tyranny – and the notion of 'patriotism' came to describe an emotional tie to the nation state. There had been *patriotes* before, groups who might vaguely identify with 'the people', but that people had never been closely defined. During the Maupeou crisis in 1770, the *parlement* of Paris was defended, amongst others, by self-styled '*patriotes*', a broad and inclusive grouping that included all those, from a range of social groups and legal estates, who favoured the immediate restoration of the *parlements* and accused the king and his minister of overstepping their powers. 'As long as one hated Maupeou and cheered the returning magistrates,' writes Durand Echeverria, one was a patriot, regardless of what other political views one held. It mattered little 'whether one was conservative or radical, reactionary or liberal, a defender of aristocracy or a democrat, a devout Catholic or an anticlerical deist'.[25] By 1789 that concept of patriotism would be dramatically transformed and, in the process, the image of the province, too, would change, to become the antithesis of the nation, veiled in privilege and reaction. But until then there were no such moral overtones. The concept of the nation implied little more than a shared interest or common purpose, while the benefits of 'patriotism' were most clearly identified in analysing the reasons for Britain's military successes in the Seven Years' War and in formulating a French response to them.[26] The words themselves were far from new: 'nation' had first appeared as early as the twelfth century, and the more emotive 'patrie' in the sixteenth. They were used in a rather different sense from today, however, in that they proposed a clear distinction between the nation and the rulers of the state. In the medieval period the nation might be the chiefs and nobles who hailed a new king on his coronation; and even in the eighteenth century Boulainvilliers clearly conceived of a primordial 'nation' that was composed principally of the Frankish nobility.[27]

The nation did not have to be coterminous with the political area of state power or with the lands controlled by the monarch; it could be more localized, and might as easily refer to a province as to the state. There were regular references in eighteenth-century texts to such provincial identities as 'the Breton nation', or the 'nations' of Provence or Languedoc. In 1694, for instance, the word is defined in the *Dictionnaire de l'Académie Française* to include 'all the inhabitants of a state or *pays*' – the political unit is quite consciously imprecise – 'who live under the same laws and use the same language'. By the 1740 edition this had been amended to say that 'it is also used of the inhabitants of the same *pays*, even where they do not live under the same laws or use the same language'.[28] This change is not insignificant, especially in a country like France where law and custom were as likely to divide inhabitants as to unite them, and where differences between common law and Roman law, *langue d'oc* and *langue d'oeil*, and *pays d'états* and *pays d'élection*, all served to dilute shared experience and accentuate the emotional tug of provincial identity. Perhaps the last distinction is the one that affected people's rights most intimately. In the *pays d'états*, where the provincial estates retained their legal right to approve taxation, there was at least a limited check on royal ambitions. But around two-thirds of the kingdom had now been reduced to the status of *pays d'élection*, where there were no representative bodies and where taxes were gathered in by royal officials or by tax-farmers without any form of consultation.[29] It is scarcely surprising that so much of the tension between the monarch and his people should have centred on the issue of taxes.

Even allowing for the contrasting histories of different parts of the kingdom, provincial identity was a powerful force which monarchical reformers would ignore at their peril. In the *ancien régime* the province was a generic term for constituent parts of the state. Each province had a governor who was the king's representative and could act on his behalf, but provinces were not constructed on any common model. Some covered vast areas, while others were tiny. Provinces had grown in a rather haphazard way across the centuries as France had expanded its frontiers; they had not resulted from any royal decree or clear administrative decision. Indeed, while this might seem to lack any coherence, there was a clear logic behind the maintenance of an apparently loose provincial structure of this kind: it was integral to the way in which the Bourbon monarchy operated, maintaining the identity of each successive conquest, and leaving its privileges and liberties largely intact. As a result, France was composed of a patchwork of provinces, with different rights and customs, different legal codes and different relationships to the crown. Some were not even precisely defined and it is impossible to be certain how many provinces there were. Pierre Doisy's dictionary in 1753 listed a total of fifty-eight, but that number was constantly fluctuating; a law of 1776, which established that each province should have a royal governor, concluded that the number of such governors was thirty-nine.[30] Even contemporaries saw provinces as insubstantial constructs; yet they were central to the character of the *ancien régime*.

One reason for the confusion is that, for the most part, the provinces were more important in people's self-perception than they were for any administrative role they might have played. They were not precise territorial units, at least until Calonne's local government reforms of 1787. Rather, as Michel Péronnet argues, their strength lay in what they stood for, in the values which they were believed to represent. From the sixteenth century, in the eyes of the state, the province had become one of three key points of sociocultural reference, the others being the court and the city of Paris. What values each of these represented varied according to the dominant mood of the moment: the province was at times equated with backwardness and superstition, at others regarded as the natural home of traditional values, honesty and virtue, high morality or religious piety.[31] Some, like Brittany and Languedoc, were ancient jurisdictions which covered substantial areas and had a long history of opposing royal despotism; they might be so large, indeed, that their territory included sub-provinces (like the Rouergue or the Velay, which were incorporated into Languedoc). Others were tiny, like Aunis and Saintonge, Sédan and Foix.[32] Their provenance, too, differed markedly. Some were the old historical divisions of the realm (like the Île-de-France, Picardy, Champagne and Burgundy); others had been added in the course of the sixteenth century (like Anjou, Auvergne, Berry or Poitou); and others again had been added still later through military conquest (generally the more peripheral territories, like Flanders and Hainaut, Lorraine and Roussillon). Together, they formed a somewhat irregular patchwork of territories; they did not constitute a rational framework for local government.

By the late eighteenth century most were fairly toothless bodies that tended to be bypassed by the crown. Their principal administrative functions had been given to the royal intendants, whose areas of competence, the *généralités*, took little account of provincial boundaries. Some provinces, indeed, seemed to will it that way, since their disparate territories proved incapable of cooperating amongst themselves and were little disposed to constitute a solid political unit. Such, notably, was the case of Gascony.[33] In all, only four of the large historic provinces – Brittany, Languedoc, Burgundy and Provence – retained their provincial estates and maintained a vestige of a representative role in their region, though twelve smaller provinces also had estates, mostly frontier provinces in the Pyrenees and to the north. But they played little part in the network of *ancien régime* administration. Even provinces endowed with estates were included in the network of *généralités* and subject to the authority of an intendant, while the provincial assemblies which were created in 1787, on the eve of the Revolution, referred not to historic provinces but to new administrative areas that were gouged out of these *généralités*.[34] All this struck enlightened contemporaries as needlessly confused and opaque, so much so that Voltaire could dismiss the province as the home of traditionalism and illogicality, a space that encapsulated 'the contradictions and confusions that resulted from the whims of the centuries'.[35] Any onlooker in 1789 could be excused for concluding that the province was already a moribund institution, waiting to be killed off by the reforms of a more rationalist age.

Yet the provinces continued to command strong levels of approval and loyalty from the population, to the extent that there was widespread support in the 1770s and 1780s for reforms to strengthen provincial government either by creating new estates where they had not previously existed or by establishing provincial assemblies. This support came largely from the local elite, who saw the province as a means of holding on to their traditional power in local government, but whose petitions and addresses also convey a sense of provincial particularism, a refusal to hand over all decision-making to Paris. They looked to their traditional rights and their role in tax collection, citing ancient constitutions which had, they argued, guaranteed their liberties against any extension of centralized power. The 'Provençal constitution', for instance, was often invoked by the notables of the Midi in defence of local privileges. This was not a constitutional document in any modern sense of the term, but rather a series of texts which had been built up since the Middle Ages, guaranteeing a number of individual freedoms and defining the structures of local government. Specifically, the people of Provence were not to be extradited to any other province but tried by their peers; they had the right to consent to taxation; and the executive and legislative authority of the Estates of Provence was defined.[36] These rights had, of course, been eroded, along with the very existence of the estates, but the constitution was frequently invoked to oppose further centralization and impede ministerial reforms. In the pamphlet literature of the day it had become a sort of mantra, ill-defined and of dubious legality, but offering some reassurance to local nobles and jurists. What is less easy to explain is the extent to which provincial liberties of this kind commanded strong popular support in many parts of the country. Ordinary people, it would seem, derived a sense of belonging from provincial customs, and could be persuaded that the province represented their interests as Bretons or Gascons or Burgundians in a way that the centralized state could not presume to do.[37] They believed that it offered a promise of legal protection and economic well-being.

The province, in other words, might have little practical role to play in the government of the country, but it still had a certain emotional appeal and helped to mould people's identities in a way that more active administrative units, most notably the *intendance*, could not. That does not mean that eighteenth-century Frenchmen necessarily saw themselves as being first and foremost Bretons or Dauphinois. For many, indeed, the province was simply too large and sprawling to offer any framework for their lives. This was especially true of the peasantry, many of whom were engaged in a subsistence economy that provided little opportunity for contact with the outside world. They were more likely to identify with what they knew, with the many smaller *pays* into which each province was divided, or, more locally still, with their town, or, in the countryside, the parish, or *seigneurie*, or *communauté d'habitants*. This last was often the most important of the three, since it was where villagers were called to discuss matters that affected them as a community, from the upkeep of local roads to common grazing lands, especially important in upland pastoral communities where these could encompass as much as three-quarters of the land area. In parts of the Pyrenees, for instance, local valleys and communities practised a primitive form of democracy in the management of their affairs, to the point where one valley could be described seriously as a 'semi-autonomous pastoral republic'.[38] In Burgundy, meetings of the *communauté d'habitants* were long-established vectors of communication with local people, where their opinions would be sought and laws and decrees announced.[39] For the pious the parish assumed great significance, even where its boundaries diverged from those of the community. In some regions, most notably Brittany, parish meetings discussed secular and fiscal matters as well as questions of faith and parish organization, while the *curé* himself enjoyed the status and trust that came with being a village notable.[40] The parish, like the *communauté d'habitants*, villagers saw as their own; it was not imposed on them from the outside. Here they could discuss issues which were of importance to local people, and they felt that sense of loyalty that came from belonging.

This was a loyalty which the *intendant* could not, by virtue of his office, hope to inspire. For however far-sighted individual *intendants* might be, they were destined to be seen as outsiders, appointed by the king to control local people, to maintain order and to see that state priorities were met. They were not local men, though in their day-to-day administration they leant heavily on the services of their *subdélégués*, who were recruited from among local notables and might be assumed to have better understanding of what local people wanted and believed. But that did not affect people's perceptions of the office: theirs was a functional relationship, the relationship between a royal civil servant and those he controlled. People were administered by the *intendances*; they did not identify with them, and complaints against both *intendants* and *subdélégués* abounded in the last years of the *ancien régime*. As Marcel Marion noted, they incurred the wrath of the same people, and especially those who viewed with suspicion any attempt to increase royal authority in the province – 'nobles irritated that they had to appear before them, magistrates, municipal officers, recalcitrant tax-payers or those seeking illegitimate favours'.[41] These were the people who had most reason to distrust the extension of royal power and to take refuge in tradition and archaism, in preserving notions of provincial autonomy.

And yet many of the *intendants* deserved better. In the later eighteenth century a number were themselves minor *philosophes* or encouraged the philosophical output of others, offering support to the arts and sciences in their region and patronizing learned societies. Chazerat, for instance, founded the Academy of Clermont-Ferrand, and Sénac de Meilhan helped organize that at Valenciennes; while in Bordeaux Dupré de Saint-Maur played a primary role in setting up the *musée* for local merchants and lawyers interested in science and *belles-lettres*. Sometimes they took the lead in supporting existing schools and conservatoires, like Blossac with the *École Royale de Peinture et de Sculpture* in Poitiers, or Dupleix de Bacquencourt with the *Société de Musique* in Amiens. Others had more social concerns and sought to relieve poverty or cut death rates – like Du Cluzel, who established a *Manufacture des Pauvres* in Tours, or Caze de la Bove, who worked to train and employ midwives in rural Brittany.[42] Or they put their improving ideas to work in ambitious schemes of urban renewal and road-building, like Tourny in Bordeaux, Montyon in Aurillac or Turgot in Limoges, all of whom made major contributions to expanding the local economy.[43] Some even used their position to fight against entrenched privilege. All in their different ways left a real mark on the communities they administered, and some were fondly remembered for their good works. But the office itself did little to forge local identity.

Nor did Frenchmen define themselves in relation to the larger clerical divisions, the dioceses and archdioceses, though those had evolved more gradually than the fiscal and administrative jurisdictions and many were of Gallo-Roman origin. This might seem curious, given the resilience of the parish as a unit of local identity in rural areas. Bishoprics, on the other hand, were unevenly distributed across the country, with huge disparities in size and importance, and this made them unsuitable units for taxation or justice. Moreover, the diocesan map was one of rare complexity and, at times, as John McManners has shown, almost comic absurdity.[44] On the eve of the Revolution there were around 130 dioceses in France, the majority of them grouped into twenty-eight provinces under the jurisdiction of an archbishop. But there, any semblance of conformity or rational distribution abruptly ceased. A few sees in the East had their metropolitans outside France, in Trier or Mainz; while Perpignan came under the jurisdiction of

Tarragona in Spain. By the same logic, French bishops found themselves in charge of foreign priests in areas where France had annexed neighbouring territory, most obviously in Nice and Savoy. And there were spectacular disparities in the size of bishoprics and the workload of their incumbents. If Rouen was the largest, with no fewer than 1,385 parishes to administer, in the South there were six dioceses with fewer than thirty each, centred on small towns like Mirepoix, Vence and Agde. Diocesan lines could be irksome and illogical, slicing through towns and villages, or retaining historic enclaves inside the territory of neighbouring sees. It was difficult to see any logic in the patchwork of dioceses that resulted, and made drawing the map of episcopal divisions particularly difficult.

The bodies which did command strong local support in the eighteenth century were the *parlements*. Again, parliamentary jurisdictions were very uneven, ranging from the *Parlement* of Paris, which sprawled across several provinces to take in a quarter of the kingdom, to the very local courts in towns like Arras and Douai in the North or Colmar and Besançon in the East. As with provincial divisions, the smallest *parlements* tended to be on the periphery, reflecting relatively recent accessions to the French crown.[45] *Parlements* were primarily courts of appeal. They were the supreme courts of each region, dispensing both civil and criminal justice, hearing appeals and registering royal decrees; subordinate to them was a network of more local *bailliage* and *sénéchaussée* courts whose verdicts were referred to the *parlements* on appeal. These activities did, of course, give them a very public profile, and at times brought them to blows with royal jurisdiction, which could in turn lead to their suspension and exile. During the 1760s, for instance, there were repeated conflicts in Brittany between the *Parlement* of Rennes and the royal governor, the Duc d'Aiguillon, over royal plans for road-building in the province, conflicts which culminated in the mass resignation of the *parlementaires* and their replacement by a new judicial court. In 1765 and 1766 relations grew heated when the court published two remonstrances denouncing the mistreatment of the *parlement*, and the King replied by arresting the *procureur-général* and rejecting all its constitutional claims in a specially convened *lit de justice*.[46] So, during the 1780s, it was through the *Parlement* of Paris and the other twelve provincial courts that the privileged orders maintained their pressure on the King. But the fact that they were called upon to stand up to royal authority brought the magistrates a degree of popularity in their own localities which neither the *intendant* nor the clerical hierarchy could match, and issues of estate and privilege melted into apparent insignificance. Discussing the popularity of the *Parlement* of Bordeaux, William Doyle notes that all social groups under its jurisdiction felt that they benefited from its protection at some time; support was not restricted to the elite. For it was by its very nature a provincial institution, one that served the interests of its province and grouped together its most prominent legal minds. 'The most distinctive public role of the parlement,' Doyle concludes, 'was as defender of the province. Its most original ideas, and those in which it ran against national currents, were all evolved in the provincial crucible'.[47]

It was this perception of the *parlements* as being composed of local notables, who understood the interests of the community and were willing to take personal risks in defence of those interests, which alone can explain their popularity. Their defiance of the king when they felt that royal decrees were encroaching on local liberties or resulting in higher fiscal demands won widespread admiration among those they represented, most notably in the long struggle between the *Parlement* of Rennes and the monarchy during the 1760s, the so-called 'Affaire de Bretagne'. Here, as in so many other conflicts, the *parlementaires* were able to claim the prestige of defending their nation against outside interference in the interests of the people.[48] On other occasions they fought for the livelihoods of local people by defending them against outside encroachment. Thus the *Parlement* of Bordeaux repeatedly advocated protection for wine-growers and the colonial market, even as it urged the liberalization of the grain trade. It went without saying that the city's prosperity came before any question of philosophical consistency, to say nothing of any personal profit that they might hope to accrue, and their action won them widespread acclaim throughout Guienne.[49] Nor did magistrates always rush to serve their own interests. When the *parlementaires* of Rouen defied Louis XV by opposing plans to deregulate the grain trade, their motive was not to amass personal fortunes, since the measure clearly ran counter to their desires as landowners at a time of good agricultural prices.[50] Rather it was to come to the aid of a starving population and help ensure that public order in the province was maintained, ambitions which enabled the *parlementaires* to claim to represent at least an important cross-section of public opinion in their region.

Where the *intendant* was often treated with cold suspicion, the *parlement* could expect to bask in popular approval when it was in conflict with the monarchy. In 1788, for instance, when all the *parlements* were summoned to register royal edicts that would have placed their independence in jeopardy, a constitutional storm erupted and, in the South-West, the *parlements* of Bordeaux and Pau were exiled. In Pau, the capital of Navarre, where local rights had always been jealously defended, the news was greeted with popular defiance and anger. Whereas the nobles were willing to disband, fearing that defiance of the King would lead to repression and possible loss of life, no such prudence overcame the townsfolk, who insisted that the magistrates dress up formally in their robes and parade through the streets. There, as a sign of solidarity, 'all the orders of the town joined them; the young people accompanied them on thirty musical instruments; the shops were closed; the church bells were rung throughout the city, and all that could be heard were sounds of joy and merriment'. The people of Pau were not just showing their support for their magistrates and for the constitution which maintained them; they were making it clear that they opposed any reforms which sought to reduce their magistrates' independence of action, and turned the scene into one of public carnival, defying the King's wishes at some risk to their lives.[51] They were hostile to any extension of royal authority and they understood the symbolic significance of their gesture.

The *parlements*, like the provincial estates, benefited from being perceived as the champions of provincial rights and guarantors of their economic interests in the face of the centralizing force of the monarchy. Often this was no more than a matter of perception: they were seen as belonging to the people in a way that royal government was not. But their appeal did not rest there. They also bestowed material benefits on their communities, since the very fact of having a *parlement* brought great distinction and wealth to the city that hosted it. This could take a number of forms, depending on the scope of the existing urban economy, but in every case they provided the town with a rich, highly educated elite, judges and magistrates who had cultured tastes and enjoyed high levels of consumption, and who, along with their families, could be expected to spend lavishly, patronize local business and inject new wealth into the community at large. As lawyers they were interested in questions of rights and prerogatives, reading newspapers, patronizing bookshops and participating in local *salons* and academies in the larger provincial capitals. Their presence attracted other forms of investment, too: in schools and colleges for their sons, in specialist crafts and trades to supply a new luxury market, in elegant town houses that could be expected to galvanize urban renewal. The practice of the law and the hearing of appeals brought others to the towns and cities where the hearings were held, as plaintiffs, defendants, witnesses and onlookers, and they, too, consumed, increasing the need for hotels and lodgings, restaurants, bars, transport and other services. In short, the presence in a town of a *parlement* was not seen only in terms of urban prestige; it also injected substantial wealth into the local economy.

Just how great a difference it made would depend, of course, on the nature of the urban community on which it was imposed. Did it have competing sources of wealth and social prestige? Were there other elite groups already established in the town with whom the legal luminaries of the *parlement* had to vie? Smaller cities like Pau and Arras owed a huge debt to the lawyers, whose arrival made all the difference between prosperity and relative obscurity. Aix, too, was an old-established legal centre where status and professional distinction went hand in hand; by the eighteenth century it boasted not just the *parlement* and its associated courts – which employed around one hundred people and ensured an important legal presence in the city – but also provincial estates, a university, a college, several libraries, and an academy, one of several in Provence.[52] Aix was a highly cultured city, where the sons of noble families attended the university to acquire the legal training that would prepare them for work on the *parlement* and the *cour des comptes*.[53] Unsurprisingly, lawyers dominated the city's elite. But even in the larger provincial capitals, cities where the legal fraternity had to compete with others for social dominance – with the clerical hierarchy of a

cathedral city or with the merchant fraternity of the local chamber of commerce – the magistrates always figured among the wealthiest inhabitants
and formed the very core of the city's elite. They were often nobles, landowners in the surrounding countryside with elegant town houses in the best
urban addresses, men whose fortunes came from several generations of legal
practice. In Bordeaux, for example, they occupied quarters like the rue des
Remparts and the Porte-Dijeaux, as well as the streets close to the *parlement*,
and were in no sense eclipsed by the Bourse or the mercantile fortunes of
the Chartrons.[54] In Dijon, too, where a relatively small number of nobles
and *anoblis* dominated local society, the more fashionable quarters were
bursting with lawyers – and not just the parliamentary elite, but a host of
others, 'magistrates on lower courts, advocates, prosecutors, clerks, court
officers, notaries and many more, who were at the same time fascinated and
rejected by the *noblesse de robe* to which so few of them would be allowed
to rise'.[55]

If a city could look to its role as a provincial or parliamentary capital as
a source of distinction, so, too, could it gain wealth and prestige through
commerce and overseas trade – sectors which underwent dramatic expansion
in the eighteenth century. While the luxury trades continued to flourish – the
silk-making centre of Lyon remained the most important city outside
Paris – and industrialization was beginning to transform the character of
artisanal production, it was overseas trade and the mercantile economy
which witnessed the strongest growth and provided a welcome boost to the
port cities which served the Mediterranean and the Levant (particularly
Marseille), and the Americas (the Atlantic ports from Bayonne to Le Havre,
and most especially Nantes and Bordeaux). It was along the coast that expansion was most concentrated, and to the ports that migrants came in the
largest numbers in search of their fortune. Growth was not, however, evenly
distributed, and different markets showed differing levels of dynamism.
This was most noticeable in Marseille, where the Mediterranean trade grew
more slowly than colonial markets, and where merchants were increasingly
attracted to the Indies and the Americas.[56] Overall, it was the Atlantic
coastline that underwent the most dramatic transformation, made rich by
the colonial trade with the Antilles, the slave trade from West Africa and a
lucrative triangular commerce with the American South. Merchants, wholesalers, shipowners and those trading in colonial produce to the Baltic and
Northern Europe all benefited hugely from France's privileged access to the
islands, to Martinique and Guadeloupe and, especially, Santo Domingo.
The most successful of them became, in their turn, provincial notables, who
bought vineyards and country estates, as well as elegant town houses, and
who took pleasure in living nobly. In a few cases merchants even won the
final accolade of ennoblement and challenged the pre-eminent position of
the law in civic affairs. In all the Atlantic ports the construction of public
buildings and elegant residential quarters created a new urban pride which
reflected both their wealth and their ambitions.[57]

This pride extended beyond the new wealth that had been created; beyond, too, the fabric of urban renewal, the classical buildings, the streets and squares, parks and public amenities. There was a new confidence in these regional centres that went with their role as provincial capitals, cities which set their own agendas and had their own intellectual and cultural life, independent of that of Paris. For with the growth of trade and the professions, the presence of courts and tribunals, came the expansion of civic life and the increased importance of the public sphere. Provincial elites had their own intellectual life by the mid-eighteenth century, one built around academies and reading circles, bookshops and masonic lodges; they published books, newspapers and political pamphlets; they attended concerts and art exhibitions; they financed essay competitions on enlightened and humanistic themes; they listened to philosophic papers – Rousseau first addressed the Academy of Dijon in the 1750s[58] – and discussed learned treatises; they built theatres and employed their own troops of actors. For lawyers and public officials, particularly, masonic lodges offered a useful forum where like-minded men could meet and network, and discuss the sorts of philosophical and anticlerical ideas that in other contexts might seem subversive. And now that men were no longer fearful of facing charges of irreligion, freemasonry achieved immense popularity, with as many as 128 members of the Paris bar highly visible members of lodges and the more 'philosophical' salons.[59] There were other outlets, too, for those wishing to embrace new ideas. 'An institution common in the great commercial towns of France, but particularly flourishing in Nantes, is a *chambre de lecture*,' noted Arthur Young approvingly, 'or what we should call a book club that does not divide its books, but forms a library'. He went on to describe the comfort of the facilities. 'There are three rooms, one for reading, another for conversation, and the third is the library; good fires in winter are provided, and wax candles'.[60] In such circumstances local people had little reason to feel beholden to Paris. Indeed, they diffused a culture and a confidence which banished any lingering sense of inferiority which life in the provinces might evoke.[61] One could make a living in the Republic of Letters, as a journalist or a minor *philosophe*, in Rouen or Toulouse as well as in Paris; while in Bordeaux the local elite made great play of the fact that theirs was the city of Montaigne and Montesquieu, characterized not just by commercial wealth but by enduring intellectual distinction.

And yet, behind all the burgeoning confidence, there was just a suspicion of fragility, a sense that their new-found wealth and comfort might be vulnerable. So much had been built on the profits of overseas trade, on a prosperity which, in spite of the resounding optimism of the age, was poorly distributed across the country and could not be assumed to last forever. France was still a country of small towns and regional administrative centres rather than of great industrial and commercial cities, and between cities communications remained slow, even if the network of roads and post-coaches had been vastly improved during the half-century before the Revolution. In 1795, for instance, it still took six days for news to travel from Paris to Bordeaux, eight to Aix or Marseille, and nine to Perpignan.[62] In village France the sense of being linked to the outside world was inevitably diminished, with poor links to the cities and infrequent postal deliveries. Indeed, in the more remote rural regions of the Massif or the Alps, roads were often rendered impassable by snows and mountain rains for months on end, leaving local communities effectively cut off from the outside world and thrown back on their own resources. It was impossible to get news even from nearby cities; here life was not lived according to the timetable laid down in Paris.

As Arthur Young was quick to remind his readers, agricultural modernization was progressing only slowly, with the result that many in the countryside still lived in fear of dearth. Peasants were blighted by high state taxes and seigneurial exactions, though the existence of a concerted 'feudal reaction' is much disputed. More probably peasant communities suffered from a reduction in paternalism in years of poor harvests, and from a greater systemization of estate management.[63] But the impact of shortage was not limited to the countryside. The severe harvest failures that preceded the Revolution were a timely reminder that even in the cities the new prosperity could not be taken for granted, as the price of bread and other staples reached levels that were beyond the reach of many working families. It was not only the poorer members of society who felt vulnerable. Even the richest *négociant* had reason to take stock, since a succession of foreign wars had shown how dangerously dependent the economy had become on the maintenance of peace and stable conditions. In times of war, ships were sunk, cargoes were seized and respected firms forced to close; insurance rates became unaffordable and even the most law-abiding merchants felt obliged to try their hand at privateering. For cities like Bordeaux and Nantes, dependent on a steady flow of men and goods between France and the islands, naval warfare always had the potential for economic disaster, the more so as France's principal naval rival, Great Britain, made no secret of its colonial ambitions or its desire to displace the French in the Antilles. At the Peace of Paris in 1763, Britain had agreed to leave France with Santo Domingo in return for the cession of French Canada, while victory in the American War had opened up American markets to French shipping. The 1780s were a decade of furious and competitive naval construction, with France aiming to build a navy that could wrest control of the seas from the British. Under Castries and La Luzerne, the French navy was expanded from its traditional strength of sixty ships of the line, until a *mémoire* of 1788 could talk of sixty-four ships of the line and an equal number of frigates, which would give Louis XVI the second greatest navy in the world.[64] But in these same years the British fleet was also being renewed, through a lavish capital building programme that far exceeded any budget which the cash-strapped Louis XVI could envisage. The threat of a future naval and colonial war with Britain seemed ever more imminent, a war that risked destroying the profitability of Atlantic trade.

Just as the major provincial cities felt threatened economically during the last years of the *ancien régime*, so they had reason to fear further administrative reforms that would centralize decision-taking and reduce local autonomy. In practice, in many towns and cities that autonomy was really a form of privilege, which benefited small elites while doing little for the mass of the citizenry. Nor was there any logic in the structures in place: municipal institutions varied from region to region and between North and South, where different legal traditions pertained. Among smaller towns there was no common tradition of municipal structures in a country that veered between the rural communities of the Paris Basin, governed by a single *syndic*, and those of Languedoc, which often had elected councils with clearly defined functions. Some of the larger provincial cities were still governed by small, tight groups of *jurats*, as in Bordeaux, or *capitouls*, as in Toulouse – elites who were answerable to no one but themselves and who had often transformed municipal office into a hereditary fiefdom. The town of Autun is a case in point. Here the posts of mayor (or Vierg) and public prosecutor lay in the gift of the crown, exercised through the Intendant of Dijon, with the function of Vierg remaining in the same family from 1740 through to the Revolution, passing from father to son in 1785.[65] And though there were repeated attempts at reform – municipal constitutions in Burgundy were revised on three separate occasions between 1772 and 1786 – even the boldest of reformers hesitated to interfere with long-held municipal liberties. The royal decree of 26 June 1778, for instance, had taken care to avoid any measure that undermined the hereditary rights of the *capitouls*.[66] Hence municipal government remained largely unreformed, a battleground between the king and his ministers on the one hand, and a somewhat motley collection of provincial and municipal elites on the other. It was a conflict that had smouldered throughout much of the century and would be reignited dramatically in the years immediately preceding the French Revolution.

Notes

1   Raymonde Monnier, 'L'image de Paris de 1789 à 1794: Paris capitale de la Révolution', in Michel Vovelle (ed.), *L'image de la Révolution Française* (4 vols, Paris, 1989), vol. 1, p. 73.
2   David Garrioch, *The Formation of the Parisian Bourgeoisie, 1690–1830* (Cambridge, MA, 1996), p. 82.
3   Dena Goodman, *The Republic of Letters: A Cultural History of the French Enlightenment* (Ithaca, NY, 1994), p. 4.
4   Jeffrey Kaplow, *Les noms des rois. Les pauvres de Paris à la veille de la Révolution* (Paris, 1974); Jeffrey Kaplow, 'Sur la population flottante de Paris à la fin de l'Ancien Régime', *Annales historiques de la Révolution Française* 187 (1967), pp. 1–14.

5 Arthur Young, *Travels in France during the Years 1787, 1788 and 1789* (London, 1889), p. 103.

6 Arlette Farge, *Dire et mal dire. L'opinion publique au dix-huitième siècle* (Paris, 1992), especially pp. 147–51.

7 Steven L. Kaplan, 'The Famine Plot Persuasion in Eighteenth-century France', *Transactions of the American Philosophical Society* 72 (Philadelphia, 1982).

8 Daniel Roche (ed.), *La ville promise. Mobilité et accueil à Paris, fin 17e–début 19e siècle* (Paris, 2000), p. 9.

9 The nature of this threat is well summed up in a pamphlet on policing published in 1764 by Turmeau de la Morandière, at the height of a state clamp-down on beggars, entitled *Police sur les mendiants, les vagabonds, les joueurs de profession, les intrigans, les filles prostituées, les domestiques hors de maison depuis longtemps, et les gens sans aveu*, and cited in Roche (ed.), *La ville promise*, p. 75.

10 Jean Tulard, *Nouvelle Histoire de Paris: La Révolution* (Paris, 1959), p. 15.

11 Jean-Pierre Poussou, *Bordeaux et le Sud-ouest au dix-huitième siècle: croissance économique et attraction urbaine* (Paris, 1983), p. 76.

12 Robert Leguillois, 'Étude de la population masculine de Paris en 1793 d'après les cartes de sûreté', in Michel Vovelle (ed.), *Paris et la Révolution* (Paris, 1989), pp. 5–7.

13 Abel Poitrineau, *Remues d'hommes. Les migrations montagnardes en France, 17e–18e siècles* (Paris, 1982), p. 5.

14 Jean-Jacques Rousseau, *Les confessions* (Paris, 1968), p. 146, quoted in Kaplow, *Les noms des rois*, p. 22.

15 Jeremy D. Popkin (ed.), *Panorama of Paris: Selections from* Le Tableau de Paris *by Louis-Sébastien Mercier* (University Park, PA, 1999), p. 23.

16 Jay M. Smith, *The Culture of Merit: Nobility, Royal Service and the Making of Absolute Monarchy in France, 1600–1789* (Ann Arbor, MI, 1996), p. 191.

17 Natacha Coquery, *L'espace du pouvoir. De la demeure privée à l'édifice public, Paris, 1700–90* (Paris, 2000), pp. 65–6.

18 Figures quoted by Jean-Pierre Poussou in a paper to the conference of the Society for the Study of French History, held in Nottingham in April 2003. For a general discussion of the demography of French towns in this period, see Jean Meyer, *Études sur les villes en Europe occidentale, du milieu du 17e siècle à la veille de la Révolution Française* (Paris, 1983), vol. 1 – France, pp. 49–76.

19 Claude Nières, 'Les obstacles provinciaux au centralisme et à l'uniformisation en France au dix-huitième siècle', in Roger Dupuy (ed.), *Pouvoir local et révolution: la frontière intérieure* (Rennes, 1995), pp. 74–5.

20 Bernard Lepetit, *Les villes dans la France moderne, 1740–1840* (Paris, 1988), p. 184.

21 Philippe Guignet, *Le pouvoir dans la ville au dix-huitième siècle* (Paris, 1990), p. 97.
22 Louis Trénard (ed.), *Histoire de Lille* (2 vols, Toulouse, 1981), vol. 2, p. 286.
23 Nières, 'Les obstacles provinciaux', p. 77.
24 David A. Bell, *The Cult of the Nation in France. Inventing Nationalism, 1680–1800* (Cambridge, MA, 2001), pp. 199–200.
25 Durand Echeverria, *The Maupeou Revolution: a Study in the History of Libertarianism. France, 1770–74* (Baton Rouge, LA, 1985), p. 38.
26 Edmond Dziembowski, *Un nouveau patriotisme français, 1750–70. La France face à la puissance anglaise à l'époque de la guerre de Sept Ans* (Oxford, 1998), p. 266.
27 Harold A. Ellis, *Boulainvilliers and the French Monarchy: Aristocratic Politics in Early Eighteenth-century France* (Ithaca, NY, 1988), p. 30.
28 Jean-Yves Guiomer, *L'idéologie nationale: nation, représentation, propriété* (Paris, 1974), p. 22.
29 P. M. Jones, *Reform and Revolution in France: The Politics of Transition, 1774–91* (Cambridge, 1995), pp. 19–20.
30 Ibid., p. 17.
31 Michel Péronnet, 'Province, Provinces', in Lucien Bély (ed.), *Dictionnaire de l'Ancien Régime* (Paris, 1996), p. 1037.
32 William Doyle, 'Provinces', in S. F. Scott and B. Rothaus (eds), *Historical Dictionary of the French Revolution* (2 vols, Westport, CT, 1985), vol. 2, p. 792.
33 Maurice Bordes, 'La Gascogne à la fin de l'Ancien Régime: une province?', in Christian Gras and Georges Livet (eds), *Régions et régionalisme en France du dix-huitième siècle à nos jours* (Paris, 1977), p. 139.
34 Doyle, 'Provinces', p. 792.
35 Voltaire, *Essai sur les moeurs* (Paris, 1763), quoted in Louis Trénard, 'Provinces et départements des Pays-Bas français aux départements du Nord et du Pas-de-Calais', in Gras and Livet (eds), *Régions et régionalisme*, p. 55.
36 François-Xavier Emmanuelli, 'La généralité d'Aix', in Gras and Livet (eds), *Régions et régionalisme*, p. 129.
37 Jones, *Reform and Revolution*, p. 18.
38 François Taillefer (ed.), *Les Pyrénées de la montagne à l'homme* (Toulouse, 1974), p. 215.
39 Pierre de Saint-Jacob, *Les paysans de la Bourgogne du Nord au dernier siècle de l'Ancien Régime* (Dijon, 1960), p. 81.
40 Timothy Tackett, *Priest and Parish in Eighteenth-century France* (Princeton, 1977), pp. 155–65.
41 Marcel Marion, *Dictionnaire des institutions de la France* (Paris, 1923), p. 520.
42 Maurice Bordes, *L'administration provinciale et municipale en France au dix-huitième siècle* (Paris, 1972), pp. 148–51.

43 Michel Lhéritier, *L'Intendant Tourny, 1695–1760* (2 vols, Paris, 1920); Jean-Pierre Poirier, *Turgot. Laissez-faire et progrès social* (Paris, 1999), pp. 80–118.

44 John McManners, *Church and Society in Eighteenth-century France* (2 vols, Oxford, 1998), vol. 1, pp. 177–82.

45 Jones, *Reform and Revolution*, pp. 21–3.

46 J. H. Shennan, *The Parlement of Paris* (London, 1968), p. 316.

47 William Doyle, *The Parlement of Bordeaux and the End of the Old Regime, 1771–1790* (London, 1974), p. 309.

48 Monique Cubells, *La Provence des Lumières: les parlementaires d'Aix au dix-huitième siècle* (Paris, 1984); William Doyle, 'The Parlements of Paris and the Breakdown of the Old Regime', *French Historical Studies* (1970), pp. 415–58.

49 Doyle, *Parlement of Bordeaux*, p. 310.

50 Olivier Chaline, 'Parlements', in Lucien Bély (ed.), *Dictionnaire de l'Ancien Régime*, p. 964.

51 *Récit de ce qui s'est passé à Pau en Béarn les 19, 20 et 21 juin 1788* (4 pp., Pau, 1788); Alan Forrest, *The Revolution in Provincial France: Aquitaine, 1789–99* (Oxford, 1996), pp. 37–8.

52 Edouard Baratier (ed.), *Histoire de la Provence* (Toulouse, 1990), pp. 376–9.

53 Donna Bohanan, *Old and New Nobility in Aix-en-Provence, 1600–1695. Portrait of an Urban Elite* (Baton Rouge, LA, 1992), pp. 125–6.

54 François-Georges Pariset, 'Les beaux-arts de l'age d'or', in F.-G. Pariset (ed.), *Bordeaux au dix-huitième siècle* (Bordeaux, 1968), p. 562–3.

55 Jean Bart, *La Révolution française en Bourgogne* (Paris, 1996), p. 69.

56 Charles Carrière, 'Le travail des hommes, 17e–18e siècles', in Edouard Baratier (ed.), *Histoire de Marseille* (Toulouse, 1990), pp. 213–14.

57 François Georges Pariset, 'Le Bordeaux de Boucher et de Tourny' and 'Le Bordeaux de Victor Louis', in F.-G. Pariset (ed.), *Bordeaux au dix-huitième siècle*, pp. 533–647.

58 David Andress, *French Society in Revolution, 1789–99* (Manchester, 1999), p. 33.

59 David A. Bell, *Lawyers and Citizens: The Making of a Political Elite in Old Regime France* (New York, 1994), p. 167.

60 Arthur Young, *Travels in France during the years 1787, 1788 and 1789* (London, 1889), pp. 133–4.

61 Daniel Roche, *Le siècle des lumières en province. Académies et académiciens provinciaux, 1680–1789* (2 vols, Paris, 1978).

62 Guy Arbelot and Bernard Lepetit, *Atlas de la Révolution Française, vol. 1: Routes et communications* (Paris, 1987), p. 41.

63 Pierre Goubert, 'Sociétés rurales françaises du dix-huitième siècle: vingt paysanneries contrastées', in P. Goubert (ed.), *Clio parmi les hommes* (Paris, 1976), p. 70; John Markoff, *The Abolition of Feudalism: Peasants,*

Lords and Legislators in the French Revolution (University Park, PA, 1996), p. 54.

64 William S. Cormack, *Revolution and Political Conflict in the French Navy, 1789–94* (Cambridge, 1995), pp. 22–3.

65 Marcel Dorigny, 'Crise des institutions municipales et émergence d'un parti patriote: l'exemple de la ville d'Autun, 1787–90', in Robert Chagny (ed.), *Aux origines provinciales de la Révolution* (Grenoble, 1990), pp. 111–12.

66 Maurice Bordes, *L'administration provinciale et municipale*, pp. 329–30.

|3|

The provinces and the crisis of the ancien régime

Against a background of mounting criticism from pamphleteers and enlightened authors, it was difficult to defend existing structures of local government. The problem was to find a workable alternative, to construct a system that would both satisfy local pretensions and make more effective use of the nation's tax base, which was seen as essential if royal finances were not to be damagingly undermined. The king was, in any case, by now much too weak to impose any uniform pattern of institutions that might appear to trample on local usages. Perhaps the best that can be said is that Louis XV and Louis XVI understood the demand for change and tried to answer it. Municipal government, in particular, was the subject of widespread grievance throughout the eighteenth century, and between the 1760s and the outbreak of revolution in 1789 there was no shortage of suggested reform programmes, each seeking to bring uniformity and legitimacy to the process. In a text published in 1764, for instance, the Marquis d'Argenson urged that municipal institutions should be strengthened and that Paris should make municipal magistrates responsible for assessing and collecting taxes, policing and public works.[1] And in two edicts dated 1764 and 1765, François de Laverdy sought to reorganize communal administration by employing representatives of the old gilds and urban corporations, a move that would allow those of even modest property to take their place in local government.[2] In those towns where they were implemented, they had the effect of introducing more standardization into municipal government and bringing new, professional men of proven ability into elected office.[3] It was Laverdy's way of breaking time-honoured oligarchies that had proved excessively resistant to reform.

These measures proved short-lived, due largely to opposition from the old municipal elites, and in 1771 Terray gave way to political pressures and repealed them. Thereafter the history of municipal reform was highly chequered. In 1775 Turgot commissioned a report on representative local government, but again the local elites opposed change, and Turgot's dismissal ensured that all attempts at reform were abandoned until 1787 when they were revived by Calonne. Under the terms of his reform programme, towns were to have councils consisting of the *seigneur*, the *curé*, and a number of councillors – three, six or nine – fixed according to their population, thus allowing a degree of public accountability and undermining the entrenched position of local oligarchies. Electors were to be chosen by parish assemblies, and members elected for three-year terms.[4] The idea, if we judge by the response in the *cahiers de doléances*, enjoyed a significant measure of popular support. But difficulties in finding appropriate personnel, and continued resistance from local notables meant that two years later, at the outbreak of the Revolution, many towns had still to reap any discernible benefit from the 1787 law.

Resistance to municipal reform paled into insignificance when compared to the outburst of vitriol that greeted Calonne's other proposal for local government in 1787, to create a network of provincial assemblies throughout the country. This involved the establishment of real administrative units at provincial level, something which the old provinces had never offered, a form of representative government with a degree of executive authority and the power to raise revenue. The assemblies were to be created in all the *généralités* and in the twenty-six provinces that were *pays d'élection*, and were to be modelled on two pilot assemblies which had been set up in 1779 in Haute-Guienne and Berry. This might appear to represent a considerable step forward. The assemblies were to consist of deputies who were themselves landowners and hence men of property. While their membership would be selected from the three orders of the clergy, nobility and the Third Estate, they were, unlike the old provincial estates, to meet as a single chamber without distinction of rank. Their numbers would be carefully balanced: since the King reserved the right to determine the number of representatives for each of the three orders, he could guarantee that the number representing the two privileged orders would never outvote those from the Third.[5] Condorcet was among the more prominent figures who welcomed this as a step towards public accountability and government by consent.[6] Even the Parlement of Paris, which regarded any proposal emanating from the King or his ministers with healthy scepticism, raised no objection to the idea of provincial assemblies, since they did not seem likely to strengthen royal administration or to threaten local elites. In any case, by 1787 the attention of the *parlement* was already concentrated elsewhere, on the threat of a *subvention territoriale* and the suggestion that a new stamp tax might be introduced to raise added revenue. These were matters that struck at the heart of its prerogatives, and it had no hesitation in declaring that they were an abuse of royal power, since only the nation had the right to decide on new taxes. Given the gravity of the state's finances, the magistrates concluded that these questions could not be solved by legislation and that they must be referred to an Estates-General.[7]

But the proposal to create provincial assemblies was not universally popular in the provinces themselves. It met with fierce opposition from the intendants, who saw the assemblies as a threat to their existing powers, and, less predictably, from some of the local *parlements*. Among the magistrates opinion was divided, some welcoming the new bodies as a device for devolving central authority, others fearing that their traditional right of remonstrance would be lost and that the assemblies would soon become little more than a power base for the provincial nobility. Their responses varied from resigned acceptance to outraged hostility, often on the grounds that their treasured privileges were being arbitrarily taken away. Some followed the example of Paris and accepted the assemblies without demur; these included such relatively docile bodies as the *parlements* of Douai and Colmar. Elsewhere enthusiasm was more muted, as in Nancy, Metz and Rouen, where it was stipulated that provincial assemblies should not be able to apportion taxes without prior approval from the *parlement*. At Aix, where the magistrates had always had a reputation for moderation and where the King appeased local opinion by decreeing that their estates should be restored to their former glory, the *parlement* declined to criticize royal policy on the assemblies, though it did enter a squeak of protest when its colleagues at Bordeaux were punished by exile.[8] But in several of the provinces which had historically had their own estates, the *parlementaires* went further, combining an angry rejection of the assemblies with the demand that the King re-institute their estates; such was the case in Dauphiné and the Franche-Comté.[9] The fiercest opposition to the reform, however, came from Guienne, where the Parlement of Bordeaux roundly denounced the royal proposals, arguing that 'as the deliberations of the provincial assemblies would be subject to royal approval, we would not be sufficiently free, or independent, or sovereign'. Behind this lay a desire to claim back powers that had long been abandoned, notably the revival of the long-defunct Estates-General of Guienne, surely an unrealistic demand born of an exaggerated sense of their own, and their province's, importance.[10]

   Calonne had thought he could appease provincial pride by the offer of these assemblies. But he had succeeded only in exacerbating regional and interregional tensions, adding to the difficulties he was experiencing with the privileged orders on the national stage. For at the same time as he was trying to impose his idea of provincial assemblies on local notables, he was also convening an Assembly of Notables at Versailles to try to achieve agreement on a package of tax measures that would help balance the nation's finances. His provincial reforms merely deepened the suspicions of the nobility, who knew that any financial package would involve their losing at least some of their fiscal privileges, and who were therefore more determined than ever to concede none of their honorary distinctions. When they convened in February 1787, therefore, it was against this background that the notables viewed Calonne's proposed assemblies as bodies which were to comprise a single chamber, without distinction as to order. This was a break with tradition which alarmed the privileged orders, and the Assembly of Notables rapidly declined to cooperate with the reform programme. This pushed the monarchy further into crisis, leading to Calonne's dismissal and his replacement as Controller-General by the Archbishop of Toulouse, Brienne.[11] As for the provincial assemblies, they duly met in November, when some of them added their weight to the mounting clamour for provincial rights. They did, as Calonne had supposed, see it as part of their role to defend the interests of their province when it was suspected that these might be under attack. That was hardly contentious. On the other hand, they were not radical bodies, and the majority of them did not wish to seek a quarrel with the monarchy. Some explained that they had no desire to extend their powers or to play a fiscal role. They recognized that they could not establish legally any direct or indirect tax, or consent to the extension of an existing levy. That, the assembly of Dauphiné was careful to point out, was the prerogative of the Estates-General, and it was therefore imperative that the estates be assembled urgently for the purpose.[12]

Indeed, many of the assemblies showed themselves to be rather timid, capable of taking little political initiative of their own; they were not well suited to represent an increasingly assertive public opinion or to assume the mantle of opposition to royal despotism.[13] Where they did intervene in national politics, it was usually in the cause of reaction, asking that the King abandon his reform plans, restore provincial liberties in their traditional form and agree to maintain all noble and clerical privileges. In the context of the 1780s, this seemed to many in the provinces to offer the only viable means of retaining a share in decision-making and blocking reforms that would only intensify royal absolutism. The Provincial Assembly of Guienne, for instance, sent a powerful address to the King in 1787. This reflected a mixture of ideas, highly conservative yet concerned to ensure participatory government. It asked for the new laws that Louis had promulgated over the previous months to be rescinded as a precondition for further negotiation, and for *lettres de cachet* to be abolished. It insisted that the *parlements* should be recalled and the deputies of the Breton nobility freed. And it asked that the traditional privileges of each province should be preserved while every province should also have its own provincial estates. It also asked Louis to call the Estates-General.[14] In other words, far from agreeing to any strengthening of royal authority in the provinces, the assembly was supporting the *parlementaires* when they came under attack.

The *parlements*, as events proved, were right to be apprehensive about their liberties and to fear royal retribution. The King needed to have his tax plans passed, and the opposition of the magistrates was proving more and more intractable. Thus, from September 1787, there were continual rumours, both in Paris and in the major provincial cities, that the government intended to reduce their powers or even to rule without them, by establishing a plenary court in Paris, consisting of provincial nobles and deputies, which would be able to judge the most important criminal and civil cases and register royal edicts without referring them to the *parlements* for approval.[15] In the spring of 1788 Brienne resurrected this measure, which passed into law as one of the six edicts drawn up by Lamoignan, the Keeper of the Seals, and was forced through, in the face of widespread opposition, on 8 May. There was no pretence that this was a negotiated solution. The *parlements* were effectively abolished, their role reduced to that of simple appeal courts, while the range of their jurisdiction was further diminished by upgrading forty-seven subordinate courts to the status of *grand bailliage*.[16] They were even denied any right to debate or vote on the measure. The edicts were imposed on the Parlement of Paris in a *lit de justice*, which the King prudently held at Versailles rather than in the capital. In the provinces the governors imposed the same laws at military sessions, where order was maintained by a show of armed force. And throughout the kingdom Louis ordered the *parlements* to dissolve and be placed on vacation. There was an immediate upsurge of anger, often supported by noisy popular demonstrations, as the *parlements* responded to what they interpreted as a brutal political *coup* by the monarchy. The edicts were denounced as a major act of provocation, intended to destroy any lingering ability they still had to obstruct royal policy. In the provinces, most *parlements* defied the King's order to disperse and reassembled to pass angry resolutions. Far from being given more autonomy through the provincial assemblies, the provinces feared that their constitutional rights had been torn up and that they had been stripped of all effective powers of opposition.

These reforms may be seen as the last attempt by the monarchy to salvage something of royal absolutism, but in fact they were a desperate gamble that succeeded neither in dislodging the privileged groups who governed provincial France nor in modernizing the country's administrative infrastructure. In the short term they merely deepened the administrative crisis and renewed the call for the Estates-General, as the action of the King's ministers was denounced in hundreds of pamphlets as the sort of monarchical despotism which had for so long been feared. Louis's own popularity plummeted, and the magistrates of Paris and most provincial cities united in expressing outrage and defiance. In contrast, the *parlements* enjoyed renewed popular support, as large crowds gathered throughout France to cheer their magistrates' defiance of royal authority or to welcome them back after periods of enforced absence. Brienne did not hesitate to order the exile of those courts which defied the King's commands, and the Parlement of Paris, most notably, found itself banished, once again, to Troyes, where the magistrates found themselves not only fêted by the people of the town, but warmly applauded by the cathedral chapter, the elite of the First Estate.[17] The magistrates had suddenly regained their authority as the focus of popular resistance, and they now saw the Estates-General as the only possible antidote to a nascent royal despotism. In Toulouse, Besançon and Metz the government tried to silence the *parlementaires* by arbitrary arrests and the use of *lettres de cachet*; and in a number of cities violence threatened, particularly in Rennes where the military lost control of the streets.[18] In Pau, when the King's representative ordered the *Parlement* of Navarre to disperse, several thousand nobles took to the streets, and crowds broke the locks on the *parlement* building to reinstall their magistrates; they defiantly held aloft, as a symbol of their liberties and their independence from France, the cradle of Navarre's favourite son, Henri IV.[19] By an act of despotic authority which was seen by many as more drastic than Maupeou's in 1770, Brienne and Lamoignan had unleashed a cascade of provincial defiance and created an unstoppable demand for an Estates-General to be summoned before any new taxes would be considered. Of course, memories of the Maupeou Parlement were still fresh, and they only strengthened the magistrates' resolve. They also conjured up images of despotism in the minds of a wider public in both Paris and the provincial cities. Louis and his ministers had handed the *parlements* a vital moral victory in the battle for public opinion and lost an important element of popular support for reform.

The most significant resistance, however, came from Dauphiné, where the May edicts were forcibly imposed by the King's lieutenant-general, the Duc de Clermont-Tonnerre, who issued a *lettre de cachet* to each of the *parlementaires*, ordering them to leave the city. But in Grenoble, opposition was not restricted to the magistrates. In a city where prosperity was closely tied to the activities of the courts, anxiety and rumour quickly spread to the general population. The municipal council, half of whose membership were either advocates or prosecutors, loudly opposed the edicts – which they saw as damaging to Grenoble's prosperity – and demanded the magistrates' return. Moreover, their views were quickly taken up by the city's trades and *corporations*, representing the business and artisan community.[20] When troops were called to disperse the magistrates, crowds rapidly assembled, the tocsin was rung and the townspeople were joined by peasants from the surrounding countryside. The outcome was violent confrontation on 7 June between the troops and the people of Grenoble, in which the populace took to the rooftops and hurled down tiles on the soldiers below. Four men were killed and Grenoble had its first martyrs, tradesmen and journeymen who had died for a principle they believed in. A year before the attack on the Bastille in Paris, a provincial city had been turned into a battleground between the people and their government. The *Journée des Tuiles* captured the popular imagination; for the Dauphinois, these were the first shots to be fired in the French Revolution, shots that would be celebrated widely in the province at the centenary in 1888.[21]

Their significance was more than symbolic, however. To prevent further loss of life, Clermont-Tonnerre felt obliged to make concessions. He suspended the exile of the *parlement*, and though the magistrates, fearful of sparking off further violence, agreed to withdraw from the city on 12 June, the demand for change did not die away. Two days later, on 14 June, an assembly of notables met in Grenoble town hall. This body, urged on by Barnave and Mounier, demanded the suspension of the edicts, the return of the *parlement*, and – crucially – a meeting of the estates of Dauphiné where the Third Estate would be given representation equal to that of the two privileged orders. The Dauphinois were not to be fobbed off with empty proclamations. In July the deputies and communities of the province met at the château of Vizille, where they repeated the demand that the estates be called to discuss the liberties of the province. That meeting was held in Romans in September, and it solemnly confirmed a broad programme of political reform, starting with the calling of an Estates-General of the entire nation. The King was helpless to stand in their way. The political leadership in Dauphiné, among them some of the best constitutional minds of their generation, had pushed France closer to transforming national as well as provincial institutions.[22]

For the crisis in the Dauphiné had not been limited to issues of local rights and representation, important as these were. It had also served to concentrate attention once again on the national financial crisis, and to raise renewed expectations that an Estates-General would be summoned. This the King and Brienne felt bound to resist, since they wanted to retain control of events for as long as possible. But they had given vital ground in Dauphiné when they approved the meeting of the provincial estates, there and in neighbouring Franche-Comté, with increased representation for the Third; and, rather more seriously, the royal treasury was now empty, the loans on which the government depended proving hard to raise after months of vacillation over reform. In the summer of 1788, moreover, violent hailstorms and harvest failures spelt out clearly the economic problems to come, making it even more difficult to persuade financiers to advance short-term loans. Brienne could reasonably feel that he had run out of options, and when, on 8 August, he at last promised an Estates-General for the following May, he did so from a position of weakness, as the final step available to the monarchy if it was to avoid the economic humiliation of bankruptcy. But it still involved a degree of political humiliation, since calling the Estates-General represented a retreat by the King, a retreat from absolutism and the principle that he was entitled to rule without any form of representative government.[23]

Tellingly, perhaps, Brienne then resigned, passing to Necker responsibility both for the economy and for the future of administrative reform. His first goal was to try to re-establish working relations with the local elites. His declaration announcing a date for the meeting of the Estates-General also took a number of palliative measures, like recalling the *parlements* which his predecessor had exiled and discarding once and for all Lamoignan's ill-advised judicial reforms. The first decree the recalled magistrates were asked to register was the convocation of the Estates-General for the following year, the very measure which they had been demanding during the previous months. Of course they did so with alacrity, even though they might have had reservations about the protocol: they were being asked to accept an Estates-General in its traditional form, last used in 1614. This meant that the three estates must convene as separate chambers and that each should have the same number of representatives. To many in the provinces these arrangements seemed outmoded and unnecessarily divisive. Those provincial estates that had met since 1778 had all accepted that the Third should have double representation, including those called the previous year in Dauphiné and Franche-Comté. Public opinion now demanded that the structures which it had seemed appropriate to implant in Dauphiné also be applied when the Estates-General met in Versailles. Some 800 petitions flowed in from all over France, demanding greater representation for the Third and denouncing the selfishness of those who sought to cling to their privilege. Finally, even the Parlement of Paris accepted the principle that the Third Estate should have twice the number of deputies – 600 rather than the 300 assigned to the other estates – though it held out for voting by order. Necker was obliged to rule on what had become the major issue of public debate, but he was reluctant to antagonize the two privileged orders. And so he offered a compromise: he agreed to the doubling of the Third, but continued to insist that the three estates meet as separate bodies. Only once the Estates-General had assembled, he argued, could the deputies of their own free will settle the issue of voting by order or by head.[24] That instruction, which was published on 27 December 1788 as the *Résultat du Conseil d'État*, laid down that deputies would be elected by *bailliages* and *sénéchaussées*, and that *curés* should have the right to sit in person in the electoral assemblies of the clergy. This promptly became a subject of heated debate throughout the country.

Though the calling of the Estates-General inevitably moved the focus of interest away from the regions and towards the national stage, the electoral process and the hustings which it generated were spread across the provinces. Just who would have the right to vote became clear with the decree of 24 January 1789, which established what was by any standards a very generous franchise. To claim the vote one had to be of French nationality and a taxpayer, be twenty-five years of age and domiciled in the area; otherwise only those in domestic service were excluded. In many parts of France this amounted almost to universal male suffrage, and it was certainly wider than any electorate during the Revolution itself. For the clergy and nobility the framework of voting was simple: there was to be only one electoral assembly for each *sénéchaussée*, and this would have responsibility for returning deputies to Versailles. For the Third Estate, however, the voting system was more complicated, and this may have vitiated the impact of the law.[25] Voting was to take place at two levels in rural communities, with parish assemblies choosing delegates who would be sent on to the *sénéchaussée*; whereas in towns there were to be three different stages in the electoral process, with assemblies of gilds and corporations, groups sharing a privileged status, choosing delegates for the city assembly, who would in turn select electors for the *sénéchaussée*. For men who had never previously had the opportunity to vote for any public authority, this must have seemed a rather daunting process, the initiation to a somewhat confusing secret rite.[26] Indeed, though the level of participation was wide, it is difficult, even today, to define the electoral principle underlying it. It certainly did not correspond to individual responsibility, since with the system of indirect voting, the gilds chose one elector for every 200 members, yet the liberal professions chose one for every hundred. This made it easy to criticize: in the view of Patrice Gueniffey, for instance, it 'was purely a matter of political expediency that contributed in no way to the invention of citizenship'.[27] This view has considerable substance, especially since, on the one issue that most aroused public opinion – the form of the chamber or chambers that would result from the process, and the all-important method of voting that would pertain once the Estates-General met – the law remained stubbornly silent.

The first electoral assemblies met in February 1789, with the double mission of choosing their delegates and drawing up the traditional *cahier de doléances* that would be presented to the King. By March the deputies of the three estates would meet in the main town of each *sénéchaussée*, where people were excited by the hustings and expected, amid the hunger and misery of that spring, to witness decisions that would herald better times. Local people could not but be aware of what was going on. There was a lively pamphlet literature surrounding the elections, as opposing candidates made a pitch for local opinion and parish priests lobbied against the delegates of the upper clergy. And everywhere the same procedure was followed, involving, once again, a degree of solemnity and public ceremonial. The deputies would first take part in a communal mass and hear a speech from the *sénéchal* calling them into session and reminding them of the gravity of the decisions before them. They would then divide into their respective orders, each meeting in a designated building, where they would draw up their *cahiers* and choose their representatives. In Agen, for instance, the deputies took over the most prominent public buildings in the town: the Hôtel de Ville and the Eglise des Pénitents Bleus for the nobility; the Eglise des Capucins for the clergy; and the Eglise des Jacobins for the Third Estate. The streets were crowded with distinguished strangers. Hotels were filled to overflowing and trade flourished. There was something of a carnival atmosphere in the streets.[28]

Or at least, that was what was supposed to happen. Occasionally the issue of voting by head or by order was already proving troublesome, as the Third Estate tried to persuade the other two orders to join them in a single meeting-place and to draw up a single document, in defiance of royal instructions. Such attempts were doomed to fail, but they are proof of both political awareness and a certain radicalism in parts of the provinces, even before the Estates-General opened in May. In Tulle, for instance, the electors of the Third Estate asked those from the other two orders to form a single chamber where they could proceed to elect common deputies and draw up a single *cahier*, unfettered by considerations of rank. There were also signs of radicalism amongst sections of the lower clergy, who were to attend their assemblies in person, along with their bishops and archbishops: monks and nuns sent representatives. In Limoges, as in several other regions, a sense of common interest appeared to tie the lower clergy, the *curés de paroisse*, to the Third Estate rather than to the privileged members of their own order.

To this end a number of the *curés* who had come to Limoges to vote improvised an illegal meeting of their own, with neither abbots nor bishops present. Their aim was clear: to draw a clear demarcation between themselves and the upper clergy, and to try to take charge of the electoral meetings that followed.[29] And though the *curés* were forced to obey the law and take part in the election as members of the First Estate, relations between them and their bishops were often cool, and sometimes openly hostile. In several dioceses the bishops had publicly questioned the wisdom of the electoral law, criticizing it for being too liberal. In Gap, for instance, the bishop rallied to the views of his conservative superior, the Archbishop of Embrun, and denounced the 'excessive liberty' which the election offered to his parish priests, adding for good measure that he thought it was 'a travesty to see an unenlightened *curé*, with neither birth nor talent, competing on a ballot with the prelates'.[30] Such tactless indiscretions were grist to the mill of the more radical parish priests, who made sure that they, too, had their representatives in the Estates-General.

The first duty of the electors was to draw up their lists of grievances, the *cahiers de doléances* which the King had requested as part of the traditional preparation for an Estates-General. The three orders met individually, just as they would do as electors, though there were a few instances where different estates came together to draw up a common document. Again the size and complexity of the Third Estate necessitated a series of local consultations before a composite list of grievances could be constructed. The preliminary *cahiers* were to be drawn up by rural parishes, gilds and corporations, and also by towns, a process which, it was decreed, should be completed by 16 March; by that date local grievances should be passed to the *bailliage* or *sénéchaussée*, where a single document could be prepared for the attention of the King. Additionally, a number of privileged towns were allowed to hold direct elections and to send their grievances straight to the King: in addition to Paris, this privilege was accorded to six provincial cities, Arles, Lyon, Rouen, Valenciennes, Metz and Strasbourg, and to the Ten Imperial Cities of Alsace, which were deemed to form one electoral district.[31] At each stage the listing of grievances was followed by the nomination of electors, since both were seen as integral parts of the electoral process. All the evidence would suggest that the three orders took this consultation very seriously, and that even in the smallest villages the people would assemble – often, as at Boissé in Maine, called by the church bell 'in the customary manner' – to list their grievances and provide the King with the information he needed to end the abuses which were blighting their lives.[32] The prospect that their views and opinions would count for something raised popular expectations throughout France, and induced many ordinary people to think that their wishes were about to be granted. They therefore looked eagerly to the Estates-General for relief from their diverse burdens.

It goes without saying that their expectations were often unrealistic, and that many would emerge from the process bitterly disappointed. The claims of the Third Estate were often at variance with the interests of the privileged orders, who were more inclined to urge the maintenance of established liberties and political institutions that would guarantee their role in decision-making. The First and Second Estates were not opposed to political change; indeed, they often urged measures that would help stem royal absolutism. Nor were the provincial nobility necessarily against economic and fiscal reform, since many of them were driven by enlightened views as much as by self-interest. But the privileged orders tended to cling to at least the more honorific of their privileges, resisted the imposition of new state taxes and insisted that the three orders continue to meet separately. They also tended to identify with their province and its established institutions, like estates and assemblies, defending them against any extension of royal imperium. By way of contrast, the final *cahiers* of the Third Estate were overwhelmingly concerned with the issue of taxation and the upcoming meeting of the Estates-General, where, they stipulated, they wanted voting to be by head. The general *cahiers* which the Third Estate sent on from the *bailliages* to Versailles showed a concern for individual freedoms and constitutional issues, which demonstrates how widely such ideas had taken hold among the lawyers and office-holders of provincial towns who so often edited the final drafts.

Constitutional concerns were less conspicuous in the preliminary *cahiers* that were drawn up at village level, which often emphasized economic and fiscal matters rather than great issues of politics or representation.[33] According to the computerized content analysis of the *cahiers* carried out by Shapiro and Markoff, the most frequently cited issues in parish *cahiers* were stubbornly apolitical – taxation questions in general, and in particular the *gabelle* (salt tax) and *aides* (taxes on alcoholic drink). They complained about compulsory labour service on the roads, denounced the *taille*, sang the praises of Louis XVI and complained of the tax benefits enjoyed by the nobles and clergy – again, issues that risked being overlooked when the *bailliage* documents were edited.[34] In part this may reflect a degree of single-mindedness among the officials who were responsible for that editing, a desire that the Estates-General should focus its attention on constitutional reform. There had, after all, been long debate on the political issues of the day, and the countryside, like provincial towns, was being canvassed by tracts and pamphlets. It may also conceal a certain contempt for the concerns of the poor and illiterate. But there were also sound reasons for treating the parish *cahiers* with a degree of caution. Many of them listed grievances that had little resonance outside their immediate localities – from plagues of rabbits to the seigneur's doves and the opening hours of the local inn – and which would have no meaning for the King. Some were clearly copied diligently from the various model *cahiers* that circulated in the countryside, as men with rather more education and *savoir-faire* attempted to gain peasant support for their cherished plans.[35] Others were the work of local *syndics* and village officials, and they spoke for a village elite, making no effort to articulate the grievances of the very poor, which they dismissed as either unimportant or insoluble. The poorest inhabitants, according to the *cahier* of Saint-Fragaire in Normandy, 'feel their sufferings without being able to identify their cause or the means of providing a remedy'; they therefore put their trust in 'people more enlightened than themselves'. In the nearby parish of Saint-Vincent-de-Nogent they had no better solution than to turn to the 'kindness, enlightenment and wisdom' of the monarch.[36] With the best will in the world it would have taken a masterly act of drafting to create a balanced *cahier*, truly representative of a cross-section of the Third Estate.

By the summer of 1789 peasant grievances in many areas would have given way to peasant violence and revolt, with outbreaks of the Great Fear along the major grain routes into Paris and increasing anti-seigneurial violence in parts of the South-West and the Massif Central. These will be examined in greater detail in the next chapter, but it is instructive at this point to consider how far rural disorder reflected the levels of anger expressed in the *cahiers*, how far, if at all, peasants had been able to use the opportunity provided to get their grievances across to those in authority. John Markoff, using his extensive database to compare the demands made in the parish *cahiers* with areas of subsequent revolt, concludes that indeed there is a correlation to be drawn. There was, he suggests, a tendency for those villages which were exercised by big national issues, like state taxation, seigneurial exactions and the need to hold an Estates-General, to be the same ones that would later turn to violence and château-burning. Equally, those villages whose grievances were largely internalized, directed at redistributing common lands or reclaiming grazing rights, were precisely those where violence did not erupt, perhaps because these were issues that reflected divisions within the local community rather than unity against outside abuses. The *cahiers*, if Markoff is right, present a pointer to future behaviour, if an imprecise one. Much changed in peasant experience and expectation between the spring of 1789 – when the *cahiers* were written – and the summer months, by which time the Estates-General had already met and a new polity had been created.[37]

Once the *cahiers* were drawn up, the assemblies turned to their principal task, that of choosing representatives to go to the *bailliage* or on to the Estates-General. So whom, finally, did they elect to represent them in the corridors of Versailles? From the identity of the deputies they chose, it is safe to assume that all three orders preferred men who already enjoyed a certain local notoriety and who could be trusted to defend their liberties and collective interests. How else, after all, would individuals be known to their electors or able to present themselves as suitable candidates? But the point is worth emphasizing, for it implies that the Estates-General, when it finally met, was more a gathering of provincial notables than an assembly of national politicians. They were well informed on the national agenda, of course, concerned by the same issues of liberty and representation, but the electors were guided by reputations formed in the regions they inhabited and the role they played in provincial society, far more than by careers in the royal service or such fame as might be generated nationally. Their experience of politics, when they had any experience, was of municipal or provincial politics. The majority of those who assembled in the Salle des Menus Plaisirs at Versailles came to their new task without previously having held any office under the crown.

That was true of all three estates, of the nobles and clergy as much as the Third. Among the nobility, indeed, the elections often spelt defeat for courtiers and those who had spent much of their time as absentees from their province, seeking office and honours elsewhere. We find a widespread reluctance to elect members of the *robe*, a repudiation of men who had formed the administrative elite under the *ancien régime*. Instead, the electors chose representatives from the *noblesse de sang*, the scions of the most distinguished families of provincial France. Of the 322 noble deputies there were four princes and sixteen dukes, eighty-three marquises and 104 counts or viscounts.[38] They included several princes of the blood and the wealthiest members of old provincial families; few had been recently ennobled and none could be classed as poor rural *hobereaux*. Indeed, if any one section of the nobility played a more prominent part than any other it was the military aristocracy, those who had made careers as army officers. The same pattern was repeated up and down France. In the Périgord, for instance, the Comte de Périgord, a prominent member of the court nobility during the 1780s, lost out to two men who were better known in the province itself and who might, it was assumed, be better able to represent it.[39] Some were, of course, deeply opposed to reform, as their upbringing and aristocratic breeding dictated. But not all the noble electors chose arch-conservatives to represent them, or men who would defend their privileged status at any price; some were liberals, eager to seek greater rights for the province or for the individual in the face of growing royal despotism. Different provinces espoused widely varying ideas of reform. The most uncompromising response came from the nobility of Brittany, an area where the provincial nobles had been locked in struggle with the urban elites during the previous year. First they demanded that their deputies be nominated by the provincial estates where they could impose their authority and when that demand was rejected they refused to participate in the election, on the grounds that the Third Estate had no right to an independent voice. But this was a rare instance of intransigence and the product of a particular local context. Unsurprisingly, the Third Estate of Brittany won a reputation for radicalism when its deputies assembled at Versailles.[40]

In the same way, the clergy – and especially the lower clergy, who were far less concerned with questions of order and precedence, and who formed around three-quarters of the electorate – looked to men with an established reputation in their locality to represent them. The clerical elections, indeed, routinely provide evidence of a class division between the parish priests and the upper clergy, with the priests favouring their own or men known to have championed *curés'* rights within the diocese. The upper clergy were often contested figures, and if in some places the bishop was returned almost as of right, in others there were angry clashes between bishops and their priests. The Bishop of Dax, for instance, made no secret of his resentment when the clergy of Lannes chose one of their own over any of the bishops in the area,[41] while in Périgueux an unpopular bishop was comprehensively beaten by two country priests, both of whom would sit with the Third Estate when the Estates-General met.[42] The lack of empathy between the parish clergy and their bishops, which had already been demonstrated in the spread of Richerism earlier in the century, could resurface acrimoniously in the clerical elections. In Normandy, for instance, several bishops declared themselves outraged by what they saw as cabals developing among the lower clergy, secret meetings to ensure that the bishops were defeated at the polls. The results would seem to bear out their suspicions, since only in Rouen were members of the upper clergy returned, and here they owed their election to the power of the cathedral chapter. In the remaining *bailliages* of Normandy the picture was very different. In three (Caen, Evreux and Alençon) all those chosen as deputies were members of the *bas-clergé*, while in the other two (Coutances and Caudebec) the *curés* were in the majority.[43] Across the whole country almost two-thirds of those elected were ordinary parish priests, whereas the forty-six bishops returned formed only 14 per cent of the clerical deputies.[44] This result was a severe blow to the clerical hierarchy and goes far to explain the radicalism of the First Estate on wide areas of the political agenda. Once again, local trust was paramount, and parish priests often favoured candidates who were sympathetic to a reform agenda.

If the elections for deputies to the Third Estate were more complex, they were generally peaceable and concluded without the virulence that characterized the clerical assemblies. In both urban and rural areas the election process was spread across several stages, whereby delegates were sent on to a higher level to record the opinion of their peers. Voting was almost universally carried out publicly, in open meetings, and exact voting lists were seldom maintained, suggesting that it was the opinion of communities more than of individuals that was being sought. With no voting registers, assemblies had to use tax rolls and gild membership lists to determine whether men were eligible as voters.[45] In urban areas the trade gilds were convoked to the primary assemblies, and the role played by the *maîtres de métiers* would prove crucial. Often they were tightly organized and eager to exercise their vote. In Moulins, for instance, we know that of the 480 *maîtres* called upon to attend, 407 took part, with some trades (*cordonniers, tapissiers* and *selliers*) recording 100 per cent attendance; the average for all the trades in the town was 78 per cent.[46] In towns this method of convoking the assemblies had the effect of excluding the poor and unpropertied, but in rural communities there was very little social differentiation, with the consequence that village assemblies were dominated by peasants and rural artisans. Thus we find that in the villages and *bourgs* of rural Provence, around 80 per cent of the electors were drawn from the popular classes of society;

in one commune, Villeneuve-Coutelas, these accounted for 100 per cent of the assembly's membership.[47] That is not to suggest, of course, that social deference played no part in the vote, or that peasants and labourers were not tempted to vote for men better educated than themselves. Levels of participation varied hugely, to the point where it is impossible to propose meaningful averages across whole regions. To take one, admittedly extreme, instance, the figures for eighteen rural parishes around Vitré in Brittany ranged from 6 to 96 per cent.[48] In Provence around half the villages for which statistics can be found recorded turnouts of less than 15 per cent, while only in a quarter did the figure rise above 25 per cent.[49]

From the results we can safely conclude that the vast majority of communities tended to select their more prosperous citizens, those to whom poorer peasants and tradesmen might look for inspiration. Only at the first stage, and in particular in rural areas, is there some evidence that the poor and uneducated were able to win a modest degree of support. In rural Artois, for instance, voters opted for the wealthier *fermiers*, who as a group accounted for over 65 per cent of those elected; but they did not exercise total control. Rural artisans numbered around 4 per cent, while even one or two of the poorest farmhands, the *ouvriers* and *manoeuvriers*, got themselves elected.[50] But no peasants or artisans got beyond the first stage of the electoral process. Those who were elected at that point had to pass to the secondary electoral assembly, and to travel there at their own expense; to have any chance of being elected, they then had to impress with their oratorical skills and their command of the issues of the day. In these circumstances it was entirely foreseeable that the men who were chosen to represent the Third Estate at Versailles should have been the product of a fairly narrow urban elite, drawn from the educated classes of provincial towns – doctors, merchants and especially lawyers – rather than those elected in rural areas. They were men versed in public speaking, well able to control meetings, men who had often involved themselves in the political agitation of the *pré-révolution* in the provinces.[51] They read newspapers and played their part in the public sphere. Some sixty of them had written books and pamphlets and contributed directly to the Republic of Letters, including a small number who might be classed as *philosophes* in their own right, and many more who had composed tracts on legal reform and legal theory.[52] And although the majority had little experience of politics outside their own area, they were committed to certain broad principles like equality before the law and equality of tax liability. United in their opposition to hereditary privilege, they constituted the revolutionary political class in the making.

Their constituents had high expectations of the Estates-General, and awaited news of its decisions with keen anticipation. They wanted change, the betterment of their lot, answers to the questions they had raised in the *cahiers*. But most had little idea of how great the changes would be or the direction they would take. They had asked for political rights, and the Estates-General duly obliged with plans to restrict the powers of the monarchy,

guarantee individual freedoms and respect equality before the law. These
policies corresponded to the broad lines of what had been demanded in the
cahiers and met with general approval. But the first year of the Revolution
would introduce measures that went far beyond that. It would set about the
task of abolishing feudalism, and with it privilege, policies that lay far
beyond the demands of the Third Estate in the spring of 1789, and which,
though again there was a wide measure of consent, attacked the very heart
of *ancien régime* society. For eighteenth-century France was constructed
around corporate notions that were dependent on the acquisition of liberties. Provinces, municipalities, trading monopolies and gild structures were
all based on liberties, on privileges that had been acquired by charter or purchased as a favour. Sometimes these liberties had been hard won, the result
of constant petitioning of the King and the ministries, and were seen as the
key to economic prosperity. The *droit de franchise* which guaranteed free-
port status to the ports of Bayonne and Dunkerque, is a case in point.[53]
Other freedoms, like those granted by charter to many of the gilds and corporations, were bitterly contested by free tradesmen, who regarded them as
harmful constraints on trade, preventing the opening up of cities to a spirit
of enterprise.[54] But abolishing them would not be easy, for they were critical to the way society worked, and to give them up would involve the sacrifice of a vital part of one's identity, whether as a goldsmith or carpenter, a
Rouennais or Lillois, a Breton or Provençal. It would mean the denial of
much that had been central to provincial politics over the centuries, a system on which jobs and prosperity depended as much as local pride and civic
dignity. If this was what the new citizenship involved, it would mean tangible sacrifices as well as greater freedoms, and the sacrifice of things that
were precious to many provincial towns and their inhabitants.

Reform of provincial administration had lain at the heart of monarchical
plans during the 1780s; in the King's eyes it was a necessary precursor
to measures of tax reform and economic regeneration. Provincial France
had become greatly exercised by questions of rights and liberties, and the
provinces, too, had put down markers for the future. In their resistance to
the proposals of Calonne and his successors, the provincial estates and *parlements* had called up their wider constituency and had claimed to speak for
provincial opinion; and in what was increasingly a conflict between state
centralism and the autonomous tendencies of the local nobility, they took
the side of autonomy, with its obvious populist appeal and claims to consti-
tutionalism. They spoke of it in terms of rights and freedoms, a language
not inconsistent with the French Revolution, although it was also a cause
that was steeped in reaction, since it emphasized the maintenance of privilege and the rejection of economic liberalism. That is certainly how it was
seen at the time by ministers and by those *intendants* and royal governors
who were attempting to construct more effective institutions for local government. It was also the message which it sent to reformers, to those lawyers,
merchants and royal office-holders who had been agitating for change and

who would form the new political class after 1789, men for whom provincial sentiment could easily become equated with peasant traditionalism and anti-revolutionary prejudice, with the self-interest of local elites, and with such reactionary ideologies as particularism, regionalism and, later, federalism.[55] These were not useful causes with which to be associated during a revolution that would place such emphasis on the sovereignty of the people and the primacy of the nation state, and they would not be forgiven easily. In any subsequent conflict that might oppose centre and periphery, Paris and the provinces, Paris had in these early months already scored some invaluable points.

Notes

1 Pierre Deyon, *L'État face au pouvoir local: un autre regard sur l'histoire* (Paris, 1996), pp. 89–90.

2 For a full discussion of Laverdy's municipal reforms, see Maurice Bordes, *La réforme municipale du contrôleur général Laverdy et son application, 1764–71* (Toulouse, 1963); an analysis of his overall philosophy, both fiscal and administrative, can be found in Joel Félix, *Finances et politique au siècle des Lumières: le ministère L'Averdy, 1763–68* (Paris, 1999).

3 Béatrice Legrand-Baumier, 'La réforme municipale de L'Averdy 1764–65): glas de la représentation patricienne au sein des corps de ville? L'exemple de Tours', in Claude Petitfrère (ed.), *Construction, reproduction et représentation des patriciats urbains de l'Antiquité au 20e siècle* (Tours, 2000), pp. 160–1.

4 Maurice Bordes, *L'administration provinciale et municipale en France au dix-huitième siècle* (Paris, 1972), pp. 339, 344–5.

5 Archives Nationales, H1-1600, 'Projet de déclaration pour l'établissement des assemblées provinciales', 1787.

6 Condorcet, *Essai sur la constitution et les fonctions des assemblées provinciales* (2 vols, Paris, 1788), vol. 1, p. 11.

7 J. H. Shennan, *The Parlement of Paris* (London, 1968), p. 321.

8 Monique Cubells, *La Provence des Lumières: les parlementaires d'Aix au dix-huitième siècle* (Paris, 1984), pp. 295–6.

9 Jean Egret, *The French Pre-revolution, 1787–88* (Chicago, 1977), pp. 125–6.

10 Léonce de Lavergne, *Les assemblées provinciales sous Louis XVI* (Paris, 1864), pp. 323–4.

11 Georges Lefebvre, *The French Revolution* (2 vols, London, 1962–4), vol. 1, p. 99.

12 A.N., C13, address of the Assemblée provinciale de Dauphiné, 1787.

13 David Andress, *French Society in Revolution, 1789–99* (Manchester, 1999), p. 39.

14 A.N., C13, address of the Assemblée provinciale de Guienne, 1787.

15 Jean Egret, *The French Pre-revolution*, p. 144.
16 William Doyle, *The Oxford History of the French Revolution* (Oxford, 1989), p. 82.
17 Nigel Aston, *Religion and Revolution in France, 1780–1804* (London, 2000), p. 109.
18 Doyle, *Oxford History*, p. 83.
19 Alan Forrest, *The Revolution in Provincial France. Aquitaine, 1789–99* (Oxford, 1996), p. 37.
20 Gérard Chianéa, 'Institutions dauphinoises, pré-révolution et identité provinciale', in Vital Chomel (ed.), *Les débuts de la Révolution Française en Dauphiné, 1788–91* (Grenoble, 1988), p. 34.
21 Philippe Nieto, *Le centenaire de la Révolution dauphinoise. Vizille, un mythe républicain* (Grenoble, 1988), pp. 59–64.
22 Jean Nicolas, *La Révolution Française dans les Alpes, Dauphiné et Savoie* (Toulouse, 1989), pp. 48–59.
23 Malcolm Crook, 'The French Revolution and Napoleon, 1788–1814', in M. Crook (ed.), *Revolutionary France, 1788–1880* (Oxford, 2001), p. 12.
24 Doyle, *Oxford History*, pp. 92–3.
25 Gabriel Désert, *La Révolution Française en Normandie* (Toulouse, 1989), pp. 51–2.
26 Jacques Godechot, *La Révolution Française dans le Midi Toulousain* (Toulouse, 1986), p. 60.
27 Patrice Guéniffey, *Le nombre et la raison. La Révolution Française et les élections* (Paris, 1993), p. 35.
28 Archives Départementales du Lot-et-Garonne, *Le Lot-et-Garonne dans la Révolution Française* (Agen, 1989), p. 34; Forrest, *Aquitaine*, p. 44.
29 Paul d'Hollander and Pierre Pageot, *La Révolution Française dans le Limousin et la Marche* (Toulouse, 1989), p. 58.
30 Timothy Tackett, *Priest and Parish in Eighteenth-century France* (Princeton, NJ, 1977), p. 255.
31 Beatrice F. Hyslop, *A Guide to the General Cahiers of 1789* (New York, 1936), p. 21.
32 A. Bellée and V. Duchemin (eds), *Cahiers des plaintes et doléances des paroisses de la province du Maine pour les États-Généraux de 1789* (Le Mans, 1881), vol. 1, pp. 205–10; J. M. Roberts and R. C. Cobb (eds), *French Revolution Documents* (Oxford, 1966), vol. 1, pp. 83–6.
33 Roger Chartier, 'Cultures, Lumières, doléances: les cahiers de 1789', *Revue d'histoire moderne et contemporaine* 28 (1981), pp. 68–93.
34 Gilbert Shapiro and John Markoff, *Revolutionary Demands: A Content Analysis of the Cahiers de Doléances of 1789* (Stanford, CA, 1998), p. 380.
35 George V. Taylor, 'Revolutionary and non-revolutionary content in the *cahiers* of 1789: an interim report', *French Historical Studies* 7 (1972), pp. 479–502.
36 Désert, *La Révolution Française en Normandie*, p. 44.

37 John Markoff, 'Peasant Grievances and Peasant Insurrection', in Shapiro and Markoff, *Revolutionary Demands*, pp. 428–34.

38 Timothy Tackett, *Becoming a Revolutionary. The Deputies of the French National Assembly and the Emergence of a Revolutionary Culture, 1789–90* (Princeton, NJ, 1996), p. 28.

39 R. Pijassou, 'La crise révolutionnaire', in Arlette Higounet-Nadal (ed.), *Histoire du Périgord* (Toulouse, 1983), p. 256.

40 John Markoff, 'Allies and Opponents: Nobility and Third Estate in the Spring of 1789', in Shapiro and Markoff, *Revolutionary Demands*, p. 298.

41 Serge Lerat, *Landes et Chalosses* (2 vols, Pau, 1983–4), vol. 2, p. 618.

42 Pijassou, 'La crise révolutionnaire', p. 256.

43 Désert, *La Révolution Française en Normandie*, pp. 54–5.

44 Tackett, *Becoming a Revolutionary*, p. 24.

45 Malcolm Crook, *Elections in the French Revolution* (Cambridge, 1995), p. 15.

46 Michel Naudin, *Structures et doléances du Tiers Etat de Moulins en 1789* (Paris, 1987), p. 203.

47 Monique Cubells, *Les horizons de la liberté. Naissance de la Révolution en Provence, 1787–89* (Paris, 1987), p. 127.

48 Crook, *Elections*, p. 16.

49 Cubells, *Horizons*, p. 131.

50 Jean-Pierre Jessenne, *Pouvoir au village et révolution. Artois, 1760–1848* (Lille, 1987), pp. 60, 270.

51 Doyle, *Oxford History*, p. 101.

52 Tackett, *Becoming a Revolutionary*, pp. 55–9.

53 Pierre Hourmat, *Histoire de Bayonne: i – Des origines à la Révolution Française* (Bayonne, 1986), pp. 500–3.

54 Bernard Gallinato, 'La crise du régime corporatif à Bordeaux à la fin de l'Ancien Régime', in Robert Chagny (ed.), *Aux origines provinciales de la Révolution* (Grenoble, 1990), pp. 46–7.

55 Albert Soboul, 'De l'Ancien Régime à la Révolution: problème régional et réalités sociales', in Gras and Livet (eds), *Régions et régionalisme en France du dix-huitième siècle à nos jours* (Paris, 1977), pp. 25–6.

4

The spread of popular revolution

The opening of the Estates-General took place on 5 May amidst great pomp and ceremonial and in an atmosphere that at times came close to euphoria. This was the moment the French public had been waiting for, both in Paris and beyond. They had expressed their wishes and grievances in the *cahiers* and their deputies had left for Versailles to discuss the financial and constitutional problems of the realm. The long years of crisis and political stalemate were at last over, and the King would learn at first hand the true aspirations of his people, unhampered by the political manoeuvrings of his ministers and the court. Or so they supposed. The work of the Estates-General was followed by an entranced public both in Paris, where the Palais Royal evolved into a major forum of agitation, and in towns and cities throughout France. Deputies wrote pamphlets for their constituents, giving accounts of the major political struggles and justification of their own convictions. In provincial cities as well as in Paris, the political debate was carried into the streets and cafés by the multiplication of handbills and pamphlets and by the burgeoning of a new political press, concerned to discuss the ideas of the day rather than to assume the mantle of the more staid and traditional provincial *affiches*. New newspapers were coming out at the rate of one a week, with the privilege of publishing reports on the Estates-General granted to named Parisian papers and extended to others in the provinces.[1] The excitement was palpable, and the threat to order barely concealed. Arthur Young, writing on 9 June, commented that 'the business going forward at present in the pamphlet shops of Paris is incredible. I went to the Palais Royal to see what new things were published and to procure a catalogue of all. Every hour produces something new. Thirteen came out today, sixteen yesterday, and ninety-two last week.' All the presses of France were equally busy, in provincial cities just as in Paris, and they went about their business without hindrance. 'Is it not wonderful,' he adds, that while the press teems with the most levelling and even seditious principles, that if put into execution would overturn the monarchy, nothing in reply appears, and not the least step is taken by the court to restrain this extreme licentiousness of publication?[2]

The issue that proved all-consuming in the first weeks was, of course, one of procedure, of how the estates should meet and vote. This was the major question that had been left unresolved the previous spring; and when they did meet, the Third Estate were in no mood simply to conform to precedent. The deputies were aware of their own importance and their potential power: they had been persuaded by the powerful propaganda of the previous months, most notably by Sieyès' pamphlet, *Qu'est-ce que le Tiers Etat?* to understand the role that they should play in the life of the new nation.[3] They knew how vital this constitutional question was if they were to have a chance of pushing through a programme of political reform, and they were supported in this by their constituents back home, alerted by months of political campaigning to the political significance of the moment. Thus, although the nobility were happy to accede to the King's demand that they verify their powers, and did so by a large majority, the clergy showed themselves to be split, while the Third held out against the move, claiming that it would be a political defeat, the first step to an acceptance of voting by order. The Third, speaking as the Commons, at first proceeded carefully, electing *commissaires* on 18 May to negotiate with the other orders. When the unity of the clergy cracked and some of their number crossed to join the Third, the tactic was shown to have worked. Events moved at breathtaking speed. On 17 June the deputies declared themselves to constitute a single National Assembly, and though the King attempted to subvert this move by ordering the doors of the assembly hall to be locked, the deputies felt strong enough to defy him, commandeering a tennis court on 20 June and taking the solemn oath not to disperse until the constitution of the realm had been established. The oath was a calculated gamble, a gesture of defiance that united all factions within the Third Estate and made each deputy individually responsible for their collective action. It was proposed by the leading *monarchien*, Mounier, and supported by three distinguished lawyers, Target, Le Chapelier and Barnave.[4] When the King attempted to use a *séance royale* on 23 June to disperse the deputies, they resisted, defying him to use force, with the result that Louis had no choice but to give ground. This he finally did on 27 June, when he ordered the two privileged orders to join the National Assembly, thus effectively recognizing its legitimacy. The move was met with loud celebration and fireworks across the capital, for this was indeed a famous victory. Already on 14 July the assembly had set up a constitutional committee to expedite the drafting of a new constitution. It was to be the instrument that would enable the deputies to carry through a true revolution in government.[5]

During the summer months of 1789 the eyes of the nation were on the Estates-General, and regional identities were played down as France struggled with the new challenge of creating the institutions of a sovereign nation. Assuming the title of National Assembly meant more than a change of name; it was a revolutionary measure which asserted the primacy of the nation over particularisms and privileges; and those who took it fully expected that it would be followed by punitive sanctions. The fact that Louis XVI felt obliged to recognize the Assembly was due to more than his personal temperament or a tendency to vacillate; it reflected the terrible weakness of his position, his desperate need for new taxes if the monarchy were to avoid bankruptcy. If he gave way, it was because he had little choice. Public opinion remained nervous, however, and suspicions of the King's motives remained, especially as the more conservative of his courtiers were urging that the deputies' action be treated as an act of sedition, and as military units were known to be taking up position around the capital. For, though the principal goal of the deputies had been to secure voting by head, the consequences of their action were far greater. The creation of the National Assembly was, in the words of one recent historian, 'clearly a revolutionary measure, converting a traditionally consultative body into a deliberative, policy-making one and it presaged the assertion of national sovereignty'.[6] But at the time there was little to herald the revolution that was soon to be unleashed. Many deputies expected that the new constitution, far from being a root-and-branch measure, could be drafted rapidly, without undue controversy, in a matter of weeks.[7] They were counting without the pressure of the streets, the extension of the revolution to the popular classes of society.

For if the summer of 1789 was the moment when the Third Estate transformed itself into the National Assembly and initiated legislation independently of the King – steps which would extend the assembly's life for another two and a half years – it was also the period when popular pressures made themselves felt with renewed force on the deputies and pushed forward the cause of reform. This was true in Paris and in most provincial cities, but also in many parts of the countryside, where poor harvests had led to grain shortages, and where unemployment and economic misery had become major catalysts of popular violence. Indeed, throughout the spring and summer, during the period of the elections and in the months that followed, the social climate in many regions of the country became more tense, and misery was turned into a political issue which called for political answers. People increasingly feared political reaction from those who might seek to deny them the fruits of their constitution or overturn the political benefits that had already been won. The need for a constitution, as a guarantor of moderate reform, was one of the few central planks on which everyone seemed agreed. In Toulouse, the city's barristers demonstrated rare unity of purpose during these months: they were committed to moderate change, and expressed the hope that 'the diverse orders that compose the nation ... are going to work in concert and without respite toward the restoration of the State, the perfection of the Constitution ...'.[8] Everywhere, it seemed, there was a new level of political awareness and assertiveness, and a new generation of political leaders was born. Many, like Bertrand Barère in Tarbes in the

Pyrenees, would continue to provide leadership, regional and national, throughout the revolutionary decade.[9]

If the elites were inclined to respond by addresses lauding the work of the Assembly and the Committee of the Constitution, peasants and urban workers were more likely to turn to direct action and violent protest. Economic hardship drove men, and to a degree, women, into the streets and markets to make their protest against high prices and put their case against feudal exactions. Bread prices soared uncontrollably in the spring and early summer as France approached its third successive crop failure, and in the granary belt around Paris shortage was soon translated into fear, panic and the constant threat of violence. At the market of Les Andelys, for instance, the price of wheat had risen by two-thirds in the twelve months from March 1788 to March 1789, and already the poor were driven to seek whatever relief they could find – whether it be through casual labouring, help from the parish poor box, begging, petty crime or seasonal migration elsewhere.[10] So great was the fear of social disorder that urban authorities tried to intervene whenever it became clear that the parish funds were exhausted. In Normandy, for instance, emergency measures were taken in virtually every major town. In Caen and Granville the authorities distributed soup to the poor, with the clergy assuming direct responsibility for this in Caen. In Evreux the council ordered the manufacture of a special low-price bread for the town's poor, stipulating that the flour should contain one-third of barley. In Cherbourg and Le Havre the city authorities held back some grain from the market so as to provide a reserve for moments of dire shortage. And both Caen and Rouen recognized the need for some economic redistribution, collecting money from the more affluent members of the community so that they could buy stocks of grain to feed the poor. Everywhere there was fear of dearth and starvation, a fear which, in the Norman case, was made worse by falling wages in the textile trades.[11]

Fear of starvation was as much a rural problem as an urban one, for high grain prices posed as much of a threat to the rural poor, the subsistence peasants who had little land and no reserves to last them throughout the agricultural year, the *bordiers* and *journaliers* and other landless labourers who already formed a rural proletariat in the wheat-growing areas of Paris's hinterland. They were without resource, poor, starving and desperate, in villages and hamlets where there was insufficient grain to keep the population alive until the following summer; they had to leave if others – women and children, and those too old to hold down a job – were to survive the worst months of hardship. They were the ones most likely to seek seasonal work in the capital, those able-bodied young men whose untimely presence as they passed through a village or market town could so easily spark off panic among local people. The communities that lay along the main roads to and from the capital were those where such fears were most naturally fostered, communities that had long been accustomed to the sight of rough, unshaven strangers, people whom no one could vouch for, passing through on their

way to somewhere else, men whose business might or might not be legitimate, men with the power to inflict harm on their inhabitants. Travellers were
a permanent sight, passing through on foot or in carts or by river, walking
lethargically through hot afternoons or travelling by night to reach market
by dawn; many, indeed, had no choice but to travel during the hours of
darkness, which made their presence even more suspect, and their hidden
threat all the more sinister. Migrant workers seldom travelled alone. From
mountain communes and the villages of the plain they moved about the
country in groups, noisy, gregarious bands of friends and companions whose
company made the long journeys seem less arduous.[12] But for the people of
the towns and villages along the way – those lying along the banks of the
Seine or on the brigand-infested *route du Nord* – the sight of bands of migrant
workers was always spiced with menace. They were, of course, integral to
the life of Paris, as of any other great city. But they are also crucial for
understanding rural panics. 'It is through them', as Richard Cobb noted,
'that radiate the shock waves of popular fears and prejudices, news and
rumours of great events, of violent political changes, of great disasters,
natural and human'.[13]

It was misery, the sheer depths of desperation to which the poor had sunk
in the winter of 1788 and through the spring and early summer of 1789,
which best explains the *Grande Peur* that swept through great swathes of the
French countryside in the course of that summer. Much of the reaction was,
of course, wholly irrational, the effect of rumour and paranoia rather than
any real threat. The sight of strangers at unseasonal times, the rural poor
returning dejectedly to their homes from a Paris where they had found neither jobs nor sustenance, was enough to spark off panics that might engulf
whole regions. The tocsin would be rung and lurid stories passed from
mouth to mouth, village to village, until two men had become twenty, and
ten had been transmogrified into a snarling mob one hundred strong. Only
the detail differed. Here drunken strangers were blamed, men supposedly in
the pay of the seigneur or even the King; elsewhere it was bands of brigands
out to hold the countryside to ransom; in one instance, close to the Norman
coast, the trouble was attributed to British soldiers, again in the pay of the
aristocracy.[14] Rural communities armed themselves in self-defence, and the
appearance of soldiers sent from Paris only served to fuel popular anxiety
further. There was, it would seem, no orchestrated peasant movement,
though the elections and the drawing up of the *cahiers* helped persuade many
peasants and rural artisans that those they thought of as their natural enemies
were turning vagabond armies against them in order to subvert the revolutionary process in the countryside. Between the winter of 1788 and the late
summer of 1789 there were peasant uprisings in Provence, Dauphiné,
Franche-Comté and Picardy, and even though not all of these were the result
of fear, news of them helped unleash fear elsewhere. By the end of the summer peasant violence and outbreaks of panic had spread through large parts
of Alsace, Lower Normandy, the Mâconnais and the Périgord.[15]

Yet to place such heavy emphasis on panic should not conceal the fact that in some parts of France peasant violence can be traced to deep-seated anti-seigneurialism – in the Franche-Comté, for instance, and in parts of the South-West, where whole communities armed themselves, often led by rural artisans with the tacit approval of wealthier farmers.[16] Here it was less strangers who found themselves the object of attack than seigneurs and their estate managers, and the objective of the rioters was often the seigneur's château, his dovecote or his armoury. In a few instances they demanded those specific feudal documents which established his claim to levy dues, or shotguns which, the peasants claimed, he had illegally confiscated from them. A succession of attacks in Dauphiné in the last days of July shows just how precise the assailants could be, scouring lawyers' offices in search of *terriers*, demanding precise legal documents of whose existence they were already aware, and burning them before the very eyes of the seigneur. At La Tour du Pin they specifically demanded the list of feudal exactions dating from 1680.[17] In other words, these were peasant movements that had a political core, movements which often, as in the Dordogne, had roots in a hatred of the system of landholding and the abuses of the lords that can be traced back to the *croquants* of the seventeenth century.[18] In some regions the violence bore the hallmarks of peasant insurrection and social conflict. Clay Ramsay suggests that the presence or absence of fear in these months may reflect the degree of social cohesion existing in the community, and the relations between the countryside and local towns. In the Cambrésis, for instance, where there was no fear, the poor of town and country were linked in shared opposition to the rich and the grain merchants, but in the Soissonnais, where there was fear, the country-dwellers were united by common animosity towards the towns.[19] Taken collectively, the outbreaks of rural violence of these months were without precedent in the eighteenth century, with the possible exception of the *Guerre des Farines* of 1775.[20] Even where rumours spread that the region was ravaged by brigands or foreign soldiers, the reason given was often political, a popular belief that counter-revolutionary nobles had hired vagabonds and other criminal elements to starve country people and force them to renounce their hard-won rights. This reasoning followed naturally from a widespread rural belief in famine pacts that united the rich and the landed against the peasantry, imagined plots that were partly explained by social conflicts in the countryside and partly by the structural weaknesses of the eighteenth-century grain trade.[21]

Rural violence had an immediate impact on the deputies at Versailles, for whom news of rick-burnings and assaults on châteaux conjured up alarmist images of the countryside in flames. It played a role in national politics by frightening many of the nobility and forcing them to make timely concessions, and it explains, at least in part, the sudden willingness of so many seigneurs to renounce their ancient privileges in the hecatomb of the night of 4 August, and of so many deputies to contemplate the reality of a world stripped of privilege.[22] Writing of an attack on his property near Argentan on 29 July, the Comte de Germiny lamented the loss of his feudal *terriers*, the historic documents that allowed him to lay claim to his seigneurial dues. Who, he asked, would ever be able to prove that he had suffered this loss, or establish the true extent of what had been destroyed? 'I appeal to your prudence for the National Assembly to set out some method to return to me what I have lost, above all the use of a common, useful to my parishioners as well as my property, of which they have burned the titles'.[23] Of course, Germiny was not alone. In areas rent by outbreaks of fear, the social fabric itself was threatened, and reports of popular violence turned the minds of property-owners to repression and measures of self-defence.

In towns the *Grande Peur* hastened the creation of citizen militias and National Guard battalions as their citizenry sought to secure their properties against attack from the countryside. Long-standing suspicion of the peasantry was rekindled, and town–country distrust exacerbated. Even very small towns reacted precipitately to the threat of violence. In the Corbières, for instance, Lézignan established its *garde bourgeoise* to patrol the neighbouring countryside, in response to 'confused and turbulent rumours that are spreading through the town and its hinterland', so as to 'prevent disorder and put a stop to such troubles as may be developing'. Or again, in Marsillargues, where a meeting was held of 'all the inhabitants, without distinction of order', it was decided to create a communal militia 'to maintain order and guarantee public safety'.[24] Overall, the effects of the fear were arguably greater in rural areas, where one result was to rearm a rural population that had been systematically disarmed by the royal authorities during the second half of the eighteenth century – in Flanders in 1777, and in Normandy and Guienne as recently as 1785–7. The creation of citizen militias to counter the *Grande Peur* largely undid this work, since many of the local militias were maintained long after the threat of insurrection had passed, and became a means of combating the authorities of the *ancien régime*.[25] In the Ille-et-Vilaine, for instance, where there were functioning National Guard units in around 30 per cent of rural communes between 1790 and 1793, membership was not confined to townsmen or those who might be classed as 'semi-urbanized', men who worked as artisans and would have had regular contact with the towns. Nor were they always voters or taxpayers, since in many communities their number exceeded the number of active citizens. In those villages where we know the professions of members of the guard, they were often peasants, country-dwellers without any obvious link to urban culture.[26]

The creation of citizen militias and National Guard units merged with another development in provincial towns during the summer of 1789, the creation of emergency municipal committees to reclaim political authority from unrepresentative bodies and to solve what local people identified as a multifaceted social and political crisis. Their agenda was dominated by fear and anxiety – fear of peasant violence and attacks on property being matched by another more political fear, that the King would ignore the popular will and dissolve the National Assembly. In addition, they faced continued problems of grain supply and feared unrest amongst the poorer sections of their population. News of Necker's dismissal on 12 July helped to fuel existing passions, so that in the weeks that followed many towns rushed to set up revolutionary committees, either to take control of municipal government or to supervise the existing elites. Some waited for Paris to take a lead before setting up a new executive; others were happy to take the initiative unaided, acting in the last days of June in response to pressure from their electors. But the setting up of municipal committees seldom occurred without the accompanying threat of popular violence. There were calls for cheaper bread, attacks on *octroi* gates and pillaging of grain stores. In Strasbourg the town hall was sacked.[27] In Troyes the authorities had to negotiate with the rioters after seven or eight thousand people demonstrated in front of the gates of the town hall 'and could have massacred all those inside'.[28] Violence also erupted in a number of cities in Normandy – Rouen, Caen and Cherbourg – starting with noisy demonstrations in the popular *faubourgs*, which were usually sparked off by high bread prices and market shortages. In Rouen, for instance – where the first crowd scenes were reported on 11 July, three days before the storming of the Bastille in Paris – rioters gathered in the suburb of Martainville, attacking granaries and the houses of the rich.[29] More commonly, provincial ferment flared when news arrived of Necker's dismissal, or within a few days of the fall of the Bastille, when municipal councils found themselves under increasing pressure to supply the mass of the people with arms.

The precise form of the municipal revolution varied from town to town, usually reflecting the degree of social turbulence in the community and the respect in which the *ancien régime* authorities had been held. In those towns where the installation of new authorities followed closely on the fall of the Bastille and where the attention of local revolutionaries was focused on developments in the capital, we find an understandable desire to imitate the Parisians. Events in Bordeaux, for instance, followed a predictable pattern when, on 17 July, the municipality was informed in a letter from Paul Nairac, a merchant and patriot who was then staying in Paris, that the Bastille had been taken. The youth of the town demonstrated noisily, adorned in patriotic *tricolor* cockades, and sought from the ninety electors of the city – the *Quatre-vingt-dix* – authority to raise a citizen militia, an *armée patriotique*, without distinction of rank or legal estate. By 21 July the proposed army had been raised, a force of 1,200 men divided into thirteen regiments and 266 companies, and in this way the city's National Guard was born. On the following day, the *Quatre-vingt-dix* reconstituted themselves as a committee, with elected officers (a president, vice-president and secretary). Almost immediately they involved themselves in the task of obtaining sufficient bread for the population, and within days the *parlement* sought their help in calming popular fears. The *Quatre-vingt-dix* thus achieved new prestige, which legitimated their role in municipal affairs to the extent that, without obtaining any formal legal recognition, they and their executive committee of fifteen members became the effective municipality of the city. They enjoyed unparalleled popular support; indeed, such was the enthusiasm for guard service in 1789 that at one point Bordeaux had some 15,000 men in arms, undergoing a fairly rudimentary training to defend the city and its property.[30] Quietly and prudently, and without any bloodshed, Bordeaux's municipal revolution had been achieved.[31]

In other places, where there was bloodshed or rioting, the municipal revolution was often an emergency measure taken to avert a worsening crisis. Property-owners, merchants and businessmen now involved themselves in municipal politics, often for the first time, in a bid to avert anarchy. What differed from one place to another was the role allowed to the former municipal officials. In some places the new committees sought to supplant the existing town councils and assume their powers of municipal government. In others they divided responsibilities more clinically, with the committee restricting its ambitions to matters of policing and public order. Or they co-opted the old councillors, working in close collaboration with them. The difference in approach is well brought out in Lynn Hunt's comparison between two nearby cities, Troyes and Reims, which responded in subtly different ways to the July crisis. She observes that in Troyes the town council quite deliberately did not invite the twenty-four town deputies to join the committee, whereas Reims, and many other larger provincial towns, did. This was because, she argues, 'the Troyes officials saw their committee as a creature of circumstance, an ad hoc formalisation of the cooperation developed in the months of crisis between the leading officials of the local Old Regime institutions'.[32] It was not intended to transform local politics, but simply to conduct a policing operation and put down popular disorder.

In every case, however, the municipal revolution brought local people, and especially the local bourgeoisie, into city politics; in some it pitted towns against the surrounding countryside and underscored their urban pride. In no case was their action deliberately directed against the centre, or in any sense anti-Parisian. Indeed, what occurred in towns like Lille and Bordeaux can best be seen as part of a countrywide movement in which events in Paris played a central role and offered an example that inspired other urban centres to follow suit. For against the backcloth of national events and the debates in the assembly, Paris, too, underwent a municipal revolution in the summer of 1789, one that would change the image of the capital in provincial France and play a key part in national politics throughout the decade. The creation of municipal institutions and the devolution of local power were crucial elements in the national revolution as well as in a purely local or regional context.

The people of Paris, as we have seen, had long been regarded by the authorities with suspicion, as a fickle and potentially turbulent populace, liable to be roused to fury by rumour and insult as much as by dearth and shortage. It was for this reason that, for so much of the eighteenth century, the city had been policed with a thoroughness and professionalism unknown elsewhere, and its people subjected to an unparalleled degree of surveillance and espionage. By 1789 Parisians lived in less fear of murder and violent assault than they had earlier in the century, and the city authorities were well equipped to deal with the periodic ravages of fire and flooding that punctuated urban life. Paris had more police and a better tradition of policing than the cities of provincial France, and far more policing than the country-side, where the *maréchaussée* did little more than patrol main roads and keep order at fairs and markets. Policing Paris was a matter of state security and it was organized by the state, under the command of the *lieutenant de police*, a post first created by Colbert in 1667, which by Louis XV's reign had developed into one of the most powerful offices under the crown. For here was a man who had ready access to the corridors of power, who would make a weekly journey to Versailles to confer with ministers, and who was on occasion received directly by the King himself.[33] Yet he also had know-ledge of Parisian low-life, the brothels, gaming dens and rooming houses of the capital, the sources of potential violence and crime; he collected evi-dence through a network of spies and informers; and he offered aid and redress to the poor and desperate of the capital. He understood the criminal underworld of Paris, and it was that which made him so valuable to those in power. His officers came to their task with certain deeply ingrained assumptions about the society they were policing, about which *quartiers* were prone to violence and which trades to acts of brutality. They knew, in Richard Cobb's phrase, 'that some trades – and people from some provinces and some villages – are more violence-prone, more brutal, more anarchic, more explosive, more easily provoked, than those from another trade or another province or village'.[34] In other words, they worked from their col-lective experience and prejudice to control the popular classes of the capital and prevent the violence that always seemed to threaten.

Yet if violence often threatened, it seldom erupted with any venom. There had been, it is true, a serious outbreak of panic and rioting in 1750 when rumours spread that officials were conniving at the abduction of Parisian children, mainly boys, so that their blood could be used to cure a royal princess who was supposedly suffering from leprosy; yet even in these extreme circumstances the anger of the crowd was directed not at the King or the government, but quite specifically at the police authorities in Paris itself.[35] But that outbreak was something of an exception. In 1775, when large areas of the North and the Paris Basin were at the mercy of rioters, Paris itself was relatively easy to control.[36] The reputation for violence, it would seem, was based not on the half-century before 1789 so much as on a previous age, especially the sixteenth and seventeenth centuries. Indeed, what is striking by the end of the *ancien régime* is how often Paris failed to riot, even when the *parlement* had been exiled or when the price of grain had risen: there were moments when Paris was a surprisingly calm and orderly city, when the Parisian crowd was strangely, almost ominously, silent. It was only in the two years of the immediate *pré-révolution*, from 1787 until 1789, that the city once more became agitated and young Parisians started taking to the streets in support of a political cause, defying the police with hails of stones, clubs and fireworks. It is legitimate to ask why Paris had been so untypically quiescent. One possible explanation lies in a loss of urban solidarity across this period, following the decision to disband the old citizen militia and replace it with police and soldiers who often came from distant provinces and shared little common culture with the Parisians. In Robert Descimon's words, this left the people of Paris 'civically alienated', 'an orphaned community'.[37] Only with the growth of the artisan trades and the immigration of workers from the provinces would this change. By the time of the Revolution there was a new sense of community among artisans and journeymen which brought them into the streets and encouraged them to demonstrate spontaneously against authority, and to do so without acknowledged leaders or social mediators.[38]

In the summer of 1789 Paris was swept by a surge of political violence that would change the character of the Revolution and restore Parisians' reputation for bloodletting and, in the eyes of many, anarchy. The violence was concentrated in a single week, starting on 12 July when news of Necker's dismissal became known in the streets of the capital and rumours of a royal coup began to spread. Necker still enjoyed popular esteem in the city and it was widely believed that his dismissal would have dire consequences: bread prices would rise still further, the state would be threatened with bankruptcy and the National Assembly would be transferred to the provinces where it could be quietly dissolved.[39] The response of ordinary Parisians was noisy and confused, with crowds gathering at the Palais Royal in search of news. In the gardens of the Palais Royal several thousand Parisians were harangued by popular orators, most famously by a young Camille Desmoulins, who raised the spectre of a new Saint Bartholomew's day directed against patriots and called on the people to take up arms in defence of their liberties.[40] Necker's dismissal was felt personally by those who had looked to him to initiate reform, and public entertainments were closed as a sign of mourning. Passing down the Boulevard du Temple, one group entered Curtius' waxworks, where they acquired busts of two of their heroes, Necker and the Duc d'Orléans, which they draped in black crêpe and held aloft, like saints in a Catholic procession. Eyewitnesses spoke of a crowd five or six thousand strong when it reached the Place Vendôme, where it was brutally scattered by an ill-conceived cavalry charge by the Royal Allemand, under the command of the Prince de Lambesc.[41] According to revolutionary legend, Lambesc not only used mercenaries to suppress the people of the capital, in the process crushing innocent bystanders, but he was also responsible for killing an old man in the process. Though this is probably untrue, Lambesc's charge provided popular Paris with a convenient martyr. Believing that the royal counter-attack had begun, the people began looting gunshops in order to arm themselves against repression, and as rumours spread that the King had ordered his troops to take control of the streets, an army unit stationed in Paris, the *Gardes Françaises*, went over to the side of the people.[42] The popular revolution in the capital had begun.

That night and throughout the next day the crowd vented their anger on the *octroi* gates, the customs barriers around Paris, which they held responsible for the mounting bread prices in the capital. The gates were torn down and around forty of the fifty-four customs posts destroyed, while the *Gardes Françaises* stood by and offered their moral support. Others attacked the prisons of La Force, the Conciergerie and the Saint-Lazare monastery, looting stocks of grain from Saint-Lazare and freeing those they found imprisoned there. There was an air of carnival and anarchy in the city, but also a deep sense of foreboding, as it was known that the King was bringing up reinforcements in the form of his Swiss regiments to defend key installations. The electors, meeting at the Hôtel de Ville, were the only *de facto* authority who could hope to exert any measure of control, and they acted incisively, decreeing the formation of a bourgeois militia in each of the sixty districts of the city. In this way Paris, too, armed itself in defence of life and property, creating a force – soon to be renamed the National Guard – of 48,000, strongly rooted in the propertied classes of the capital, in whose ranks the common people were not immediately welcomed. Indeed, its first task in patrolling the city would be to prevent anarchy and arrest looters, and that at a time when the crowd was still anxiously roaming the streets and when each day brought fresh rumours of troop movements. Its significance should not be overlooked. Amid disorder and the threat of anarchy, Paris, too, had initiated its municipal revolution.

It was on 14 July, of course, that popular violence in the capital came to a head, with the attack on the Bastille by a large and angry crowd. Already that morning a smaller crowd had attacked the royal armoury at the Invalides, hopeful of finding arms and gunpowder; cannon and small arms had been seized, but the people turned their attentions to the Bastille on learning that significant powder stocks had been moved there the previous day. By the early afternoon several thousand had gathered, fuelled by drink and the excitement of the moment, demanding that the governor, de Launay, hand over the weapons and ammunition stocked in the building. They were, as we know from police records, largely local men, artisans and journeymen from the east of Paris and the nearby Faubourg Saint-Antoine, and, though they were clearly stirred by the words of popular orators, all attempts by the authorities to prove that they had been manipulated or bribed by radical troublemakers failed.[43] The ensuing events are well known. Infuriated by rumours of royal plans to use force to repress Paris, and further stirred by the apparent attempts by Flesselles, the *ancien régime* mayor of the city, to deny them the arms they needed to defend themselves, the crowd was in angry mood. Fear mingled with their anger; fear for their lives, their families, their homes. That was why all attempts to find a compromise solution that could end the *journée* peacefully proved fruitless, and when troops guarding the fortress – significantly, they were Swiss troops, foreign mercenaries in the pay of the King – fired towards the crowd, their anger spilled over into violence.[44] The crowd, still calling for arms, forced an entry into the inner courtyard, whereupon the troops panicked and opened fire, killing around one hundred attackers and wounding a further seventy. At one point de Launay threatened to blow up the powder stocks, destroying both the fortress and much of the surrounding neighbourhood; but his garrison persuaded him that an atrocity on that scale would be self-defeating. They knew that the prison gates could not withstand the force of the crowd, and so, reluctantly, de Launay surrendered.[45]

What followed, in the eyes of royalist and conservative observers, was little better than lynch law, the unbridled savagery to which undisciplined crowds can give way in moments of high tension. First Flesselles and then de Launay, both suspected of trying to trick the people and expose them to danger, were brutally hacked to death, their heads triumphantly held aloft by the crowd on pikes as they processed through the streets in celebration of their victory. Three officers and three soldiers of the Bastille garrison were also denounced, for treason and for firing on the people; they, too, were massacred. It was an act of hatred and popular vengeance, the response of the crowd to the brutality they had witnessed and justified to those involved by their fear of treason, the betrayal of Paris and its people. The Bastille was widely detested as a symbol of tyranny, an impregnable prison to which the King condemned those who threatened his autocracy, innocent victims of arbitrary justice or *lits de justice*. In fact, when the crowd burst in, the Bastille contained only seven prisoners, none of whom could reasonably be seen as victims of royal absolutism. But that barely mattered. What counted was its power as a symbol, a fortress overshadowing the popular streets of the capital, a store for weapons and powder with which to oppress the people, a prison so secure that it was impossible for any prisoner to escape. That image was already well established before the end of the *ancien régime*, as public fascination with the daring escape of Latude in 1756 bears witness. In all Latude would spend a total of thirty-five years locked in the Bastille, and he was already something of a folk hero in the Paris of the *ancien régime*. Through his association with the dark symbolism of the Bastille, the Revolution could be said to have relaunched his popularity, and in 1789 his portrait by Vestier was one of the great successes of the Paris Salon.[46] When, the following year, he published a memoir on his escape under the provocative title of *Le despotisme dévoilé*, the book would go through twenty editions in four years, so well did it capture the mood of the moment. In the *Mercure de France* it was praised as a graphic struggle between liberty and tyranny, and the paper even suggested that it should be required reading for the young.[47]

The *journée* of 14 July ensured that the Bastille would acquire a new symbolic value in the history of the French Revolution. Overnight its destruction

became a symbol of liberty itself. Prints and etchings celebrated the overthrow of royal tyranny, while the presses ran off pamphlets singing the
praises of the brave Parisians who had fought and sacrificed themselves in
the cause of liberty. De Launay, it was generally assumed, had earned his
fate; there was little sympathy for the vanquished, while criticism of the
crowd was muted. Far from being bloodthirsty cannibals driven by a primordial bloodlust – the image presented by royalist opponents – the Parisians
were portrayed as a noble people, inspired by a philosophy of freedom and
a desire to liberate their fellow men. And their actions were given an epoch-
making significance. The freeing of the prisoners from the royal fortress,
which had been little more than a casual afterthought on the day, was now
elevated into a central part of the legend, one that both tainted the monarchy and brought lustre to the people. Everything was painted in black and
white. As the event was reported in *Révolutions de Paris* – and the same
tone was adopted by journalists and pamphleteers across France – 'It is
impossible to describe all the horrors that were found in this detestable cave;
machines of death were found previously unknown to man'.[48] It hardly
mattered whether these accounts were true; indeed, by obscuring the truth
and offering a heroic and symbolic representation, contemporaries merely
hastened the mythification of the event. Parisians rushed to demolish what
was left of the building, among them Pierre-François Palloy, who made his
fortune by making mementoes of the prison and sending stones seized from
the rubble of the Bastille around the provinces of France.[49] The storming of
the Bastille rapidly became one of the defining moments of the Revolution,
and it was one which placed Paris and the people of Paris at the very heart
of revolutionary identity.

It certainly seemed so to contemporaries, as news of the people's triumph
spread from town to town. The young, in particular, identified with the
Parisian crowd and urged their own civic leaders to emulate the example of
the capital. In La Rochelle, for instance, people flocked to the post offices to
find out what had happened, and when the details of the *journée* became
known, the news was greeted with rapture, especially the report that the
King had accepted the national cockade to symbolize a new and more har-
monious relationship between the monarch and his people.[50] Often the news
led to a revolution in civic institutions and the formation of municipal committees on the model of the Paris Commune. In some of the larger provincial cities the crowd tried to imitate Paris by attacking their own 'bastilles',
their own symbols of tyranny. In Lyon, for instance, they mounted an
assault on the fortress of Pierre Ancise in August 1789, and in the following
spring the people of Marseille attacked two royal forts in the city, Saint-Jean
and Saint-Nicolas. Paris noted these events with satisfaction, seeing them as
inspired by their own example. On this occasion the editor of *Révolutions
de Paris* was specific. 'Citizens of Marseille,' he wrote, 'your cause cannot
be separated from that of the Parisians … You have walked in their footsteps'.[51] Everywhere the fall of the Bastille gave the people of the capital a

new public recognition. Theirs was a real revolutionary achievement which allowed them to present themselves as the saviours of the nation, preventing the victory of reaction that was so widely feared. Overnight they became heroes. But the key question remained. Could that achievement legitimate the *fureurs* and violence of the crowd? Or were the people of Paris forever to be identified with lynching and murder? Few questioned that the taking of the Bastille was one of the founding acts of the Revolution, but not everyone could approve the actions of a crowd when they favoured uncontrolled violence and 'a sacrilegious anarchy'.[52]

Of course, the assault on the Bastille was one of the founding acts of the French Revolution; and it was not for nothing that 14 July would be chosen by the politicians of the Third Republic as France's national day.[53] Events moved very swiftly thereafter. On 15 July the King, fearful that his soldiers would not obey his commands, informed the National Assembly that he would withdraw the army from Paris and Versailles. The news was received by the deputies amid scenes of joy and ecstasy. On the same day the electors transformed themselves into the Paris Commune, a new and permanent ruling council for the city, with an elected mayor. As their first mayor they chose Jean-Sylvain Bailly, with the Marquis de Lafayette as commander of the National Guard. Both were highly symbolic figures, men who had become indelibly identified in the public mind with the revolutionary cause. Bailly, an astronomer and member of the Académie des Sciences, represented the city of Paris in the National Assembly; on 3 June he had already achieved a certain notoriety when the Third Estate had elected him as their president.[54] Lafayette was widely fêted as the 'hero of two worlds', the general whose troops had defeated the British and contributed to the independence of the American colonies. During the 1780s he had been largely marginalized for his liberal views, but he played an important role in the National Assembly, where, as vice-president, he would propose the first clauses of the Declaration of the Rights of Man on 26 August.[55] Now both men were at the centre of the revolutionary stage, a fact tacitly accepted by Louis when he was welcomed by Bailly at the Hôtel de Ville on 17 July, before symbolically donning the *tricolor* cockade. On the previous day he had made a still greater concession to the will of the Paris crowd when he had accepted the inevitable and recalled Necker.

Just as important was the general change of political culture which this heralded – the move during 1789 and the early months of 1790 to elected bodies, working in the name of the people and answerable to the people, and the rejection of the organic image of society, the quest for precedent and respect for seniority which had been so critical to the workings of the *ancien régime*. For local politics in Paris this change had crucial consequences, leaving the city far more open to radicalism. It destroyed once and for all the influence of the traditional Parisian power-brokers, the vestries, gilds and fraternities, replacing them with elected bodies, from revolutionary committees to National Guard units and justices of the peace. In the process it transformed the concept of a Parisian political class, encouraging those of a more ideological bent, those capable of appealing to the wider population and undermining the tight, self-perpetuating elites who had held sway in the past. The new men were less hierarchical and submissive to authority, so that it became more difficult, in David Garrioch's words, 'for one occupational group, one family or one clique to dominate'.[56] For the authorities this had the effect of making the city more difficult to control, since they could no longer operate through the traditional corporate structures. Along with the effective ending of censorship, it helped ensure that the people of Paris would go on to play a formative role in the escalation of revolutionary radicalism.

The move towards greater radicalism also implied the acceptance of higher levels of violence, since increasingly the Parisian revolution was being played out in the city's streets and markets. We have seen how in the week of 12 July that violence was quickly turned to political ends, and how both the Assembly and the King were forced to take account of it. Direct action by the *menu peuple* of the capital, whether for their own ends or in support of the more radical factions in the assembly, had immediate political repercussions – gaining concessions on bread prices, for example, and even forcing changes in government policy – and with the passage of time the Parisians became well aware of their political muscle. During 1789 popular violence became almost endemic in the life of the capital and was a major factor in the radicalization of the revolutionary movement, with the consequence that throughout the year key political moments were marked by the intervention of the crowd. A few examples may suffice. Back in April, again in the Faubourg Saint-Antoine, there had been stormy scenes in the Sainte-Marguerite electoral district as the Third Estate were discussing their *cahier* and some poorer artisans tried unsuccessfully to have their demands included. It was at this meeting that a wallpaper manufacturer, Réveillon, urged that bread prices be fixed so that poorer members of society could afford to eat. But his words were misunderstood to mean that he was proposing wage reductions, and the crowd responded angrily, by sacking the factories of the two largest employers in the area, Réveillon's own and that of a manufacturing chemist, Henriot.[57] Here the people exerted political as well as economic pressure. The electors and the newly elected deputies would take note of their demands, as the destruction of property spread further alarm amongst the possessing classes. The early debates were held in the shadow of popular violence.

Violence did not cease once the Bastille had fallen and political gains had been registered. Throughout the rest of the year Paris remained a nervous, edgy city, with the threat of violence ever present. Flesselles and de Launay were not the only prominent figures to die at the hands of a lynch-mob. Only a few days later, on 23 July, the *intendant* of Paris, Bertier de Sauvigny, and his father-in-law, Foulon, were first murdered and then decapitated by a crowd angered by rumours that they had tried to starve the population; and again the crowd put their severed heads on pikes and paraded them through the streets.[58] Popular politics still had something of the carnival about it, and the deaths were integrated into a kind of macabre street theatre, designed to impress the deputies in the Tuileries as much as ordinary Parisians going about their business. Like the traditional public executions on the Place de Grève, the deaths of Bertier and Foulon were played out in the street, challenging and involving onlookers. The deputies, too, were challenged. The National Assembly had no choice but to take cognizance of the crowd's fears and wishes, knowing that violence was now part of the language of politics, with the Parisian crowd one of its principal players.

In October, some 7,000 women from the Paris markets, many armed and dragging cannon, marched to Versailles to demand bread and the punishment of speculators. Once again the people attempted to exert political as well as economic pressure; they linked food shortages with political corruption and sought redress from the assembly. On this occasion the disturbances had their origins in bread queues and cuts to food supplies to the capital; but very soon the rumour spread that shortage was caused by speculation and a conspiracy of the rich, another manifestation of the belief that the Parisians were being deliberately starved. Once at Versailles, the women confronted the Assembly before demanding an audience with Louis himself. Then followed a new demand: that the royal family accompany them back to the capital. By this time the marchers were backed by armed force, as Paris sent Lafayette and units of the National Guard to contain the more violent excesses of the crowd. But the call for Louis to return to the capital only grew louder, and on 6 October the King agreed. By bringing the royal family to the Tuileries, the crowd forced Louis, and with him his ministers and courtiers, into the heart of their city, where they knew that they could at any time bring popular pressure to bear on him. A few days later the National Assembly felt bound to follow.[59] Political decisions would henceforth be taken very publicly, under the eyes of the Parisian crowd, ending the symbolic division between court and people, between Versailles and Paris, which Louis XIV had favoured as a means of keeping Paris at bay. From this point on, Paris could bring its influence to bear on the national revolution in a way that no other city could rival. This would prove a crucial development in a revolution which emphasized the devolution of political authority. It meant that local power struggles in Paris would now have a significance in national politics, and brought new levels of violence into political life. It also transformed the balance of power between Paris and provincial France.

Notes

1 Hugh Gough, *The Newspaper Press in the French Revolution* (London, 1988), p. 22.
2 Arthur Young, *Travels in France during the Years 1787, 1788 and 1789* (London, 1889), p. 153.

3 Emmanuel Sieyès, *Qu'est-ce que le Tiers Etat?*, ed. Jean Tulard (Paris, 1982).

4 Albert Goodwin, *The French Revolution* (London, 1953), p. 58.

5 Jean Egret, *La Révolution des Notables. Mounier et les Monarchiens, 1789* (Paris, 1950), *passim*.

6 Michael P. Fitzsimmons, *The Remaking of France: The National Assembly and the Constitution of 1791* (Cambridge, 1994), p. 42.

7 Ibid., p. 52.

8 Lenard R. Berlanstein, *The Barristers of Toulouse in the Eighteenth Century, 1740–93* (Baltimore, MD, 1975), p. 160.

9 Leo Gershoy, *Bertrand Barère, A Reluctant Terrorist* (Princeton, NJ, 1962), pp. 60–6.

10 Olwen H. Hufton, *The Poor of Eighteenth-Century France, 1750–89* (Oxford, 1974), pp. 69–127.

11 Gabriel Désert, *La Révolution Française en Normandie* (Toulouse, 1989), p. 60.

12 Abel Poitrineau, *Remues d'hommes. Essai sur les migrations montagnardes en France aux 17e et 18e siècles* (Paris, 1983), p. 69.

13 Richard Cobb, *Paris and its Provinces, 1792–1802* (Oxford, 1975), p. 27.

14 Georges Lefebvre, *La Grande Peur de 1789* (Paris, 1932), pp. 152–6.

15 P. M. Jones, *The Peasantry in the French Revolution* (Cambridge, 1988), pp. 67–70.

16 Jean Boutier, 'Jacqueries en pays croquant. Les révoltes paysannes en Aquitaine', *Annales: ESC* 34 (1979), pp. 765–6, 769–70.

17 Jean Nicolas, *La Révolution Française dans les Alpes, Dauphiné et Savoie* (Toulouse, 1989), pp. 86–8.

18 For a magisterial study of peasant violence in seventeenth-century Périgord, see Yves-Marie Bercé, *Histoire des Croquants. Étude des soulèvements populaires au XVIIe siècle dans le Sud-ouest de la France* (2 vols, Geneva, 1974).

19 Clay Ramsay, *The Ideology of the Great Fear. The Soissonnais in 1789* (Baltimore, MD, 1992), p. 26.

20 Anatoli Ado, *Paysans en Révolution. Terre, pouvoir et jacquerie, 1789–94* (Paris, 1996), p. 139.

21 Steven L. Kaplan, 'The Famine Plot Persuasion in Eighteenth-century France', *Transactions of the American Philosophical Society* 72 (Philadephia, 1982), especially pp. 66–72.

22 Jean-Pierre Hirsch, *La nuit du 4 août* (Paris, 1978), pp. 116–24; Michael P. Fitzsimmons, *The Night the Old Regime Ended: August 4, 1789, and the French Revolution* (University Park, PA, 2003), p. 220.

23 John Roberts and Richard Cobb (eds), *French Revolution Documents*, (Oxford, 1966) vol. 1, pp. 140–1; for the translated version see David Andress, *French Society in Revolution* (Manchester, 1999), pp. 171–2.

24 Robert Laurent and Geneviève Gavignaud, *La Révolution Française dans le Languedoc méditerranéen* (Toulouse, 1987), p. 47.

25 Ramsay, *Ideology*, pp. xvii–xviii.
26 Roger Dupuy, *La Garde Nationale et les débuts de la Révolution en Ille-et-Vilaine, 1789–mars 1793* (Paris, 1972), p. 253.
27 William Doyle, *The Oxford History of the French Revolution* (Oxford, 1989), p. 71.
28 Letter from mayor and aldermen of Troyes to the *intendant* in Châlons-sur-Marne, 20 July 1789, quoted in Lynn Hunt, *Revolution and Urban Politics in Provincial France. Troyes and Reims, 1786–90* (Stanford, CA, 1978), p. 73.
29 Désert, *La Révolution Française en Normandie*, p. 69.
30 Michel Lhéritier, *Liberté, 1789–90: les Girondins, Bordeaux et la Révolution Française* (Paris, 1947), p. 107.
31 Pierre Bécamps, 'Le peuple souverain', in François-Georges Pariset (ed.), *Bordeaux au dix-huitième siècle* (Bordeaux, 1968), pp. 381–3.
32 Hunt, *Revolution and Urban Politics*, p. 74.
33 Alan Williams, *The Police of Paris, 1718–89* (Baton Rouge, LA, 1979), p. 17.
34 Richard Cobb, *The Police and the People: French Popular Protest, 1789–1820* (Oxford, 1970), p. 19.
35 Arlette Farge and Jacques Revel, *The Vanishing Children of Paris. Rumour and Politics Before the French Revolution* (Cambridge, MA, 1991), pp. 3, 104–11.
36 Cynthia Bouton, *The Flour War: Gender, Class and Community in Late Ancien Regime French Society* (University Park, PA, 1993), pp. 88–9.
37 Robert Descimon, 'Milice bourgeoise et identité citadine à Paris au temps de la Ligue', *Annales: ESC*, 48 (1993), p. 906.
38 Thomas Manley Luckett, 'Hunting for Spies and Whores: A Parisian Riot on the Eve of the French Revolution', *Past and Present* 156 (1997), pp. 116–19.
39 Jacques Godechot, *The Taking of the Bastille* (London, 1970), p. 187.
40 Jean-Paul Bertaud, *Camille et Lucie Desmoulins* (Paris, 1986), p. 40.
41 Godechot, *The Taking of the Bastille*, pp. 188–9. Godechot's analysis of the violence in Paris on 12–14 July is much the most detailed and I have relied on it heavily for the account that follows.
42 Paul G. Spagnoli, 'The Revolution Begins: Lambesc's Charge, 12 July 1789', *French Historical Studies* 17 (1991), pp. 466–97.
43 George Rudé, *The Crowd in the French Revolution* (Oxford, 1959), pp. 194–5.
44 Alain-Jacques Czouze-Tornare, 'Les troupes suisses à Paris', in Michel Vovelle (ed.), *Paris et la Révolution* (Paris, 1989), p. 244.
45 Hans-Jürgen Lüsebrink and Rolf Reichart, *The Bastille, a History of a Symbol of Despotism and Freedom* (Durham, NC, 1997), p. 43.
46 Michel Vovelle (ed.), *La Révolution Française, images et récit* (5 vols, Paris, 1986), vol. 1, pp. 148–9.

47 Claude Quétel, *Escape from the Bastille: The Life and Legend of Latude* (Cambridge, 1990), pp. 155–6.

48 Lüsebrink and Reichart, *The Bastille*, p. 77.

49 Ibid., pp. 117–47.

50 Jean-Noël Luc (ed.), *La Charente-Maritime: l'Aunis et la Saintonge des origines à nos jours* (Saint-Jean-d'Angély, 1981), p. 291.

51 Raymonde Monnier, 'L'image de Paris de 1789 à 1794: Paris capitale de la Révolution', in Michel Vovelle (ed.), *L'image de la Révolution Française* (4 vols, Paris, 1989), vol. 1, p. 75.

52 Colin Lucas, 'Talking about urban popular violence in 1789', in Alan Forrest and Peter Jones (eds), *Reshaping France: Town, Country and Region during the French Revolution* (Manchester, 1991), p. 123.

53 Jean-Pierre Bois, *Histoire des 14 juillet, 1789–1919* (Rennes, 1991), p. 9.

54 Edna Hindie Lemay (ed.), *Dictionnaire des Constituants, 1789–91* (2 vols, Oxford and Paris, 1991), vol. 1, pp. 48–9.

55 Claude Manceron, 'Galerie de portraits', in Michel Vovelle (ed.), *L'état de la France pendant la Révolution* (Paris, 1988), pp. 275–6.

56 David Garrioch, *The Formation of the Parisian Bourgeoisie, 1690–1830* (Cambridge, MA, 1996), p. 156.

57 R. B. Rose, *The Making of the Sans-culottes* (Manchester, 1983), p. 37.

58 Godechot, *The Taking of the Bastille*, p. 244.

59 Doyle, *Oxford History*, pp. 121–3.

|5|

The promise of devolution

The attention of the deputies remained focused on what they saw as the main function of the Revolution, to create a new constitution that would recognize the rights of the French people and impose strict controls on the power of the executive. This proved a lengthy and somewhat complex process, since the deputies were divided about the nature of their mission. Was it to resurrect and define an existing constitution which guaranteed the rights of the people, as so much of the pamphlet literature of the 1780s had suggested, or was it rather to defend the people against royal despotism by creating a new document, based on ideals like the separation of powers and the rights of man? Even the wording of the Tennis Court Oath had been confused and uncertain on this point, which explains why the assembly had seen it as a major priority to set up a committee, the Committee of the Constitution, to draw up a draft constitution for the new order and to report back to the Assembly.[1] The committee was set up on 14 July, the same day as the attack on the Bastille, and its members were among the best legal minds in the Assembly. They were also predominantly monarchist in their outlook, with conservatives like Mounier, Bergasse, Lally-Tollendal and Clermont-Tonnerre outnumbering more radical deputies like Talleyrand, Sieyès and Le Chapelier.[2] Their cause was that of reform rather than democracy, and those who did dare to speak the language of democracy, like Mirabeau, earned a degree of suspicion and notoriety.[3] In their original mandate it was assumed that the committee could report back in only ten days, which was to prove something of a miscalculation; as its chairman, Champion de Cicé, told the Assembly on 27 July, there was much work to be done in consulting local opinion and examining the *cahiers*. In the event it would be 1791 before the draft of the constitution was complete and the work of the committee was done.

The idea of a constitution that would guarantee the rights of all, like the concept of citizenship itself, offered the promise of unity and uniformity, a bond that would tie all Frenchmen to a single political nation. It was a generous concept, built on the foundations of the Rights of Man, and there is no doubting its appeal in a country that sought an end to privilege and in a world where rights had been dependent on legal status. Optimism was rife in these early months. Frenchmen throughout the country, whatever their occupation or social origins, looked to the committee to provide the foundations of a better world, just as they had looked to the Estates-General back in 1788. Then there had been a stream of addresses from all over France, taking an obvious pleasure in the new language of the nation, a clear pride in the qualities that united them. From the Pays des Cévennes, for instance, had come a clarion call to the nation and the unity of all the people. 'Citizens of all estates and all orders', it read, 'a single spirit incites us; and in spite of the diversity of our religious opinions; there are no differences in the feelings we hold in our hearts: we are all our fellow-citizens and brothers'. They recognized themselves as citizens in a world that was suddenly united, with Paris assuming the role of unquestioned capital of the nation, associated by many with the future of mankind and with political and civic innovation. At Villeneuve-de-Berg in the Vivarais, 'the young people of the town built a triumphal arch of laurel leaves, on which they hung inscriptions in Latin praising the city of Paris, discharged muskets, and formed a military procession to the door of the church', marching to the sound of military music behind a white flag, 'decorated with red and blue ribbons'.[4] That enthusiasm had not faded; under the Constituent Assembly it was focused on civil rights and the abolition of privilege, and especially on the work of constitution-building.

The tone of addresses to the Assembly did change, however, over the summer of 1789, in so far as the provinces' faith in their deputies, and in the efficacy of legislative change, was more strongly expressed, and the concern for purely local interests visibly gave way to greater self-awareness as a nation. The municipal revolutions of July and August 1789 should be seen as local reaffirmations of the legitimacy of the Assembly, and the setting up of National Guard units at least partly as statements of support for the new polity. Even more impressive, though, is the tone that was adopted by local people when addressing the Assembly – the assumptions they made about the mandate they had given to their deputies, the widespread opposition to self-serving local oligarchies, the belief that reform must come from the centre rather than from any local or municipal bodies. Overnight, it seemed, the focus of the people had shifted away from estates and *parlements*, and instead of trying to guide the deliberations of the Assembly – as they had still tended to do through their deputies to the Estates-General – power was increasingly handed over to the deputies, the people expressing their confidence in the Assembly to deliver legislation that would answer their needs. Some wrote to renounce their provincial traditions as vestiges of a moribund order; others urged blind obedience to such decrees as the deputies in their wisdom might propose. Amongst the privileged orders were some who showed irritation with the reluctance of their representatives in Paris to renounce their privileged status. The Second Estate of Saint-Flour, for instance, responded to a request for new powers by their deputy, the arch-conservative Duc de Caylus, in June 1789 with the observation that progress could only be made by general agreement of the deputies of the three orders and that they, as nobles, had greeted news of the union of the three orders with undisguised joy.[5] Little by little, a large part of provincial France was beginning to give definition to the idea of the political nation.

Not everyone, of course, could be integrated into the political nation. Not all those with privileges to lose were as idealistic as the nobility of Saint-Flour, and already in these early months we see something of the fissures that would increasingly afflict the Revolution and undermine any sense of national purpose. During 1789 and 1790 the King made it clear that he accepted his limited executive role only reluctantly, that he found the revolutionaries' insistence on legislative control tiresome and demeaning, and that he was insulted by the abolition of clerical privilege and by what he rightly interpreted as an attack on the Catholic Church. In December 1789 the first Church lands were sold off, and by February 1790 the Assembly had prohibited monastic vows and suppressed religious orders. Committed monarchists and devout Catholics might both feel that the generous and consensual nation did not include people like them, and that the generous discourse of the Revolution was less inclusive than it liked to pretend. Moreover, the economic grievances that were so frequently raised in the *cahiers* had not been addressed – the harvest of 1789, like its two predecessors, was poor, resulting in yet another rise in bread prices; and the government experimented in the use of paper money, issuing the first *assignats* on 19 December, the same day as the decree ordering the sale of Church lands.[6] The Revolution was now seen to be doing more than giving people rights; it was imposing measures which some sections of the population found damaging and ideologically challenging. Even in 1789 some members of the French nation took the decision that the Revolution was not for them, and they began to seek salvation in emigration.

As yet, of course, their number was small. A contingent of prominent courtiers followed the Comte d'Artois, who fled from Versailles on the morning of 17 July; they included the Princes de Condé and de Conti, as well as various Rohans, Broglies and Polignacs, all luxuriously decked out as they and their wealth moved inexorably to the frontiers of Italy or the Rhine. A few others followed in response to the Great Fear, as it became apparent that their privileges were at risk and their old lifestyle gone for ever. But it was the march to Versailles in October and the virtual imprisonment of the King in the Tuileries, that really set alarm bells ringing among the aristocracy, leading to the emigration of men like Breteuil and Choiseul, who then convinced themselves that the institution of the monarchy had little future. Shortly behind them came the first of the many army officers whose loyalty was to the person of the King and who had little tolerance for politicians or constitutions. By 1790 and 1791, of course, their numbers would swell, especially after the King's own botched attempt to leave the country ended in humiliation at Varennes. And the Revolution's assault on seigneurial privilege would persuade many thousands of noble landowners that there was

no place for them in the new order. In the early months, however, their numbers were still small, as was the effect that their departure could have on
local opinion. Some châteaux, it is true, were boarded up and abandoned,
or estates were left in the charge of an estate agent or factor, whose job was
simply to ensure that the seigneur's income was collected. But in most regions
the effect on the landscape and on local opinion was limited, especially since
many of the wealthiest émigrés had long been absentees. The exceptions
were those parts of the country where the Great Fear had not passed into
memory rapidly, and where the countryside remained marked by peasant
jacqueries and violent attacks on seigneurialism – regions like Burgundy,
Languedoc and the Franche-Comté. Here, early emigration was a far more
widespread phenomenon, the impact of which was felt both by the local
elites and the rural economy.[7]

The extent of opposition should not be exaggerated: the majority of provincial Frenchmen remained committed to the revolutionary ideal and looked
to Paris to provide both a uniformity of rights and a greater degree of devolved
control. But that should not be taken to mean that there was general agreement on the steps that were necessary to implement the Revolution, or that
everyone shared the same view of where that Revolution was going. The
local notables from whom the new political class was drawn were in broad
agreement about the desirability of liberty and municipal reform, but they
were still men of very different temperaments and persuasions. They included
both radicals and conservatives, political firebrands and men out to defend
their municipal dignities. Important political questions remained unanswered.
Was the management of the Revolution to be an affair of the local elites, of
those with a demonstrable stake in society? How far should popular involvement be encouraged and how far should the rights of citizenship extend?
Should popular violence be tolerated – as it clearly had been in Paris in 1789 –
or should the anger of the people be curbed by firm policing? And if all privileges were to be abolished, including those that had been conferred on
provinces and municipal bodies by royal charter, what effects would such
abolition have on the major cities of France, on their regional influence and
their economic prosperity?[8]

The new polity emerged from months of frenetic legislation and was finally
given legitimacy in the constitution of 1791, where the decisions that had
been taken by the Committee of the Constitution over the previous eighteen
months acquired the status of constitutional law. But the broad outlines of
the constitution were already clear in 1789. At national level the revolutionaries insisted on the primacy of the legislature and on the strict application of the separation of powers: the King was to be styled 'king of the French',
and his decisions were subject to legislative review; so was the amount of
the civil list, while his choice of ministers was also constrained. The last vestiges of royal absolutism were thereby abandoned.[9] The Assembly, in turn,
was to be answerable to public opinion through elections, though these
elections remained indirect – electors chose one of their number to act as an

elector – and participation was restricted to active citizens. The definition of the *citoyen actif* was that offered by Thouret in the suffrage proposals he presented to the Assembly on 29 September. To qualify one had to have been born a Frenchman or to have been naturalized; to have reached the age of 25; to have lived in one's canton of residence for a minimum period of twelve months; and to pay direct taxes to the value of three days' unskilled labour.[10] Standing for office required a higher tax qualification, the equivalent of ten days' wages. In the France of 1789 there was much talk of liberty and the rights of man, but there was no hint of democracy, and the deputies demonstrated their fear of ordinary people by introducing a noticeably more limited suffrage than the one that had operated for the elections to the Estates-General. Here they remained loyal to enlightened ideas of citizenship, to d'Holbach if not to Rousseau. Electoral participation, like admission to the National Guard, was to be restricted to men of some substance, to those who had a stake in the preservation of order and the protection of property.

Elections were not confined to the national sphere, to the choice of deputies to serve in the Assembly. On the contrary, the electoral principle was seen as fundamental in legitimizing office-holding at every level, local as well as national, judicial as well as administrative. It was the mechanism through which the sovereignty of the people was to be expressed. Mayors and town councillors, judges, magistrates, *juges de paix*, all were subject to election and to regular re-election, as were bishops and many parish priests after 1790, under the terms of the Civil Constitution of the Clergy. In 1790–1 the principle of election was even extended to the military, used to designate officers, first in the National Guard, then in volunteer battalions.[11] In this way the old offices, with their traditions of venality and favouritism, were swept away and power was shown to emanate from below. This was particularly true of the legal process, where a system constructed on privilege and venality was rapidly replaced by one founded on election. Before the end of 1789, the sovereign courts of the *ancien régime*, the *parlements*, had been placed on permanent vacation, and with them went a whole raft of lower courts, along with the privileged status of barristers, who lost their corporate rights and their monopoly position at law. Henceforth the district tribunal would be the cornerstone of criminal justice, and its judges would be elected for a limited period only before they had to submit their record to public scrutiny. It was a symbolic moment when the law was freed from the old, corrupt system of appointment, breaking with the traditional concept of royal justice and transferring sovereignty to the people.[12]

Local government reforms aimed to produce a uniform system and one that would increase levels of accountability and trust.[13] They were a major priority for the National Assembly and the subject of two major pieces of legislation in December 1789. The decree of 22 December set up electoral and administrative assemblies throughout France.[14] It also established the distinction between active and passive citizens, and thus defined the electorate for the early years of the Revolution. The old administrative and judicial divisions – provinces, *généralités*, *sénéchaussées* and the like – were swept aside, to be replaced by new units of local administration which still remain in place today. The territory of the kingdom was divided into *départements*, units which were supposedly equal in area and population, and which were smaller than many of the old provinces so that the people of France would have readier access to the various functions of administration. The final number that the committee alighted upon was eighty-three, a figure that would increase slightly during the Revolution with the addition, through annexation, of the Vaucluse – the papal states of Avignon and the Comtat Venaissin – in 1790, the division of Corsica into two departments in 1793, and the subdivision – as an act of political vengeance – of Lyon's department, the Rhône-et-Loire, following Lyon's involvement with federalism. There would also be a number of new departments which resulted from annexations in war.[15] But the overall departmental structure remained intact, testimony to the foresight of the assembly in carving France into viable units of local government. They took over the administrative tasks of the royal *intendants*, especially in matters of taxation, and the policing powers of the *parlements*; and they were rapidly given responsibility for enforcing a massive range of legislation handed down from the centre. They were called upon to collect information about the economy, taxation, public opinion and conscription, a range of demands without parallel in *ancien régime* France. That they succeeded in carrying out these functions says much for the quality of the administrators on the ground, and it is largely explained by the fact that the departments looked to those who had previous experience of administration, to those who had served the crown and the *parlements* under Louis XVI. Not until 1793 and the Jacobin republic was there any serious attempt to replace them.[16] Moreover, much was done by delegation. The elected *conseil-général* met only periodically as a body; it passed most of the day-to-day business to a *directoire* of eight of its members, who worked closely with the *procureur* and became effectively salaried administrators in each department.[17]

The effectiveness of the departments was also dependent on close liaison with the district authorities, the principal units into which each department was subdivided. The districts were smaller and more manageable areas; and, like the departments, they had elected *conseils-généraux* that were answerable to their electors, as well as an executive *directoire* of four members and a *procureur*. Theirs was an important role, providing a key link between the department and the village, the state and the citizen. They collected information from the communes in their area, assigned tax and military quotas, and scrutinized local budgets. They enforced requisitions and implemented the Revolution's religious policy. And they did these things with commendable efficiency. But here their influence stopped: for it was not part of their brief to make policy of their own, merely to implement laws and carry out the policies of others. They were, says Alison Patrick sympathetically, 'awkwardly poised between the upper and lower levels, with no tradition and no right to their own opinions, being mechanisms merely, without direct access to interpretation of the law'. But that did not make them ineffective. 'If the departments were the hinge between Paris and the periphery,' she suggests, 'the districts were the hinge between the department and the populace'.[18] Nor were their members always politically passive. When in 1793 the Jacobins became suspicious of the conservatism shown by many departmental administrations, it was to the districts that they would turn to provide militant republicans for local administration.

Below the district, and answerable to it in the revolutionary chain of command, was the municipality or commune, each with its mayor and *conseil municipal*. These were established by another major piece of legislation, the decree, on municipalities of 14 December, though in many areas the new law merely legitimized and regularized the position of the revolutionary municipalities which had sprung up spontaneously in the summer of 1789.[19] The whole land area of the country, rural as well as urban, was divided into some 44,000 communes, each of which would receive copies of laws and decrees, and would be expected in their turn to report to the district on such matters as the condition of the harvest, the numbers of beggars and vagabonds and the state of public opinion. Some, of course, had tiny populations scattered across the countryside, but even they had to have three elected officers to conduct municipal business. At the other extreme were cities with more than 25,000 inhabitants, which were given the right to divide themselves into *sections* for reasons of administrative convenience. Lyon, for instance, was divided into thirty-two sections, as was Marseille; Bordeaux got twenty-eight, Toulouse fifteen; other cities were allocated smaller numbers. Paris, which attracted special attention both because of its size and the turbulence of its sixty electoral districts, was allocated forty-eight. Again, the measure aimed to create a single system throughout France, to get rid of a multiplicity of local privileges inherited from the *ancien régime*, and to ensure that the Revolution would have a continuing presence at village level. The law emphasized once again the importance of uniformity, of common institutional ties between government and people; and mayors had a responsibility both to report up the line to the district authorities and to keep local people informed of their obligations under the law. Here the Revolution was being rather ambitious, particularly in the smaller communes and in remote rural areas where there were no men with any administrative experience, where communications were often poor and literacy levels low. In communes of fewer than 5,000 inhabitants it was difficult to recruit an *agent communal* or an *adjoint*.[20] Predictably, it was in just such communes, especially in mountain areas and close to frontiers, that local communities remained most recalcitrant and that, even at the height of the Terror, laws remained unread and unenforced.[21]

The position of Paris was the subject of particular debate. Since it now housed both the King and the Assembly, and thus had an increased importance in the affairs of the realm, could it be treated like any other city, or did it require a special statute? The question seemed more pressing in the light of the capital's reputation for political violence, especially since the events of 1789, which had spread a degree of terror and anti-Parisian feeling throughout much of the provinces. Could Paris be trusted to run an elected assembly like other towns? Or did its increased importance in national politics mean that it had to be more tightly regulated from the centre? After a lively debate, the Assembly voted to give Paris the same freedoms as other towns, which represented a considerable victory for the capital. A law of 21 May 1790 made Paris answerable to the common law, and replaced the institutions that had been hastily thrown up by the municipal revolution with a new municipality with a mayor, sixteen administrators, thirty-two councillors and ninety-six notables. Paris was also, as we have seen, divided into forty-eight sections, which would act as electoral assemblies. It would, in other words, have institutions that were comparable with those of other cities, and on 2 August 1790 Bailly was duly elected as the first mayor with 12,550 of the 14,000 votes cast. But distrust lingered on, along with a measure of jealousy, and the idea of Paris as the capital of a large department frightened those in provincial France who believed that the city already had disproportionate influence. Whereas the Parisians demanded a department large enough to provision the city, the communes of the Île-de-France hesitated to pass such power to their turbulent and unruly neighbour. After a long debate it was decided to create a department of Paris – or of the Seine – that would be restricted to little more than the city and its immediate suburbs, with three districts, located in Paris itself, Saint-Denis and Bourg-la-Reine. Any expansionist ambitions that Paris might harbour would thus be held closely in check.[22]

Though the commune was the basic unit of local government, efficiency dictated that the smallest of them should be grouped together for certain of their functions, and so, between the commune and the district, the Revolution created a further unit, the canton. In the administrative structure this could be overlooked easily, since the canton had no administrative authority and no elected body at its head. It was, quite simply, an area of about four square leagues of territory, grouping together a handful of communes, which was used for elections – it hosted the primary electoral assemblies[23] – and had a crucial role in the administration of justice, where it was the seat of the local *juge de paix*. This office was created in 1790 as part of a package of judicial reforms aimed at replacing the system of seigneurial justice, which had served the French people under the *ancien régime*, a system which effectively collapsed in the wake of 4 August and which was regarded by the revolutionaries as deeply corrupt. The judges had often used their position as a source of profit, and they were perceived as seigneurial officials, their loyalty to the lord rather than to the public. In contrast, the new *juge de paix* was a paid official elected by local people, a man who often had no formal legal training but who enjoyed a wide degree of public confidence. His job was less to interpret the law than to offer conciliation, to mediate between the villagers and get them to settle their disputes amicably and without recourse to the courts. Disputes could be settled quickly and cheaply, and the fact that the judge might be an amateur in legal matters does not seem to have reduced his authority. The system proved popular, helping settle minor disputes and ending the disincentives to pursuing more serious crimes which had bedevilled the countryside in the eighteenth century. A high proportion of the *juges* were re-elected. Not for nothing did the revolutionaries believe that this was one of their most significant reforms for improving the quality of life of ordinary people.[24]

Creating this new system of local government and making it answerable to a local electorate was supposed to ensure that France was governed by consent and to produce stable and moderate administration. To a great extent this was indeed the outcome, particularly in the early period of the Revolution, but there were, even in 1790, notable exceptions to the rule, towns and cities where, as in Paris, violent or extreme factions were able to exercise disproportionate influence, and where any initial spirit of consensus was rapidly lost. This was especially true in parts of the Midi, where local elections often produced an extreme factionalism that divided opinion and went on to blight the years that followed. Yet in the *cahiers* and in the run-up to the Estates-General there had seemingly been a substantial degree of unanimity about the sorts of reforms which people wanted to see. The Midi did not appear very different in its response to questions of privilege, for instance – whether of the seigneurs or of the Catholic Church – from other parts of France. But these appearances were misleading, for there were significant differences, and these would mark the subsequent history of the region. In particular, there was little continuity between the municipal elites of the pre-revolutionary period and those who emerged in 1789 and 1790. The *parlements* in the region, Aix, Grenoble and Toulouse, had all held to their particularist traditions and were among the most vocal opponents of revolution in 1789, signing inflammatory protests against the actions of the National Assembly which forced the former magistrates into exile and emigration. By 1793, indeed, twenty-eight of the seventy-one presidents and counsellors of the Parlement of Aix had emigrated, twenty of the fifty-three members of the Parlement of Grenoble, along with thirty-seven from the Parlement from Toulouse.[25] In the first elections, moderates were rejected by the electorate in favour of radicals and other more ideological candidates, in stark contrast to results in other regions of France, where local people showed by their choice of deputies their deep-rooted commitment to shared community values, and a desire to govern by consensus. In parts of the South – rather as in the sections of Paris – local voters showed no wish for political harmony, and no desire to avoid the risks of confrontation. Often they returned men calling themselves Patriots, who, as early as 1790, expressed their lack of faith in constitutional monarchy and sought to establish more radical institutions.

Examples of advanced radicalism abound, and some cities established an early reputation for their advanced ideas. Patriots on the newly elected municipal council of Marseille lost no time in boasting of their ideological purity, and from 1791 they were openly declaring their republicanism, claiming their rightful position as the first French city to rise against despotism and defend the rights of man. Others were expected to listen – 'Marseille has seized the right to give an example to others'[26] – both in Paris and in the villages of their rural hinterland, to which they sent missions to preach a more egalitarian republicanism and whip up opposition to the Catholic clergy. Indeed, from the very beginning of the Revolution the Marseillais flaunted their reputation for patriotism and revolutionary radicalism, showing an expansionist impulse which alarmed many of the city's richer citizens. When others proved more cautious, or, worse still, threatened to resist revolutionary change, the radicals of Marseille saw no reason to stay within the boundaries of their jurisdiction. They claimed their right to proselytize and preach the ideals in which they believed, thus gaining the city a reputation for extremism and hot-headedness. And they did not feel constrained by the law. In the last days of July 1789, for instance, a band of several hundred militants seized arms at the Hôtel de Ville and marched on neighbouring Aix to free seventy men gaoled for rioting. By the following May the city was urging delegates from adjacent departments to take common action to defend the Revolution, reporting on royal troop movements, seizing arms from state arsenals and offering to deploy its National Guard units wherever they might be required. In these circumstances, it is scarcely surprising that the Municipality of Marseille was accused of trying to take control of the Midi, of wishing to set up a southern republic under its tutelage; nor that the government viewed such initiatives, and the city that spawned them, with the deepest distrust.[27]

Intolerance could easily turn to bloodshed and massacre. In Nîmes, a bitterly divided town both socially and culturally, which pitted aristocrats against bourgeois manufacturers and Catholics against Protestants, the election quickly assumed a confessional as well as a social dimension, with the winners seeking to purge local government of their opponents. This was the land of the Wars of Religion, a country with a long history of sectarian hatred, where confessional factions used the language of revolution and reaction but continued to fight their traditional religious battles. The 1790 elections were won by the Catholic establishment after a long and bitter anti-Protestant campaign; but that in turn led to a hatred between the two communities of murderous intensity. Protestant peasants and textile workers from the rural Cévennes flocked to the city to support their co-religionists, and the outcome was a bloody massacre, the so-called *bagarre de Nîmes* in which some 300 Catholics were slaughtered.[28] That was not, of course, the end of the matter. Protestant extremism necessarily created a violent Catholic backlash, and communities from neighbouring departments responded by sending delegates to a meeting at Jalès, where royalism and anti-Protestantism moulded a programme of Catholic counter-revolution that would undermine the stability of the region for a quarter of a century.[29] Religion, indeed, proved to be something of a litmus test for revolutionaries across the Midi. In Avignon, newly annexed to France after several centuries as a papal state, overjoyed Patriots turned their anger on the Catholic population of the neighbouring Comtat, rounding up scores of Catholic villagers and herding them into the tower of La Glacière. Fears of counter-revolution were all-pervasive, as were popular cries for vengeance. In October 1791, months of paranoia reached a violent climax when the Patriots declared martial law in the city and dragged some sixty prisoners from their cells, among them members of the former town council, before butchering them in the court-yard.[30] Again the radicalism of home-grown Patriots had flowed over into vengeance, resulting in a cold-blooded massacre. Terror had come early to Avignon, and it had occurred without any encouragement from Paris, the result of local rather than national initiative.

Terror and intolerance were not, of course, the monopoly of the Left, and where royalist and arch-conservative factions triumphed in these early months, they behaved in very similar ways, denouncing and rooting out their opponents and looking to émigré nobles and clergy for support. Hatred was not confined to any one side, nor yet to the popular classes of society. In Nîmes, for instance, there is little doubt that Froment and his Catholic reactionaries would have slaughtered the Protestant faction with just as much relish if they, rather than their opponents, had been presented with the opportunity to do so. And in Montauban, where the first elections did give power to declared royalists, men committed to the social values of the *ancien régime* and the rights of noble landowners, violence immediately threatened, especially when the government attempted to nationalize Church lands. The royalists, too, set about arresting their opponents, and would doubtless have made Montauban into a fortress of counter-revolution had the revolutionaries of surrounding cities not spotted the danger and reacted. That, at least, was what alarmed Patriots reported. In this case it was left to the new municipality in Bordeaux to take the initiative, sending a force of 1,500 National Guardsmen against Montauban to restore the city to the revolutionary cause.[31] For the Bordelais it proved a valuable investment, since it not only halted the spread of counter-revolution, but also established Bordeaux's reputation in the South-West as a fulcrum of revolutionary values. The Montauban expedition won praise from the National Assembly and became an important part of Bordeaux's patriotic legend, a justification for its claims to leadership in the region and proof of sacrifice made in the revolutionary cause.[32]

Even in the first months of the Revolution it was clear that municipal leaders were no longer united, and that serious divisions were emerging between conservatives and radicals, and between town and country. At the heart of these wrangles were issues of influence and local power, questions of status within a wider region, the future of what many cities assumed to be their natural sphere of influence. Ideology could, of course, exacerbate these tensions where rival towns had different outlooks on the Revolution or different kinds of social elite; or quarrels about power and self-interest, which were never the most respectable of causes, could be judiciously cloaked in a discourse of idealism or humanist rationality. But there was usually little that was idealistic about these quarrels. By choosing to abolish long-established units of local government and traditional legal jurisdictions, the Revolution opened a hornets' nest of griefs and ambitions. It might indeed be making the system more accessible, bringing administration closer to the people and ridding provincial France of some of its more entrenched resentments; but it was also creating new ones, born of a sense of loss and insult, and some at least of these new resentments would continue to fester locally throughout the entire period of the Revolution.

For the government was not simply – as the revolutionaries sometimes liked to claim – stripping away privilege, creating a logical system of local government based on the *cadastre* rather than on tradition or sentiment. That idea was utterly utopian, and the only attempts to develop it into a practical scheme for administration were the highly intellectual mathematical models of Sieyès and Dupont de Nemours – based, in Sieyès's case, on departments of equal area, each of 324 square leagues.[33] The practice had to be very different, for though, in theory, the new administrative divisions were supposed to be created equal, both in their land area and in their population, common sense decreed that, between, say, the Paris Basin and the Massif Central, this was a dream that could not reasonably be delivered. The result was inevitably a series of compromises, in which departmental and district boundaries played more than lip-service to tradition, and reflected the major administrative divisions of the *ancien régime*. And provincialism did not simply wither away; the old provinces were in many cases the preferred basis for the new divisions. The major administrative units, the *départements*, demonstrate this very clearly. In the new order, the old provinces of Angoumois, Quercy, Rouergue, Périgord, Armagnac and Roussillon remained more or less intact, while some of the smallest of the provinces – like the Aunis and Saintonge, Bresse and Bugey, Béarn and Pays Basque – were amalgamated to form single units. By the same logic, the biggest of the old provincial territories were simply subdivided into roughly equal chunks to form an appropriate number of departments – five for Brittany, three for Burgundy, seven in the case of Languedoc. Usually this was achieved without difficulty and with a wide measure of consensus. It was where historical precedent was confused and where there were competing claims to local dominance that the greatest doubts, and the bitterest squabbles, resulted.[34] In the South-West, in particular, the committee was unable to decide how best to cut up the somewhat inchoate area composed of Guienne, Gascony, Béarn and Navarre, and left the number and location of the future departments open to local debate and lobbying.

Provence was one area where the whole debate about local government was dominated by a sense of provincial identity, and where the years from 1787 to 1790, with their successive reform plans and the re-establishment of the provincial estates, had encouraged the growth of a sense of particularism. Indeed, until the old province finally disappeared on 20 July 1790, there were continued attempts to influence the assembly in the direction of provincialism, of preserving some form of traditional authority in the South-East, and even of extending the liberties of Provence to other areas of France. The deputy for Aix, Charles-François Bouche, intervened repeatedly in debate to urge that local liberties were precious to the people and should be maintained, in the process gaining considerable popularity in Provence and earning himself the sobriquet of 'defender of the provinces'.[35] Another Provençal deputy, Mirabeau, also argued fiercely that departments should be formed as subsections of provinces in order to make the change more palat-able to local opinion; on this basis he argued, vainly, for a France of 120 rather than eighty-three departments. With time, of course, the new depart-ments did achieve popularity, and provincial particularism receded, in part, perhaps, because the *départements* were run by *conseils généraux*, by elected bodies which helped to maintain the illusion of democracy and a measure of local autonomy.[36] But there is equally no doubt that provincial sentiment remained strong and would re-emerge at moments when – as in the summer of 1793 – the actions of central government could be portrayed as being authoritarian or inimical to local interests.

Decisions about where best to draw administrative frontiers were not ones that could simply be made in Paris and imposed by decree on unwill-ing provincials. The early revolutionaries believed in the value of consensus wherever possible, and took care to involve local people – or at least the elites among them – in the decision-making process. To have acted other-wise would have been to court electoral repudiation. They therefore created a structure of departmental commissions which would consult locally and give due weight to the opinions they collected. But who was chosen to serve on these commissions? Almost universally it was the same sorts of people – aristocrats and significant landowners on the one hand, on the other, lawyers, public prosecutors, men versed in public affairs, those whom the nineteenth century would term *les capacités*.[37] These were the same groups that the Revolution courted in an attempt to create an active political class in provincial cities, men who would make the national revolution work at local level. But in the precise context of the administrative subdivision of the territory it had another important consequence, since these were men whose background and culture made them rather conservative. The Constituent Assembly handed the job of advising on the new administrative and judicial system, on the boundaries of the *département* and the number of districts into which it should be split, and on the exact geographical location of adminis-trative bodies, courts and tribunals, schools and colleges, to those men who best represented the local elites and who, for that reason, had most reason to cling to their historic distinctions and identities.[38] The advice they gave tended to stress the value of history, control and law-enforcement, the role of the town in the life of the surrounding countryside; they respected a long legal tradition and favoured towns where local people had been in the habit of going to plead for justice; they looked for suitable infrastructure in the form of passable roads, adequate hotels and decent restaurants. In other words, they looked to the existing capability of a town and the administrative expertise it had acquired under the *ancien régime*.[39]

In broad outline it must be said that the committee did its work well, and that the administrative and judicial units set up in 1790 have largely stood the test of time. But not all were satisfied. By organizing the administrative division of France in this way, the Constituent Assembly opened up a raft of claims and counter-claims between local areas, creating winners and losers and producing new levels of animosity among those who saw their dreams of status evaporate, or could only watch as their most bitter rivals emerged from the lottery with some prized honour or source of future wealth. This could, of course, favour compromise as much as outright victory. Take the question of district authorities, where each department was allowed to choose the number of districts into which its jurisdiction most logically fell. Even the smallest departments had to have three districts, while a case could be made for a higher number, up to a maximum of nine. Most went for some number between these two limits, but a few sought to maximize the number of districts, often because of local rivalries or family disputes rather than from any rational concept of the *cadastre*. The picture that emerged was thus wildly variable. Of the smallest departments, some, like the Ariège and the Haute-Loire, had no difficulty in nominating three district centres without any apparent ill feeling, while as many as eighteen departments chose to spread their honours as widely as possible, opting for the full quota of nine districts, each with its elected *conseil-général* and its paid functionaries. They were not always the biggest departments, either by area or population: indeed, the larger departments, like the Nord or the Gironde, often settled for a lesser number. Among those which did choose to form nine districts we find the Meurthe and the Morbihan, the Sarthe and the Oise, the Ain, the Dordogne and the Lot-et-Garonne.[40] No principle was at issue here, no reference to centrality or the dictates of the *cadastre*. The only plausible explanation is that they chose the route of least resistance, avoiding conflict by recognizing that local aspirants could best be bought off and hence attracted to the new political order by the offer of an honour or jurisdiction of their own.

Everyone wanted to gain from the redistribution of responsibilities, from the breakdown of privileged jurisdictions and the promise of decentralization that came with it. Everyone recognized that their future prosperity was tied in with these changes, and that to miss out brought with it the threat of becoming marginalized from the economic mainstream. For this reason the work of the committee attracted enormous local interest and stimulated a cascade of petitioning. More than a hundred special commissioners travelled to Paris to plead the cause of their town or city, while from the ends of the kingdom petitions flooded in, making the case that each of 1,508 towns and *bourgs* should have their place on the new administrative map, whether as the seat of a department or district – some, uncertain of their chances, were careful to hedge their bets and ask for both – or as home to a court or tribunal. A few were major regional centres which feared the loss of prestige and

influence under the new system; no department, after all, would have anything like the jurisdiction of the *Parlement* of Paris, while the great provincial capitals like Rennes and Toulouse necessarily lost influence through the
break-up of provincial units. Most were small to middling towns that would
have had very little independent authority in the *ancien régime* but were
now eager to establish their administrative credentials.[41] They battled to
publicize their cause in Paris, whether by ridiculing their rivals or by praising
their own most treasured features. And though they scrupulously adhered
to the discourse of the new order, expressing their enthusiasm for citizenship
and the principles of the Revolution, these were ill-concealed statements of
interest, often harking back to the privileges they had enjoyed under the
monarchy. The mindset they reveal was deeply conservative.

Where they could exert political pressure, through a patron or a member
of the Assembly, they did not hesitate to do so, for this was a time when
communities felt the need for influential deputies to support them, men who
might bring influence to bear on their behalf. Often there was no compelling
reason that they could cite other than naked ambition; indeed, this was one
moment when self-interest was poorly concealed and rational argument
played a very secondary role. Having a powerful voice to support one's cause
could prove especially precious, as Bertrand Barère demonstrated in his tire-
less efforts on behalf of the city of Tarbes.[42] There were, after all, so many
open questions to which there was no obvious logical response. Should the
capital of the Bouches-du-Rhône be in Marseille or in Aix; and should that
of the Charente-inférieure, forged out of the old Saintonge and Aunis, go to
Saintes or to La Rochelle? If Rouen got the department of the Seine-
inférieure, where did that leave the port of Le Havre? And if there was general agreement that Bordeaux should head the new department of the
Gironde, what of the claims of Libourne or Bazas? These questions could
not be settled by logic alone and lobbyists quickly got to work. So at the level
of district and canton, and in the competition for every local court and school,
towns vied relentlessly with one another, pointing to their historic eminence
or claiming that they had the most solid links with the surrounding countryside. They tried to adapt to the language of the Revolution, arguing that
they had made sacrifices for the new order or that they had a greater moral
right to distinction than their rivals. Castres, for instance, could point to a
line of *ancien régime* offices which had been lost because of the onset of revolution – gone were its seneschal, its diocesan administration and its tax
administration; with the Civil Constitution it was now threatened with further losses: its cathedral chapter, its *collégiale*, its bishopric, and the Maison
des Chartreux, 'which is of infinite value because of the amount it consumes
and the amount it distributes in alms'. Could it not be compensated with the
chef-lieu of the Tarn?[43] Towns also petitioned for a coveted administrative
position on the basis of their success in raising voluntary contributions for the
government, as though large gifts or substantial tax revenues could themselves
demonstrate a town's revolutionary commitment. They rushed to boast of

what they had achieved: 600,000 *livres* from Le Havre, 303,265 from Lorient, more than 117,000 from Fontainebleau, 85,000 from Rochefort. Some drew comparisons with less generous neighbours in case the committee overlooked them. 'As townspeople from Saint-Brieuc explained, their gift of over 100 *marcs* of silver and their *contribution patriotique* of 120,000 *livres* proved that they were in the forefront of the Revolution'.[44]

But boasting of their generosity could sound dangerously like boasting about their wealth, which did not necessarily suggest sacrifice or revolutionary virtue. A central geographical position could be more useful; so could the argument that peasants came to town for market and therefore could conveniently transact administrative or judicial business there without incurring additional or unnecessary expense. Besides, commercial wealth could be a two-edged sword, for many rural communities eyed the wealth of merchants and the great seaports with considerable suspicion. Small towns feared being stifled by their powerful neighbours; having a modest economy and few visible 'interests' could give a claimant an advantage in the eyes of villagers, while the egalitarian spirit of the Revolution made it difficult to discriminate against mediocrity. Mercantile cities like Marseille and Le Havre were too distant from ordinary people, too cosmopolitan, their interests facing the ocean rather than their hinterland. The rural communes around Le Havre expressed this suspicion memorably when they argued against the location of any major administration in the city. Le Havre, they insisted, was irrelevant to the majority of rural people, a city of sailors and port workers, soldiers and foreigners; and they added that it was really nothing more than an entrepôt for foreign goods that would then be redistributed across the country. They preferred by far to see the district located in their midst, in the market town of Montivilliers, 'which would redistribute the fruits of its position amongst the local population'. This trend was repeated in a number of departments, where richer trading cities found themselves the object of local prejudice and lost out to seemingly lesser rivals. Aix was preferred to Marseille in the Bouches-du-Rhône, legal tradition counting for more than commercial wealth. The claims of commercial Castres were thrown out in the Tarn in favour of the cathedral city of Albi. And Bayonne was not only denied the *chef-lieu* of a department; such was local antipathy to its merchant status that even its claims to a district were rejected in favour of the more 'mediocre' town of Ustaritz.

If such arguments flared between major centres vying for major responsibilities – a department or a district authority – they were every bit as intense at a more local level, where the prize might be a *collège* or a tribunal or even a *justice de paix*. These were important to local people, as they represented status and gave a degree of authority over their immediate neighbourhood. They were also, for smaller towns and bourgs, prizes worth having, the tangible fruits of devolution which promised to bring in their wake a higher level of economic activity, or simply to save a failing local economy from being condemned to misery. Some aspiring towns made their case almost

solely on the basis that without some administration they would lack any
other means of resource. Saint-Lizier (Ariège), in claiming a local tribunal in
1789, put its case plaintively: 'The town of Saint-Lizier', it informed the
committee, 'languishes in an honest mediocrity, and you will find it infinitely
more just and reasonable, by allocating a *tribunal de justice*, to give a certain
well-being to a town that has little than to increase the wealth of a neighbouring town that is already well endowed through trade'.[45] Such cases were
often listened to, and it must be recognized that large numbers of smaller
centres did do rather well out of the Revolution. Paris did not always see it
as politic to invest too much power in a few big provincial cities, and at the
height of the Terror the Montagnards, fearful that some departments were
taking a militantly moderate line, preferred to shift responsibilities away from
the departments to the districts. For smaller district *chef-lieux* – places like
Cérilly in the Allier, Loudéac in the Côtes-du-Nord or Saint-Mihiel in the
Meuse – this meant an influence and involvement in national affairs that
would have been unthinkable in the *ancien régime*.

It also made it even more galling to be left out. Not all those seeking local
distinction could be successful, and some communities that had set out with
high hopes of improving their lot through the Revolution's administrative
reforms ended up with nothing. The administrative decisions made in 1790
would not easily be forgotten, or the imagined slights forgiven, to the point
where the politics of particular towns would continue to be dominated
throughout the 1790s by a desire to rectify what they regarded as a massive
injustice. Most notably, the divisions between Girondins and Montagnards
in 1793 often reflected long-standing personal rivalries and agendas, both
between towns and between local families, and these rivalries were frequently exacerbated by anger over disappointed dreams. How else can we
explain the bitterness of local quarrels between towns that had been rivals
for the departmental *chef-lieu* – the likes of Mâcon and Châlon-sur-Saône,
Aix and Marseille, Albi and Castres, Mende and Marvejols, Foix and
Pamiers, Saintes and La Rochelle, or Aurillac and Saint-Flour? At district
level, too, there were repeated exchanges between such entrenched rivals as
Bourg and Blaye in the Gironde, Martigues and Salon in the Bouches-
du-Rhône, Montpon and Mussidan in the Dordogne. Even applicants for
tribunals and cantons continued their campaigns under the guise of
republicanism and political integrity. In some places the desire for revenge
seemed unassuageable, and the decisions made by the Committee of
Division had a lasting resonance, giving a distinctive and embittered flavour
to local politics throughout the revolutionary decade.

Notes

1   Keith Michael Baker, *Inventing the French Revolution* (Cambridge,
    1990), pp. 252–3.

2 Eric Thompson, *Popular Sovereignty and the French Constituent Assembly, 1789–91* (Manchester, 1952), p. 27.

3 Guy Chaussinand-Nogaret, *Mirabeau* (Paris, 1982), pp. 132–3.

4 Jean-Pierre Donnadieu, '1789, motions et adresses. Le Languedoc écrit à Paris', in M. Vovelle (ed.), *L'image de la Révolution Française* (4 vols, Paris, 1989), vol. 1, p. 29.

5 Michael P. Fitzsimmons, *The Remaking of France: The National Assembly and the Contitution of 1791* (Cambridge, 1994), p. 149.

6 For a useful chronology of government action during the final months of 1789, see Colin Jones, *The Longman Companion to the French Revolution* (London, 1988), p. 13.

7 Donald Greer, *The Incidence of the Emigration during the French Revolution* (Cambridge, MA, 1951), pp. 21–3.

8 For examples of such privileges, see the case of Bayonne, discussed at some length in Alan Forrest, *The Revolution in Provincial France. Aquitaine, 1789–99* (Oxford, 1996), pp. 17–19.

9 William Doyle, *The Oxford History of the French Revolution* (Oxford, 1989), pp. 123–4.

10 Malcolm Crook, *Elections in the French Revolution* (Cambridge, 1996), p. 31.

11 Bernard Gainot, 'État des questions', in S. Aberdam, S. Bianchi, R. demeude, E. Ducoudray, B. Gainot, M. Genty and C. Wolikow (eds), *Voter, élire pendant la Révolution Française, 1789–1799* (Paris, 1999), p. 36.

12 Hervé Leuwers, 'Élire les juges: l'exemple des juges des tribunaux de district du Nord et du Pas-de-Calais, 1790–1792', in Robert Chagny (ed.), *La Révolution Française: idéaux, singularités, influences* (Grenoble, 2002), p. 303.

13 Isser Woloch, *The New Regime. Transformations of the French Civic Order, 1789–1820s* (New York, 1994), pp. 38–40.

14 John Hall Stewart, *A Documentary Survey of the French Revolution* (New York, 1951), pp. 127–37.

15 Stewart, *Documentary Survey*, p. 141n.

16 Alfred Cobban, 'Local Government during the French Revolution', in *Aspects of the French Revolution* (New York, 1970), p. 117.

17 Woloch, *New Regime*, p. 39.

18 Alison Patrick, 'French Revolutionary Local Government, 1789–92', in Colin Lucas (ed.), *The French Revolution and the Creation of Modern Political Culture, vol. 2: The Political Culture of the French Revolution* (Oxford, 1988), p. 404.

19 Stewart, *Documentary Survey*, pp. 120–7.

20 Jacques Godechot, *Les institutions de la France sous la Révolution et l'Empire* (Paris, 1968), p. 474.

21 Clive H. Church, *Revolution and Red Tape: The French Ministerial Bureaucracy, 1770–1850* (Oxford, 1981), pp. 85–6.

22 Jean Tulard, *Nouvelle Histoire de Paris: la Révolution* (Paris, 1989), pp. 131–9.

23 Godechot, *Institutions*, p. 108.

24 Anthony Crubaugh, *Balancing the Scales of Justice: Local Courts and Rural Society in South-west France, 1750–1800* (University Park, PA, 2001), pp. 119–56.

25 Hubert C. Johnson, *The Midi in Revolution. A Study of Regional Political Diversity, 1789–93* (Princeton, NJ, 1986), p. 125.

26 Jacques Guilhaumou, *Marseille républicaine, 1791–93* (Paris, 1992), pp. 22–3; also his 'Fédéralisme jacobin et fédéralisme sectionnaire à Marseille en 1793: analyse de discours', *Provence historique* 36 (1987), p. 195.

27 William Scott, *Terror and Repression in Revolutionary Marseilles* (London, 1973), pp. 26–8.

28 Gwynne Lewis, *The Second Vendée: The Continuity of Counter-revolution in the Department of the Gard, 1789–1815* (Oxford, 1978), pp. 23–6.

29 Ibid., p. 231.

30 René Moulinas, *Histoire de la Révolution d'Avignon* (Avignon, 1986), pp. 202–3.

31 Daniel Ligou, *Montauban à la fin de l'Ancien Régime et aux débuts de la Révolution, 1787–94* (Paris, 1958), p. 240.

32 Alan Forrest, *Society and Politics in Revolutionary Bordeaux* (Oxford, 1975), pp. 45–6.

33 Emmanuel-Joseph Sieyès, *Observations sur le rapport du Comité de Constitution concernant la nouvelle organisation de la France* (Paris, 1789).

34 Marie-Vic Ozouf-Marignier, *La formation des départements. La représentation du territoire français à la fin du dix-huitième siècle* (Paris, 1989), pp. 45–75.

35 Thérèse Gourel de Saint-Pern, 'Particularisme et provincialisme en Provence, 1787–90' (mémoire de maîtrise, Université d'Aix-en-Provence, 1969), p. 134.

36 Ibid., p. 160.

37 Yannick Le Marec, *Le temps des capacités. Les diplômés nantais à la conquête du pouvoir dans la ville* (Paris, 2000), pp. 7–10.

38 Decree of 26 February 1790, in John Hall Stewart, *Documentary Survey*, pp. 137–41.

39 The correspondence of these local commissions is to be found among the papers of the Committee of Division, a subcommittee of the Committee of the Constitution established to define the exact boundaries of local jurisdictions. They are filed in Archives Nationales, series D-IVbis. Much of the detail that follows is taken from the papers of the committee. Some of the local examples cited in the following paragraphs can be found in Alan Forrest, 'Le découpage administratif de la France

révolutionnaire', in Centre Méridional d'Histoire, *L'espace et le temps reconstruits. La Révolution Française, une révolution des mentalités et des cultures?* (Aix-en-Provence, 1990).

40 A.N., BB30 157, Comité de Division, correspondence of the Garde des Sceaux.
41 Ted W. Margadant, *Urban Rivalries in the French Revolution* (Princeton, NJ, 1992), p. 8.
42 J.-B. Laffon and J.-F. Soulet (eds), *Histoire de Tarbes* (Roanne, 1982), p. 186.
43 A.N., D-IVbis1, petition from Castres (Tarn) to the Comité de Division, 1790.
44 Margadant, *Urban Rivalries*, p. 172.
45 A.N., D-IVbis 20, petition from Saint-Lizier (Ariège) to the Comité de Division, 1789.

|6|

The diffusion of revolutionary politics

Throughout France, the early years of the Revolution witnessed a huge effort of political mobilization, as people who had never previously been involved in the process of politics saw opportunities for self-expression and for influencing events. Men who had enjoyed no voice in public affairs in the *ancien régime*, who might at most have dabbled with pamphleteering in the 1770s and 1780s, were now able to express their views freely and partici-pate in public life. A political forum had been created, almost overnight, and many who had interested themselves in political questions – who had been lawyers or journalists or had preened themselves as minor *philosophes* – now stepped forward into the political arena. For some, politics spelt opportunity, the chance to take part. Increasingly, however, participation was also an obligation, something that was expected of public-spirited citizens. In a rev-olution where the people were sovereign, it was hardly an option to remain indifferent, to stand apart and leave the time-consuming business of politi-cal activism to others. That might easily be mistaken for social disdain, a contempt for the honest efforts of the people, or else it could suggest a lin-gering sympathy for the old order. By the time of the Jacobin republic, involvement in the Revolution came to be seen as a duty, something that people ought to do for the benefit of their fellow citizens, part of the civic obligation that fell on everyone alike. Standing aside from politics, a lack of interest in the affairs of the nation, or of one's municipality or local club, brought the risk of a charge of *égoïsme*, the crime of putting one's own self-ish interests above the interests of the republican community.[1] Or, as Patrice Higonnet has expressed it, 'Jacobins yearned for togetherness', a notion that extended across the community of citizens.[2]

The promotion of wider participation was not a monopoly of the Jacobins, nor was it always laced with menace. For the revolutionaries it was a neces-sary corollary to that most 'profound revolutionary act', the proclamation of the sovereignty of the nation, since ways had to be found to permit the nation to exercise its sovereignty.[3] This presented them with something of a challenge, since large sections of the French population were still illiterate and were plunged in a kind of local autarchy, with no experience of politics and no understanding of the workings of the state. This is not, of course, a subject on which it is easy to generalize, since in the larger towns and rural pockets across the country there were many who followed political events in 1789 with a concern that came close to passion. Through the *cahiers* and the hustings for the Estates-General, many had been awakened to the potential benefits of the new order, and they looked to the Assembly to answer their pleas. But rural areas still suffered from poor communications, receiving news that was days if not weeks old, and relying too often on communication by word of mouth; there were many villages where information from the outside world was more likely to come from itinerant pedlars or transhumant shepherds than through the postal service.[4] It was far easier to be involved if the political stage was erected on one's doorstep, and there is little doubt that from 1789 the main stage was elsewhere, with the nation's attention increasingly turned to Paris – to the decrees of the Assembly, the responses of the King, the demands of the Paris markets or the direct action of the crowd. It was in Paris that political initiatives were concentrated, in Paris that popular sovereignty was fought over, in Paris where the crowd rapidly acquired its own organization and a new political vocabulary. The gulf between the level of participation in the capital and that of small towns and *bourgs* in the provinces was, it might seem, as great as ever it had been under the *ancien régime*.

And yet was that really so? Many towns and cities had, as we have observed, experienced their own revolution during 1789, establishing municipal committees to take over the functions of government that had previously fallen to urban elites, and bringing a new political language into the local community. In the process, as Lynn Hunt has shown, they brought new men into the political arena, most notably drawn from the merchant classes, but spreading down to include less prosperous groups like artisans and shopkeepers.[5] Fear of rural violence and a concern to protect their homes and businesses led owners of even modest property to volunteer for service in a bourgeois militia or a unit of the National Guard, while many towns imposed their own conditions on entry, some accepting 'all citizens of known probity', others demanding a minimum level of *taille* or tax payment.[6] But though the *garde* was born of violence and panic – often in the days following the arrival of news of the Bastille – few units would be employed in combat. Theirs would be a largely symbolic role, involving such ceremonial functions as participation in festivals, guarding public buildings and parading, resplendent in the blue uniform of the new order. It proved an effective schooling in civic values, both for the *gardes* themselves and for the society in which they lived and whose members they impressed. Besides, in 1789 it was no longer possible to ignore the national arena, such was the feeling of liberation that had spread across France during the summer.

It soon became clear, even in the smaller towns, that local people would have to produce their own political class, men who were literate and who had at least a modicum of education, on whom the burden of responsibility would rest. Of course this would prove easier in some places than in others – in provincial cities, for instance, where a literate and cultured elite was already established. But even the smallest of communes – and the process of administrative subdivision had given communal status and substantial responsibility to some minuscule communities of under fifty inhabitants – had duties to perform, duties like the assessment of property for taxation, the maintenance of the commons and local roads, and the upkeep of the church and cemetery. Mayors and their councillors were kept aware of their place within the wider world of revolutionary administration, something which could only help instruct and educate villagers about their new-found rights and obligations.[7] By the deployment of the new administrative machine the revolutionaries believed they could help to mobilize opinion in each one of the 44,000 communes in France.

Administration may have been the most direct way of bringing the Revolution, and later the Republic, into local communities, but it was far from being the only way. The revolutionaries' passion for elections was not just a natural reaction to the years of autocracy that had gone before. It was also a means of involving a large part of the population in the fundamental processes of the Revolution and familiarizing a wider public with the affairs of government, goals which they equated with the apprenticeship in citizenship which they were so eager to inculcate. Elections, like the administrative structure they supported, were to be uniform across France, the decree of 14 December 1789 creating a single system of directly elected councils for town and cities, as well as for villages and rural parishes. The only city excluded from that law was Paris, where a separate piece of legislation was required, and this had to wait until 21 May 1790.[8] The law laid down that voting should be reserved for active citizens – essentially those males aged twenty-five, resident in the community for at least one year and paying taxes equal to three days' wages – and that the mayor, the municipal council and various other municipal office-holders should be chosen by election. If that sounded straightforward, however, the practice the laws introduced was less so, with the consequence that the process of election was complex and time-consuming. Towns were to be subdivided into *sections* or *quartiers* in proportion to their population. Primary assemblies would be called in these sections to elect their *bureau*, which would then have responsibility for conducting the election; and again, a president and secretary had to be elected before the process could get under way. And though being an active citizen gave a man the right to vote, it did not permit him to stand for election; so they voted not for the deputy himself, but for *éligibles*, men of greater wealth and property from whose number the final choice would be made.[9] In Paris, where the average daily income was high and where the barrier was thus more difficult to jump than in smaller towns and rural communes, this meant that only those paying the equivalent of ten days' wages in tax had any direct input into the electoral process.[10]

It was, in short, a cumbersome and, for many people, a rather confusing system, one that was quite different from anything they had experienced in the *ancien régime*. In particular, they were to vote as individuals, as citizens – not, as they had in the past, as members of a gild or corporation – while the primary assembly could be called for any of a multiplicity of reasons. If they were called upon to vote for the mayor and municipal council, so, too, they would have to vote for members of the departmental, district and cantonal authorities, for deputies to the Assembly and for *suppléants* who would replace them should their seats fall vacant, for municipal *procureurs*, and for a raft of judicial offices ranging from judges on local courts to *juges de paix* in every canton. The meetings of the primary assemblies could become quite protracted, as they passed from one election to another; and the density of business, in October 1790 in particular, led to a certain confusion, surely understandable in view of the general ignorance of the legislative texts.[11] The government, however, remained unshaken in its commitment to the electoral principle. In the years following the Civil Constitution it extended election to the clergy, with bishops elected by departmental assemblies and *curés* by district ones.[12] Even in the army a proportion of both officers and *sous-officiers* were to be elected by the men in the grade immediately below them; the only exception was at the very highest level, that of *général de brigade*.[13] If the people were to be sovereign, it followed logically that officials had to be answerable at all times to the people, and that meant being answerable at the polling booth. It also followed, however, that with such recurrent calls on the people to vote, there was a real and constant risk of civic fatigue among those asked to exercise their civic duty. Any sense of liberation, of joy at being invited to take part in the electoral process, soon wore off. In many areas, the high point of electoral participation was not during the Revolution at all, but during the immediate pre-revolution, when local communities were called upon to choose their deputies to the Estates-General. Thereafter the electorate would be more circumscribed, and public enthusiasm, at least in so far as it can be judged by the rate of participation, more restrained.

The number of active citizens – computed by the National Assembly itself at around four million people, or around 15 per cent of the population – varied considerably between departments and from city to city. The highest percentages were often in the countryside and in small towns, where the population was relatively stable and there were not the great extremes between wealth and poverty that were to be found in the larger cities. In Burgundy, for instance, the vast majority of farm workers and small *vignerons* were active citizens, though the money they earned barely kept them above the breadline. Around Versailles, too, most countrymen were classed as *actifs* though few either owned or leased their land. And the Massif Central, an area of great poverty and high seasonal migration, again recorded high numbers of active citizens.[14] But voting levels within rural areas also varied greatly to reflect the peculiarities of the fiscal system and local landholding patterns at the end of the *ancien régime*. In Upper Artois, Jean-Pierre Jessenne notes that enfranchisement was higher in areas of large-scale farming than in those where the land was subdivided into tiny smallholdings.[15] In any case, local councils made their own estimates of the value of a day's wage, which could be differently interpreted in different parts of the country and inevitably led to inequities. And cities tended to come off badly, with one of the lowest figures that for Paris. This meant that peasants and country-dwellers were more likely to enjoy the use of their civic rights than were the inhabitants of the larger cities, and it helps explain why turnouts in elections during the Revolution were often much higher in rural areas. None of the great provincial capitals recorded high levels of voting, even in 1790, because not even the *citoyens actifs* had an automatic entitlement to vote. Further restrictions were often applied. In Lille, for instance, the franchise was restricted to men aged twenty-five or over who, besides the tax qualification, were not domestic servants, had served in the National Guard, and had sworn an oath of loyalty. As a result, out of Lille's population of around 66,000 there were only 5,464 active citizens entitled to exercise their vote.[16]

Those who did not exercise their right to vote, and who became categorized as passive citizens, were not necessarily excluded from the electoral rolls on economic grounds. Many stayed away through apathy; it was easy to lose interest. Or they were deterred from voting by the sheer frequency and complexity of electoral consultation.[17] The example of the Bas-Languedoc is perhaps instructive in this context, an area of France where around two-thirds of adult males were classed as *actifs* and where still more could have voted had they chosen to do so. In one department, the Hérault, we know that thirty-one out of every hundred adults ended up in the category of passive citizens, yet only 3 per cent were excluded by the modesty of their tax payments. By way of contrast, nine of the thirty-one were domestic servants who, for that reason, were denied the vote, while the other nineteen, the overwhelming majority, were simply negligent, men – often of humble means – who had failed to register with their municipality and were thus excluded by their own inaction. Of those who did register, a large number omitted to vote when the municipal elections were held. In the election of 1790, indeed – and of all municipal elections this was the one that commanded most popular interest – it is noticeable how it was the bourgeois, the merchants and professional men who were most assiduous about casting their votes, while others stayed away from the polls in large numbers. There were exceptions: in the municipal and cantonal elections of that year, the highest percentage vote of the entire Revolution, an astonishing 61 per cent, was recorded in the Landes.[18] But modest turnouts were far more typical. Of those inscribed on the electoral register in Lodève, for instance, only 23 per cent took the trouble to vote; in Montpellier the figure was less than 20 per cent.[19] This pattern was reproduced across France. It explains both why the elections themselves were largely trouble-free and why municipal government and local office-holding passed rapidly into the hands of a stable, educated political class, united behind the more moderate ideals of liberty and the rights of man.

Of course, elections were an important manifestation of citizenship, and one which allowed at least a substantial part of the local population to offer views on government policy and municipal affairs, or to express their preference between candidates for municipal or judicial office. And 1790 was undoubtedly the high point of electoral participation. But even then voters were presented with ideas rather than candidates; there were no political parties to help organize opinion; and political societies did not yet enter the fray. Those in power remained an elite, and if it is true that the elections resulted in the virtual elimination of the aristocracy from local government, at least in the major cities, there were exceptions, like the Marquis d'Estouteville in Rouen and the Comte de Fumel in Bordeaux. Besides, the social spectrum from which mayors and councillors were chosen remained relatively narrow, with the big provincial towns opting for men of property and standing, merchants or businessmen, or those with professional expertise, especially lawyers. It was not immediately obvious that the new voters were being given a real choice or being invited to become part of the political class. Only gradually did clearer political factions develop, so that the larger cities might choose between radicals and moderates, those who could be identified with the Montagne or the Gironde. More commonly, in 1790, they were presented with contests between *magistrats* from the local *parlement* or between the scions of prominent local families.[20] The Constitution of 1793 would also abolish the legal distinction between active and passive citizens, and hold out the prospect of a democratic electoral system; but that prospect proved illusory, since no elections were ever held. The heyday of electoral politics had already passed.

What elections did achieve was to give the new administrative bodies, the districts and departments as well as the municipalities, a status to which they could not otherwise have aspired. They could claim, plausibly, to represent local people, and not just to take their place within the administrative framework, answering up the line to the minister of the interior. And they were not expected to remain mute, or simply to toe the line laid down in Paris. They could, in the name of their people, respond to national policies, passing resolutions and publishing political statements as the interests of their electors demanded. During the Constitutional Monarchy towns and cities were expected to take initiatives and defend their local economy: this was a period of genuine devolution, when centralism was still rather suspect, liable to be equated with the absolutism of the Bourbons. Armed with National Guard and bourgeois militias, some towns also sought to spread their influence and hegemony across the surrounding countryside. In particular, Marseille believed that it had a mission to spread radical politics in its region, outflanking Paris where necessary to keep alive revolutionary truths and sending out *commissaires* to proselytize in the villages of the South-East. In the same spirit, the city's radicals 'liberated' the Patriots of Arles and Avignon by armed force.[21] Elsewhere towns provided regional leadership by moving to crush incipient counter-revolution, most notably, perhaps, when Bordeaux sent 1,500 National Guardsmen against the supposed royalists of Montauban in 1790, winning prestige and near-universal acclaim from the assembly and from revolutionaries across the length and breadth of France.[22] These towns and their municipal authorities had no reason to accept a Parisian model of revolution, one where policy was made at the centre and where the provinces had a largely executive role. Paris had no monopoly of policy-making, nor was it the only centre of patriotism or political radicalism. As important regional centres, many of which had been provincial capitals earlier in the century, they felt that it was their duty to act in defence of the Revolution.

Many provincial towns launched initiatives of another kind in joining regional *fédérations* to celebrate the anniversary of the Fall of the Bastille and to mark their shared commitment to the ideals of the Revolution. This movement had its origins in the provinces, in the immediate wake of the Grande Peur, when there were attempts to form defensive pacts between the militias and guard units of neighbouring towns and villages to help repress rural aggression. But the need for mutual defence soon passed, and by 1790 federations had changed in character, becoming more ceremonial than functional, and taking the form of a show of solidarity or a demonstration of fraternity. There was little common pattern: some of the earliest manifestations drew inspiration from the popular festivals of folkloric tradition. In Bourges, a bonfire was lit in the centre of town on 25 June, the day of the traditional *Feux Saint-Jean*, and local people danced around the flames to indicate their solemn participation in the civic oath. Or two neighbouring villages might come together to celebrate their fraternity, some inventing new rites to rid themselves of centuries of animosity.[23] There was no fixed rite or format, no authoritative text or message, and the government took fright lest local *fêtes* sink into uncontrolled violence and debauchery. But they could not be ignored, for even these spontaneous gatherings on village squares often had a serious revolutionary purpose. In the autumn of 1789, a scheme had been mooted by the city of Angers for correspondence to be established among the *milices* of all the provinces in the kingdom – a very premature idea as things turned out, but one which, in recognizing the need for a hierarchy of militias and a national framework, was already pointing the way forward to future forms of collaboration.[24]

During the winter of 1789 and the first six months of 1790, there were reports of federations of the National Guard in most regions of France, but with a particular density in the Rhône valley. It was here that one of the first federations met, at Étoile in the Drôme, on 29 November, bringing together 12,000 National Guardsmen from around twenty communes to swear a solemn oath, 'to remain forever united, renouncing in future any provincial distinctions'. By the end of January, when another federation was called at Valence, National Guardsmen arrived from a one-hundred-mile radius, from over 240 communes, and the scene was set for further major assemblies in Lyon, Nancy and Strasbourg, each involving a military spectacle, a solemn act of oath-taking, and a sumptuous celebration in the form of a popular festival.[25] The 'pacte fédératif' had changed from being a mode of self-defence against an unruly peasantry to become a patriotic ceremony which provincial towns vied with one another to host. Cities were flattered to be invited to take part, and some, like Bordeaux and Toulouse, were given honoured status in each other's federations – on 17 June and 4 July – as a sign of close friendship.[26] At this time, it should be emphasized, there was nothing disreputable about the idea of regional collaboration of this kind; for many it seemed an obvious way of protecting their achievements against counter-revolutionaries or other enemies. It was the National Assembly which, fearing a proliferation of local ceremonies, solved the problem by making the *Fête de la Fédération* into a single official festival, to be celebrated on the symbolic ground of the Champ de Mars in Paris, where all the local federations could celebrate together in an act of national harmony. This was, as Mona Ozouf describes it, a deeply conservative response, one that aimed to restore order and impose authority. It was also a statement of national power, of the essential unity of France and the centrality of Paris. By proposing an official national ceremony, the assembly was effectively undermining future provincial initiatives, and the role of the capital as the fulcrum of the Revolution was again emphasized. From all over France the *fédérés* would approach Paris – the city that housed the King and the Assembly, and which now epitomized the Revolution – as pilgrims of old, visiting a holy city.[27]

Once inside its walls, they would be enveloped in the sumptuous ritual of the festival itself, with its heavily normative imagery and magnificently choreographed presentation. The revolutionaries were conscious of the power of such visual images; attendance at festivals was seen as an important way of educating the populace and mobilizing public opinion. They were also conscious of the need to sway opinion and win minds, something that elections alone could not hope to achieve. *Fêtes* were one obvious and highly visual form of propaganda that could influence the widest spectrum of society, the illiterate as much as the lettered, and under the Jacobin republic they would be developed into an art form, most notably by David. By then the festivals were national days of celebration, organized from the centre by the Committee of Public Instruction; like the revolutionary calendar into which they were integrated, they helped to forge the ideal of a single national revolution, bereft of localism or regional diversity. But earlier festivals were quite different. Many were organized locally along traditional lines, taking the form of long processions snaking their way from the town hall to the church or cathedral, and incorporating an important clerical presence. Moreover, they were usually planned locally, without reference to Paris. In Bordeaux, as in other provincial cities, most festivals culminated in a mass and in the singing of a solemn Te Deum as the celebrants sought to expiate their sins. They were variable in purpose, some continuing to celebrate the religious festivals of the *ancien régime* – the fires of Saint-Jean or the processions of the *Fête-Dieu* – others celebrating major moments of the Revolution, whether national events like the Bastille and the death of Mirabeau, or more local ones like the installation of the new bishop or the blessing of the flags of the National Guard. All retained a strong spiritual element alongside the reminder of civic responsibility. And they retained a certain diversity, until 1793 when the Festival of Reason marked a new turning point in revolutionary symbolism.[28]

From these early festivals provincial opinion did not always derive the same political message as the government, nor did local people necessarily recognize their debt to Paris. The same is true of the other major conduit of political ideas, the printed word, which had a profound impact in the provinces. For while in the early years of the Revolution the capital witnessed an extraordinary burgeoning of print culture, with pamphlets and newspapers pouring from its presses, Paris never enjoyed a monopoly of publication, as other towns and cities produced unprecedented quantities of political ephemera. This was only to be expected. As we have seen, most provincial cities were centres of vigorous intellectual life in the eighteenth century, with their academies and cathedrals, their masonic lodges and reading circles; and the new technologies of printing made it easy and relatively cheap to circulate tracts and prospectuses. Towns like Rouen, Toulouse and Besançon were significant publishing centres before the Revolution, while Troyes and Epinal had an established reputation for making cheap, brightly coloured prints. Newspapers flourished in most sizeable towns, owned and edited by local men who, naturally, wanted to inform their readers about national events, but who also wished to offer local news and discuss municipal affairs. Bookshops had sprouted in most larger cities, where readers would browse, drink coffee, discuss the latest publications, or order books from Paris. And printers, far from being obscure artisans working in constant fear of the censor, were often a prosperous and rising group within urban society, men of some substance who enjoyed wealth and property and might be linked by marriage to the elite families of provincial society. Urban France was admirably prepared to share in the enthusiasm for the printed word which greeted the outbreak of the Revolution.[29]

The most characteristic and arguably the most potent form of publication was the newspaper press, a medium which, under the *ancien régime*, had been restricted by censorship laws and judicial constraints, to the point where some of the more openly political comment had to be introduced into France from abroad, in French-language newspapers like the *Gazette de Leyde*. Here one could find what French publishers did not dare to provide – open criticism of government policy, soberly expressed sympathy for enlightened ideas and support for the *parlements'* attempts to resist the extension of royal authority.[30] That there was a market for such ideas was not in doubt, and with the advent of the Revolution that market expanded many times over. French journalists and newspaper proprietors no longer contented themselves with the reporting of events, but offered comment and editorial opinion, comparing revolutionary measures with the pre-revolutionary context, and offering a vision of history that provided legitimation for the ideas and achievements of the new order.[31] The lifting of censorship – the letter of 19 May from Maissemy, the *directeur-général de la Librairie*, which allowed certain 'authorized' papers to cover the debates in the Estates-General and was Louis XVI's last attempt to control the press[32] – combined with the sense of excitement and expectancy both in Paris and throughout France, made the years from 1789 to 1791 ones of free expression and journalistic diversity. France seemed gripped by a seemingly insatiable appetite for up-to-the-minute information. Journalists were aided by low publishing costs; they could afford to take risks, to appeal to minority markets. Of course, Paris was the centre of political agitation, and it was out of the cauldron of the Paris pamphlet wars of 1787 and 1788 that the revolutionary periodical press emerged. The meeting of the Estates-General served as a call to arms, with journalists quick to respond, new titles sprouting up on all sides and representing contrasting strands of opinion. Between the beginning of May and the end of July alone forty-two new periodicals were launched in the capital, with the *journée* of 14 July bringing a sudden multiplication of the number of titles.[33] In 1790 over 300 new papers appeared in Paris alone, and almost as many again in the first nine months of 1791. These covered the whole gamut of opinion to include radical papers and moderate papers, republican ones and – perhaps rather more slowly – royalist ones. Both right and left were represented, as well as important client groups like merchants, lawyers, peasants and women. At the same time, the politicization of the Paris press had a galvanizing effect on the rest of the country. In provincial towns and cities prospectuses promised a new political discourse and new papers were launched – some lasting for only a single issue, and relatively few surviving into their second year, but keeping the debate alive in the furthest recesses of the country. And many existing local papers took up the challenge which the Revolution held out to them, changing their format from that of the *affiches* of the *ancien régime* to provide a new, politically committed regional press. By autumn 1791 the provinces, too, had witnessed a print revolution, with some 200 newspapers launched to vie for the affections of local people.[34]

In the euphoric early months there was little sign in this new and volatile press of conflict between Paris and the provinces, or between government and people. The press was seen as part of the revolutionary process, a key mechanism for keeping the population informed of the debates in the assembly and mobilizing support in the country. The revolutionaries believed in the importance of openness and transparency; 'publicity', in the words of the mayor of Paris, Bailly, in August 1789, was 'the people's safeguard', without which they could easily be betrayed; secrecy could only encourage plotting and aid counter-revolution.[35] Thus a free press was to be encouraged as a major guarantor of open government, of what the Revolution liked to term *franchise*. That view, of course, would look somewhat utopian in the years that followed, as France lurched from regime to regime and became increasingly intolerant of dissent. In their turn, royalists, constitutional monarchists and moderate republicans found their thoughts unwelcome or their presses closed down, until by 1793, the Jacobin republic had become so paranoid about supposed counter-revolutionary cells that virtually any criticism, whether of the Jacobins, government policy or their allies in the Paris *sections* was seen as seditious. This was a particularly dangerous time for journalists; as in so many revolutions, they were always among the first to be arrested for abusing their position and misleading others, for undermining public morality and revolutionary virtue; and the spread of 'federalism', anti-Jacobin politics in many provincial cities in the summer of 1793 made the position of provincial journalists especially exposed. Clubs and popular societies began to run their own official papers in many cities and denounce their rivals, with the consequence that the free press became the object of increasing suspicion. And since provincial journalists were often themselves political figures in their communities, a significant number of them became implicated in the federalist revolt and would pay for their opinions with their lives. Mathon de la Cour and Fain in Lyon, Marandon and Duvigneau in Bordeaux, Schneider in Strasbourg, Lambertie in Limoges and Pipaud Desgranges in Périgueux were among the more notable provincial journalists to die on the guillotine.[36] Others, like Ferréol Beaugeard, the politically committed editor of the *Journal de Marseille*, were quick-witted enough to abandon their newspapers and go into hiding until it was safe to emerge.[37] That way, at least, they survived.

Newspapers were one of the most effective ways of diffusing the revolutionary message because of the loyalty they built up: editors were appreciated for their opinions, readers customarily subscribed for three months or more, and members chose which cafés and reading circles to frequent by the sorts of papers they stocked. Papers were pitched at target audiences – merchants, lawyers, radicals or conservatives, Catholics or anticlericals, popular militants or (in the case of the Jacobins' rural flagship, the *Feuille Villageoise*) the more politically aware of the peasantry and others in village society. Writing for peasants was a particularly demanding task, and Cérutti, the *Feuille*'s editor, used a wide range of techniques to get through to people who might not have any prior interest in Jacobin politics, including the printing of educative almanacs and uplifting songs which their readers might sing in the fields or at the village *veillée*; he also took care to print news of the harvest and agricultural prices, things that were uniquely important to village society.[38] Papers were also relatively affordable. They were compact enough to be printed quickly and cheaply, like the pamphlets so many of them resembled, and might either be posted to subscribers or distributed to passers-by through street vendors and hawkers visiting local markets or selling their wares at the Palais Royal or on the Pont Neuf. Like pamphlets and handbills – other successful media for the popular diffusion of politics – newspapers came into local communities and sought out their readers. Most frequently they came through the post, arriving at regular times and eagerly awaited by the faithful; they were read by men of different social classes and they were discussed in bars and on public squares. This was itself enough to guarantee that successful journalists enjoyed an impact many times greater than the circulation numbers of their papers. Moreover, as the Revolution became more popular and politics appealed to ever wider sections of society, so the style of the press became more pithy and often more humorous. Pamphlets might have the benefit of immediacy and sensationalism, as instant publications responding to crucial political events; but newspapers were regular publications, conveying the trusted opinions which their readers wanted to hear. Their popularity is not in doubt: indeed, their further expansion was limited only by levels of illiteracy and poverty in the local population and by the state of technology in the printing and paper-making trades.[39]

Subscribing to the right newspaper or joining the right reading circle was a way of demonstrating one's involvement; choosing the wrong allegiance was something that was often taken to indicate a lack of *civisme*. As the regime grew increasingly intolerant of individualism, so a man's choice of paper or pamphlet came to be seen as an indicator of a more general attitude, a symbol of the kind of person he was and the sorts of actions of which he was capable. During the Terror, when arrests were made and seals placed on the property of the accused, the authorities took a close interest in these matters, just as they carefully noted the titles on his bookshelves: what a man read could tell so much about his revolutionary credentials. So, increasingly, could other forms of leisure – in particular the plays he attended and the theatres he patronized. This was especially the case in Paris, of course, where many of the boulevard theatres developed a reputation for rowdiness and disrespect for the authorities, and where the unlighted expanse of the stalls could provide shelter and anonymity. Particular theatres were known to stage plays of a certain political persuasion – radical or counter-revolutionary, republican or royalist – and to attract a politically minded audience, many of whom went for the tumult in the pit as much as for the presentation on stage. Not for nothing did Paris theatres provoke the anger of Robespierre or provide such a natural setting for the dramatic antics of the *jeunesse dorée* after Thermidor, when actors who had identified with the Republic were reviled and ridiculed.[40] It was true also of the larger provincial cities, where theatre-going became one of the principal pastimes of the young and was a favoured activity for the sons of wealthy families. For them the theatre was a place to see and be seen, a symbol of the luxury and make-believe they craved, a stage on which they, too, could act out their role as part of the city elite. What many of them experienced in the theatre was a coded version of revolutionary politics.[41]

But in the atmosphere of *franchise* that characterized the early Revolution, there was no need for political involvement to be concealed behind codes or relegated to leisure time. Writing journalistic articles, penning pamphlets and attending radical or anticlerical plays, all were forms of commitment that could go hand in hand with other political activities, such as electioneering, serving in the National Guard or addressing the crowd in squares and markets, on the Pont Neuf or at the Palais Royal. In Paris and other towns, those wishing to involve themselves in politics soon had the opportunity to join a club or popular society, which could provide a meeting of like-minded people who would talk about current political issues, discuss the latest news from the National Assembly and act as powerful pressure groups on the local political scene. Some sprang up in the very first weeks of the Revolution, a reflection of the avid interest shown in many of the larger cities; and though they were new creations, products of their immediate context, historians have looked for their antecedents in the *sociétés de pensée* of the eighteenth century and in the humanist traditions of the Grand Orient. Some early clubs, indeed, took over both the premises and much of the membership of masonic lodges, before rebadging themselves in the new idiom of the Revolution.[42] Or, like the aptly named *Club du Café National* in Bordeaux, they were formed in cafés to provide their members with an opportunity to read the Paris papers and discuss more radical politics.[43] But there any resemblance to the sociability of the *ancien régime* ceased. Unlike the reading circles and masonic lodges of the eighteenth century, the new societies were exclusively focused on politics, the spread of information and the exercise of influence. Most were fiercely patriotic. And many – like the most influential among them, the clubs in the Jacobin network – were sufficiently committed to openness that they held their sessions in public.[44]

Clubs provided an outlet for expression that further widened participation in revolutionary politics, bringing merchants, lawyers and tradespeople into political life and offering a more immediate forum for activism and involvement than was provided by elections. In Paris, of course, they built upon the political excitement which life in the revolutionary capital had evoked, and it is no accident that the first clubs were formed by deputies within the ambience of national politics. The Jacobins, for instance, had started life in 1789 as the Club Breton, formed by a number of future deputies to the National Assembly who were planning ahead of the meeting of the Estates-General and organizing themselves into an effective caucus for more advanced ideas. They first met at Versailles, and when the assembly was transferred from there to Paris, they went, too, opening new premises in the convent of the Jacobins in the rue Saint-Honoré. But what is most significant is the timing: they had come into being spontaneously, informal gatherings of men determined to exercise what influence they could on the affairs of state. They were not alone. Other political clubs sprang up in the capital in a similar spontaneous way as men reacted to the fluid political situation in which they found themselves. And if they did so in Paris, so groups formed in towns across France, in Lyon, Dijon, Lille, Saint-Malo and Perpignan, and soon what began as informal *cercles* became formalized into political societies, with presidents and secretaries, a fixed membership, rules and agendas and subscription fees. They were local men produced by a local political context and maintaining an allegiance to their local communities, 'local worthies aiming to elucidate the decisions of the National Assembly to their fellow citizens'.[45] But their attention was also focused on the capital, and increasingly they saw their role as more interventionist, providing support locally for the club's role nationally. In turn, the Paris society, understanding the strength that this gave it on the national stage, sought to inform and educate like-minded clubs in the provinces. By this means it became a rallying point for Patriots across the country, to the point where its influence was disproportionate to its original purpose and it was the centre of a tightly structured network of clubs united behind the Jacobin cause.[46]

That, however, was for the future, for 1793 and 1794. Paris might provide leadership and organization, but its domination of the club movement in the early stages of the Revolution was far from complete. Societies came into being through local initiative and in response to local needs, and only later did some gain what many sought, the affiliation to the Paris Jacobins that gave them access to the pamphlets, speeches and other printed materials that threw light on the politics of the Assembly or the Convention. By 1793 the Paris club used the privilege of affiliation as a weapon to gain influence and extend its imperium over a national network of local societies. But that should not blind us to the real nature of these local societies or the extent of local initiative, not just in the larger provincial cities but in several thousand towns and *bourgs* throughout the country. One of the most salient features of the club movement, indeed, was its diversity: they did not all speak with the same voice, nor did they look consistently to Paris for leadership. At one time or another towns might boast several different clubs, often with conflicting political aims. Paris itself had a rich variety of societies, set up to espouse particular causes and champion political ideals, royalist and monarchist clubs as well as more republican and democratic ones, the counter-revolutionary *Amis du Roi* and the Girondin *Cercle constitutionnel* coexisting with the radicals of the Jacobins and the Cordeliers. Brissot and Condorcet founded the *Amis des Noirs* to further the cause of slave emancipation, while by 1793 women could enter this largely male bastion through membership of the *Club des citoyennes républicaines révolutionnaires*.[47] Such diversity was not restricted to the capital; in the larger provincial cities, too, men of opposing political views expressed them through club membership. Bordeaux, for instance, at one time or another boasted a moderate republican club, the *Amis de la Constitution*, which, perhaps mistakenly, retained its affiliation with the Paris Jacobins, despite glaring political disagreements; but it also had the radical *Club National*, the *Société des surveillants zélés de la Constitution*, and the *Société Patriotique*, or *Club de la Merci*. On the monarchist right, too, the city offered choice: the *Club monarchique (ou des Amis de la patrie ou de la paix)*, the *Club des Impartiaux* and, later, the *Société de la Jeunesse bordelaise*. Patriotic women could attend the *Amies de la Constitution*, the sister society of the *Amis*.[48]

People chose to join a club for its ideology, of course, but also as a form of educated sociability, a place to meet friends and kindred spirits. In the early months, indeed, they were often open and welcoming to newcomers, a broad church where men of differing views could mingle and debate. What mattered was patriotism. National Guards took the initiative in forming the club in Marseille, and at first only guardsmen and municipal councillors could join; yet within a week over 800 guards had signed up.[49] Until that moment when the Jacobins insisted that their members had to renounce membership of other societies, there was no reason to restrict oneself to a single club; one could sample the riches of several different societies, and some of France's newly enfranchised citizens eagerly did so. Equally, there was diversity and a range of opinion within many popular societies, including even the Paris Jacobins. Many clubs suffered from schisms and harboured internal factions: the Paris Jacobins were themselves rent by two great internal battles which sent shock waves through the entire club movement and, in Michael Kennedy's words, 'well-nigh dismembered the network'.[50] These were the Feuillant schism in 1791 and the Girondin-Montagnard schism in 1793, and they were reflections in the club movement of the searing divisions within national politics. Often political divisions of this kind resulted in the appearance of rival societies, until even some of the smaller provincial towns could offer their citizens a choice. Libourne, for instance, had three societies by 1793, vying with one another for subscriptions and loyalties, and introducing the spice of competition into the politics of a smallish provincial town. Unsurprisingly, given its geographical position, Libourne was a predominantly Girondin town, and the relative strength of its societies reflects this. The more moderate of its republican clubs, referred to by local people as 'club number two', had a membership running into many hundreds – 468 members recorded their votes at a meeting in January 1793 – while the radicals of 'club number one', glorying in their claims to be 'Robespierristes' or (worse still) 'Maratistes', could attract only around twenty brave souls to their meetings.[51]

Popular societies were not the exclusive preserve of town-dwellers. They sprang up in *bourgs* and villages, too, especially in those parts of the South-East and South-West with strong traditions of community and *sociabilité méridionale*. And they appeared in two main phases. Between 1789 and 1792, clubs formed by local militants might then seek affiliation with the Paris Jacobins to gain access to information and influence; by the end of the period there were around 1,500 affiliated societies, with the strongest implantation in three very different areas: a 'vast Midi' that extended from Bordeaux to Toulon and up into the Massif Central from the South and the West; the Saône axis between Lyon and Dijon; and a small area of the North between Dunkerque and Cambrai. These areas were still important during the second phase of expansion, between the autumn of 1793 and the summer of the Year II, but at this point, when the Jacobins were already in power and when club membership might also be a means of ingratiating oneself with the authorities, a dense network of clubs also grew up in the Paris Basin, the lower Seine valley and Artois. In all there were around 6,000 clubs by the end of this period, of which some 3,400 had been established during the Jacobin republic.[52] But what remains most astonishing is the density of popular societies in small rural communities in the South-East and the Rhône valley. In the Drôme, of 356 communes, 268 had a popular society at some moment between 1789 and the Year III; and every single *chef-lieu de canton* had its club. In the Bouches-du-Rhône that was true of 85 per cent of all communes and 100 per cent of *chef-lieux de canton* – again, astoundingly high figures for activism in villages, even if they were at Marseille's back door. In the Vaucluse, almost one hundred of the department's 132 clubs were set up by 1792, before fear and political fashion set in.[53] Club activity was not limited to the plain or to river valleys. In the Pyrenees, for instance, where a long tradition of community politics already existed under the *ancien régime*, clubs were formed in small villages and even in some pastoral valleys, often clustered around the popular society of the local town to whom they looked for inspiration. By 1793 the department boasted over a hundred societies, more than sixty of them affiliated to the Jacobins.[54] Remoteness, it seemed, did not constitute a barrier to the expansion of the club network. Even the villages of the southern Ardèche, far removed from the main arteries of communication – villages like Burzet, Chassiers, Jaujac and Thueyts in the *garrigues* of the newly formed District du Tanargue – felt the need to form clubs so that they might assume their role within the political nation.[55]

The larger towns were divided for administrative purposes into sections, and these, too, took on a political life of their own. As we have seen, Paris had forty-eight, Lyon thirty-two, Bordeaux twenty-eight; but medium-sized towns, too, were divided into a smaller number of sections, often at the behest of the new municipal authorities; in late 1790, for instance, Caen was divided into five sections and Limoges into four, while smaller departmental *chef-lieux* like Agen and Périgueux acquired two or three each.[56] Unlike clubs, they were not societies which people applied to join or for which they paid a subscription. They were simply subdivisions of cities, like the electoral wards of towns today, intended to facilitate day-to-day administration, and every citizen who lived in the area defined by the section had the right to attend its meetings and take part in its debates. But whereas initially they were given no right to participate actively in politics except when called into session by the municipal authorities, by 1791 the more radical assemblies in Paris were already calling for the right to sit permanently, to discuss subjects that they chose and to petition both the city and the Assembly. With the support of the more advanced republicans in the clubs, they assumed the rights they demanded, challenging the government to overrule them, so that soon sections, both in Paris and elsewhere, sat in regular session and began to initiate policy. It was a huge change, one that dispersed political decision-taking across urban society and created another forum for activists. But whereas in Paris the sectional movement created a powerful voice for radicalism and support for direct action by the crowd, in provincial cities Jacobin sympathizers were often a small, if vocal, minority. Here the balance of political power was different from that in Paris, and it was unusual for the rich and educated – most notably the lawyers, doctors and merchants – to be excluded from sectional office, as they came to be in Paris. The sections of cities like Lyon and Marseille were to prove deeply suspicious of the Montagnards, both nationally and locally, and would help steer municipal politics in the direction of a more moderate republicanism, one that was solidly based on the local elite. As with the membership of provincial clubs, there was generally only a minority who adopted the language of the Paris Jacobins or the Paris Commune, or who shared their commitment to fraternity, popular sovereignty or programmes of price-fixing and social equalization. Indeed, in the summer of 1793 it would be the sections which often took the lead in pressing for the provincial cities to adopt a more openly anti-Jacobin and anti-Parisian stance, and even to take up arms against the capital.[57]

A study of clubs and sections in provincial France shows how different milieux developed different political and social priorities while still proclaiming their loyalty to the goals of the Revolution and to the constitution, and supporting the patriotic effort on the frontiers. It made them different from the Parisians in their interpretation of the law, and especially of popular sovereignty. It made them suspicious of direct action and the notion that deputies might serve as the delegates of those who had elected them. It caused them to distrust anarchy and street violence, which they associated uniquely with the capital, encouraged by a complaisant government and their accomplices in the Paris Commune. But it did not, except in the jaundiced eyes of the Montagnards and their Parisian allies, make them any less republican, or less committed to the rights of man. Many in the provinces still looked for a lead to national politics, whether to their *frères* in the Paris club or to their deputies in the Convention. Some amongst the provincial Montagnards took pride in standing shoulder to shoulder with the Paris sections, and in their adoptive title of *sans-culottes*. But in most towns they were a minority. More generally, people feared the violent extremism which they associated with the streets and sections of the capital. They were mobilized by their clubs and sections to defend the Revolution, but the Revolution as they understood it. It was they, they explained, who fought consistently for clear, unadulterated ideals, and the Parisians who had allowed theirs to be forgotten, their integrity to be defiled.[58]

Opinion was mobilized in other ways, too, ways over which central government had little control and which often ran counter to the official desire to seek consensus. In many parts of rural France, for instance, rioting and château-burning continued long after the panics of the *Grande Peur* had subsided. The Great Fear may have seemed to most townsmen to constitute little more than blind panic, peasant bands spreading terror and destruction in response to rumours and ill-defined threats. And so in many regions it was. But in some parts of the countryside a more radical political message took root in 1789, which would continue to inspire local people throughout the revolutionary years. This was particularly true in large parts of the South-West and the Massif Central, where anti-seigneurial feeling combined with social grievances and an abiding hatred of privilege to create a tradition of revolutionary violence among the peasantry which was more specifically targeted against landlords and large estates than the relatively random violence of fear. There were, even in 1789, isolated outbreaks of peasant violence which seemed to demonstrate a certain political maturity and a new awareness of the import of national events. At Sousmoulins in the Saintonge, for instance, 400 peasants invaded the château of the local seigneur, forcing him to wear the national cockade and drink the health of the Third Estate before tearing up his feudal *terriers* and insisting that he sign a document in their presence renouncing his family's feudal claims.[59] In July such action was still remarkable, but after the night of 4 August the level of political awareness to be found among the peasantry was visibly strengthened. First seigneurialism was their main target, then, in 1791 and 1792, their anger turned against some of the Revolution's own reforms, those insisting that feudal dues could only be redeemed by purchase – a law widely condemned for offering a shabby and unnecessary compromise with the *ancien régime* – or favouring agrarian individualism at the expense of the traditional commons.[60] Rural France had been brought into the political nation, and its consent could not be taken for granted.

Sporadic peasant protest would continue in some regions of France throughout the Revolution, surfacing even at the height of the Terror. In the Bas-Limousin, for instance, there was an explosion of renewed violence in the spring of 1790, focused primarily on what local people saw as the indefensible remnants of seigneurial control and the failure of the Revolution to free them from oppression. The gains of 4 August, they claimed, had not been delivered, and the peasantry responded in time-honoured fashion, using violence to drive home their demands. They were not, they insisted, opposed to the Revolution; they were trying to diffuse its ideology and force their landlords to abide by its ideals, and in a number of villages they consigned their demands to paper. In the village of Cornil, for instance, eleven peasants wrote a petition to the *lieutenant-général-criminel* at Tulle, condemning the 'caprices' of their seigneur and his refusal to relieve them of the 'feudal despotism' he exercised over them. This might seem the classic stuff of rural protest, indistinguishable from their demands in the *cahiers*, until they went on to talk of the context of their action. 'It is only now,' they explained, 'when a new constitution has changed the nature of the state or more especially of its antique laws, when they see themselves as being a little more free and less exposed to the rigour of the tyranny of their *seigneurs*, that they are beginning to test their liberty to complain of the unjust vexations which they have experienced'.[61] There was nothing random about such protest: it was a calm and calculated attempt to remove the last vestiges of feudalism, to compel the legislators to enforce the spirit of the Revolution in the country-side. In some cases the peasants took advantage of the moment to scorn and humiliate the seigneur and – in the more anticlerical areas – the *curé*, stig-matizing them as bastions of *ancien régime* privilege. In more isolated instances there is even evidence of outside involvement by organized groups of radicals. In the Dordogne, for example, village and small-town clubs were already assuming an active part in the organization of anti-seigneurial violence during the winter of 1789–1790.[62]

Though seigneurial abuses were the most frequently cited cause of peasant uprisings, there were, of course, other issues that stirred country-dwellers to action in the revolutionary years and helped ensure that popular violence continued to be a form of political expression in rural France. Among them were religion and hunger, both of which were serious questions for the peasantry of the southern Massif, where rural communities reverted to vio-lence and château-burning throughout the revolutionary decade. The Lot and the Cantal were particularly affected, with serious outbreaks of *jacquerie* tak-ing place in 1792, a time when much of rural France seemed resigned and quiescent. Hunger and shortage lay at the heart of much of the unrest, as year followed year without the good returns the peasants craved. By 1792, penury and high prices threatened to reduce large sections of the population to starvation, as yet again the harvest failed. On the market at Aurillac the price of a *setier* of wheat had risen from twelve *livres* in May 1789 to thirty-two *livres* in January 1792, while at Salers the price rose a staggering 50 per cent between February and May.[63] But not all the unrest could be put down to hunger, the natural fears of small peasant farmers who relied on the market if they were to have enough to eat. By this time other forces were at work in areas like the Cantal, from the pressure exerted by émigrés and refractory priests to the rhetoric and propaganda of local revolutionary activists. The most violent outbreaks of rioting were not necessarily sponta-neous outpourings by the peasantry. Rather they might be responses to measures that antagonized local people, like dechristianization or levels of recruitment for the military; or they might be fed by rumours of émigré activity. Peasants still expressed themselves as they had always done, through violence. That remained their most effective way of making their views heard. Increasingly, however, that violence was now being orches-trated by others, men who knew the mentality of the peasant and under-stood how much their agenda differed from that of Paris and the Assembly. It is surely no coincidence that the most violent outburst of 1792 in the Cantal, the peasant insurrection that swept the canton of Montsalvy, was largely inspired by the intervention of the Jacobin deputy, Milhaud, and his National Guard, who sought to interfere in parish affairs.[64] Milhaud succeeded only in creating a backlash, though he had little reason to regard that as failure. Driving the peasantry to riot was yet another way of diffusing revolutionary politics, a time-honoured method of communication. Indeed, in rural departments like the Cantal, far removed from the world of radical journalism and the Paris sections, it still proved a highly effective form of mobilization, one that took account of rural difference and played on the fears and jealousies of the French countryside.

Notes

1 For a definition of 'égoïsme', as used by the Revolutionary Tribunal, see William Scott, *Terror and Repression in Revolutionary Marseilles* (London, 1973), p. 199.

2 Patrice Higonnet, *Goodness beyond Virtue. Jacobins during the French Revolution* (Cambridge, MA, 1998), p. 240.

3 Isser Woloch, *The New Regime. Transformations of the French Civic Order*, 1789–1820s (New York, 1994), p. 60.

4 Peter Jones, *Liberty and Locality in Revolutionary France. Six Villages Compared, 1760–1820* (Cambridge, 2003), pp. 40–2.

5 Lynn Hunt, 'Committees and communes: local politics and national revolution in 1789', *Comparative Studies in Society and History* 18 (1976), pp. 321–46.

6 Georges Carrot, *La garde nationale (1789–1871): une force publique ambiguë* (Paris, 2001), pp. 52–5.

7 Woloch, *New Regime*, p. 34.

8 Serge Aberdam *et al.*, *Voter, élire pendant la Révolution Française, 1789–99. Guide pour la recherche* (Paris, 1999), pp. 146–54.

9 Melvin Edelstein, 'Electoral behaviour during the Constitutional Monarchy (1790–91): a "community" interpretation', in Renée Waldinger, Philip Dawson and Isser Woloch (eds), *The French Revolution and the Meaning of Citizenship* (Westport, CT, 1993), p. 105.

10 Guillaume Métairie, *Le monde des juges de paix de Paris, 1790–1838* (Paris, 1994), p. 129n.

11 Ibid., p. 130.

12 Nigel Aston, *Religion and Revolution in France, 1780–1804* (London, 2000), p. 142.

13 Rafe Blaufarb, 'Démocratie et professionalisme: l'avancement par l'élection dans l'armée française, 1760–1815', *Annales historiques de la Révolution Française* 310 (1997), pp. 613–14.

14 Patrice Gueniffey, *Le nombre et la raison. La Révolution Française et les élections* (Paris, 1993), p. 92.

15 Jean-Pierre Jessenne, 'De la citoyenneté proclamée à la citoyenneté appliquée: l'exercice du droit de vote dans le district d'Arras en 1790', *Revue du Nord* 72 (1990), p. 822.

16 Gail Bossenga, *The Politics of Privilege: Old Regime and Revolution in Lille* (Cambridge, 1991), pp. 108–9.
17 Guéniffey, *Le nombre et la raison*, pp. 191–2.
18 Edelstein, 'Electoral behaviour during the Constitutional Monarchy', pp. 110–12.
19 Robert Laurent and Geneviève Gavignaud, *La Révolution Française dans le Languedoc méditerranéen* (Toulouse, 1987), pp. 60–3.
20 Jocelyne George, *Histoire des maires, 1789–1939* (Paris, 1989), p. 32.
21 Scott, *Terror and Repression*, p. 20.
22 Daniel Ligou, *Montauban à la fin de l'Ancien Régime et aux débuts de la Révolution, 1787–94* (Paris, 1958), p. 240.
23 Mona Ozouf, *La fête révolutionnaire, 1789–99* (Paris, 1976), p. 54.
24 Pierre Arches, 'Le premier projet de fédération nationale', *Annales historiques de la Révolution Française* 28 (1956), p. 256.
25 Yoichi Uriu, 'Espace et Révolution, enquête, grande peur et fédérations', *Annales historiques de la Révolution Française* 280 (1990), pp. 157–9.
26 Yannick Butel, 'Fêtes et divertissements en Bordelais au dix-huitième siècle' (mémoire de maîtrise, Université de Bordeaux-III, 1978), p. 26.
27 Ozouf, quoting Edgar Quinet, in *La fête révolutionnaire*, p. 59.
28 Butel, 'Fêtes et divertissements', p. 27.
29 For a detailed discussion of these issues in a major provincial city, see Jane McLeod, 'A Social Study of Printers and Booksellers in Bordeaux from 1745 to 1810' (PhD, York University, Toronto, 1987).
30 Jeremy D. Popkin, *News and Politics in the Age of Revolution: Jean Luzac's* Gazette de Leyde (Ithaca, NY, 1989), p. 15.
31 Pierre Rétat, 'La légitimation du discours révolutionnaire dans le journal de 1789', in Michel Vovelle (ed.), *Aux origines provinciales de la Révolution* (Grenoble, 1990), p. 279.
32 Claude Labrosse and Pierre Rétat, *Naissance du journal révolutionnaire, 1789* (Lyon, 1989), p. 9.
33 Claude Bellanger (ed.), *Histoire générale de la presse française* (4 vols, Paris, 1969), vol. 1, p. 428.
34 Hugh Gough, *The Newspaper Press in the French Revolution* (London, 1988), p. 44.
35 Jeremy D. Popkin, *Revolutionary News. The Press in France, 1789–99* (Durham, NC, 1990), p. 3.
36 Gough, *Newspaper Press*, pp. 102–3.
37 For an analysis of the colourful career of Beaugeard and his newspaper, see René Gérard, *Un journal de province sous la Révolution: 'Le Journal de Marseille' de Ferréol Beaugeard, 1781–97* (Paris, 1964). This is one of the fullest modern studies of a provincial newspaper across the period of the Revolution.
38 Melvin Edelstein, *La Feuille Villageoise. Communication et modernisation dans les régions rurales pendant la Révolution* (Paris, 1977), pp. 331–6.

39 Popkin, *Revolutionary News*, p. 82.

40 François Gendron, *La jeunesse dorée. Episodes de la Révolution Française* (Montréal, 1979), pp. 110–12.

41 See, for instance, Paul Courteault, *La Révolution et les théâtres à Bordeaux* (Paris, 1926).

42 Ran Halévi, *Les loges maçonniques dans la France d'Ancien Régime. Aux origines de la sociabilité démocratique* (Paris, 1984); and the same author's doctoral thesis for the École des Hautes Etudes en Sciences Sociales, 'La sociabilité maçonnique et les origines de la pratique démocratique' (EHESS, 1981). Halévi writes in the tradition of Augustin Cochin, whose *Les sociétés de pensée et la démocratie: études d'histoire révolutionnaire* (Paris, 1921) was reissued in 1978 under the title of *L'esprit du jacobinisme*.

43 Jeanne Melchior, 'Histoire du Club National' (thèse de doctorat, Université de Bordeaux, 1951), pp. 15–18.

44 Woloch, *New Regime*, p. 78.

45 Higonnet, *Goodness beyond Virtue*, p. 172.

46 Jean Boutier and Philippe Boutry (eds), *Atlas de la Révolution Française, vol. 6: Les sociétés politiques* (Paris, 1992), p. 16.

47 Olwen Hufton studies this club in some detail in *Women and the Limits of Citizenship in the French Revolution* (Toronto, 1992), pp. 25–39. She draws particular attention to the discomfiture which the *citoyennes* caused for male republicans.

48 Pierre Bécamps, 'Le peuple souverain', in François-Georges Pariset (ed.), *Bordeaux au dix-huitième siècle* (Bordeaux, 1968), pp. 388–9.

49 Michael Kennedy, *The Jacobin Club of Marseilles, 1790–94* (Ithaca, NY, 1973), p. 30.

50 Michael Kennedy, *The Jacobin Clubs in the French Revolution, 1793–95* (New York, 1999), p. 7.

51 Michael Kennedy, *The Jacobin Clubs in the French Revolution. The Middle Years* (Princeton, NJ, 1988), p. 56.

52 Boutier and Boutry (eds), *Atlas*, vol. 6, pp. 16–17.

53 Ibid., pp. 99–103.

54 Jean Annat, *Les sociétés populaires: la période révolutionnaire dans les Basses-Pyrénées* (Pau, 1940), pp. iv–v.

55 Boutier and Boutry (eds), *Atlas*, vol. 6, p. 79.

56 Paul Hanson, *Provincial Politics in the French Revolution. Caen and Limoges, 1789–94* (Baton Rouge, LA, 1989), pp. 217–19.

57 See, most notably, W. D. Edmonds, *Jacobinism and the Revolt of Lyon, 1789–93* (Oxford, 1990).

58 This view is consistently expressed by some of the richer and more influential sections of the Bordeaux waterfront, always ready to see the Paris Club and the Commune as the playthings of violent demagogues. See Alan Forrest, *Society and Politics in Revolutionary Bordeaux* (Oxford, 1975), pp. 84–6.

59 Jean-Noël Luc (ed.), *La Charente-Maritime: l'Aunis et la Saintonge des origines à nos jours* (Saint-Jean-d'Angély, 1981), p. 292.
60 Anatoli Ado, *Paysans en révolution. Terre, pouvoir et jacquerie, 1789–94* (Paris, 1996), pp. 257–73.
61 Jean Boutier, *Campagnes en émoi. Révoltes et Révolution en Bas-Limousin, 1789–1800* (Paris, 1987), p. 81.
62 Henri Labroue, *L'esprit public en Dordogne pendant la Révolution* (Paris, 1911), p. 18.
63 Jonathan Dalby, *Les paysans cantaliens et la Révolution française, 1789–94* (Clermont-Ferrand, 1989), p. 64.
64 Ibid., p. 77.

|7|

Revolutionary priorities in Paris and the provinces

Although in 1789 the new nation appeared firmly united behind the ideals of the National Assembly, that unity would prove fragile as interest groups emerged within the new polity. People not unnaturally sought different things from the Revolution and emphasized different priorities, depending on whether they were young or old, religious or secular, urban or rural. Squabbles rent whole communities and came to dominate the local agenda – whether between religious denominations, as happened in Nîmes and the Gard, or between towns and their close hinterland, the territory which the urban elites, backed by substantial sums in revolutionary *assignats*, increasingly colonized.[1] The larger provincial cities thus found themselves locked in battle with the country-dwellers of their regions, eyeing one another's political initiatives with mounting distrust. And so it was with Paris, the biggest city of them all, though here the nature of the squabble was more variable. Paris came to symbolize different things to provincial Frenchmen at different moments of the Revolution, depending on whether it was perceived as the capital city of France, the seat of administration and revolutionary government, or the city of Paris, with its heaving, impatient and increasingly radical population. Both sparked hostile reactions from provincial rivals. *Paris-ville* and *Paris-capitale* both made a deep impression on the rest of the country, and neither could expect that its actions would be greeted with blind loyalty or complete indifference. Paris was, quite simply, too important to ignore.

As a capital city, revolutionary Paris was the centre of government and the seat of an assembly which represented the sovereign people of France. It enjoyed fiscal and administrative powers of which no city under the *ancien régime* could have dreamt, especially after the overthrow of the Constitutional Monarchy and the declaration of the Republic. Whereas under the Bourbons the court had been at Versailles and the locus of power had been divided deliberately – Louis XIV had little affection for Paris and established Versailles as an alternative seat of political decision-making – under the Revolution there was no such ambivalence. The ministries and the state bureaucracy were now concentrated back in Paris, where Parisians had long felt that they belonged. At the same time, government became more centralized, and provincial France only too often found itself at the beck and call of government, of myriad decrees on matters like policing, taxation, military service or requisitions, which were despatched from Paris to the departments, before being reprinted and distributed through the districts to every *mairie* in the land. The result was administrative overload, with heavy demands and impositions made on local people who were generally unpaid, who combined their public office with their normal employment, who might be barely literate, and who had little of the administrative expertise needed to cope with the explosion of government paper. Much, of course, was simply ignored, for lack of time or competence.[2] But it is hardly surprising that the constant stream of demands and intrusions came to be resented in the provinces or was mistaken for the cold hand of the capital.

Ministries like Finance, Police and the Interior so bullied the departments and districts to fill in regular administrative reports and act as the eyes and ears of central government that it was often difficult not to resent it. And the war only made things worse. Paris, it seemed, had an insatiable appetite for paper, statistics, indeed any information that could be turned to the advantage of the state. Even in the early years, before the Revolution's taste for statistical tables fully matured, there were attempts to collect statistics on demographic distribution (1790), to enumerate the poor (1790) and to draw up *mercuriales* tabulating food prices; there were also enquiries into the condition of agriculture, manufacturing, roads and mines.[3] There were censuses of grain stocks, farm animals, horses and mules, carts and carters, all at the behest of the Ministry of War.[4] And all that happened before the Jacobin dictatorship, and before that period of the Directory which can be termed a 'golden age' of statistics. In all, Isabelle Guégan has shown that the period between 1789 and 1795 saw some 446 *enquêtes* requiring detailed statistical input from the provinces – their frequency rising from four in 1789 to thirty-five in 1791 and fifty-seven in 1793, before hitting a peak of 177 in the Year II.[5] Repeatedly the government returned to mayors and town hall staff with more and more minute questioning as they tried to determine the state of the economy and, even more significantly, that of public opinion. To judge by the improbably well-rounded numbers that many communes returned, we may assume that local people viewed these exercises with irritation and disdain, devoting very little time to their replies. But that does not mean that they had no effect, for in the process Paris itself could become an object of resentment, shorthand for state interference and unwelcome intrusion.

Paris-capitale was not only about government and administration, important though these were in the city's relations with the rest of France. It was also about style, and elegance and luxury. Already in 1789 Paris was a capital of fashion, whether the fashion of *haute couture* and *articles de Paris*, or of art through the biennial *salons* that did so much to set the tone for collectors and people of taste throughout the kingdom. That was, of course, a culture of the elite, a culture that was soon internationalized and which came to mark off the upper classes from the rest of the population. They enjoyed a social and cultural influence that extended across Europe, so that the fashion-conscious and those wishing to ape the manners of the day looked increasingly to Paris for inspiration.[6] And provincial consumers, whether of fashion clothes or paintings and sculpture, looked to Paris as the cultural capital of the nation. Indeed, a substantial part of its economy depended on leisure and the luxury trades. To many Paris signified fun and frivolity as much as the more serious business of government, and because it signified fun, because anyone could dress up and pretend to glamour for a day, because the constraints on dress and appearance were so lax – the last sumptuary law excluding certain forms of dress dated from 1665[7] – it also breathed a sense of freedom, of equality, which many in the provinces could only regard with envy. Demand for luxury goods was not confined to the rich. Paris by the later eighteenth century saw a soaring demand for semi-luxury imports like cotton goods, porcelain and lacquer ware, and for those cheaper 'populuxe' products that could be bought by families of modest means.[8] Consumer culture had been democratized, to the point where most households owned some consumer goods – tools and kitchen utensils, bedding and clothing[9] – especially clothing, that ultimate signifier of standing and respectability, clothing that would be passed on to domestic servants or sold in the city's flourishing second-hand market, the province of the *fripier* and *regrattière*.[10] All classes seemed conscious of style and colour, and in this regard, too, Paris spelt opportunity, a world freed from many of the customs and traditions which so constrained provincial life.

To take advantage of such opportunity did, of course, require money; 'a poor man', in Mercier's words, 'cannot be happy in Paris', as he was denied access to the entertainments of the capital and excluded from the community of leisure.[11] For those without the material means to exercise their freedoms, the curious equality of Paris could be a source of anger and frustration, a force that helped galvanize their desire for change. So if the more prosperous of the capital's inhabitants were often anxious not to lose their cherished lifestyle – revolutionary Paris would produce conservatives as well as radicals – the poorer quarters of the city were quick to demand their share of political rights and influence. But theirs was more than just the politics of deprivation or envy; their demands were also based on a powerful sense of justice and a sense of their own worth. The people of the capital seemed to contemporaries to be unschooled in that deference that so often held back others. Labourers, carters, even messenger-boys showed little respect for those they served, addressing them with a casualness that suggested they saw them almost as social equals. This was not simply a question of popular attitudes. It was ingrained in the legal system, and in the language of gilds and journeymen's confraternities. The law quite specifically gave journeymen and apprentices rights in the workplace which they could, and did, exercise in their relations with their masters, showing no hesitation in leaving one workshop for another or in regarding their position as being bound by nothing more than a cash contract. Artisans, like the gilds themselves, were notoriously litigious in eighteenth-century Paris; they cited custom and usage, denounced the alleged despotism of employers, and appealed, often successfully, to the conventions of natural law.[12] In a society based on credit and reputation, masters had to exercise care in how they treated their employees; their honour, reputation and the credit-worthiness of their business were at stake. However much the state tried to tighten up the regulation of workshops and introduce disciplinary measures through the gilds, these were widely flouted and led to a new flurry of dissent and litigation.[13]

Paris was a difficult city to regulate or repress, as it also had a long tradition of violence, especially around the city's markets; indeed, it was that propensity to violence which was most worrying for conservative opinion, the fear that the city would erupt again at the first opportunity. It was not in the Parisian character to be docile or to accept authority. Even domestic servants, who would be treated with a degree of contempt during the Revolution as flunkeys open to the corrosive influence of their masters and mistresses, were portrayed in eighteenth-century prints as being assertive, acting with a certain swagger, cocky and insolent towards their social betters. Like the rest of the *menu peuple* of the city, they were self-confident and sure of their position within the social fabric of the city. This confidence, as David Garrioch has recently argued, goes far to explain the advanced patriotism and the 'precociously egalitarian' character they demonstrated in the first months of the French Revolution, and the presence of many thousands of them in the recurrent popular *journées* of 1789. In particular, he suggests that the involvement of thousands of women in popular protest, drawn from the central market area and from the Faubourg Saint-Antoine, demonstrates the importance of work ties in mobilizing the populace and hence of 'the influence of the urban environment on political events'.[14] Egalitarianism had its roots deep in the consciousness of the city.

It followed that ordinary Parisians had their own political agenda during the revolutionary years, the artisans and shopkeepers, the men and women of the docks and markets, even the casual floating population of unskilled workers and immigrants from the provinces who soon found themselves drawn into the culture of the capital. They often had a developed sense of their own rights; and they were accustomed to the role of political actors – in grain riots like those of 1725 and 1775 – and to a presence at the great events of the eighteenth century that took place in the capital, whether they be royal processions, parliamentary remonstrances or public executions, like those of Cartouche and Damiens.[15] Eighteenth-century Parisians had a shared identity born of a community which lived and did business in the street, a city where the crowd took an active part in the ceremonies of Church and state. Parisians could hardly avoid politics. They discussed the political news of the day in the bars, taverns and markets, including the latest scandals and the more sordid affairs of court; they gossiped about the Queen's sex life and whispered about the

reported death of the King. They exchanged hearsay about alleged poison-
ings and gave credence to famine plots, often to the outraged alarm of police
spies and undercover agents who reported the conversations they overheard.
There was nothing sinister about this. An interest in politics followed naturally
from gossip about neighbours, trade, issues of disease and public health, scares
and alleged conspiracies, from the normal sociability of Paris life. As Arlette
Farge expressed it, 'the city was an informational sphere whose inhabitants
organised themselves so as to *know* more and unravel the secrets of king and
monarchy. Public curiosity was not a character trait, but an act which brought
each and every individual into politics'.[16]

It was out of this public curiosity that the Paris crowd of 1789 was born, and
though as a crowd it may have been driven forward by its own dynamic, it
cannot be forgotten that it was composed of individuals, and of different
individuals depending on circumstance – often tradesmen and apprentices,
as at the Bastille or in the attack on Réveillon's wallpaper factory in April,
but at other times the market-women of Les Halles, most notably in the march
to Versailles in October. Indeed, to describe them as a 'crowd' seems barely
adequate, since each crowd was specific to the issue of the moment, a response
to immediate pressures and provocations. And on each occasion it was
an assembly of men and women whose political instincts had already been
aroused and who shared a common culture that resulted from living and
socializing in Paris, with its distinctive values, varied itineraries and profound
sense of neighbourhood. It is these qualities that most clearly distinguished the
menu peuple of the capital from their counterparts elsewhere, and which
gave substance and direction to the popular politics of the city. The crowds
that formed so rapidly and apparently so spontaneously in 1789 were composed of individuals drawn from the poorer quarters of the capital, whose
outlook had been shaped by their experiences there – by their relationship
with the police and with authority in a city where policing and information-
gathering were ubiquitous, but also, more generally, by the forces that
formed the 'fragile lives' of Arlette Farge's study, what one recent historian
of popular Paris has aptly termed 'the intricate interlacing of family and neighbourhood relations, gossip and opinion, work-culture, religion and superstition'.[17] Their mentality had been forged by years spent living and working in
Paris, by its excitement and vitality, and by the uncertainty and instability of
their existence.

Their instincts were, of course, aroused by revolutionary discourse, but
they were not the creation of the Revolution. What the vigorous pamphleteering and public oratory of the early months of the Revolution achieved
was to reorientate popular anger and give a new focus to their grievances.
The official municipal leadership of Bailly and Lafayette, with its strong
emphasis on the maintenance of public order, had never enjoyed the confidence of ordinary Parisians, and Lafayette's vocal support for the repression
of the army mutineers at Nancy in 1790 only hastened his fall from grace.
By the end of 1791, Bailly had resigned, wearied by months of factional

struggle, and Paris municipal government passed into more radical hands. The mayoral election of November 1791 was won by Jérôme Pétion, a man who commanded greater respect among ordinary Parisians – a lawyer who had first been elected to the Estates-General, who was known for his condemnation of slavery and his close association with Robespierre. By the summer of 1793, however, he, too, was out of favour, pushed increasingly by his distaste for popular violence and his revulsion at the September Massacres towards more moderate politics and an alliance with the Girondins. He took to flight after the Jacobin coup of May 1793 and, rather than face his enemies, chose to commit suicide. What Pétion's tragic story confirmed was just how far Parisian politics had moved from the high-minded radicalism of 1791, and how powerless the office of mayor had become in the face of popular violence. Under the Jacobins the victory of popular politics in Paris would be complete, with the choice of the new mayor, Jean-Nicolas Pache, one of the plotters of the Jacobin coup and a man who identified with the cause of popular democracy. By the spring of 1794 he would be too extreme even for the Montagne; he was an intransigent egalitarian who had sympathies with the *enragés* and gave his support, and that of his city, to the cause of the *Hébertistes*. The mayor had become little more than a pawn of the radical faction.[18]

In any case, the radicals had ceased to look to the *Hôtel de Ville* for either their leadership or their inspiration. By 1791, as we have seen, clubs and sections provided the organization which the early crowd had lacked, while journalists vied with one another to capture the voice of the people; between 1789 and 1791 there were as many as 1,400 papers in the capital, even if many survived for no more than a single issue.[19] As a consequence, Paris was flooded with news and information, gossip and rumour, much of it highly inflammatory. Radicals like Marat and Hébert spoke to a Parisian popular audience with a directness and, often, a peculiarly stylized rhetoric which they quickly assumed as their own, and nameless pamphleteers and street orators took their message into the taverns and markets. They brought national politics to the streets of the capital in a sensationalized and often alarmist register, playing on popular prejudices and raising the spectre of foreign invasion and a terrible vengeance. The themes were not new, but the changing political context gave them a new immediacy – the threat of a famine plot; speculation in the revolutionary paper currency, the *assignat*; the supposed influence of nonjuring priests with the King and Marie-Antoinette; and, as ever, plots and conspiracies, treason, the work of foreign agents inside Paris and, particularly, inside the government. Word of the King's abortive flight to Varennes only increased the atmosphere of suspicion, as news seeped out of his abandonment of his people; and popular anger mounted when it became clear that the assembly was prepared to absolve him of all responsibility, even offering credence to the somewhat risible story that he had been kidnapped against his will. Priests and foreigners were attacked. Clubs and sections denounced what they saw as the deputies' cowardice, while across Paris radicals demanded that the King should be put on trial. Already the Cordeliers were calling for a republic. A call to the people to petition the Assembly led to around 50,000 people gathering on the Champ de Mars on 17 July, where over 6,000 had signed before violence erupted. Two men found hiding under the *autel de la patrie* at the heart of the ceremony were dragged out and lynched as spies; and when Bailly sent in the National Guard to restore order, they opened fire on the crowd, killing around fifty unarmed Parisians.[20] Once again Paris had its martyrs, and the schism between the authorities and the people of the capital had never been wider. The people increasingly looked to the radicals for leadership.

Among radical leaders, Jean-Paul Marat, in the guise of *l'Ami du Peuple*, was uncompromising in his attacks on moderation, taking every opportunity to point to the dangers which threatened the virtuous Parisians. He shared the pathology of many in the crowd, at once fearing conspiracy and betrayal, and denouncing the machinations of enemies real and imagined, including spies, foreigners, royalists and assorted counter-revolutionaries, hoarders, speculators and those in the pay of the British government. The more radical Parisians followed his counsels slavishly, believing in the most recent plot that he had unearthed and concurring in his judgment that courtiers or corrupt politicians must lie at the heart of every attack on their rights. In Marat the people of Paris had found their champion, someone on whom they could depend to defend them through thick and thin. For three years he wrote unflinchingly against all forms of weakness and compromise, usually in letters addressed directly to the Parisians or to their National Guard. Whatever their cause – whether it was over their petition on the Champ de Mars, the more radical pronouncements of the Paris Commune or the bloody excesses of the prison massacres – they could look to *l'Ami du Peuple* as one of their own, a bold and resolute voice that would defend them against outside criticism.[21]

Hébert wrote in a very different register, but again he succeeded in talking to the *menu peuple* of the capital in a manner with which they identified, and again he took up his pen in defence of their radicalism and their virtue. Like a number of journalists and pamphleteers of his day, Hébert preferred to address his readers through an assumed persona, that of a Parisian furnace-maker, the 'Père Duchesne', an ingenious character who might have been borrowed from the stage of one of the many theatres along the boulevards, a brave, patriotic, egalitarian figure who was at the same time funny, foul-mouthed and deliberately outrageous. Through the Père Duchesne and his family, living simply and virtuously in their artisanal garret, Hébert hoped to recreate many of the prejudices of the back streets of the capital and to enflame the anger of his readers against those he identified as their enemies. As a *brave sans-culotte*, Hébert assured them, Duchesne had nothing to fear from the authorities, neither arrest, denunciation, nor nocturnal visits from the local *comité de surveillance*. He could sleep peacefully in his bed, virtuous in the knowledge that he had done a good day's work in the cause of the Revolution, happy in the bosom of his somewhat idealized family. 'He can go everywhere with his head held high. In the evening, when he comes home to his pad, his wife throws herself on his shoulder, his little brood come to give him a kiss, his dog jumps up to lick him. He tells them the news he has learned at his section. He takes an infernal joy in recounting a victory over the Prussians, or the Austrians, or the English; he tells how they have guillotined a general for treason, or a Brissotin; and quoting the example of these rascals, he makes them promise always to be good citizens and to love the republic above all else'.[22] The device worked so well that many of the Parisian radicals, self-styled *sans-culottes* of the *faubourgs* and the inner-city sections, soon identified with the language of the Père Duchesne and looked to him to express, in his rather literary Parisian *argot*, their deepest aspirations. Indeed, through his pages he not only helped to politicize his readers, but also he became a trusted mentor for many of them at a time when the sections were still forging their new political identity.

But what was that identity? What was a *sans-culotte*, the stereotype to which popular Paris seemed so committed after the full-blooded entry of the sections into national politics in late 1791 and 1792? He certainly cannot be defined in clear social terms as a member of a precise social class, though many of them came from the ranks of the Paris trades, and those who were perceived as being either too rich or too highly educated might have found themselves excluded. Vingternier's famous definition points to a certain simplicity of lifestyle, a rejection of luxury and ostentation and a respect for the usefulness of manual work. 'He's someone who always goes on foot, who does not have millions as you'd all like to have, no castles, no footmen to serve him, and who lodges very simply with his wife and children, if he has any, on the fourth or fifth floor'.[23] There was something almost moral in this insistence on simplicity, even down to their place in the topography of a Paris tenement block. But it did not make them any less of an elite among the Paris workforce, an elite who numbered only three or four thousand out of a population of over 600,000, and who defined themselves by their patriotism and by the sacrifices they had made for the Revolution. They turned up to their sections, served in the army or the National Guard, manned the revolutionary committees or joined in the police work of the *armées révolutionnaires*. These were seen by the *sans-culottes* as important moral as well as political qualities, defining a political attitude, 'a certain moral approach to political problems'.[24]

How did the *sans-culottes* define their cause and their aspirations? And what were the political objectives they strove to achieve through their participation in crowd violence, their membership of the more radical sections, their relentless pressure from the tribunes of the Convention? There is no doubt that the defence of the nation and the Revolution headed their agenda: they were fiercely proud of the achievements of the Revolution and willing to use any means – especially direct action and violence – to protect the gains it had brought them. Fear of plots and conspiracies, of foreigners and counterrevolutionaries, only deepened their resolve and made them prone to outbursts of violent panic. They were proud, in particular, of their own Parisian revolution, the movement based on the Paris Commune and the more radical sectional assemblies, which, since declaring themselves permanent in the last months of 1791 and early 1792, could initiate political debates on subjects of their choosing. The sections soon showed that they had distinct priorities of their own. They shared with much of popular Paris a deep-seated distrust of the Catholic Church, particularly of monasteries and the clerical hierarchy; so they pressed for effective policing of the clergy and took a leading part in mounting a campaign of terror against nonjurors. They urged severe punishments for hoarders and speculators, anyone whom they suspected of profiteering from popular misery or of starving the people into submission. They demanded price controls on foodstuffs and tight policing of markets, and they urged the strict implementation of the General Maximum. And they showed little sympathy with the ideas of political and economic individualism which had been championed by the Assembly, notably the Le Chapelier law that had effectively outlawed workers' movements to improve wages and working conditions. Liberalism, for the *sans-culottes*, was less important than securing a measure of economic equality, and that implied a degree of redistribution, something that the government was reluctant to offer. They championed the more symbolic policies of the Republic, too, taking their place at the many revolutionary festivals and glorying in the orgy of destruction that accompanied dechristianization – the so-called 'vandalisme révolutionnaire' of the Year II, which targeted everything from saints in their medieval niches on street corners to the tombs of the kings of France at Saint-Denis.[25] They were enthusiasts for rational innovations, like the new metric weights and measures, and the imposition of the revolutionary calendar; and they were not without a certain puritanism, as was shown by their determined assault on brothels and prostitution. Above all, they prided themselves on being democratic and egalitarian, seeing their elected deputies as delegates who were answerable to their constituents and accepting the need for direct action and violence as part of the political process.[26] That image came to characterize the entire Parisian revolution.

It was, however, a form of popular radicalism which did not travel well, and which was largely restricted to the *sans-culottes* of the capital. There were, of course, radicals in provincial cities who joined Jacobin clubs and sought to imitate the politics of the capital, looking for inspiration to the Cordeliers or the Père Duchesne, and trying relentlessly to import the world of the Paris sections into Lille or Toulouse or Marseille. But their efforts were usually fruitless, failing to win over mass opinion and fighting a losing battle against the well-entrenched local elites. If radical politics swept a majority of the Paris sections and ensured their support for the Commune, elsewhere its appeal remained limited. It was usually 1792 before the sections of provincial towns began to emulate their Parisian counterparts by demanding rights for their members, and then only at the behest of local clubbists. At their height they amounted to little more than a small hard core of radicals in half a dozen sections in cities like Lyon and Bordeaux, linked to and schooled by local Montagnards, while in medium-sized towns like Dieppe and Le Havre the *sans-culottes* could muster only a tiny minority, some twenty or thirty men doggedly turning up to sectional meetings with little hope of creating a popular base.[27] Indeed, the most influential sections were often among the more conservative, offering support to the municipal authorities rather than seeking to undermine them. In Bordeaux, for instance, the most powerful sections were those in the city centre and the merchant quarter of the Chartrons, composed of the same kinds of people – lawyers, doctors, merchants, clerks and accountants – as sat on the municipal council itself.[28] They had little reason to attack municipal and departmental decisions. Indeed, they remained solidly moderate in their republicanism, united in what they saw as the defence of their city's interests.

They were typical of the many provincial Frenchmen who believed that there were limits to the legitimate use of violence, and for whom the violence of *sans-culotte* language and obloquy, combined with the physical threat posed by the Paris crowd, seemed menacing and destructive. Too often the image that provincial France chose to retain of popular activism in the capital was not the noble picture of idealism which the Jacobins favoured, but rather an image of bloodthirsty crowds hauling prisoners out of the gaols to lynch, of baying mobs around the guillotine and of units of the Parisian *armée révolutionnaire* scouring the countryside, bullying peasants into parting with their grain, stripping bells and silverware from village churches and ordering arbitrary arrests of those they considered suspect.[29] Most townsmen, whatever their trade or social background, showed little desire to follow Paris down that path, and the more extreme claims made by their own local Patriot or Jacobin spokesmen kindled fear and revulsion rather than popular enthusiasm. Nor were the heroes of the Paris sections automatically hailed as role models. Marat, in particular, came to symbolize for many a taste for blood and indiscriminate killing, especially when news of the September Massacres, and of paler imitations in a scattering of provincial towns, brought home the frightening reality of such killing. In the face of such images the *sans-culotte* was always liable to be seen as little better than an urban thug.

Much depended on the respect which local people retained for their own elected representatives, and that in turn reflected the tone and purpose of local politics. It is noticeable, indeed, how in many provincial towns the first municipal elections returned moderate politicians, men who were well established in their communities, lawyers, merchants, professional men who already enjoyed a degree of personal standing. Where that respect was not immediately dissipated, it could result in a continuity of municipal personnel that stood in stark contrast to the recrimination of the capital. It could also serve to unify local people behind their city and the causes for which it stood: its place within its department or region, its role as a centre of commerce or industry, law or public administration. Further removed than Parisians from the hurly-burly of national politics, people in provincial cities tended to care more about the local economy and the prosperity of their community, about their place in the administrative hierarchy after the changes of 1790. Here Jacobin militants and their *sans-culotte* allies had the greatest difficulty in winning wider support or persuading people to risk their economic well-being by adopting vengeful or socially divisive policies. The elites found it very much easier to stay in control, and this they did in Rouen, Nantes, Bordeaux or Toulouse until national politics intervened and the government in Paris was able to impose its values on them. As the years passed, local councils often became more socially inclusive, welcoming some artisans or shop-keepers to join the clutch of lawyers, merchants and professional men who were so dominant on departmental, district and municipal bodies. This occurred, for instance, in Limoges; but markedly less so in Caen.[30] Where it happened, it provided local government with an important safety valve, guaranteeing a smoother evolution in local politics and cutting the risk of violent change. Even in those cases such as Lyon where the Jacobins did come to power, they did so through violence and terrorization as much as through the ballot box. The evidence of the poll which brought Joseph Chalier to power in November 1792 shows how effectively the Lyon radicals mar-shalled their vote, but it also demonstrates their dependence on a very small number of sections, like Hôtel-Dieu and Port Saint-Paul, where their sup-porters had already established a powerful stranglehold.[31]

If provincial cities did not always follow the Parisians' revolutionary agenda, how much more was that true of rural areas, where the priorities of the club and the radical sections often seemed remote from the needs of agriculture and the concerns of farming? Parisians talked and acted as urban consumers, eager to impose price controls and to insist that peasant com-munities part with their grain to feed the cities and the military. For many in the countryside that could only spell disaster. The *sans-culotte* belief in the need for a maximum on prices was translated into poor returns and no surplus with which to pay for their own needs, while the Parisians' assump-tion that rural households were guilty of hoarding if they held back part of the harvest for use in the spring and summer months left them exposed to reprisals and terror. *Sans-culotte* discourse could seem deliberately hostile, directed against a countryside that was at once distrusted and despised, especially when Paris was swept by panic or when dearth threatened.[32] Here *Paris-capitale* had never interfered greatly in their lives in the past, in a system where authority was located in a variety of towns and cities, those housing the *intendance* and the *parlement*, the bishopric and the *bailliage*. Central government had impinged relatively little: taxes had been owed to tax farmers, feudal dues to the local seigneur, and even army recruitment and militia service had been organized regionally. Conversely, many rural communities had enjoyed a degree of democracy that would have been sur-prising to any townsman, whereby village meetings would discuss matters of shared concern – road-building, the management of common lands and affairs of the parish – and would spend the small amounts of money that were reserved for communal use. There is little either in the *cahiers de doléances* or in subsequent petitioning from rural areas to suggest that they wanted the government to interfere extensively in the management of their affairs. True, they might complain about isolation and poor communications, especially in mountain areas where entire communities could be cut off by snowfalls or mud slides during the winter season; or they might feel aggrieved that postal links with the outside world were so poor, at least beyond the *chef-lieu de canton*. Prats-de-Mollo, the last village before France gave way to Spain in the pastoral uplands of the Vallespir, complained that the post which had once come as far as Prats had been cut back and now stopped at Arles-sur-Tech, with serious implications for local trade along the frontier.[33] But they showed no desire to be beholden to central government; they relished the independence and autonomy which they had enjoyed – which, in the more far-flung corners of France, like the valleys of the Pyrenees and the Alps, had been virtually total[34] – and they still resented what they saw as gratuitous interference by Paris in their communal affairs.

Rural France might not wish to be ruled from Paris, but that does not mean that country-dwellers were indifferent to the rights and values which the Revolution offered and inculcated. *Cahiers* from the farthest provinces of the kingdom had demanded constitutional reforms and had looked to the Estates-General to rid them of seigneurial privileges and feudal exactions, labour service and salt taxes; they wanted the right to hunt for rabbits and shoot game birds; and they had looked to a decent return from agriculture that would offer them a degree of economic security. In some regions, as we have seen, anti-seigneurial feelings ran especially deep, adding an ideological element to the outbursts of rioting that constituted the *Grande Peur*. Rural areas now expected the revolutionaries to deliver on these issues; had not the law of 4–11 August 1789, passed in the atmosphere of delirium and high tension that followed the night of 4 August, rather unwisely proclaimed that 'the National Assembly destroys in its entirety the feudal regime'? Of course it had, and for many in the countryside, that was all they wanted to know. Unfortunately for the peasantry, and for rural calm, the reform proved to be much more circumspect, the 'destruction' of feudalism limited by restrictions and explanations. The same clause that appeared to abolish feudal obligations went on to explain that 'of the feudal rights' it was 'those which are derived from real or personal *mainmorte* and personal servitude' that were to be abolished outright, while 'all others are declared to be redeemable, and the price and method of their redemption shall be fixed by the National Assembly'. Hunting, on the other hand, was thrown open to all, and this, combined with uncontrolled land clearance, heralded an ecological nightmare for large parts of the countryside.[35] But the 'fatal ambiguity' of the decree remained, and it would continue to bedevil relations between peasant France and the revolutionary authorities.[36] For many seigneurial dues, high redemption charges meant that they continued to be exacted well into the revolutionary years; and tithes, particularly heavy in parts of the South-West, were abolished only gradually, in stages, with payments in

1790 being made to the nation instead of to the Church. Country-dwellers had every right to feel let down.

This was scarcely a recipe for rural harmony. Many peasants simply assumed that all their obligations had ended, payments of tax to the state as well as dues and tithes, with the consequence that the levels of tax collected in 1790 and 1791 were well down on previous years. But in some areas anger was harder to assuage, and this led to years of rioting and sporadic château-burning, violence generally turned against what remained of the feudal nobility.[37] The epicentres of this anti-seigneurial violence were not necessarily the areas that had suffered most in the *Grande Peur*. Rather they were concentrated in the South-East, a broad tranche of territory stretching from the Gard to the Var and northwards into the Drôme and Ardèche; in parts of the centre around the Nièvre and the Allier; in the Gâtinais, especially the Yonne and the Loiret; in Upper Brittany; and in the Quercy, principally the Lot and Dordogne, with tentacles spreading also into the western Massif Central, to the Corrèze and the Cantal.[38] Peasant anger had been rekindled, affecting in particular areas that had a long tradition of *jacquerie*. In March 1792, for instance, a peasant insurrection broke out in the mountain villages around Jaujac in the Ardèche, attacking the châteaux of Castreville and Bruget. Soon, if contemporary reports are to be believed, nearly 2,000 peasants were in arms, and the whole of the Vivarais was threatened. In the 'austere Cévennes,' says Anatoli Ado, this new violence recalled the region's bloody past, the *jacques* of 1792 stepping into the shoes of the Camisards and the *masques armés* of previous generations.[39]

Tradition had an important part to play in the politics of rural communities, in shaping their responses to revolutionary initiatives and their propensity to violence and riot. Different regions had varying traditions, contrasting crop patterns and different patterns of settlement. The Midi was generally more urbanized, a land of villages and aggregated settlement, with the strongly communitarian values which that represented. This contrasted dramatically with the settlement patterns in the North of France, whether in the great granary belt of the North-East, stretching from the Île-de-France to Artois and Picardy, or in the areas of small subsistence farming, like much of Brittany and the West, lands dominated by small farmsteads, isolated from one another and set in the midst of fields. Subsistence farmers were, by definition, less geared to the market, less concerned to maximize return; indeed, often they were more concerned to achieve price stability that would see them through the agricultural year than to seek to sell in September at the highest rate. They therefore had little interest in the policies of economic liberalism which Paris preached, an ideology that was largely irrelevant to them and their world. Nor did the majority of the pastoralists who bred sheep and goats on the mountain pastures of the Pyrenees or the rough *garrigues* of the Cévennes. They worked the slopes which their forefathers had worked, taking their flocks on the traditional winter transhumance to seek sweeter grazing land elsewhere, and they were overwhelmingly dependent on the commons to eke out a meagre income. Theirs was a world far removed from the prosperous and enclosed farms of the Aisne or the Seine-et-Marne, a landscape given over to wheat and the production of flour for the Paris market; or from the sandy soils of the Gironde, transformed by an eighteenth-century 'fureur de planter' into compact estates, owned by wealthy Bordeaux families and producing some of the finest and most prized clarets. There was little in common between their interests or their social relationships: some areas were scarred by deep inequalities, or by bitter tensions between town and country as they competed to purchase rural land; others were more egalitarian, facing a future in shared poverty and heavily dependent on common lands and grazing rights to survive. Where some areas were dominated by peasant proprietorship of the land, in others the poor were landless labourers, *brassiers* or *journaliers* with little security and dependent on a daily wage.

There was, in other words, no social or economic template for the French countryside, and no such thing as a typical 'peasant'. Yet Paris persisted in seeing the countryside as a single problem for which it should be possible to legislate a single set of solutions. The revolutionaries took measures which, in their view, answered the needs of the peasantry. But with few exceptions they had little direct experience of peasants – peasants were not represented on the various revolutionary assemblies or in the Convention – and the politicians' approach was a paternalistic one, one that sought to educate the peasantry and to bring revolutionary values to the countryside.[40] They spoke of the peasantry as people whose lives were steeped in ignorance and superstition and who were in danger at every turn of being misled by others, men better educated in political matters than they were. It followed that part of the mission of the Revolution was to save the peasantry from themselves, to bring them out of their condition of isolation and integrate them more fully into the nation. Newspapers like *La Feuille Villageoise* were designed with a peasant readership in mind, as a means of winning over rural areas to revolutionary policies and the notion of citizenship. But there were shortcomings in such a policy. Paris continued to be seen, as the *Feuille* itself recognized, as the centre of a largely urban revolution, which had issued paper currency and introduced the Maximum in order to serve the interests of urban consumers, often at the expense of producers. Countrymen simply could not accept that bread prices had to be controlled while the price of industrial products and the things they had to buy was allowed to rise with the market.[41] There was, in other words, a problem of mutual understanding. For just as they believed that the evils of seigneurialism had been rooted out by the legislation of 1789, so the revolutionaries thought they could resolve the land question in the countryside by two other measures: the subdivision of the commons and the auctioning of *biens nationaux*, measures which the Jacobins, in particular, saw as a means of promoting economic redistribution in rural areas.

Of the two, the sales of clerical, royal and seigneurial lands seized by the state as *biens nationaux* probably achieved more, though whether it constituted the huge social revolution that some historians have claimed is open to question. The first sales, in 1792, were mooted in order to raise revenue for the exchequer rather than to encourage more democratic landholding. Estates – mainly ecclesiastical ones – were sold in large blocks, with the result that land changed hands between men of property, with urban bourgeois purchasers making strong inroads into the agricultural areas nearest to their homes. But that, for the local peasantry, might imply little more than a change of *châtelain*, and the arrival in their village of new money and exploitative attitudes born of urban capitalism. Only in 1793 was some attempt made to split up the estates into smaller holdings for which ordinary peasants, and even the rural poor, might hope to bid. Under a law of 22 November, all seigneurial property and such ecclesiastical land as remained unsold was to be split up into smaller plots and sold at auction.[42] Again the smaller peasantry often found themselves squeezed out, but at least an attempt was made to ensure a more equitable redistribution of agricultural land and to rebuild rural society on the basis of small proprietorship, a goal which the Jacobins were eager to pursue. And the amount of land sold was certainly impressive. Between the first sales in 1792 and the end of the Directory, over 10 per cent of the land area of France had been put on the market and sold, often at exceptionally low prices. Just how much gain the peasantry made from this vast operation varied hugely from one area of the country to another, depending on such contingent questions as the proximity of large towns, the opportunism of local bourgeois, and the willingness of peasants to club together to bid. In the Nord, Georges Lefebvre estimated that the peasantry did make some overall gains, but noted the contrast between Flanders, where the urban bourgeois swept all before them, and Hainaut and Cambrésis, where the bourgeois were more discreet and where a strong tradition of anti-seigneurialism inspired the peasantry to buy up as much land as possible.[43] And even where so-called 'peasants' did well out of land sales, it was often those who already had property, the rich *laboureurs* who had savings to invest. The poor, the landless, day-labourers and *travailleurs agricoles* were left with nothing.[44]

Overall, the land sales subdivided large estates, created new rural proprietors, and contributed to the retention of a sizeable population in the countryside, all important achievements which would mark the French countryside during the following century. There were, of course, losers: the Church was effectively stripped of its landholdings, while the nobles emerged from the Revolution with their position dented rather than destroyed. As for the peasantry, they sustained their position in the market – they had to content themselves with around one-third of the purchases – but the real winners were the bourgeoisie, particularly those from neighbouring towns who could, by dabbling in the land market, both increase their wealth and bask in the sweet glow of republican virtue. Although they did not, of course, outnumber peasants amongst the purchasers, their acquisitions were usually much more substantial.[45] For small-town Jacobins, in particular, *biens nationaux* seemed a very worthwhile investment to make, one that let them take advantage of an artificially bloated market in agricultural land and increase their standing with their urban *confrères*. In the process they often caused bitter town–country antagonisms as they squeezed local families out of the rural land market and threatened the very sustainability of the village economy. This antagonism is seen by some historians as a major cause of peasant rejection of the Revolution and the strength of counter-revolutionary sentiment in the departments of the West.[46]

Global figures are, however, somewhat misleading, since they take no account of landholding patterns locally. There were many parts of rural France where urban influence was small, and where the sale of *biens nationaux* affected only the rural community. In such places it is clear that land did get substantially redistributed, helping to extend peasant landholding and thus to entrench the peasant economy. A typical example is the village of Balazuc in the Ardèche, where lands owned by a local émigré, Julien de Vinézac, were put up for sale by auction in February 1794 in nearby Joyeuse. Balazuc was not a prosperous village; indeed, earlier sales of land had been slow because of a lack of bidders. But in the more democratic climate of the Jacobin republic it was decided to subdivide Vinézac's estates, valued collectively at over 33,000 *livres*, into small parcels of land, forty-six lots in all, composed of some arable land, meadow, gardens along the river, vineyards, and some oak, walnut and mulberry trees, as well as several village houses. This time bidding was brisk. The auctioneer lit candles in the traditional manner, which he allowed to burn down until the last bid had been heard, and when the auction was over, most of the lots had been purchased and the Vinézac estate had been dispersed. As there were no bourgeois to compete with local people, it was mostly the villagers themselves who bought up small pieces of land to extend or complement their existing holdings. In all, of the twenty-five purchasers, twenty came from Balazuc. The consequences of these sales, as John Merriman notes, were considerable, not so much for helping to destroy the last vestiges of feudalism (for these had largely gone), but for making possible a shift in the village's agricultural base from the production of grain to that of silk and wine, which were to be the mainstays of the village economy in the nineteenth century.[47] The southern Ardèche may seem an extreme case, remote from both towns and major communication routes. But even in places with much better communications, urban purchasers were not always dominant. In the countryside around Amboise, for instance, Anne Jollet found that urban incursion into the land market was limited to the town itself and the lands that skirted the main trade arteries, the river Loire and the road out of town. Elsewhere, though the amount of land changing hands rose considerably, the transactions mostly followed a traditional course, the buying and selling of pieces of land between local peasants and winegrowers, forced by debt and the exigencies of cash flow.[48]

If the rural population generally welcomed the Revolution's policy of selling off *biens nationaux*, the plan to divide up village common lands as a further inducement to agrarian individualism – known as *partage* – caused much more controversy. *Partage* lay at the heart of Jacobin agrarian policy, and it was hoped that by distributing the commons amongst the rural population, the government would give over two million peasants the chance to own their own property, and thus create the basis for a property-owning democracy in the countryside – the so-called 'voie paysanne', seen as a way of empowering rural *sans-culottes* and blocking the pretensions of the richer farmers. It would, the Jacobins believed, satisfy the aspirations of the poorer, landless peasants of the grain belt to the north and east of Paris, from which so many of the Jacobin activists themselves had sprung, an area where sporadic rioting had broken out in support of some form of *partage* as early as 1791, and where peasant individualism was a political cause almost as popular as anti-seigneurialism.[49] The Île-de-France was, however, one of relatively few regions where the shortage of land to put under plough made this a pressing issue; there were also isolated calls for *partage* in the South-East and South-West. In many other areas the law commanded little support, since, if it was to operate effectively, virtually all the commons would have to be suppressed, and in many areas of subsistence farming, life without common grazing rights was inconceivable. Their destruction would mean the removal of an essential mechanism for survival. The law, to be fair to the government, recognized that it would not be applicable everywhere, and that communities must therefore be allowed to decide whether they wished to hold on to their commons. The law, almost uniquely, was permissive; it was limited to grazing lands and non-wooded common land, and it stipulated that at least one-third of the inhabitants must support the reform.[50] In those communities where it did go ahead, moreover, all the villagers had a right to their share, from the richest to the poorest. The response across the country was predictably mixed, with violence and rioting in some places. Others, especially communities in mountain areas where the graziers depended so heavily on the commons for pasturing their flocks, rejected any form of agrarian individualism. Here the prospect of *partage* had appeared as a threat from people who did not understand how their economy worked. By taking up the cause so passionately the Jacobins ran the risk of being seen, yet again, as distant Parisians, taking decisions for the whole country that had relevance only to Paris and its immediate hinterland.

Issues like the abolition of feudal privilege, the auctioning of *biens nationaux* and the division of the village commons were largely economic questions with a direct bearing on rural incomes. Peasant households looked to Paris for understanding and for measures that would help to secure their livelihoods. They had expressed their views in the *cahiers*; commonly, it would seem, they then expected their wishes to be granted, and they frequently declared themselves unsatisfied with the measures that ensued. But laws on feudalism and land were not the only ones which had particular resonance for rural departments. The Maximum, as we have seen, became a particular source of grievance in areas producing for the urban market; so was the government's insistence that peasants accept payment in *assignats* when they

were fulfilling contracts for Paris or for the armies, since the serial devaluation of paper currency further jeopardized their earnings and was seen by
many peasants as akin to a form of fraud. And the declaration of war made
relations between the peasantry and central government more precarious as
Paris demanded ever greater sacrifices in the name of the war effort – requisitioning grain for the troops; conscripting their sons and depriving of them of
much-needed labour in the fields; and insisting that they hand over their carts
and carters, their horses and mules to the military authorities. Rural communities responded in contrasting ways. Many grumbled or pleaded to be
exempted, hid their sons from the recruiting sergeant or provided casual labour
to deserters. Always, they complained, Paris acted without taking account of
the needs of agriculture, extending the arm of the state into their communities
and interfering in their traditional way of life. Particularly in the more isolated
rural communities, peasants responded with mundane acts of defiance to show
how much they resented the intrusion of the state into their world.[51]

That intrusion was even more angrily refuted when it interfered with their
faith or ran counter to their most deeply held beliefs, and in many parts of the
country the Revolution's religious policy served to drive a further wedge
between local people and their government. Catholic France had never found
it easy to come to terms with the general principles of the Revolution – its
intolerance of privilege, its predilection for eighteenth-century rationalism
and its suspicion of monarchy and those who appeared too closely allied to
the Bourbon cause all militated against easy relations between the Church and
the revolutionary state. To the revolutionaries, after all, the Catholic Church
was, first and foremost, a privileged corporation that should be stripped of its
privilege in a world where religious worship was a matter for the individual
conscience. At first the revolutionaries concentrated on denying Catholicism
any privileged status in the new order, whether by nationalizing Church lands,
reforming parish administration or opening up government office, both civil
and military, to Protestants and other non-Catholics. In 1790 the state prohibited the taking of monastic vows and imposed an oath on secular clergy 'to
watch carefully over the faithful of the diocese or parish entrusted to them, to
be faithful to the nation, to the law and to the King, and to maintain with all
their power the Constitution decreed by the National Assembly and accepted
by the King'.[52] If the creation of the Constitutional Church was difficult for
committed Catholics to accept – and Timothy Tackett is surely right to see the
widely varying levels of oath-taking as a test of local opinion as well as of clerical conscience[53] – what followed was very much worse. Under the Republic,
nonjuring clergy were expelled from France and mercilessly hounded as suspects if they dared to return; several hundred priests and nuns lost their lives
to the guillotine. At the same time the government turned from regulating
Catholicism to undermining religious belief itself, first with a nationwide
programme of dechristianization, involving the closure of churches and the
prohibition of public worship, and finally, at Robespierre's behest, by the creation of a civic religion, with festivals of reason celebrated in the cathedrals

and parish churches of Paris and major provincial cities. In the space of only five years the government had ceased to sustain Christianity, relegating Christian worship to the private sphere.[54] There could have been no greater test for devout Catholics. Could they remain at one and the same time Christians and revolutionaries?

This test also placed a new strain on relations between Paris and the French provinces, and especially with those parts of the countryside where Catholicism was deeply rooted in popular culture and where, to this day, attendance at communion is highest. It was here that the number of refractories was most considerable and here, too, that illegal services continued to be held on hill-sides beyond the reach of the authorities. It represents on the map a clear zone of Catholic resistance, a 'France du refus' that stretches from rural Flanders to Brittany and the Loire valley, from the East (Alsace, Lorraine and much of the Franche-Comté) to the Massif Central and the enclaves at either end of the Pyrenees, the Pays Basque and Catalonia. These were regions, many of them lying along France's periphery, where religion belonged in the community, where devotional works and simple woodcuts of saints were common currency, and where parish priests were most likely to be local men, men who were respected as community leaders. There were other parts of the countryside – notably the South-East and the South-West – where sons were not so strongly encouraged to seek a clerical vocation, and where priests had to be brought in from regions with a natural surplus; such was the case, for instance, in Guienne, where the departments of the Gironde and the Dordogne produced only half the number of parish priests needed to keep the faith alive.[55] Many towns, Marseille among them, had already demonstrated their alienation from the Church and its clergy. After 1789 the rift between Catholic France and the politics of Paris widened further as many rural Catholics interpreted the Revolution as a movement driven by urban extremists pursuing their own anti-Catholic agenda. Some denounced it as wicked and atheistic, a view which was given added force by republican rhetoric. The priesthood, reflected the Director La Révellière-Lépeaux in 1797, was a form of blasphemy, an assault on individual liberty; for through the intervention of the priest 'the believer is transformed into the stupid and servile executor of the minister's wishes'.[56] In areas where memories of the Wars of Religion still rankled, Protestants were frequently blamed. The devastation wrought by anticlerical deputies-on-mission brought home the full meaning of anti-clericalism to rural communities as they closed churches, vandalized cemeteries and imposed the revolutionary calendar with such obvious relish, such mocking pleasure. The more radical of them openly despised Christianity, with its emphasis on faith and divine mystery. As late as 1798, the administrators of the department of the Yonne were still denouncing Catholicism as 'a cult which had as its only goal to make men into beasts'.[57]

For many Catholics, Paris was the capital not just of the Revolution but also of apostasy, a centre of anticlericalism and atheism that was destroying the spiritual faith of the entire nation. There was more than a grain of truth in this charge. The Paris Basin was a region where numbers of clerical vocations were low, and where the clergy were relatively alienated from the laity. Paris was also a city that had been profoundly affected by the Jansenist tradition earlier in the century. There was no lack of clergy or of religious foundations in the city – in 1768 the clerical population stood at around 8,000, servicing fifty-three parish churches, forty-seven monasteries and sixty convents – but, although Parisians enjoyed the great feast days, like that of their own patron, Sainte-Geneviève, many fewer engaged with the spiritual life of the Church or fasted at Lent.[58] After 1789, Paris was one of the principal centres of anticlericalism, and in the autumn of 1793, the Commune and the more radical sections enthusiastically embraced dechristianization, outlawing the wearing of clerical dress and ordering the removal of carvings of saints and apostles from church buildings. In the Faubourg Saint-Antoine, the Section des Quinze-vingts symbolically asked that their suburb be rebaptized to rid it of its Christian connotation as part of a campaign to liberate Paris from Christianity.[59] The *sans-culottes* were proud to be the first to cleanse France of priests and end religious worship, and there was a flamboyance about their actions which sent a frisson of revulsion around the Catholic heartlands. The Section des Gravilliers, for instance, marched in strength to the Convention to announce that its churches were now closed and that huge amounts of silver had been confiscated for the exchequer and the war effort. The procession to the Convention, organized by Léonard Bourdon, was spectacular, a joyous celebration of the removal of Christian worship from the city. Michael Sydenham takes up the story.

> Behind a splendid canopy surmounting a bust of Marat marched the section's companies of the National Guard, some grotesquely clad in clerical costume and some carrying ornaments taken from the churches, while the musicians of the *Société des Jeunes Français* played appropriately lugubrious airs. The Convention was then addressed by one of Bourdon's pupils, the seven-year-old Paulin, 'whose ears have not yet been polluted by lies'. Raised aloft, the child explained that by closing its churches the section had destroyed 'the lairs of foul beasts, dens built and maintained by the blood and subsistence of the people'.[60]

The Commune went on to order the closure of all churches in the city on 22 November; henceforth Paris was to be a religion-free zone. In the city itself there were few dissenting voices, since the Parisians were already largely dechristianized. But when the *sans-culottes* tried to export their vision to the countryside, the response of the Catholic peasantry was ominous. The loss of their religion was a major element in turning their misgivings into open revolt.

Notes

1 Gwynne Lewis, *The Second Vendée. The Continuity of Counter-revolution in the Department of the Gard, 1789–1815* (Oxford, 1978), pp. 18–20.

2 Alison Patrick, 'French Revolutionary Local Government, 1789–92', in Colin Lucas (ed.), *The French Revolution and the Creation of Modern Political Culture, vol. 2: The Political Culture of the French Revolution* (Oxford, 1988), pp. 399–400.

3 Jean-Claude Perrot and Stuart Woolf, *State and Statistics in France, 1789–1815* (Chur and London, 1984), p. 100.

4 Alan Forrest, *The Soldiers of the French Revolution* (Durham, NC, 1990), p. 143.

5 Isabelle Guégan, *Inventaire des enquêtes administratives et statistiques, 1789–95* (Paris, 1991), pp. 9–11.

6 Cissie Fairchilds, 'The Production and Marketing of Populuxe Goods in Eighteenth-century Paris', in John Brewer and Roy Porter (eds), *Consumption and the World of Goods* (London, 1993), pp. 228–48.

7 David Garrioch, *The Making of Revolutionary Paris* (Berkeley, CA, 2002), p. 286.

8 Colin Jones, *The Great Nation. France from Louis XV to Napoleon* (London, 2003), p. 356.

9 Annik Pardailhé-Galabrun, *La naissance de l'intime. 3000 foyers parisiens, xviie–xviiie siècles* (Paris, 1988), pp. 137–8.

10 Daniel Roche, *A History of Everyday Things. The Birth of Consumption in France, 1600–1800* (Cambridge, 2000), pp. 213–16.

11 Daniel Roche, *The People of Paris. An Essay in Popular Culture in the Eighteenth Century* (Leamington Spa, 1987), p. 234.

12 Michael Sonenscher, *Work and Wages. Natural Law, Politics and the Eighteenth-century French Trades* (Cambridge, 1989), p. 251.

13 Michael Sonenscher, 'Journeymen, the courts and the French trades, 1781–91', *Past and Present* 114 (1987), pp. 77–109.

14 Garrioch, *The Making of Revolutionary Paris*, pp. 287, 294–5.

15 On the ritual of public executions, see Michel Foucault, *Discipline and Punish. The Birth of the Prison* (London, 1977), especially the telling description of the opening pages.

16 Arlette Farge, *Subversive Words. Public Opinion in Eighteenth-century France* (Cambridge, 1994), p. 197.

17 David Andress, *Massacre at the Champ de Mars. Popular Dissent and Political Culture in the French Revolution* (London, 2000), p. 25.

18 For short biographies of Bailly, Pétion and Pache, see David Andress, *French Society in Revolution, 1789–99* (Manchester, 1999), pp. xx, xxix.

19 Jack Censer, *Prelude to Power. The Parisian Radical Press, 1789–91* (Baltimore, 1976), pp. 7–8.

20 Andress, *Massacre at the Champ de Mars*, *passim*; William Doyle, *The Oxford History of the French Revolution*, (Oxford, 1989), pp. 153–4.

21 Olivier Coquard, *Jean-Paul Marat* (Paris, 1993), p. 301.

22 *Père Duchesne*, issue 313, quoted in John Hardman (ed.), *French Revolution Documents, ii, 1792–95* (Oxford, 1973), pp. 218–19.

23 Walter Markov and Albert Soboul (eds), *Die Sansculotten von Paris. Dokumente zur Geschichte der Volksbewegung, 1793–94* (East Berlin, 1957), p. 2.

24 Richard Cobb, 'The people in the French Revolution', *Past and Present* 15 (1959), p. 67.

25 Michel Morineau, 'L'enquête sur le vandalisme révolutionnaire', in Simone Bernard-Griffiths, Marie-Claude Chemin and Jean Ehrard (eds), *Révolution française et 'vandalisme révolutionnaire'* (Paris, 1992), pp. 127–9; also Serge Bianchi, 'Le "vandalisme" anti-féodal et le "vandalisme" anti-religieux dans le sud de l'Île-de-France', ibid., pp. 157–67.

26 R. B. Rose, *The Making of the Sans-culottes* (Manchester, 1983), especially pp. 170–1.

27 Richard Cobb, *The Police and the People. French Popular Politics, 1789–1820* (Oxford, 1970), p. 126.

28 Alan Forrest, *The Revolution in Provincial France. Aquitaine, 1789–99* (Oxford, 1996), p. 113.

29 Richard Cobb, *Les armées révolutionnaires: instrument de la Terreur dans les départements, avril 1793–floréal an II* (2 vols, Paris, 1961–3), vol. 2, pp. 664–8.

30 Paul Hanson, *Provincial Politics in the French Revolution: Caen and Limoges, 1789–94* (Baton Rouge, LA, 1989), pp. 199–203.

31 W. D. Edmonds, *Jacobinism and the Revolt of Lyon, 1789–93* (Oxford, 1990), pp. 138–43.

32 Richard Cobb, *Terreur et subsistances, 1793–95* (Paris, 1965), pp. 144–9.

33 *Cahier de doléances* of the Third Estate of Prats-de-Mollo, in Etienne Frénay (ed.), *Cahiers de doléances de la Province de Roussillon, 1789* (Perpignan, 1979), p. 180.

34 E. Goyeneche, *Le Pays basque: Soule – Labourd – Basse-Navarre* (Pau, 1979), especially pp. 374–7.

35 Peter McPhee, '"The misguided greed of peasants"? Popular attitudes to the environment in the Revolution of 1789', *French Historical Studies* 24 (2001), pp. 247–69. See also, on the issue of land-clearance, the same author's *Revolution and Environment in Southern France. Peasants, Lords, and Murder in the Corbières, 1780–1830* (Oxford, 1999), pp. 121–47.

36 Sydney Herbert, *The Fall of Feudalism in France* (London, 1921), pp. 111–13.

37 See, for instance, A. Richard, 'Les troubles agraires dans les Landes en 1791 et 1792', *Annales historiques de la Révolution Française* 4 (1927), pp. 568–71.

38 P. M. Jones, *The Peasantry in the French Revolution* (Cambridge, 1988), p. 112.

39 Anatoli Ado, *Paysans en révolution. Terre, pouvoir et jacquerie, 1789–94* (Paris, 1996), p. 269.

40 Harvey Mitchell, 'Resistance to the Revolution in Western France', *Past and Present* 63 (1974), p. 96.

41 Melvin Edelstein, *La Feuille Villageoise. Communication et modernisation dans les régions rurales pendant la Révolution* (Paris, 1977), p. 281.

42 Jones, *Peasantry*, p. 155.

43 Georges Lefebvre, *Les paysans du Nord pendant la Révolution Française* (Bari, 1959), cited in Jones, *Peasantry*, p. 157.

44 A. Le Boterf, 'La vente des biens nationaux dans le District de Saint-Sever, 1791–an X' (mémoire de maîtrise, Université de Paris-I, 1971), pp. 177–81.

45 Bernard Bodinier and Eric Teyssier, *'L'événement le plus important de la Révolution': La vente des biens nationaux (1789–1867) en France et dans les territoires annexés* (Paris, 2000), pp. 439–41.

46 Charles Tilly, 'Local conflicts in the Vendée before the Rebellion of 1793', *French Historical Studies* 2 (1961), pp. 209–31.

47 John Merriman, *The Stones of Balazuc. A French Village in Time* (New York, 2002), pp. 68–9.

48 Anne Jollet, *Terre et société en Révolution. Approche du lien social dans la région d'Amboise* (Paris, 2000), p. 512.

49 Jones, *Peasantry*, pp. 145–7.

50 The fullest discussion of the law on *partage* and its implementation is G. Bourgin (ed.), *Le partage des biens communaux: documents sur la préparation de la loi du 10 juin 1793* (Paris, 1908).

51 Alan Forrest, *Conscripts and Deserters. The Army and French Society during the Revolution and Empire* (New York, 1989), pp. 219–37.

52 John Hall Stewart, *A Documentary Survey of the French Revolution* (New York, 1951), p. 182.

53 Timothy Tackett, *La Révolution, l'Église, la France* (Paris, 1986), pp. 207–28.

54 Nigel Aston, *Religion and Revolution in France, 1780–1804* (London, 2000), p. 189.

55 Timothy Tackett and Claude Langlois, 'Ecclesiastical structures and clerical geography on the eve of the French Revolution', *French Historical Studies* 11 (1980), pp. 352–70.

56 Claude Petitfrère, 'Un anticlérical angevin: La Révellière-Lépeaux et sa religion, 1753–1824', in Jean-Clément Martin (ed.), *Religion et Révolution* (Paris, 1994), p. 80.

57 Suzanne Desan, *Reclaiming the Sacred. Lay Religion and Popular Politics in Revolutionary France* (Ithaca, NY, 1990), p. 8.

58 Aston, *Religion and Revolution*, pp. 51–2.

59 Albert Soboul, *Les sans-culottes parisiens de l'an II* (Paris, 1962), p. 293.

60 Michael Sydenham, *Léonard Bourdon. The Career of a Revolutionary, 1754–1807* (Waterloo, Ontario, 1999), p. 209.

8

The revolt of the provinces

In 1793 the young Republic faced a year of crisis, when the war on the frontiers was going badly, conscription was leading to ever greater acts of popular defiance, and large parts of provincial France were driven to reject the authority of the Convention. Though it may seem rather exaggerated to define the year as one of provincial revolt – after all, large tracts of the country stayed loyal – it was the moment when many in the provinces, whether out of republican purism or a royalist distaste for everything the Revolution represented, turned to open insurrection. And while it is true that the revolt remained localized, it was sufficiently widespread to spread fear among the Jacobin majority among the deputies. By the late spring and early summer, the social climate had seriously deteriorated, to the point where the sorts of resentments which had previously resulted in no more than grumbled dissent now sparked open criticism of Paris, along with the rejection of its increasingly radical agenda. The declaration of war against Austria and Prussia in 1792, and its further extension in March 1793, brought provincial fears to a head, especially as the war began badly for the French, with their young army and its inexperienced officers thrown into a conflict fought under rules of war which they barely understood. French territory was invaded and the country was apparently at the mercy of the enemy. By the summer, news that foreign armies were entrenched both in Flanders and French Catalonia – much of the department of Pyrénées-orientales had fallen and the Spaniards had pushed right up to the gates of Perpignan[1] – spread panic in the interior, while the occupied areas showed little reluctance to collaborate with the invader. In military terms, the Republic had reached its lowest ebb.

Moreover, the fact of being at war seemed to justify almost any act of arbitrary centralization. The declaration of the *patrie en danger* led to a further erosion of local powers and allowed the revolutionaries to capitalize on the accompanying release of nationalist sentiment. The safety and integrity of the nation were now, more than ever, accorded an almost religious veneration;

the nation, 'one and indivisible', had to be protected at any cost. Dissent and difference were more difficult to tolerate, and the Convention began sending deputies out on missions to the provinces to ensure that the law was strictly enforced. Refractory priests were hunted down, and those attending illegal Catholic services were treated with greater severity. There was more policing, more regular intrusion into the lives of local communities. And personal sacrifices were called for in the name of national defence, heavier requisitions of grain and military supplies, new and more exigent forms of recruitment. By the spring of 1793, the government had given up all pretence that it could recruit its army by relying on volunteers, and the *levée des 300,000* allocated local quotas to departments, districts and, ultimately, communes, which they and their mayors were obliged to honour. In August, following the Jacobin *coup d'état* on 31 May–2 June in the Convention, the whole population was placed on a war footing through the *levée en masse*. The French people were now declared to be in a state of 'permanent requisition'. In a famous phrase the decree went on to spell out just what this meant for individuals.

> The young men shall go to battle; the married men shall forge arms and transport provisions; the women shall make tents and clothes, and shall serve in the hospitals; the children shall turn old linen into lint; the old men shall repair to the public places to stimulate the courage of the warriors and preach the unity of the Republic and hatred of kings.[2]

The result of greater intervention was often mutual incomprehension or open violence, especially in rural areas. Communities which had, under the *ancien régime*, become accustomed to managing their affairs without undue pressure from outside, saw the demands of the state as intolerable intrusions upon their autonomy. Why should officials from the towns have the right to force their sons into uniform, to leave their *pays* to fight on some distant frontier for an abstract concept like the 'nation' which many of them still barely understood? Why should urban *sans-culottes* be at liberty to seize their grain or requisition their livestock in the name of some ill-defined national interest? And why should rabidly anticlerical townsmen have the right to invade their space to impose the clerical oath, close down religious services or arrest refractory priests and those unfortunate enough to be caught sheltering them? The town–country division was often magnified by the self-righteous tone and sense of cultural superiority exuded by townsmen when they had dealings with their country brethren. Country-dwellers felt pressurized by those from nearby towns, who increasingly used the language and authority of central government, of the clubs and sections and municipal authorities who elected them, entrusted them with responsibility and legitimized their prejudices, against those they saw as simple villagers.[3] Relations between cities and the rural communities of their immediate hinterland were poisoned by assumptions of superiority, the product of an active urban revolutionary culture. Countrymen, it was inferred, had no interest in public affairs like the constitution, individual freedoms or liberty. They had little interest in the

Revolution, little loyalty to its central tenets. They were, it was arrogantly suggested, scarcely worthy of the title of 'citizen'.

Some areas witnessed a serious degradation in relations between urban officials and the inhabitants of surrounding villages as a result of the Revolution's religious policies. Jacobins could be especially crass in their response to rural Catholicism, and they frequently vented their own anticlericalism on the rural population, driving out nonjurors and invoking martial law to prevent devout villagers from worshipping, or prohibiting processions of villagers to churches in remote hamlets or to meetings on isolated hillsides to celebrate mass. In 1791, the towns of the Loire valley imposed constitutional priests on rural communities by the use of armed force; there was nothing subtle about the way they went about it. Troops and National Guardsmen were mobilized against what they held to be rural 'fanaticism', since many clubs and municipalities believed, like the District of Nantes, that the new *curés* could be imposed only by armed force, both for their own safety and that of the displaced refractories, given the danger of disorder and violence. They took no chances. On 22 May, for instance, one hundred National Guardsmen were sent to oversee the installation of the new priest in the parish of Saint-Herblain, and a hundred more to Sucé. The following weekend it was the turn of four other villages, with a hundred guardsmen in La Chapelle-sur-Erdre, a hundred in Pont-Saint-Martin, fifty more in Causson, and twenty troops of line sent to garrison Saint-Aignan.[4] Popular persecution of refractories in the cities grew apace, sometimes accompanied by wanton violence and the studied sadism of true zealots, and with it came the beginnings of Catholic violence in defence of their priests, something akin to a genuine counter-revolutionary reaction for the first time in revolutionary France. It was a counter-revolution made in the popular societies of Nantes and Angers; it had little contact with Paris, far less with the émigré princes in Turin.[5] Communities that had no ideological reason to oppose the Revolution discovered that they were alienated from Paris, not by the wording of decrees and laws, not even by the rumours they had heard about anarchy in the capital, but by the intolerant and thuggish initiatives of local militants who came into their communities acting in the name of the government. And though such interventions would become more brutal and were more resented after the Jacobins came to power and revolutionary government was instituted, that was only a matter of degree. Resistance to urban intrusion had begun much earlier. In 1791, in the South-East, royalist National Guardsmen had met at a second *camp de Jalès* in the Gard, uttering imprecations against a revolution in which they saw the work of the devil.[6] Meanwhile, in the depths of the Breton *bocage*, the Comte d'Antraïgues was already building on his émigré associations and making his first strenuous efforts to raise a force of disaffected peasants against Paris.[7] Parts at least of the French provinces were turning their thoughts to rebellion.

That does not mean, of course, that their rebellion had its roots in provincialism, or in a desire to undermine the unity of the nation state. Though some at least of the provinces had a strongly felt sense of their own identity, it did not follow that they sought to establish regional governments or to query the legitimacy of the nation. Nor did communities which responded with violence to the intrusion of the state necessarily demonstrate their opposition to the Revolution as a whole, or to key aspects like the constitution or the Republic. But it does imply a degree of popular alienation from the political agenda of Paris, and from the image they held both of the aspirations of the Parisians and of the tenor and direction of national policy-making. It was only too easy to interpret what was, in many ways, an urban revolution as being a Parisian revolution, influenced by the Paris crowd and pandering to the whims of the Paris sections. Had not Danton implicitly acknowledged this when he announced that 'Paris is the centre where everything comes to a head; Paris will be the focal point that receives all the rays of French patriotism, burning all its enemies with them?'[8] And the government only increased the suspicion that the Revolution was being conducted in the interests of Paris when it proposed the Maximum on foodstuffs or suggested emergency requisitions to supply Parisian markets. It all served to deepen urban–rural antagonism and to make the Revolution seem terribly remote to country-dwellers.

There were, during the revolutionary decade, hundreds of individual incidents that could be taken as evidence of counter-revolutionary intent, which were in fact nothing more than protests against particular policies, or angry responses to what was perceived as unwonted intrusion by the state. In Picardy and parts of the Île-de-France, the moment when the clergy had to take the constitutional oath sparked fierce outbreaks of rioting, while in 1793, the imposition of measures of dechristianization had similar results, with peasants in the Brie, to the east of Paris, sacking the local Jacobin club as they demanded the right to say mass.[9] In southern Brittany, rumours that there had been a secret movement of grain supplies brought both peasants and urban workers on to the streets of Vannes, making common cause against the municipal authorities whom they blamed for the introduction of a new fiscal regime in the area.[10] There were village riots over military recruitment as early as 1792 in parts of the Aude, and in the spring of 1793 in the Morbihan.[11] But these were generally brief incidents built around a single grievance; and they often took place in areas with an established revolutionary pedigree, Picardy and the Brie being obvious instances. Such riots can best be understood as a refusal by local people to associate themselves with particular policies of the Revolution, which antagonized elements in local society or which had little relevance for them, as acts of *refus* rather than of political antagonism – anti-revolution rather than counter-revolution. Discussing the region around Vannes, Tim Le Goff points out that violence spelt a lack of opportunity rather than any deep-seated ill will. 'It was not that there were no potential revolutionaries,' he concludes; rather their attitudes stemmed from their isolation from the capital, from pure contingency. 'It was simply that they had no chance to fit their aims into the course of the Revolution as it was evolving in Paris and elsewhere in France'.[12] Nor, we should remember, was peasant violence always a sign of conservatism or disapproval of the Revolution. There were incidences of peasant radicalism, too, in this period, and of violence against known counter-revolutionaries and presumed spies.

Only in a limited number of instances did local violence reflect a generalized sense of grievance, and it was here that riots over taxes or religion might blend into a larger, more intransigent movement against the revolutionary authorities. Most notably this was the case in the West, where the major rural revolt of the Vendée was initially sparked by the demands of the recruiting-sergeant for the *levée des 300,000* of March 1793, and by the refusal of the young men of the community to leave for the battalions. Yet the military issue was just a pretext, a trigger to general revolt, for the problem of draft-dodging was no greater in this area than in some other parts of the country where counter-revolution did not ensue. Indeed, military recruitment in the villages of the Vendée and Loire-inférieure, Sarthe and Maine-et-Loire, soon became engulfed in much broader social and cultural questions, in popular outcry about a range of economic and religious grievances that would plunge the departments of the West into a bitter civil war. By the summer the rebels had raised their own army to face the Republicans and troops were transferred from the eastern frontier to face the threat of the Vendean army.

The question has often been asked: why the West? Other areas of France, like the Pyrenees and parts of the Massif Central, had at least as much difficulty getting their young men into uniform. But in the Loire valley, and among the *chouans* of Brittany, whole communities mobilized against the Republic, hiding and protecting their warriors and threatening the French armies with all the terrors and unpredictability of a guerrilla campaign. What was it about this area of thickets and *bocage*, of scattered farms and isolated hamlets, that condemned it to such violence against the Republic, and to such a brutal martyrdom at republican hands that the events of the 1790s would turn it into a symbol for succeeding generations? For many republicans that question was easily answered. The Vendée, in the words of Turreau, 'that asylum of robbery and crimes, is like an extensive fortress, where the agents of royalism and aristocracy can concert their plots and meditate their horrid projects in security, and nature, misled, seems there to have exerted all her power to protect the guilty resistance and the fatal independence of the domestic enemies of the Republic'. The Vendée, in other words, should be viewed as a single unity, cut off from the rest of France and protected by its dense, impenetrable landscape.[13] But in reality the Vendée was not united: the ten years of civil war that began in 1793, noted General Gouvion in 1804, divided families and left whole communities torn by hatred.[14] So searing and indelible was this experience that the Vendée came into existence as a region whose memories and wounds marked it apart, a *pays martyr* shaped by a culture of civil war and by the popular myths which that culture helped create.[15] For many Vendeans, in the twentieth century as in the nineteenth, the kernel of their region's identity would remain its piety and devotion to the Catholic Church, its faith and tenacity in the face of godless urban revolutionaries who sought to tear them away from their priests. The Vendée of legend was engaged in the most eternal of ideological battles, for Christ against Antichrist, for King against Republic, a chiliastic conflict about political and spiritual ideals. They alone, while other Catholics accepted the state's imposition of the Civil Constitution, stood by their priests against the revolutionaries, against the godless elites of Paris and nearby towns. Theirs was a true counter-revolution, a movement of men and women who fought for their rural, Catholic culture.[16]

There is doubtless a lot of truth in that self-image; it would be difficult to deny, for instance, the part of religion in the Vendean cause. But the extent of the town–country animosity in the West should not be overlooked, for if this was a movement of ideals, it was also one of social forces and self-interest. The contempt shown by the Jacobins of Nantes or Poitiers for peasant religious sensibilities was only one aspect of a wider antagonism, one rooted in land and the economy, and Timothy Tackett is surely right when he argues that the Civil Constitution here had something of the character of a referendum, the refusal of country clergy to swear loyalty to the state reflecting the ideas of their parishioners as much as the dictates of their conscience. Priests who did take the oath in the hope of hanging on to their livings risked the contempt of the villagers to whom they ministered, who often ostracized them and abandoned their services, and might, in more extreme cases, shout abuse, threaten them with violence or physically attack them. Constitutional clergy imposed by outsiders were not regarded as men worthy of trust, whereas the old priests had generally enjoyed widespread confidence and affection. When it was announced in the village of Erbrée that a constitutional priest was about to be imposed on them, the village reacted by saying that they could only have confidence in priests who were known to them, priests who understood their community. The municipal council replied in measured tones. 'The parishioners think and say that since it is their duty to worship and to serve God, they have the unarguable right to give their confidence only to those of whom they have perfect knowledge and whom they regard as worthy'.[17] It was, they believed, nothing short of their way of life that was under attack, their daily routine, their most intimate thoughts, their entire rural culture; and it is telling that those who took the leading part in the defence of that culture were often women, respectable mothers of families who took their religious devotions seriously and reacted angrily to outside interference.

The church had already become something of a feminine public space, and one which the women of the parish claimed as their own. Later in the Revolution, when churches were closed during the campaign of dechristianization, or when the Directory allowed congregations to open their churches for worship, it would often be the parish women who demonstrated most noisily and demanded that the authorities allow them to worship freely. It was noticeable that in these local demonstrations the central issue was often the sacred character of the church and its use for public worship. This was about more than the special symbolism of a particular building; it was, as Olwen Hufton has observed, about reconstructing the traditional devotional patterns of the local community, a process which involved a number of discrete steps: restoring the church to its recognized usage as a place of Christian worship; procuring sacred vessels for the communion service; and bringing back Sunday – rather than the *décadi* – as the periodic day of rest. In these separate stages, women, and especially widows, played a prominent part.[18] And so over the oath, it was often women who took to the streets, invaded the church during the swearing-in ceremony, or attacked the person of the *constitutionnel*. In Normandy, for example, they were widely reported to be among the noisiest protestors. At Balleroy they howled for half an hour in the church to drown out the ceremony; at Vendes they rushed forward to stop the entire proceedings; and at Les Moutiers they threatened to hang the local councillors if they tried to install the constitutional priest.[19] The *abbé* Grégoire even declared that the Constitutional Church was strangled by the intervention of 'foul-mouthed and seditious women'.[20]

If the strength of religious belief goes some way to explain the outbreak of revolt in the West, it cannot supply the whole answer to the conundrum of why civil war took place there rather than in other seemingly devout areas of the Catholic countryside. There was also an important social dimension in a region of France where agricultural land was increasingly under pressure, and where peasants had to compete with outsiders when land was sold or auctioned. This, too, was something that struck at the very core of the rural community, since it affected the peasants' right to continue to follow their traditional lifestyle without impediment, and more especially their ability to secure sufficient land to safeguard the viability of the village economy for succeeding generations. Their future security and autonomy were at stake as much as their faith. Sociological studies of the West have placed great emphasis on the role of townsmen and outsiders, men with money to invest and a patriotic ideology that drove them to buy up *biens nationaux*, which in some parts of the region resulted in the poorer peasants being marginalized and proletarianized, deprived of the land they needed if they were to maintain a buoyant peasant agriculture in the countryside. In either case, a sociological interpretation appears to beckon, suggesting that the politics of the area were dominated by questions of social power. In those western areas which had been virulently anti-feudal, Paul Bois suggests that peasant ill will was often, during the revolutionary years, turned against the new power-brokers, the landowners from neighbouring towns. The nobles, he argues, had little day-to-day impact on the lives of villagers in this part of France, overshadowed as it was by the urban centres that had sprung up along the river Loire. In contrast, the bourgeois from Nantes, Angers, Saumur and other cities had become the chief rivals of the peasantry in the market in rural land; they now owned over 50 per cent of land in the communes along the Loire, and their unpopularity was only increased by their image as a grasping, rapacious class of men with no ties to the soil and little interest in farming. In such communities, outside investors were seen as an unwelcome blight, and the fact that they were often committed revolution-aries who had profited materially from the Revolution only served to increase the sense of rural grievance.[21] During 1793, town–country conflicts became inflamed across the region, revealing an anti-urban feeling that was easily transferred to the capital and to the Revolution itself. If townsmen made lit-tle effort to hide their contempt for villagers' feelings, so peasant resentment helped fuel anti-urban prejudice and contributed towards the bitterness of the violent eruption that followed.

The Vendée began as a popular insurrection, a peasant rising in defence of their conscripts and their priests, a rising not so different from many of the other peasant movements during the 1790s that briefly turned to violence before being snuffed out. But unlike the others, this insurrection turned into a full-scale civil war which, like all civil wars, was fought with unremitting vigour and cruelty, with hundreds of thousands of casualties and the massed force of government repression. The brutality of Turreau's *colonnes infernales* as they conducted a scorched-earth policy across the villages of the region became legendary, as was the mutual hatred between republicans and rebels in the many split communities in the region which contained families devoted to both causes. The desire to eradicate counter-revolutionary and pro-Vendean sentiment was so vitriolic that it has led some historians sympathetic to the rebels to condemn the government response as a policy of extermination, 'the most atrocious of the wars of religion and the first ideological geno-cide'.[22] Few would deny that the death toll was uniquely heavy: perhaps 115,000 or 120,000 people in a relatively sparsely populated region. But why did what started as a revolt end so tragically? Perhaps it is, as the Vendeans themselves claim, that their dedication to the true Church and belief in the cause of the *sacré-coeur* gave the conflict in the West an ideo-logical intensity that was without parallel elsewhere. Or perhaps the responsibility should be laid at the door of local extremists, men on both sides who refused to compromise, and a state which, after the massacre of republicans at Machecoul by peasant insurgents, showed no wish for a compromise.[23] Whatever the reason, this was one outbreak of violence that was not allowed to die; the violence of the government's response stirred the embers of hatred and ensured that the Vendée became a place of martyr-dom, a *lieu de mémoire* for all French Catholics. An obscure region of the West which had started the Revolution without much sense of its own history or identity, had become by 1793 a symbol of rural resistance and a beacon for Catholic France in its struggle against the secularism of the nation state.

Elsewhere the legitimacy of the state might be challenged, especially after the Jacobins' seizure of power on 31 May–2 June, but there was little danger of a repeat of the horrors of the West. The scale of violence was more muted, and the extent of anti-revolutionary and anti-republican sentiment strictly limited. And only in the Vendée, in the lands to the south of the

Loire where the insurrection was anchored, did peasant discontent produce open warfare. That does not mean that other regions remained unaffected by issues of royalism and religion, landownership and proletarianization, nor yet that town–country divisions were exclusive to the West. But elsewhere peasant uprisings were rapidly repressed and their threat snuffed out. In 1793, neither the *chouannerie* of southern Brittany, nor the violence in rural Alsace, nor yet the anti-revolutionary outbursts that characterized the countryside around Le Puy in the Massif Central ever posed a real threat to the integrity of the nation. They were mostly of short duration, outbreaks of anti-revolution provoked by economic hardship or religious agitation which the army or local units of the National Guard were well able to disperse. Unlike the Vendée, they did not lead to military engagement or deflect troops from the frontiers. And yet they shared many of the grievances of the Vendeans and much of the religious passion. If they remained local events with relatively little resonance on the national stage, it is surely because in these regions relations with neighbouring towns were less venomous, the local Jacobins and revolutionary bourgeois less prone to ram the decrees of the Republic down unwilling rural throats. For in the last analysis, that is perhaps the most distinctive trait of the West, the relish with which the republicans from the towns went into the countryside on political missions that offended and brutalized the local peasantry. In 1793 they were paying the price for months, and in some cases years, of systematic abuse.[24]

The West was, in other words, an exception, a rural region which was committed to counter-revolution rather than just apathetic or opposed to state intrusion. Distrust of Paris did not cease with the fall of the Jacobins, and the region carried on its struggle in a series of insurrections throughout the 1790s before transferring its hatred of secular republicanism into nineteenth-century politics and beyond. The Directory was forced to send troops to the region, and Napoleon in his turn would experience grumbling resistance from the same rural districts that had defied the republicans. The concordat with the papacy played a part in resolving the issue of Catholicism, allowing the people of the region to pursue once again their religious devotions without fear of disruption. But the government lived in constant fear of renewed violence, of another *petite guerre* that would divert its troops from the defence of the frontiers. In the winter of 1803–4 there would be renewed turmoil in the Vendée, with bands of draft-dodgers offering violence to the gendarmerie and threatening once more to raise a popular insurrection in the countryside. Napoleon, however, had learned the lessons of 1793, and he was in no mood to treat with the rebels. His response was uncompromising. He strengthened the military presence in the region, ordering a sweep of those rural communities where rebels were known to be hiding, instituting a huge road-building programme to ease the passage of troops, and building a new administrative centre in the heart of the Vendée, a whole new town at Napoléon – La Roche-sur-Yon.[25] By these measures he hoped both to pacify

the Vendeans and to persuade them that there were concrete advantages to
be gained from obedience to the law.

There were many back in 1793 who saw the principal threat to the security of the state coming from urban areas rather than from the countryside,
from those major provincial cities – among them Lyon and Marseille, Caen
and Limoges, Bordeaux and Toulon – which declared themselves in a state of
insurrection against the authority of the Convention and which the Jacobins
chose to categorize as 'federalist'.[26] Yet when the word entered the nation's
political vocabulary, there were few who were willing to lay claim to it, and
with good reason. If taken literally, federalism implied a desire to break
away from the centre, to put local or regional interests above those of the
nation, even to withdraw that part of national sovereignty which the people
of each city or department had invested in the National Assembly. It was
primarily used as a term of abuse, its most salient quality being a willingness
to sacrifice national unity for selfish gain, and to risk breaking up the political integrity of France in pursuit of sectional advantage. It was a form of
egotism and as such was held in deep contempt by republican centralists,
and most especially by the Jacobins, who seized every occasion to hurl
abuse at those whom it suspected of this gravest of political crimes. Some,
noting that Lyon had handed over command of its defences to Précy, a former noble and émigré, chose to accuse all the rebel cities of royalism, when
actually the most notable aspect of Lyon's revolt was its quite horribly inept
timing.[27] While it is true that in their public statements the rebel cities did
criticize the actions of their masters in Paris and denounce the increasing
dominance of central government directives, there is no hint of counter-
revolutionary ideology, far less of full-blown royalism. Indeed, the federalist
leaders responded by redoubling their protestations of loyalty to the Republic.
Their battalions continued to serve in the armies and defend the frontiers.
Some, like Bordeaux, urged their troops to stay in the Vendée to fight what
they regarded as true counter-revolution.[28] They insisted that they made no
common cause with royalists.

It is at least arguable that federalism, in the sense in which the word was
used and understood by contemporaries, was a political invention. There was
no ideology of federalism, no political movement in provincial France that
sought autonomy from the centre or expressed a desire to split the Republic.
The leaders of the cities that stood accused took great care to distance themselves from any such idea, especially since the country was in a state of war
and they had no desire to be cast in the role of traitors or foreign agents.
'What is it that we are proposing to you?' asked two deputies from the rebel
cities in an address to their colleagues in the Drôme. 'Is it to break up the
Republic or to attach you to a section of the French people; is it to isolate
you from the common interest and build up within the state a number of
centres of power and political action? For it is only in these characteristics
that we can recognise federalism'.[29] The question was, of course, rhetorical;
they were, they insisted, committed republicans, men who had often suffered

in earlier periods for their support of the rights of man and their belief in the sovereign people. Some went further, claiming that they were the true republicans, fighting for the rights of the French people under the constitution at a time when these were being eroded by the Jacobins. The means they had adopted had been forced upon them and were not of their own choosing.[30] Of course, such protests fell on deaf ears, and during the summer and autumn months of 1793, 'federalism' came to be seen as a peculiarly dangerous form of sedition. In vain did the Girondin deputies protest that the word was meaningless, a polemical device and the product of a concerted campaign of abuse and denigration. In vain, too, did they point out that it was being fashioned into a major terrorist weapon by their Montagnard opponents, one which would provide the excuse to purge municipal and departmental councils and send substantial numbers of provincial republicans to their deaths, especially in the South-East and South-West.[31]

The choice of the term 'federalism' was itself very telling, emphasizing as it did the desire to break away, to jeopardize the nation in favour of local ties and loyalties. It suggested a tension between centre and periphery, between the Republic and the region, which had not been present in the early years of the Revolution. We have already seen how, in 1790, the National Assembly had actively encouraged the creation of regional federations of towns and of National Guards, and how the *Fête de la Fédération* became the first secular festival, a national celebration of the infant Revolution. At that stage there had been no suggestion that Dijon or Rennes or Toulouse was showing a lack of patriotism by staging a regional federation; on the contrary, their initiatives were widely praised and encouraged. Indeed, it was the presence in Paris during the summer of 1792 of *fédérés* from Marseille and Brittany which had allowed the Parisians to mount such a sustained assault on Louis XVI at the Tuileries and had led to the overthrow of the monarchy; and the marching song of the *fédérés* of Marseille, brought to the capital by National Guardsmen from the Bouches-du-Rhône, had become the battle-hymn of the new Republic, the anthem of revolutionary France.[32] As recently as 1792, federations were still portrayed as both patriotic and revolutionary, instances of public celebration and instruction that spread enthusiasm amongst the people of the smaller towns of the hinterland. Nor were Jacobin clubs themselves always hostile to taking part in large regional gatherings to make their collective voice heard. Clubs from departments across the Midi, for example, met in a series of federations in Valence in the summer of 1793, while republican societies in the Nord were still calling regional meetings – effectively federations – as late as October and December.[33] These meetings were, it is true, often called to counter the threat of federalism, so that the popular societies of neighbouring towns could formulate a common response. But were they really so different in kind from earlier federations? Clubs had been getting together on a regional basis ever since 1790, when, to cite one instance, the Lille club had called its neighbours to a meeting to discuss the dangers they faced along the northern frontier. In 1792, moreover, the popular societies of Burgundy held a series of regular congresses in their region, with the stated aim of spreading republican politics and enlightened views. Theirs was a clearly structured movement, planned and executed by leading figures in the Jacobin movement locally who had the will and the means to mobilize the clubbists and provide them with a coherent and integrated organization.[34]

Increasingly, however, the Paris Jacobins and their allies in the sections came to regard all such initiatives with suspicion and to be wary of any movement in the French provinces that could be construed as acting on its own initiative or as critical of central government. This represented something of a sea-change in revolutionary politics, the abandonment of the early concessions to decentralization and a steady move towards an authoritarian centralism. That change coincided almost precisely with the declaration of the Republic. 'The fact is,' writes Michael Sydenham, 'that in the late summer of 1792, probably in mid-September, the word "federal", which had hitherto signified patriotic unity, became a term of political opprobrium and proscription'.[35] With the sovereign people now represented in a single chamber and no separation of powers, the Republic stood for unity, for 'the one and indivisible nation', and political pluralism could no longer be tolerated. Festivals changed in character so that even the annual *Fête de la Fédération*, on the Champ de Mars in the capital, had been transformed into a public display of unity and national solidarity, the representation of a nation strong in defence of its republican institutions. In its previous form it had gloried in the diversity of the French people, but this was distrusted by the Jacobins, who wished only to reaffirm the unanimous support of all for Paris and the Convention. They queried the inclusion of local dress and local dialect, and contested the representation of different towns and provinces.[36] Henceforth it became the business of those who designed and organized festivals to use the occasion to portray the unity of the French people in the face of their common enemies. Any criticism of the government, any denunciation of Paris, risked being equated with counter-revolution. It is this rejection of pluralism by the Jacobins and their allies in the Paris sections, more even than the threat which they posed to the war effort, which explains the levels of outrage that greeted the revolts in Lyon and a handful of other cities in the summer of 1793.

How real was that threat, and how far did it extend? It was certainly real to the degree that a number of cities and their surrounding departments declared themselves in a state of insurrection, refusing to recognize the legitimate authority of the Convention and withholding, as they said, their portion of sovereign authority. Generally they did this by setting up a new and supposedly sovereign body within the department, usually called a *commission populaire*, composed of representatives of the department and of the major municipal councils involved in the revolt; judicial tribunals and chambers of commerce might also have representatives on the commission, largely, it appeared, to extend its somewhat delicate authority and give it a degree of legitimation. In a number of towns they were reacting to news of the Jacobin seizure of power in Paris, and they justified themselves on the basis that their deputies had been coerced or bullied into silence, that the Girondin leaders had been arrested, in short, that the Convention was no longer 'free' but was 'under the yoke' of hot-heads from the Paris sections. That was the case, for instance, in Bordeaux and in Caen, both of which counted several of their own deputies among those put on trial, and had more reason than most to distrust the Paris Jacobins. They were also towns where there was little organized popular movement, and where a small number of militants sympathetic to Paris could easily be muzzled.[37]

But if in these cases federalism can be shown to have developed out of national politics, it would be rash to equate the movement as a whole with the Girondin interest nationally or with the growth of factions in the Convention. That was the story which the Jacobin leaders chose to put around, a central plank of their propaganda campaign against the provincial cities. Elsewhere, the anti-Jacobin tone of much of the discourse of revolt had its roots less in national than in local politics, in the turbulence of the early Revolution and the rise of faction-fighting locally. It is this, for instance, that explains the uprisings in Lyon and Marseille – initiated by moderate republicans on the municipal council and in the sections against local Jacobin cliques – which took place in the last days of May, before news of events in Paris could possibly have reached them.[38] If the Lyonnais were anti-Jacobin, it was their own Jacobins, like Joseph Chalier, who were the target of their disaffection, men who, they believed, had abused their influence with a small minority of the city's sections to seize power and impose their views on their fellow citizens. Here, as in much of the Mediterranean, the origins of the revolt lie less in relations with the capital than in the bitterness of indigenous politics. In Toulon, to take another example, the revolt can be explained as the legacy of a bruising struggle between radicals and moderates in July and August of 1792, which had allowed the radical faction to seize power, leaving a number of prominent conservatives murdered on the city's streets. Here, as in other southern cities, the 'federalist revolt' was as an act of vengeance, pursued with little reference to the wider world.[39] It is perhaps best seen as part of a dialectic of recurring violence throughout the revolutionary decade.[40]

Federalism did not, of course, turn into a national movement, nor did it give provincial France any real measure of unity. It remained geographically restricted to a small number of departments and trading centres, to Lyon and Marseille in the Rhône valley, to the naval port of Toulon, and to several major commercial cities along the Atlantic seaboard and in parts of Normandy and Brittany. In all, forty-three departments – around half of the total – uttered words of encouragement or declared some degree of verbal support for the insurgents; but of these only a small minority actually withdrew their adherence to the Convention or threatened military resistance to Paris. Those that did contribute military support were mostly in the North and West – the Eure, Orne, Sarthe, Côtes-du-Nord, Finistère, Ille-et-Vilaine, Loire-inférieure and

Mayenne – while only six took the ultimate step of raising departmental armies and declaring themselves in armed revolt. Caen, Bordeaux and Nîmes all raised a military detachment, but in each case their action soon fizzled out and they posed no real threat to the capital.[41] More seriously, Marseille raised an army of 3,500 men, took Avignon, and marched northwards up the Rhône valley to join forces with the Lyonnais. But others stood in their way and their force was dispersed before it could reach its target, so that the threatened assault on Paris by a federalist army from the Midi remained nothing more than a figment of the southern imagination. Its importance did not rest there, however, since it provided the Jacobins with a powerful weapon for their propaganda campaign against the federalist cities, pointing to it as yet more evidence of the unpatriotic and seditious ambitions of greedy provincial elites. When, in August, Toulon handed over the dockyard and the Mediterranean fleet to the British and Spanish navies, their case looked even stronger, since the insurgents could now be more plausibly tarred with the brush of treason.[42]

The federalist cities, too, turned to propaganda to fight off these accusations and to strengthen their own morale. They felt increasingly isolated and vulnerable and had every interest in attracting other towns to join them in what they saw as their crusade against central authority. They knew that their actions were fraught with risk, and that what they claimed as a defence of republican values could easily be interpreted by their opponents as treason or counter-revolution. Their leaders were, understandably, fearful of being singled out for retribution or cut off from their natural hinterland; and they knew only too well that their defiance would not be forgiven. They desperately craved the support of their fellows, both as a sign of reassurance and as a source of mutual defence in the event of attack. Indeed, there were constant reports of federalist agents, often travelling in pairs, spreading a gospel of revolt across wide swathes of the country, and inspiring a widespread anti-Parisian discourse in provincial towns as they urged them to follow in their footsteps. They attempted to win over doubters, to convince municipal and district authorities that they shared a common interest in defying central authority. In the process they tended to exaggerate the level of their own support, or to imply that with just one more push they would be in a position to win a majority in the Convention. Reports circulated, and were widely believed in the federalist centres themselves, that some fifty or sixty departments had been converted to their cause, so that theirs was truly a campaign by provincial France against outside tyranny. The Lyonnais even claimed, on the flimsiest of evidence, that they commanded support in sixty-nine of the eighty-three departments.[43] It might be untrue, an expression of hope rather than of fact, built on little more than a casual nod of agreement or a polite word that implied sympathy and understanding, but it was still suggestive of threat at a time when the war on the frontiers was going badly and when the Vendée was siphoning off French battalions to fight a civil war in the West. It all helped to convince the Parisians that the

Revolution was safe only in their hands, and to deepen the gulf that separated opinion in the capital from that in provincial France.

For with the Jacobins in power in the Convention and increasingly dependent on support from the sections and the Paris crowd, there were now very different views of how revolutionary politics should evolve. In the bigger provincial cities, well endowed with newspapers, clubs and colleges, and home to a diverse and educated intellectual elite, it was widely accepted that the Republic was a project that they could help shape. Their republicanism was something active, a movement in which they expected to participate. And just as they could read in their newspapers about events in Paris and on the frontiers, so, too, they exchanged news with other provincial cities, reporting one another's initiatives in the regional press.[44] It seemed only natural that they should confer with their counterparts in other towns, join them in regional meetings of popular societies and, where possible, make common cause with them. Missions were sent out from Lyon and Marseille to scour Provence and the Rhône valley, from Caen to the department and district centres of Normandy, from Bordeaux to Dax, Périgueux and other towns throughout Aquitaine. They sought, they said, to explain their position and justify their actions to their peers, even if Paris quickly interpreted this as a dangerous form of sedition, as 'preaching federalism'. They did not always convince. In Valence – where opinion had initially been divided – the *commissaires* were met with hostility and pragmatic arguments from the *procureur*, Payan, against any step that could open local people to a charge of sedition.[45] And in the Dordogne local Jacobins forbade departmental troops from the Gironde to enter their territory.[46] But they also chalked up successes which Paris interpreted as threatening. When the Lyonnais arrived in Saint-Étienne, for instance, seeking guns for their army from the government armoury in the city, they also explained to local people the circumstances that had led them to resist. The response they elicited was rather gratifying, and they reported that a majority of Saint-Étienne's republicans seemed ready to rally to their cause. They were not counter-revolutionary and they remained proud to be called republicans, but they were prepared to support Lyon, not simply out of friendship or commercial interest, but because the Lyonnais seemed to be offering what many of them wanted most passionately, an end to revolutionary violence and the establishment of stable republican institutions.[47]

That, to Jacobin eyes, constituted counter-revolution, and it helps explain why they and the Montagnard deputies in the Convention were less prepared to compromise with local opinion and increasingly intolerant of claims to provincial difference. The Republic, they believed, was the political expression of the sovereign people, and as such it was indivisible. At the same time, the threat posed by external war made a display of solidarity all the more essential, just as it advanced the cause of French nationalism, that popular nationalism and patriotic unity which had accompanied the initial outburst of revolutionary enthusiasm in Paris and which was now part of revolutionary ideology.[48] And although the radical leaders themselves tended to be of provincial origin and had, like Robespierre or Saint-Just or Babeuf, left their *pays* – often the expansive cornlands of Artois and Picardy – to make their way to Paris in the time-honoured tradition of provincials seeking their fortune, it was as Parisians that they saw revolutionary events and judged them. As Parisians they sent out deputies-on-mission to the provinces to sort out problems and enforce decrees – a measure that had begun during the previous winter when the Girondins were still in power, but which intensified in the first months of the Jacobin republic. As Parisians, too, they came increasingly under the influence of the people, those of the markets and the radical sections, the *sans-culottes* with their ideas of popular sovereignty and their egalitarian sympathies. With the Jacobins in power, France would become more centralist and the Revolution more intolerant of difference, accentuating the role of the nation state and the concentration of power in the capital. As a consequence the balance of authority shifted away from the provincial cities, leaving many of their leaders feeling impotent and resentful. In the months that followed the Jacobin seizure of power, Paris would reinforce its position, not only as the political capital of the French nation, but also as its ideological capital, the position it would go on to hold in the memory and affections of nineteenth-century republicans. Paris had reinvented itself as the undisputed capital of revolution.[49]

Notes

1 Michel Brunet, *Le Roussillon. Une société contre l'État, 1780–1820* (Toulouse, 1986), pp. 177–9.

2 John Hall Stewart, *A Documentary History of the French Revolution* (New York, 1951), p. 473.

3 Christine Peyrard, *Les Jacobins de l'Ouest. Sociabilité révolutionnaire et formes de politisation dans le Maine et la Basse-Normandie, 1789–99* (Paris, 1996), p. 364.

4 Roger Dupuy, *De la Révolution à la chouannerie. Paysans en Bretagne, 1788–94* (Paris, 1988), p. 188.

5 Timothy Tackett, 'The West in France in 1789: The Religious Factor in the Origins of Counter-revolution', *Journal of Modern History* 54 (1982), pp. 715–45.

6 R. de Chabalier, 'Les camps de Jalès', *Revue du souvenir vendéen* 95 (1971), pp. 5–17.

7 Jacqueline Chaumié, *Le réseau d'Antraïgues et la contre-révolution, 1791–93* (Paris, 1965), pp. 19–20.

8 Keith Michael Baker (ed.), *The Old Regime and the Revolution* (Chicago, 1987), p. 329.

9 Nigel Aston, *Religion and Revolution in France, 1780–1804* (London, 2000), p. 189.

10 T. J. A. Le Goff, *Vannes and its Region. A Study of Town and Country in Eighteenth-century France* (Oxford, 1981), pp. 339–43.

11 Alan Forrest, *Conscripts and Deserters. The Army and French Society during the Revolution and Empire* (New York, 1989), pp. 79–80.

12 Le Goff, *Vannes and its Region*, p. 343.

13 Louis-Marie Turreau, *Memoirs for the History of the War of la Vendée* (London, 1796), p. 29.

14 Jean-Clément Martin, *La Vendée de la mémoire* (Paris, 1989), p. 27.

15 Jean-Jacques Becker, 'Y a-t-il une culture de guerre civile?' in *La guerre civile entre Histoire et Mémoire* (Nantes, 1995), pp. 33–8.

16 Raoul Girardet, 'La Vendée dans le légendaire national français', in Alain Gérard and Thierry Heckmann (eds), *La Vendée dans l'histoire* (Paris, 1994), pp. 161–8.

17 Donald Sutherland, *The Chouans. The Social Origins of Popular Counter-Revolution in Upper Brittany, 1770–96* (Oxford, 1982), p. 239.

18 Olwen Hufton, *Women and the Limits of Citizenship in the French Revolution* (Toronto, 1992), p. 123.

19 Timothy Tackett, *La Révolution, l'Église, la France* (Paris, 1986), p. 197.

20 Olwen Hufton, 'The reconstruction of a church, 1796–1801', in Gwynne Lewis and Colin Lucas (eds), *Beyond the Terror. Essays in French Regional and Social History, 1794–1815* (Cambridge, 1983), p. 23.

21 Harvey Mitchell, 'The Vendée and counter-revolution – a review essay', *French Historical Studies* 5 (1968), pp. 407–8.

22 Pierre Chaunu, *avant-propos* to Reynald Secher, *Le génocide franco-français. La Vendée-vengé* (Paris, 1986), pp. 21–4.

23 Alain Gérard, *La Vendée, 1789–93* (Paris, 1992), pp. 126–33.

24 Jean-Clément Martin, *Révolution et contre-révolution. Les rouages de l'histoire* (Rennes, 1996), p. 122.

25 Roger Lévêque, *Napoléon, ville de Vendée. La naissance de La Roche-sur-Yon* (La Roche-sur-Yon, 1998), pp. 58–60.

26 The most comprehensive and up-to-date analysis of federalism is Paul Hanson, *The Jacobin Republic Under Fire. The Federalist Revolt in the French Revolution* (University Park, PA, 2003). For other general discussions of federalism as a political phenomenon, see W. D. Edmonds, 'Federalism and urban revolt in France in 1793', *Journal of Modern History* 55 (1983) and Alan Forrest, 'Federalism', in Colin Lucas (ed.), *The French Revolution and the Creation of Modern Political Culture, vol. 2: The Political Culture of the French Revolution* (Oxford, 1988), pp. 309–27.

27 C. Riffaterre, *Le mouvement anti-jacobin et anti-parisien à Lyon et dans le Rhône-et-Loire* (2 vols, Lyon, 1912–28), vol. 1, pp. 456–61.

28 Alan Forrest, *Society and Politics in Revolutionary Bordeaux* (Oxford, 1975), p. 143.

29 'Adresse des citoyens Hallot, député de la Gironde, et Fonvielle, député des Bouches-du-Rhône, à leurs frères du département de la Drôme' (1793), pp. 8–9.

30 Antonino de Francesco, *Il governo senza testa. Movimento democratico e federalismo nella Francia rivoluzionaria, 1789–95* (Naples, 1992), p. 230.

31 Donald Greer, *The Incidence of the Terror during the French Revolution. A Statistical Interpretation* (Cambridge, MA, 1935), pp. 148–53.

32 Hervé Luxardo, *Histoire de la Marseillaise* (Paris, 1989), pp. 40–1.

33 Anne-Marie Duport, 'Les congrès des sociétés populaires tenus à Valence en 1793', and François Wartelle, 'Contre-pouvoir populaire ou complot maximaliste? Les fédérations montagnardes dans le Nord de la France, octobre–décembre 1793', both in *Existe-t-il un fédéralisme jacobin?* (111e Congrès National des Sociétés Savantes, Poitiers, 1986), pp. 21–38, 59–90.

34 Marcel Dorigny, 'Les congrès des sociétés populaires de 1792 en Bourgogne: défense révolutionnaire et ordre social', in *Existe-t-il un fédéralisme jacobin?* pp. 102–4.

35 Michael Sydenham, 'The Republican revolt of 1793 – a plea for less localised local studies', *French Historical Studies* 12 (1981), p. 124.

36 Mona Ozouf, *La fête révolutionnaire, 1789–99* (Paris, 1976), pp. 336–7.

37 Paul Hanson, *Provincial Politics in the French Revolution. Caen and Limoges, 1789–94* (Baton Rouge, LA, 1989), p. 244.

38 For convincing analyses of events in Lyon and Marseille, see W. D. Edmonds, *Jacobinism and the Revolt in Lyon, 1789–93* (Oxford, 1990), and J. B. Cameron, Jr, 'The Revolution of the Sections of Marseille – Federalism in the Department of Bouches-du-Rhône in 1793' (PhD thesis, University of North Carolina at Chapel Hill, 1971).

39 Malcolm Crook, 'Federalism and the French Revolution: the revolt in Toulon in 1793', *History* 65 (1980), pp. 384–5.

40 Hubert C. Johnson, *The Midi in Revolution. A Study of Regional Political Diversity, 1789–93* (Princeton, NJ, 1986), pp. 229–30.

41 W. D. Edmonds, 'Federalism and urban revolt in France in 1793', *Journal of Modern History* 55 (1983), pp. 23–5.

42 For a full account of the circumstances leading to Toulon's revolt, see Malcolm Crook, *Toulon in War and Revolution. From the* ancien régime *to the Restoration* (Manchester, 1991).

43 Henri Wallon, *La Révolution du 31 mai et le fédéralisme en 1793* (2 vols, Paris, 1886), *passim*.

44 Eric Wauters, 'La dialectique province-Paris dans la presse des départements: entre vie politique locale et réseaux nationaux d'opinion', *Annales historiques de la Révolution française* 330 (2002), pp. 71–85.

45 The debate within the Department of the Drôme is analysed in Roger Pierre (ed.), *240,000 Drômois aux quatre vents de la Révolution* (Valence, 1989), pp. 179–81.

46 Alan Forrest, *The Revolution in Provincial France. Aquitaine, 1789–99* (Oxford, 1996), p. 204.
47 Jacqueline Bayon, 'Saint-Étienne et les Stéphanois face à la crise fédéraliste lyonnaise', *Cahiers d'histoire* 38 (1993), p. 300.
48 David Garrioch, *The Making of Revolutionary Paris* (Berkeley, CA, 2002), p. 294.
49 Patrice Higonnet, *Paris, Capital of the World* (Cambridge, MA, 2002), p. 47.

|9|

Jacobinism, centralism and Terror

If, ever since 1789, Paris had laid claim to a position of primacy within the revolutionary state – a claim bolstered by the declaration of war and the spread of a strongly nationalistic interpretation of popular sovereignty – it was the Jacobins who forged the city as the capital of the Revolution. In their rhetoric they made continual reference to the need to create national unity and maintain solidarity with the political leadership. It was not that a majority of the Jacobins in the Convention themselves came from Paris. One of their political strengths in the Convention derived, indeed, from the fact that they represented virtually every region of the country, in marked contrast to the Girondins, who became too tightly identified with the Atlantic seaboard and with a relatively small number of commercial centres. Both in their geographical catchment and in their social and professional backgrounds, the Jacobins could claim to be more representative of the country as a whole. Most significantly, that Jacobin country included Paris, where they enjoyed strong electoral support – something which again distinguished them from the Gironde, who failed to make any political impact on the capital, a fact which, as Alison Patrick showed, proved a major source of political weakness.[1] Thus when in September 1792 new elections were held for the Convention, those returned in Paris were, almost to a man, strongly anti-Girondin and on good terms with the Paris Commune, which would subsequently be important in strengthening the domination of the Montagne and marginalizing the Gironde.[2] Paris increasingly saw itself as a Jacobin city.

It was also the home of the Paris Jacobin Club, the *société-mère* for the Jacobin movement, which devoted a large proportion of its time to proselytizing in the provinces and building the national network of clubs into a forceful and united movement. From the Paris club bulletins, pamphlets and printed speeches rained down on its provincial brethren, spreading ideas and inducing a degree of conformity throughout the Jacobin movement. But who were the Paris clubbists? From what parts of society did they spring? From an examination of such fragments of information as we have we can conclude that they were largely distinct from the *sans-culottes* of the sections, and that they came from virtually all sectors of Paris society, even including some members of the nobility. Of Paris Jacobins who were deputies, over half were lawyers of some kind, with significant contingents of doctors, clergy and public administrators, as well as men drawn from journalism and the arts. The information that we have for those members of the club who were not in the Assembly is much more sparse, but on the basis of 206 individuals, Rositza Tacheva has concluded that they came from a very wide spectrum, including lawyers, administrators, architects, artisans of all kinds, small businessmen – indeed, virtually every occupation is represented except agriculture.[3] They were not particularly tied to the professions, or to trade, and certainly they were not poor. The Jacobins could, with some justice, claim to be representative of the population of the capital, and to that extent to represent Paris and Parisian opinion.

For many in the provinces this was not a reassuring association. They had their own clubs and sections, their own pockets of hardline Jacobins, whose behaviour, as we have seen, often proved deeply divisive and made local politics uncharacteristically acrimonious. The Jacobins nationally were often judged by their local counterparts, and provincial dislike of the Paris club could be little more than the extension of local animosities on to the national stage. In cities where politics had sunk into bitter feuds and acts of personal vengeance, that meant that Paris Jacobinism was understood in terms of such factious terrorists as Joseph Chalier in Lyon or Jourdan Coupe-Têtes in Avignon.[4] Besides, local Jacobins were eager in the wake of the federalist revolt to gain the recognition and approval of Paris; it was seen both as a source of security and a form of respectability, and in the last months of 1793 the Paris society was swamped with applications for affiliation. The loss of the archives of the Paris Jacobin Club means that we often do not know the outcome of these applications; and it would seem that many of the letters went unanswered, whether because of the laxity of the Jacobins' correspondence committee or because of the atmosphere of paranoia which made virtually any provincial society open to charges of federalist infiltration.[5] But there is no doubt that once the Jacobins had seized power in the Convention in June 1793, many provincial clubbists were careful to take their cue from the centre and looked more and more to the Paris society for inspiration and leadership.

They also tended to join the Parisians in quoting and praising their heroes, those who had expressed radical views, written stirring addresses, or who had suffered and sacrificed themselves for the cause. For the Paris club had its heroes, whom it held aloft – often literally in processions and festivals – as exemplars to others, secular saints to take the place of Catholic icons, martyrs in the most glorious traditions of antiquity. Lepeletier de Saint Fargeau was one of these martyrs, a deputy and regicide who was fatally stabbed by a royalist protestor as he dined in a restaurant near the Palais Royal on the eve of Louis XVI's execution.[6] Provincial opinion was often slower to accept him as one of their own. But he was not demonized in the manner of that other Parisian martyr, Jean-Paul Marat, the radical journalist and deputy who was famously stabbed in his bath by Charlotte Corday and immortalized in the painting of David. Marat, more than any other revolutionary figure, divided opinion, and especially he seemed to divide Parisians from their provincial cousins. In Paris, Marat enjoyed a particular popularity, being regarded by many Parisians as one of their own. His newspaper was always printed in the capital and intensely read by Parisians; he lived there from 1790, in the heart of the revolutionary district of the Cordeliers; and when he was elected to the Convention he was carried there in triumph by his constituents. In Olivier Coquard's words, Marat seemed to enjoy 'a privileged relationship' with Paris.[7] He enjoyed no such relationship with provincial France, where only the most extreme and egalitarian of Jacobins claimed him as their own, and where identification with Marat was equated with loyalty to the Paris Jacobin Club. In Marseille, when the lawyer Hyacinthe Bertrand was accused of federalism, he defended himself by pointing to his republican record, and went on to denounce the egotism of the rich before adding this final profession of faith: 'Salut et fraternité in the name of Marat, who was my favourite philosopher back in 1791 and who has always remained so'.[8] This was a desperate last throw of the dice, a vain attempt to persuade his judges on the Revolutionary Tribunal. Even to them it must have sounded unconvincing, since for the majority of provincial Frenchmen Marat was something of a hate-figure, who had come to symbolize all that was most extreme and most sanguinary about the Parisian revolution.

That equation of Paris with extremism was one of the most persistent themes of provincial discourse during 1793 and 1794. Paris, once the city of light and philosophy, was now most commonly identified with savagery and bloodletting. The lynchings of 1789, the prison massacres of 1792, and now the repeated images of Terror all served to convince provincial France that murder, too, had its capital. The language of the *sans-culottes*, the violent denunciations of the rich and moderate, the threats uttered by the militants of the Commune, all provided a reminder, if indeed one was still needed, that the Parisians were a people apart, a people whose violent instincts risked turning the Revolution into a vengeful bloodbath. Here the changing image of the city in the course of the eighteenth century played a significant part, since, as we have seen, even before the outbreak of Revolution, Paris had assumed the mantle of a dangerous city as well an enlightened one, where order and regulation had broken down, where the people were angry, prone to violence and insurrection, and where the community had lost any sense of restraint and was no longer capable of averting disorder.[9] This was a view shared by many Parisians, and by people outside Paris as well. Images of the excesses of the Terror, of tumbrils grinding over the Parisian cobblestones and of heads falling on the Place de la Révolution before the gloating stares of Parisian *tricoteuses*, all helped to add substance to the notion of Paris as a dark and dangerous place where savagery and bloodlust lurked in the shadows.

The stridency of the radical sections of the capital in demanding ever greater repression and more stringent terrorist laws only accentuated the impression that Terror had been made the order of the day at the behest of the Paris Commune, in a bid to appease the vengeful bloodlust of the people of the city.

If Parisian men became equated with popular terrorism in the Jacobin republic, the image of the city's women was even more disturbing. They could seem particularly terrifying, and were routinely portrayed as crazed harpies braying for blood to be shed. The role of the *tricoteuse* was unambiguous; in the words of the nineteenth-century historian Lairtullier, these were women who had cast aside every last trace of feminine sensitivity in their pursuit of blind vengeance. They were, he conceded, when viewed from afar, ordinary Parisian women, indistinguishable from thousands of others: they were 'young, perhaps pretty, able to feel love; but all that was brutally repressed by their soiling contact with the world'. Their sympathetic natures were stifled in their pursuit of violence and repression, till 'that corner of cruelty too often concealed in the human heart overflows in them and like the flood of a devouring poison invades the whole of their minds'.[10] This was, in many ways, a conventional response to the spectacle of women venting their collective anger in public and laying claim to participation in acts of bloodletting. There was something deeply disturbing about it, something which many found perverted and unnatural. But if their role in revolutionary violence evoked horror, so did their apparent identification with political extremism, as when the Society for Revolutionary Republican Women in Paris took to the streets for Marat's funeral, holding a wake over his body, collecting the blood that continued to flow from his wound and casting flowers on his coffin.[11] They did not hesitate to adulate their hero, an action that helped incarnate his immortalization. It was a moment of powerful symbolism, and a peculiarly Parisian moment, which for republicans in the provinces inspired fear as well as a certain feeling of awe. For the Paris it depicted was not just violent and bloodthirsty, intent on inverting the normal social and political order; it was also a city marked by deep corruption, by a perverse desire to overturn all kinds of moral certainties as well. In the process, the *tricoteuses* came to symbolize a much deeper malaise in Parisian society, a malaise that distanced the capital from other towns and cities and especially from the broad acres of the French countryside.

They were the extras in the terrible drama of the Terror, a drama played out in public in the streets of the capital. They had drunk in the unbridled hatred expressed in Hébert's *Père Duchesne*, modelling their behaviour on the journalist's fictional hero and their values on those of the most egalitarian of *sans-culottes*. These values left little room for sympathy with the victims of Terror, no place for the milk of human kindness, and provincial onlookers were often shocked by the sheer venom that was emitted by the crowds that thronged the Place de la Révolution to participate in the public spectacle of killing. They hissed and jostled the victims as they made their terrifying last journey through the streets to the place of execution, savouring their humiliation. And the more famous the victim, the greater the levels of interest and hatred. Hordes turned out, for instance, to see Marie-Antoinette die, eager to participate in a day that signally marked the end of the royal family; eager, too, to celebrate the victory of the Republic. But the predominant mood was a desire for vengeance, a joy at being present on a day which they treated as a sort of popular carnival. Chantal Thomas describes a scene in which little dignity was allowed to the victim, whose tumbril took a full hour to make its faltering way to the foot of the guillotine.

> Very early on, the crowd rushed to the route the condemned woman was to follow. The Place de la Révolution was swarming with people. To pass the time while they waited, the people ate, drank, chatted. Chortling, they read out loud the most pornographic passages from the latest scandal sheets against her: *The Queen's Farewells to her Sweethearts, Male and Female; Marie-Antoinette's Great Disease*; or *The Testament of Marie-Antoinette, the Widow Capet*.[12]

Nothing was left out, neither the details of her treason nor the by now hackneyed vilification of her as a lesbian. It was a scene given over to popular hatred.

The Parisian malaise, it was argued, had its roots in the sections and in the temperament of the Paris *sans-culottes*. It was here that radical extremists were nurtured, here that the most egalitarian policies were enunciated, often threatening to bring down popular vengeance on the rich and privileged. The language varied – at one moment or another they were 'terroristes' or 'anarchistes', 'exclusifs', 'exagérés'[13] – but the import was the same, the sense that the sectional radicals came from a different political world, one marked by the envy and savagery that typified the popular classes of the capital. And yet they were often such ordinary people in their daily lives, artisans and shopkeepers who suddenly found themselves armed with the authority of *juges de paix* or of *commissaires révolutionnaires*, the authority to pass judgement on others and arrest their fellow citizens in the name of the regime. In their sectional meetings they often showed themselves to be far from ordinary, mouthing the most sanguinary threats and urging the intensification of terror against those they perceived as the enemies of the people. They included wholesalers and grain merchants, nobles and courtiers. For some, like the radical leadership of the Section des Gravilliers, they also included the clergy, and the section rushed to close all the churches in its bailiwick, 'those dens occupied by the foul beasts that devoured our families' food and brought discord and desolation into our homes'.[14] Gravilliers was not, of course, a typical section. Perched on the Plateau de Beaubourg, it shared with the Faubourg Saint-Antoine and Faubourg Saint-Marcel a deserved reputation for radicalism; and for much of the Revolution its popular society was dominated by the fiery presence of Jacques Roux, the *enragé* priest who sowed ideas of egalitarianism and social levelling.[15] Roux, like Jean Varlet and a handful of other sectional radicals, preached violence and direct action, the duty of sectional personnel to maintain constant vigilance lest the political leadership forget their obligation to the people. It was this that finally brought him into conflict with the Jacobins, when he launched a demagogic campaign against monopolists and urged sectional militants to avenge themselves by carrying out a new September Massacre against their oppressors. His younger associate, Théophile Leclerc, went even further, promising an army purge and death to hoarders, and wallowing, or so it appeared, in the shedding of blood. Leclerc urged pitiless terror and ruthless vigilance, insisting that 'a revolutionary ought, if necessary, to be prepared to sacrifice a hundred thousand scoundrels to the Revolution'. He had no understanding of the notion of compromise. 'I predict,' he wrote, 'that you will be led to a point where it will no longer be possible to hesitate between the death of your enemies and your own'.[16]

Sectional militants did not restrict themselves to threatening language; they also helped to enforce terrorist policies and spread fear in the local population. They staffed the revolutionary committees of their sections and organized house-to-house searches, swooping on suspects at dawn or waking residents after nightfall. And the powers of these committees continued to grow as they were given yet further responsibilities by a government increasingly paranoiac about spies and counter-revolutionaries. By 1794 they supervised food queues and policed wine shops; they issued passports and personal papers; they controlled the distribution of *certificats de civisme*; and they were entrusted with the task of raising and equipping troops to send against the rebels in the Vendée. In these roles they inspired fear as much as respect among local people, who hesitated to fall foul of committee members. For revolutionary committees could also denounce suspects to the authorities, a task which some of them approached with relish. Indeed, when in March 1793 the Revolutionary Tribunal was established, at least one sectional committee, in the Section de la Croix-Rouge, saw it as its mission to feed the tribunal regular batches of suspects.[17] Some clearly exceeded their assigned duties and antagonized local residents. A number of sections recorded dismissals for over-zealous searches and arrests, a sign that even the *sans-culotte* leadership were becoming anxious in the face of terrorist excess.

If sectional militants helped to spread Terror on their own doorsteps, how much more vigorously did they intervene when they were playing away from home, beyond the gates of the capital. Thousands of *sans-culottes* demonstrated their patriotic zeal by volunteering for one of the most characteristic institutions of popular repression, the *armées révolutionnaires* that were raised by the sections and popular societies of the capital to enforce the law on the inhabitants of Paris's hinterland. They were civilians in uniform, united by a certain *esprit de corps* and by a crusading mission, to separate the peasants and villagers of the Île-de-France from their grain and ensure that the Paris markets were provisioned and the armies on the frontier fed. Needless to say, their presence was not appreciated by local people, who saw them, with some justice, more as thugs and bullies than as principled revolutionaries. For the armies were, almost by definition, a blunt political instrument to enforce conformity and obedience, and they showed little subtlety in ensuring that their will was carried out. Even their commander, Ronsin, admitted that the principle on which they were based – the somewhat novel idea of enforcing requisitions by employing for the purpose the very men who had most to gain from them – was a 'vicious' one and was fraught with tensions.[18] They were often billeted on local people, since few villages had barracks of their own, or else they were housed in disused abbeys or monasteries. From there they fanned out into the local community, frightening people into silence by a mixture of their demands and their reputation. For they came as Parisians, as *sans-culottes* with wide powers of arrest and denunciation, prepared at any moment to punish rash protests or launch accusations of counter-revolution. Country people had every reason to be afraid. As Richard Cobb expressed it, 'they represent Terror on the move, Terror in the village; they spread fear, as was the intention of their creators; they are instruments of vigilance and vengeance, charged with punishing the guilty, striking fear in those whose commitment is luke-warm or who remain indifferent, regenerating public opinion by force'.[19] For those unfortunate enough to be terrorized, it was an experience that would stay with them for the rest of their lives. And the armies, with their egalitarian ideas and their brutal demands, were the face of revolutionary Paris that they would continue to remember, one which, inevitably, would colour their impression of Paris as the capital, not just of revolution but of repression and terror.

The activities of the Paris *armée* rarely extended beyond the departments of the Île-de-France and the villages and small towns that lay along the high roads to and from the city. Here consumer met producer, town met countryside, in encounters that allowed the Jacobins and Hébertistes of the more radical sections the opportunity to impose their views on men less politically aware or more steeped in tradition. The encounters could be unsympathetic, even on occasion brutal, but they seldom degenerated into mindless killing, and after their incursion into the countryside the Parisians returned home. But there was one notable exception to this pattern when, following the federalist revolt in Lyon, the Paris *armée* was asked to provide a force of nearly 2,000 men to help restore France's second city to sound republican principles. This was a very different sort of mission, a punitive police operation requested by Fouché and Collot d'Herbois, who specifically sought a political force to enforce their revolutionary programme in the defeated city. The result was the despatch of a rather motley army of *sans-culottes* – the entire Second Battalion, augmented by men from the Third, Fourth and Fifth, all recruited from the Paris sections – on a mission that took them hundreds of miles from home and billeted them on a city of which they knew little except its recent reputation. They found themselves, often reluctantly, far removed from their familiar world, from their friends and political allies, from the sections that gave them so much of their *raison d'être*, their mission to pacify a city that had violently denounced Paris and taken up arms against the Convention. To make matters worse, they left their families behind in the capital, while their contentment was not improved by the tight moral controls to which they were subject, as their political bosses ensured that 'the mob of wives, mistresses, *cantinières* and prostitutes' who regularly accompanied them on their travels around the capital were now kept firmly at bay.[20] This had the effect of raising still further the political temperature as the Parisians took out their frustrations on the hapless population of Lyon.

The *armées révolutionnaires* were the bluntest instrument of the Terror, used to impose new laws and enforce obedience in a country where there was – outside Paris, at least – little tradition of professional policing. If they looted wine cellars and beat up suspects, and the evidence is that they did, it was partly because they acted as political militants, with no police training and a healthy disregard for the rights and opinions of those with whom they had to deal. Initially the *armées* were not peculiar to Paris, but were created in different parts of France in response to local needs. Montpellier and Lyon were among the localities discussing raising an *armée* in the months before the whole issue of the municipal and departmental deployment of force became enmeshed in the federalist crisis. Despite Jacobin fears of locally controlled forces, there were various experiments in raising local armies – in the Haute-Garonne, for instance, the local army which has been most exhaustively studied;[21] in a number of areas where there was a strong Jacobin club movement, like the Doubs and the Hautes-Alpes; in the republican hinterland of the Vendée; and in the solidly revolutionary departments of the East, notably the Moselle and the Bas-Rhin. Everywhere, however, there was a dispute about control, particularly in the light of the recent experience of federalism. Were these to be separate departmental armies, as some of their originators would have liked, enjoying a strong measure of local autonomy? Or were they parts of a national, federal force?[22] Paris increasingly insisted on the latter interpretation, and soon all regional initiatives were prohibited in the name of national unity. At the height of the Great Terror there was only a single *armée révolutionnaire* still in existence, the one raised in the sections of Paris – a fact which goes some way to explain the close identification which many made between terror and the politics of the capital.

The abolition of the last vestiges of local autonomy over the *armées* is just one aspect of a much wider phenomenon, the trend towards ever greater centralization. This was a major theme of provincial comment in the Year II, both about the Jacobins as a political grouping and about the new structures of revolutionary government. Much of the freedom which they had been granted back in 1790, with devolution and the creation of elected authorities, now seemed to be slipping away, as all decision-making came to be centred on the Convention and its committees. For many, the claims of centralism, of *Paris-capitale*, represented a serious threat, since Paris itself was seen as harbouring ambitions to dominate the rest of the country. Under the

Jacobins, Paris had a double image problem. On the one hand, popular Paris risked being identified with extremism and the needless shedding of blood; on the other, Jacobin Paris became equated with uncompromising centralization. Neither brought any premium in popularity in areas which were the victims of Parisian attentions. It was all too easy to equate the capital with their own experience, and to see in the Parisians not the fervent idealists of their own propaganda, but something far more banal, men driven by petty ambition to subject others to unspeakable acts of cruelty. In so many cases, after all, that was the true face of the terrorist, the face that showed when, after Thermidor, some among them stood in the dock to face their accusers. Most expressed no regret, but hid behind the ubiquitous excuse of the executioner, that they had been left with no choice, that they either killed and tortured their victims or were killed and tortured themselves. What makes it all so tragic, as Patrice Gueniffey reminds us, is that they were not consciously lying. Rather they must be seen as mediocre, rather unimaginative men, trapped and overwhelmed by the system they served. 'Ideological belief hardly ever explains the atrocities committed in 1793 and 1794. It is the mediocrity of the terrorists, the emptiness of their lives, their desire for power and their instinct for survival which help to explain them'.[23]

The centralist ambitions of the Republic showed in many different ways. In 1790, much of the attraction of the Revolution to provincial Frenchmen lay, as we have seen, in the levels of authority that had been given to departments and municipalities, and to the unwanted freedoms of citizenship like voting in elections or forming popular societies. But these freedoms had been gradually eroded, until, after the Jacobin coup in the Convention, provincial difference was treated with increasing disdain, and central government became more and more dismissive of local opinion. Increasingly it restricted its confidence to the small groups of Jacobin militants who were to be found within each region, those who were most prepared to stifle local demands in pursuit of the national agenda. That does not mean that it ignored local people entirely; effective government was dependent on finding loyal supporters from within. But it does mean that it relied on an ever narrower range of opinion. The government turned more and more to its agents in the provinces to guide and advise, and they were ever prone to suspect the worst of local people, to see counter-revolution where there was nothing more than legitimate disagreement. Secret agents listened in bars and inns, in markets and on street corners, picking up snatches of gossip and conversation which they then turned into politics. They were, as always, more interested in urban opinion than the views of peasants, and most concerned with the rumours that flew around the streets of the capital. Take, for instance, this account, filed on 10 February 1794 by one such spy, Latour-Lamontagne, who was careful to assess the state of public opinion as it had been expressed in his hearing. Paris, he reported, was seething with anxiety, afraid that all across the provinces the Republic was being consistently undermined. 'They continue to spread the most alarming rumours,' he reported; 'they persist in saying that the troops of the Republic have suffered an important defeat before the walls of Valenciennes, that the Vendée is again rising from its ashes, and that the number of insurgents is growing daily in a frightening manner'.[24] Paris, he implied, had reason to be alarmed; events in the provinces were out of control.

The image of the Jacobin republic as a period of single-minded centralization, when the will of the centre was ruthlessly imposed on the provinces by myriad agents and deputies sent on missions from the Convention, has become one of the great commonplaces of revolutionary history. Government was declared revolutionary until the peace, and the authority of the two great committees of government, Public Safety and General Security, was extended to every corner of the land. This had immediate implications for the relationship between central and local administration, with the consequence that local autonomy was seriously undermined, most particularly through the law of 14 *frimaire* II (4 December 1793), which explicitly attempted to convert the system of local government into the executive arm of Paris. This legislation was seen by many as undoing all the administrative devolution by which the early revolution had won so much goodwill. The elected *conseils-généraux* of departments were abolished, along with their presidents and public prosecutors; and to restrict further the autonomy of departments, an important part of their authority was passed on to the districts. At municipal level, too, independent action was reduced, and again the *procureurs* were abolished, their tasks being allotted instead to *agents nationaux*, who were answerable to Paris and had to report on their activities every ten days. There was near-paranoia about local officials taking independent action, and this was reflected in the endless reporting and purging which the decree demanded. Municipal councils were to be purged, as were revolutionary committees, whose presidents and secretaries had to be renewed every fortnight; local *armées révolutionnaires* were disbanded; and sections could no longer correspond among themselves or send sectional delegations to make common policy with others. Or, as the law pointedly expressed it, 'the right of interpreting decrees appertains to the Convention alone, and one may address oneself only to it for such purpose'.[25]

A key part of this exercise in centralization, it is often inferred, was played by those members of the Convention who accepted, during 1793 and 1794, to go out to the provinces as deputies-on-mission, usually to troublesome departments or to the armies on the frontiers. Their presence was generally unwelcome to local authorities, who were understandably apprehensive and felt themselves under scrutiny. More moderate municipal and departmental bodies were particularly at risk, especially since the arrival of deputies from Paris was invariably sparked by some perceived failure or shortcoming – a lack of tax revenues, a failure to provide recruits for the army, the refusal of local people to part with grain for the cities. And even in the earliest missions, those dating from the spring of 1793 when the Girondins were still in government, it is noticeable that it was those deputies who sat with the

Montagne, many of them members of the Paris Jacobins, who undertook what were often hard and dangerous journeys to the farthest-flung corners of France to goad unwilling peasants into parting with their grain, or to enforce the religious or economic decrees of the Convention. Indeed, of the 176 deputies who went out on missions in the first six months of 1793, the period before the Jacobin seizure of power, Alison Patrick concludes that as many as 131 can be linked to the Mountain or the Jacobins, as against only twelve Girondins and thirty-three who were aligned with the Plain.[26] This Jacobin preponderance is particularly noticeable in the men who were selected for the mission of 9 March 1793, at a moment when the Girondins were already losing control of the assembly and when a majority of the secretaries nominated to choose deputies for the provinces were themselves committed to the Montagne. For the Gironde, handing over such massive authority to their opponents proved a costly mistake; it did not guarantee, as some hoped, that they would retain control in Paris.[27]

Local people were always ready to claim that the deputies followed a Montagnard political line, tried to impose a Jacobin ideological imperative and were prone to crush any opposition they might encounter. They were, it was claimed, the 'proconsuls' of central government, extremists with a strongly personal agenda who arrived from Paris armed with unlimited powers and backed by force. In the words of the Girondin Jean-Baptiste Louvet, they repressed local initiative in the name of an intolerant centralism. Discussing their role in the repression of the federalist cities, he wrote:

> Vomited forth from the capital as from a modern Rome, the most vile henchmen of disguised royalism, the most infamous agents of corruption arrived with chains in the conquered provinces which were already prepared to prostrate themselves before the bloody proconsulate. What had once been the proudest of cities began to bow before two or three Jacobins.[28]

The image of blind centralism, of provincial France as the helpless victim of Parisian ambition and power, could hardly be more brutally expressed.

But is this image itself not the product of a particular revolutionary discourse, a strain of anti-Jacobin propaganda? Of course it is not difficult to find examples of committed Jacobins imposing their egalitarian or anticlerical views on local people, and backing their policies with sanguinary threats and summary arrests. Indeed, some of the best-known and best-researched of the deputies-on-mission are also among the most extreme, studied for their ruthlessness and their terrorist mentality. There are excellent monographs on their missions: Le Bon spreading Terror in the Nord and Pas-de-Calais,[29] Saint-Just with the armies of the Rhine and the Nord,[30] Javogues paying off old scores on his home patch in the Loire,[31] Collot d'Herbois sorting out the debris of federalism in Lyon[32] or Carrier mixing sadism and extremism in equal measure in Nantes[33] – all seem excellent examples of a terrorist pathology introduced from Paris to shatter the calm of provincial life. But it is important to note that in almost all these cases – faced with federalism in

Lyon, a civil war in the Vendée, and discontent and insubordination in the armies – the circumstances of these missions were exceptional, and the deputies sent to these areas at least had the excuse of believing that exceptional measures were justified if political order was to be restored. The levels of violence they used certainly inspired terror throughout the provinces, and among them were men who clearly could be described, in Jacques Godechot's words, as 'artisans of Terror'.[34] But they were in no sense typical – perhaps 20 per cent of those sent out on mission, while the other 80 per cent were more concerned with fairness, equity and justice, even if the methods they used to attain these goals were inevitably controversial.[35]

The deputies sent out in September and October 1793 were given wide-ranging responsibilities: to organize the departure of conscripts, purge local committees and municipal councils and take any measures they thought justified to energize local authorities in the revolutionary cause.[36] The majority sought to complete their tasks efficiently; they relied on the cooperation of local people to do so and introduced them to the everyday virtues of sound administrative practice. Laplanche, for instance, might boast of the 'unlimited powers' vested in him by the Convention, but he used it to authorize local men to act on his behalf in carrying out national policies – taking action against 'mauvais prêtres', authorizing revolutionary taxes and helping to root out the evils of egotism, fanaticism and aristocracy.[37] Among those who offered their assistance were the revolutionary committees, and these often did consist of militants over whom little control was exercised; this was the period when the deputies could still with some justice be called 'proconsuls'. But for much of the Revolution, deputies acted under severe restraints, making regular reports to Paris, and always acting in pairs so as to forestall excess and individual ambition. Many come over as modest men serving the Revolution as best they could: Joseph Lakanal trying to introduce basic schooling in the Dordogne,[38] Jean-Baptiste Bo patiently explaining the laws to illiterate mayors in the mountains of the Cantal,[39] or Chaudron-Rousseau limiting revolutionary taxation to those who already appeared on the tax rolls as the wealthiest of the town's inhabitants.[40] These men were skilled negotiators, offering arbitration and presenting themselves as mediators between local interests. However much the law of 14 *frimaire* risked turning them into simple agents of central government, it could never entirely succeed in that aim. Throughout the years of these missions – and it should not be forgotten that they continued after Robespierre's fall into the Year III and beyond – the *représentants* played a double role, that of mediator as well as government enforcer.[41]

If there was an anarchical phase of the Terror, one where individual localities found themselves at the mercy of extremist deputies with uncontrolled powers, it happened in the early period of Jacobin rule, during the summer and autumn of 1793, rather than during the months of the Great Terror that followed. Indeed, there is some evidence that Robespierre and his closest allies on the Committee of Public Safety were becoming increasingly wary of the degree of independence which the deputies enjoyed, and sought wherever possible to rein in their powers. Their distrust showed itself in various ways: in their insistence on regular reporting, even on the most mundane routine matters; in their encouragement of denunciations, particularly of deputies suspected of being too moderate or too closely linked to the local elites; and, finally, in the decision to recall many of the deputies to Paris in the summer of 1794. As we know from their reactions once they returned to Paris, many were horrified by the fear and suspicion that reigned, the lack of free speech and the ubiquitous sense of being overheard and spied upon. They detected a new extremism in the capital, one which they explained by the attitudes and mindset of Robespierre and his cronies, by his desire to dominate all around him and a blank refusal to listen to criticism. As the returned deputies breathed in the repressive atmosphere of the capital, they imagined themselves as the Terror's next victims and, where Robespierre talked of a plot, they created one. They were not moderates; among them were men who had been denounced in the provinces for their Jacobinism, who had openly espoused the cause of political terror, men like Collot and Fouché, Tallien and Billaud-Varenne. But that had been in the particular circumstances of Lyon or Bordeaux; now they saw themselves as defending the central tenets of the Revolution against extremist elements that sought to pervert it. Some wished to take advantage of the overthrow of Robespierre to make their utopia permanent, Robert Lindet, for instance, arguing both that they should return to the principles of 1789 and that they must retain the institutions and dynamism of the Jacobin republic.[42] Men like Lindet believed intensely in the values of the Revolution they had helped to create.

Virtually all the deputies-on-mission sent to the provinces between 1793 and 1795 shared that basic belief, though not all were terrorists. Nor can all departments be said to have had a terrorist experience, even in the summer of the Year II when terrorist legislation was most savage and government interest in the provinces most intrusive. In six departments, indeed, no death sentences were passed, including two in frontier areas (the Basses-Alpes and Hautes-Alpes) and two, even more surprisingly, that fell within the Paris Basin (the Aube and Seine-et-Marne). In a further thirty-one departments the number of executions did not exceed single figures. By way of contrast, Donald Greer listed five departments where there were more than a thousand executions, all, except for Paris itself, areas close to the civil war zone in the Vendée or to federalist Lyon; these five departments account for over 70 per cent of the executions ordered by the Revolutionary Tribunal and the other exceptional courts and military commissions set up to deal with political crimes and to enforce the special terrorist legislation.[43] Seen through this prism it is the unevenness of the terrorist experience across the French provinces, not its conformity, that makes the greater impression. Local revolutionary committees used contrasting levels of enthusiasm in their approach to repression. And where deputies-on-mission were sent out to departments, their impact, too, was demonstrably unequal.

In part, this inequality reflected the diverse temperaments of the deputies and the very different aims they sought to achieve. Some went with personal agendas, seeking to right alleged abuses of power or – a common desire among the sizeable minority of Jacobins who had been educated in seminaries or had entered the priesthood – to push through a programme of dechristianization. Claude-Alexandre Ysabeau was one such, a generally moderate deputy who nonetheless showed passion in denouncing refractory priests; but then, his was an anticlericalism that burned deep, since he was a former Oratorian who had accepted the Civil Constitution and made no secret of his contempt for the Catholic priesthood.[44] Again, both Pinet and Monestier, who took a certain pleasure in targeting refractory clergy during their missions to the Landes and the Pyrenees, had strong personal reasons to ratchet up anticlericalism: Monestier, in his youth in Clermont-Ferrand, had prepared for the priesthood and served for five years as a *curé* before the Civil Constitution; while his colleague Pinet came from a well-known Protestant family in the Périgord.[45] Neither came to the clerical issue without prejudice or deep-seated intellectual baggage. But the problem was not restricted to the few, or to those trying to escape from the legacy of their youth. Dislike of priests and the equation of Catholicism with superstition were common themes among the earlier *missionnaires*, the deputies who scoured much of the countryside in the winter months of 1793–4, and some, notably Joseph Fouché in the Nièvre and Claude Javogues in the Loire, took their anti-religious fanaticism to almost pathological extremes, closing down parish churches and committing a host of local acts of *vandalisme révolutionnaire*. A few moved rapidly from commune to commune, leaving swathes of abdications from the priesthood behind them as proof of their passage. This was the case, for instance, with Albitte in the Ain, Chateauneuf-Randon in the Massif Central or Joseph Maignet in Provence.[46] But they were not typical. More commonly, dechristianization is difficult to lay at the door of a single deputy or to ascribe to Paris alone. Like so much of the Terror, it had more of the character of a negotiation, the interaction of the deputy with militants on local revolutionary committees and in battalions of the revolutionary armies, as well as a tight connivance with local Jacobin activists and *sans-culottes*. The local community cannot be simply absolved of responsibility.

Some of the deputies sent out from the Convention earned a very different reputation, as moderates, men eager to explain their purpose to local officials and to work constructively with the local population. Nor can they all be dismissed, as some Jacobin apologists were wont to do, as being ineffectual, or as craven appeasers of local interests. There was often little reason to take extreme measures or set up exceptional jurisdictions: their value was greatest in regions of crisis, where there was civil war or foreign invasion, or where the federalist revolt seemed poised to threaten the authority of the Republic. Elsewhere the deputies' role was less intrusive, just as their stay was often shorter, a passage measured in days between longer sojourns in more troublesome areas. Take, for instance, the department of the Isère, a department which lay close both to the frontier with the kingdom of Piedmont and Sardinia and to federalist Lyon – the popular Lyon suburb of La Guillotière, like the rest of the land across the Rhône from the Presqu'ile, was part of the Isère, and since this was a separate police area, it was an eternally popular refuge for criminals and other fugitives from the second city[47] – but nonetheless succeeded in limiting the degree of political repression. One reason was that the behaviour of its population did little to arouse the authorities' suspicion. Its territory was not invaded; there was no suggestion of an uprising or armed conflict; and if Grenoble did mouth some sentiments that risked tarring local people with the brush of federalism, they were careful to limit the damage that was done and did not lift a finger in defence of Lyon. The reward, for the Isère, was a series of short missions which had a necessarily limited impact, often carefully targeted or with a clearly stated objective. Thus Amar and Merlino came in the spring of 1793 to help raise men for the *levée des 300,000*; then Albitte and Dubois-Crancé were sent with two colleagues to ensure the provisioning of the Armée des Alpes, while also maintaining general surveillance on the citizenry. Others followed, usually with military priorities, and sometimes very precise ones: in the autumn of 1793, for instance, Deydier was given the specific task of visiting the forges at Rives to ensure that sufficient supplies of steel were released to the state armouries at Paris and Saint-Étienne.[48] No special tribunals were set up in the Isère, no military commissions or terrorist courts. Florent Robin may well be right in supposing that this was a department where the presence of deputies from the Convention was not seen by local people as threatening, but rather as a source of reassurance, the more so as Grenoble still enjoyed considerable prestige in Paris for its role as the 'cradle of liberty' back in 1788.[49]

Contrasts between mild and extreme Terror, between the experiences of such neighbouring departments as the Isère and the Rhône, remind us that even at the height of the Robespierrist regime not everything can be explained in terms of an unambiguous tension between Paris and provincial France. Experience of Terror varied dramatically from moment to moment, from town to town, even from club to club, and it varied as much because of the views and temperament of local revolutionaries as it did through the intervention of deputies-on-mission. Jacobin clubs were not all alike, even if they shared a certain ethic, a moral code which valued probity and sacrifice and which became increasingly exclusive with the evolution of the Republic.[50] Some were ultra-moderate, even throwing in their lot with the Girondins in the summer of 1793 and almost inviting the inevitable purge that followed. Others were openly *Maratiste*, keen to advance the Revolution in their community and to use all the power of the law to that end. Such clubs were highly critical of any sign of moderation on the part of deputies from the Convention, looking to them to stiffen local resolve rather than seek harmony or compromise. When the deputy-on-mission to the Hérault, Boisset, showed signs of wishing to moderate the Terror by dissolving the departmental *comité de surveillance*, he met bitter opposition from both the club in Montpellier and the Jacobin-dominated *comité de surveillance* at Agde. They saw him as a dangerous moderate and urged the Convention to increase the intensity of Terror in the area rather than reduce it. 'You seem intent, Boisset,' they addressed the hapless deputy, 'on stretching to the limit the tolerance of the Maratistes of Agde. All right, we declare ourselves in a state of open war with you. We denounce you to the Montagne which had chosen you to be the exterminating angel of those bastards whom you are openly favouring and whom you are stirring up, even against us'.[51] For Boisset this onslaught was a sobering experience, a timely reminder that Paris had no monopoly of radicalism. It also led to his removal.

This is a salutary tale, a reminder that, however insistent local clubbists were in their praise of Paris as the fount of revolutionary truth and virtue, they also responded to more local stimuli, and it could be argued that terror could only really grab the popular imagination where it built on local prejudice and popular sensibilities. In many towns the club membership represented a spread of such prejudices – since Jacobinism was essentially an urban movement, the same claim can less often be made for rural areas – and dechristianization and sacrilegious vandalism often originated among local militants as much as with deputies from the capital. Levels of dechristianization varied hugely from place to place, and if in some areas it was actively encouraged by the deputies-on-mission, elsewhere it was the work of mayors, councillors and club militants, who burned documents and destroyed holy relics. At Corbeil, for instance, it was a local deputation of 'the mayor, the municipal officers and the president of the popular society' who went to the church of Saint-Spire to remove the bones of Saint-Yon and the other contents of the local reliquaries. What followed was a clear act of public instruction, a lesson in the absurdity of superstition. The relics were taken on the cart normally used for removing the town's refuse, placed on a pyre in the main square and solemnly burned; the ashes were then transported on the same cart to the bridge across the Seine where they were tossed into the river.[52] In this case, local leaders may have been inspired by the anticlerical mood of the moment, and what they did was not inconsistent with what Paris was urging them to do; but the form which their vandalism took, their choice of targets, and the venom with which the ceremony was performed had their roots in local politics and the history of local communities. However dechristianization is defined, whether by acts of vandalism or clerical abdications, by addresses lauding the Supreme Being or the institution of the Cult of Reason, its intensity varied from region to region. The areas that were most marked by the movement, besides the Paris Basin, were the North and Picardy, Normandy, Berry and the Morvan in the centre, the valley of the Rhône and the departments of the South-East.[53]

For history played a significant part in defining the local configuration of Terror, both more distant history, like memories of struggles with the *Parlement* of Paris or of the Wars of Religion, or the early history of the Revolution itself. Where communities had long experience of conflict, or where the Revolution had introduced such conflict – most notably, perhaps, through the administrative division of the territory back in 1790 – they might pit themselves against a regional rival rather than against the capital: such was the case, for instance, with Bordeaux and Libourne, or Aix and Marseille. The seizure of property, the loss of land and status, the destruction of châteaux and the emblems of nobility, the emigration of leading families to Turin or Mainz, or across the frontier into Spain, all contributed to such divisions and stoked the fires of repression.[54] Or earlier atrocities were remembered, creating bitterness, hatred and a thirst for revenge that might later be assuaged under the guise of revolutionary justice. In the Gard, where Catholics and Protestants had battled in the streets of Nîmes in 1790, leaving over 300 dead and hundreds more bereaved, the Terror would again be steered by local militants, stirred by the threat of counter-revolution in the Cévennes and eager to exact their vengeance.[55] Similarly, in the Vaucluse, the atrocities of the early months of the Revolution had pitted Patriots against Catholics, Avignon against Carpentras, and had created a climate of intolerance that almost guaranteed the vigorous pursuit of a terrorist agenda.[56] And in the West, the legacy of civil war combined with the bullying, hectoring approach of many urban clubs to create a natural backdrop for terror and repressive excess. For the peasant, argues Paul Bois, the perceived enemy took the form less of a Parisian *sans-culotte* than of his counterpart in western towns and *bourgs*, a town–country animosity which he believes helped to turn peasants into counter-revolutionaries.[57] And though Bois's view has been challenged for being too extreme, even his critics would accept that urban radicals in the West and in Brittany helped to intensify feeling and deepen antagonisms.[58] The divisions within local society, in other words, already ran deep, so that communities which had witnessed serious political infighting in 1789 and 1790, or which had come through a violent, faction-ridden municipal revolution, were often prey to federalism in 1793, which in turn guaranteed that they would go on to endure a brutal and vengeful experience of Terror.

Not all provincial towns followed down this path, however. Faced with the reality of Terror – with the establishment of special courts and tribunals and the sight of neighbouring towns consumed by faction-fighting – many thought it prudent to stay silent. In the District of Apt, for instance, the chief investigator for the terrorist Commission d'Orange met with silence and a lack of cooperation from local people. No one spoke out; no denunciations were received; and there was no way in which the authorities could take action against the population.[59] Or local political leaders might take a hand to ensure that their towns were not subject to harsh persecution. Examples abound of Jacobin mayors and clubbists in provincial towns who allowed themselves to be swayed by sympathy and friendship when the letter of the law was quite clear. In Tarbes, Bertrand Barère offered a degree of protection to men who might otherwise have risked punishment. In Dax, the Jacobin leader, Samson Batbedat, knowingly refrained from sending his moderate predecessor – and former schoolmate – to the Revolutionary Tribunal in Paris.[60] There were many such communities, places where a degree of caution prevailed and the political classes closed rank to avoid repression, or where local militants were moved by humanity when they might otherwise have given way to the call of ideological purity. Despite the centralizing aims of the state, there was still room for manoeuvre, room in which to protect one's opponents or wilfully expose them to danger, to follow the dictates of Paris to the letter or listen to one's social conscience. If provincial societies responded very differently to that challenge, it demonstrates that even Jacobin centralism had its limits, and that Terror was a malleable idiom through which local politics continued to find expression.

Notes

1 Alison Patrick, *The Men of the First French Republic. Political Alignments in the National Convention of 1792* (Baltimore, 1972), appendix 4, pp. 340–58.

2 Ibid., p. 35.

3 Rossitza Tacheva, 'Sur certains aspects de l'activité sociale des Jacobins parisiens, 1792–94', in Michel Vovelle (ed.), *Paris et la Révolution* (Paris, 1989), p. 136.

4 For an analysis of the contributions of Chalier and Jourdan, see the excellent local studies of W. D. Edmonds, *Jacobinism and the Revolt of Lyon, 1789–93* (Oxford, 1990) and René Moulinas, *Histoire de la Révolution d'Avignon* (Avignon, 1986).

5 Michael L. Kennedy, *The Jacobin Clubs in the French Revolution, 1793–95* (New York, 2000), p. 56

6 A. Kuscinski, *Dictionnaire des conventionnels* (Paris, 1916), p. 400.

7 Olivier Coquard, 'Le Paris de Marat', in Michel Vovelle (ed.), *Paris et la Révolution*, p. 173.

8 William Scott, *Terror and Repression in Revolutionary Marseilles* (London, 1973), p. 186.

9 David Garrioch, *The Making of Revolutionary Paris* (Berkeley, CA, 2002), p. 302.

10 E. Lairtullier, *Les femmes célèbres de 1789 à 1795 et leur influence dans la Révolution* (Paris, 1840), pp. 200–1, quoted in Madelyn Guttwirth, *The Twilight of the Goddesses. Women and Representation in the French Revolutionary Era* (New Brunswick, NJ, 1992), p. 323.

11 Dominique Godineau, *The Women of Paris and their French Revolution* (Berkeley, CA, 1998), pp. 143–4.

12 Chantal Thomas, *The Wicked Queen. The Origins of the Myth of Marie-Antoinette* (New York, 1999), pp. 148–9.

13 Albert Soboul and Raymonde Monnier, *Répertoire du personnel sectionnaire parisien en l'an II* (Paris, 1985), p. 8.

14 Walter Markov and Albert Soboul (eds), *Die Sansculotten von Paris. Dokumente zur Geschichte der Volksbewegung, 1793–94* (East Berlin, 1957), p. 208.

15 Roland Gotlib, 'Les Gravilliers, plate-forme des enragés parisiens', in Michel Vovelle (ed.), *Paris et la Révolution*, pp. 115–16.

16 R. B. Rose, *The Enragés: Socialists of the French Revolution?* (Melbourne, 1965), p. 53.

17 R. B. Rose, 'The revolutionary committees of the Paris sections in 1793: a manuscript in the John Rylands Library', *Bulletin of the John Rylands Library* 35 (1952–3), pp. 95–8.

18 Richard Cobb, *Les armées révolutionnaires: instrument de la Terreur dans les départements, avril 1793–floréal an II* (2 vols, Paris, 1961–3), vol. 1, p. 83.

19 Ibid., vol. 1, p. 2.

20 Richard Cobb, *L'armée révolutionnaire parisienne à Lyon et dans la région lyonnaise (frimaire–prairial an II)* (Lyon, 1952), pp. 8–9.

21 Pierre Gérard, 'L'armée révolutionnaire de la Haute-Garonne, septembre 1793–nivôse an II', *Annales historiques de la Révolution française* 155 (1959), pp. 1–37.

22 Cobb, *Les armées révolutionnaires*, vol. 1, p. 232.

23 Patrice Gueniffey, *La politique de la Terreur. Essai sur la violence révolutionnaire, 1789–94* (Paris, 2000), p. 266.

24 Pierre Caron (ed.), *Paris pendant la Terreur: rapports des agents secrets du ministre de l'intérieur* (7 vols, Paris, 1910–78), vol. 4, 21 pluviôse II–10 ventôse II, p. 25.

25 John Hall Stewart, *A Documentary Survey of the French Revolution* (New York, 1951), p. 484.

26 Patrick, *Men of the First French Republic*, p. 115.

27 Michel Biard, 'La mission du 9 mars 1793', in Christine Le Bozec and Eric Wauters (eds), *Pour la Révolution Française. Études en hommage à Claude Mazauric* (Rouen, 1998), pp. 273–80.

28 Jean-Baptiste Louvet, 'Quelques notices pour l'histoire et le récit de mes périls depuis le 31 mai 1793', quoted in Michel Biard, *Missionnaires de la République: les représentants du peuple en mission, 1793–95* (Paris, 2002), p. 231.

29 Ivan Gobry, *Joseph le Bon: la Terreur dans le Nord de la France* (Paris, 1991).

30 Jean-Pierre Gross, *Saint-Just: sa politique et ses missions* (Paris, 1976).

31 Colin Lucas, *The Structure of the Terror. The Example of Javogues and the Loire* (Oxford, 1973).

32 Paul Mansfield, 'The Missions of Collot d'Herbois. A Study in his Political Career' (unpublished PhD thesis, Macquarie University, 1985).

33 Gaston-Martin, *La mission de Carrier à Nantes* (Paris, 1924).

34 Jacques Godechot, *Les institutions de la France sous la Révolution et l'Empire* (Paris, 1951), p. 308.

35 Jean-Pierre Gross, *Fair Shares for All: Jacobin Egalitarianism in Practice* (Cambridge, 1997), p. 17.
36 John Black Sirich, *The Revolutionary Committees in the Departments of France, 1793–94* (Cambridge, MA, 1943), pp. 118–19.
37 J. M. Roberts and John Hardman (eds), *French Revolution Documents* (Oxford, 1973), ii, pp. 151–2.
38 Henri Labroue, *La mission du conventionnel Lakanal dans la Dordogne en l'an II* (Paris, 1911).
39 Roberts and Hardman (eds), *French Revolution Documents*, ii, p. 179.
40 Gross, *Fair Shares For All*, p. 131.
41 Biard, *Missionnaires de la République*, p. 279.
42 Bronislaw Baczko, *Ending the Terror. The French Revolution after Robespierre* (Cambridge, 1994), p. 122.
43 Donald Greer, *The Incidence of the Terror during the French Revolution. A Statistical Interpretation* (Cambridge, MA, 1935), pp. 145–7.
44 A. Kuscinski, *Dictionnaire des conventionnels* (Paris, 1916), pp. 612–13.
45 Ibid., pp. 460–1, 495–6.
46 Michel Vovelle, *The Revolution against the Church* (Cambridge, 1991), pp. 124–5.
47 Richard Cobb, *Reactions to the French Revolution* (Oxford, 1972), pp. 45–6, 238–9.
48 Florent Robin, *Les représentants en mission dans l'Isère: chronique d'une Terreur 'douce'* (Paris, 2002), pp. 43–4.
49 Ibid., pp. 417–18.
50 Michel Vovelle, *Les Jacobins de Robespierre à Chevènement* (Paris, 1999), p. 54.
51 J.-C. Gégot, 'Le rôle des représentants-en-mission sous la Révolution dans l'Hérault', in *Les pratiques politiques en province à l'époque de la Révolution Française. Actes du colloque tenu à Montpellier les 18, 19 et 20 septembre 1987* (Montpellier, 1988), p. 273.
52 Serge Bianchi, 'Le "vandalisme" anti-féodal et le "vandalisme" anti-religieux dans le sud de l'Île-de-France de 1789 à l'an III', in Simone Bernard-Griffiths, Marie-Claude Chemin and Jean Ehrard (eds), *Révolution Française et 'vandalisme révolutionnaire'. Actes du colloque international de Clermont-Ferrand, 15–17 décembre 1988* (Paris, 1992), p. 161.
53 Claude Langlois, Timothy Tackett and Michel Vovelle (eds), *Atlas de la Révolution Française, vol. 9: Religion* (Paris, 1996), pp. 40–1.
54 Donald Greer, *The Incidence of the Emigration during the French Revolution* (Cambridge, MA, 1951), pp. 92–4.
55 Gwynne Lewis, *The Second Vendée. The Continuity of Counter-revolution in the Department of the Gard, 1789–1815* (Oxford, 1978), pp. 71–9.

56 Martine Lapied, *Le Comtat et la Révolution Française: naissance des options collectives* (Aix-en-Provence, 1996), especially pp. 105–28, 199–201.

57 Paul Bois, *Paysans de l'Ouest* (Paris, 1971), p. 356.

58 Roger Dupuy, *De la Révolution à la chouannerie. Paysans en Bretagne, 1788–94* (Paris, 1988), p. 326.

59 Jonathan Skinner, 'Republicanism and Royalism. The Conflicting Traditions of Peasant Politics in the Department of the Vaucluse, 1789–1851' (PhD thesis, University of Manchester, 1988), pp. 166–7.

60 For these and other examples of the diversity of provincial Terror, see Alan Forrest, 'The local politics of repression', in Keith Michael Baker (ed.), *The French Revolution and the Creation of Modern Political Culture, vol. 4: The Terror* (Oxford, 1994), pp. 81–98.

|10|

Centre and periphery under the Directory

Discontent both with terrorist legislation and the Jacobins who imposed it was already widespread before the palace revolution in the Convention which brought Robespierre's control of revolutionary politics to a close. Yet Terror had been very unevenly applied across the departments. In some regions local clubbists had vented their scorn for religion on the Church and its priests; in others they had tempered their reactions to maintain a vestige of social harmony. Taxes and military levies had been imposed with varying degrees of urgency, and their imposition had encountered widely different levels of resistance. And the more ferocious clauses of the Maximum law – like that obliging all merchants holding goods defined as essential commodities to send lists of their stocks to their local commune on pain of death – were applied only spasmodically.[1] Hatreds had been most inflamed in those areas where more extreme egalitarian views prevailed in the local club, or where the Paris *armée révolutionnaire* intervened to extort cheap grain to provision the capital. In some of the poorest districts of the Île-de-France, for instance, like Senlis, Mantes and Compiègne, the Jacobins paid a heavy price in local hatred for their policy of delivering cheap bread to Paris.[2] But outside the capital and its immediate hinterland there had been no shared experience of Jacobinism, with the result that Jacobins were perceived differently in different parts of the country; and when news filtered through in late July or early August of 1794 that the Jacobin government had fallen, people reacted with varying levels of excitement. In some communities, those which had suffered particularly from Jacobin rule, the relief was palpable, as in Lyon or much of the West. But others, like much of Picardy, had remained staunchly Jacobin throughout the months of the Terror, and here the news could only fill local leaders with apprehension. In any case, the full significance of what had happened was not immediately evident. Factions had fallen before; there was no reason to believe that this necessarily signalled a dramatic turning point. The Ninth of Thermidor did not have the same resonance for everyone, and it took time for the realization to sink in that the Terror, as it had been practised during the previous twelve months, had indeed come to an end.

Though in Paris the overthrow of the government seemed short and incisive – a series of carefully orchestrated speeches in the Convention, the arrest of Robespierre, Saint-Just and a few of their closest henchmen, a rapid and formulaic appearance before the Revolutionary Tribunal, and the journey to the guillotine, all completed within twenty-four hours – news took some time to filter down to the rest of the country. In the South-West, for instance, it would be 15 *thermidor* before it reached Bordeaux, 18 *thermidor* for Bayonne, and into *fructidor* by the time the mountain communities of Catalonia learned that the ordeal of the Terror was finally over.[3] The news was often followed by the sorts of rumours and justifications which had been circulating in the capital, carefully nurtured by Billaud-Varenne, Collot d'Herbois and others, claiming that Robespierre and his associates were 'conspirators', planning to destroy liberty and overthrow the Convention, to seize power and rule France despotically without any reference to the people, to organize a new 'Saint Bartholomew's Day' that would see their opponents and rivals massacred. Pamphlets circulated in Paris and some of the major provincial cities delighting in the unmasking of this plot, denouncing a supposed alliance of Robespierre and Hanriot and revealing plans to assassinate all the deputies so as to leave Robespierre supreme. In the confusion that followed just about anything seemed credible, no story too exaggerated, no detail too far-fetched. Robespierre was a counter-revolutionary; he was bent on destroying the Convention; he was in league with France's enemies. There were even rumours that he had aimed to marry Louis XVI's daughter, seize the throne and put 80,000 revolutionaries to death.[4] Hence it was hardly surprising that provincial France tended to rejoice with the new regime, rushing with greater than customary alacrity to send messages of congratulation and to side with the Thermidorians. Addresses flowed in from municipal councils and popular societies across the country, expressing shock at the latest revelations, denouncing the 'hated triumvirs', and thanking the deputies for their vigilance in unmasking a horrible act of treason.[5] Even those who had, only a few days earlier, sided with Robespierre now expressed unqualified relief at his overthrow.

The provinces had been spectators to Robespierre's fall; they had had no direct input into what was a peculiarly Parisian *journée*, a palace revolution made in the heart of the Convention and in the clubs and bars and smoking dens where deputies went to socialize. It was an intra-Jacobin coup, the work of men who thought of themselves as good and committed republicans, members of the Jacobin club, many of them former terrorists who had returned from missions in the provinces. For the first time in months they breathed the atmosphere of a Paris that they barely recognized, where sectional radicals had acquired unparalleled power and where no one could be trusted: every corridor, it seemed, hosted a conspiracy and every pillar concealed a spy.

Robespierre was known to distrust the deputies and to rely more and more on personal agents – men like Marc-Antoine Jullien, whom he had sent to Nantes and Bordeaux to report to him directly on the failings of deputies sent out by the Convention.[6] Paris was riddled with police agents and spies: the police made routine use of the evidence of informers, paying an army of *mouchards* in the markets, bars and prisons of the capital, anywhere where they might hope to overhear indiscreet talk, and pressurizing barmen and innkeepers, concierges and prostitutes to report on the activities and the associates of suspects.[7] The stepping-up of the activity of such spies in the summer of 1794 was a clear sign that a new wave of Terror was in the offing. Robespierre stayed away from the Convention, shunning its debates for six long weeks before returning to mouth vague threats of further purges, threats that were so imprecise and all-embracing that they were a challenge to everyone. Paris, in short, seemed to be breathing fear and distrust, stoked by a handful of men loyal to Robespierre and by the more extreme Maratistes of the Paris Commune. The conspirators believed that they had no choice: either they made a pre-emptive strike against Robespierre and his inner circle, or they waited until he turned the screw of Terror still tighter, with themselves the likeliest victims. There was nothing terribly principled about their actions. They saw the coup as being necessary if they were to save their own necks and acted swiftly to neutralize their opponents.[8]

Yet 9 thermidor was not quite a Parisian *journée* in the classic mould. That would have involved more than the manoeuvrings of politicians and scheming in the galleries of the Palais Royal. The *journées* of 31 May to 2 June 1793, which toppled the Girondins and brought Robespierre to power – the Parisian revolution, incidentally, to which contemporaries most frequently compared Thermidor – might have started in that way, as groups of politicians used their influence and their connections in the Club and the sections to build up their power base and prepare to seize power. But then, as on all previous *journées*, they were supported by the people of the capital, by violence and popular emotion which contributed elements of threat and brute strength to the process. And if, back in 1789, popular involvement in politics had generally appeared fairly spontaneous and unplanned, increasingly the people of the capital had found their leaders and their organization, to become an effective ally of the Jacobins in Parisian politics. They had been present at all the key moments when the Jacobins had increased their stranglehold over political life, present and exigent as they demanded greater economic controls, harsher Terror against the rich and against moderates, more egalitarian social legislation. But on 9 *thermidor* the sections barely mobilized, and the response of the National Guard was poor. Those who did congregate on the Place de Grève allowed themselves to be persuaded to disperse with little protest or violence.[9]

Why did the sections and especially the Commune stand by in this way? There are two possible explanations. The first is the more political, that there was little reason for the sections to support the government after the events of the previous months had driven a wedge between them. Their agenda and Robespierre's had never been the same, and their alliance was little more than a temporary one of convenience, useful to both sides in their common struggle against moderate opposition. They had little common ideology beyond a deep patriotism and devotion to the Republic. The split between those who wanted economic intervention and those who sought further liberalization, between advocates of sectional autonomy and those of centralization, was only too predictable, and it was made explicit when, in March 1794, the Terror was turned against Jacques-René Hébert and others whom the radical sections saw as heroes and role models. Few doubted that the 'conspiracy' for which he and eighteen of his associates went to the guillotine was a crudely fabricated affair, or that their trial was simply a way of ridding the government of men it saw as troublesome. It caused deep animosity in popular areas of the capital, and led the more radical sectional leaders to quit office or to withdraw discreetly from politics. The Cordeliers were silenced, and long before Thermidor the popular, democratic phase of the revolution was effectively over.[10] And so, when his enemies lined up to claim their turn to denounce Robespierre, the Paris radicals stayed off the streets, seeing little interest in maintaining an unloved regime in power. The second explanation is more prosaic, the result of circumstance rather than planning. The Convention acted swiftly to accuse Robespierre of treason, a charge that may have warned off possible supporters in the popular movement, who were taken by surprise and left in a state of some confusion. It may also have been raining. The *sans-culotte* was an activist, driven by ideological fervour, and the circumstances of the Ninth of Thermidor were not such as to engage his enthusiasm.[11]

The immediate impact of Thermidor was also greatest in the capital, where the new rulers set about their proclaimed aim of dismantling revolutionary government and abolishing the institutions of Terror. Within weeks the Convention had taken steps to re-establish its authority and to destroy the close-knit executive infrastructure that had made Terror possible. At the heart of the problem lay the Committee of Public Safety, which had extended its power over virtually every aspect of government; and though it was not abolished, its influence was greatly reduced. From 24 August executive power divided between sixteen different committees, each with a rotating membership and a strictly defined brief. The new Committee of Public Safety was left to run the war and foreign affairs, but responsibility for internal policy was deliberately split between several committees: General Security still had control of internal order and policing, while the Finance Committee retained its independence in money matters, and the Legislative Committee was given responsibility for internal administration and justice.[12] The Convention was, quite specifically, taking back powers which had been alienated and reimposing its authority on politics. In the same spirit it sought to reduce the power of Paris, and the influence that had been enjoyed by the Paris Commune and the radical sections, using the argument of normalization to ensure that they could never again trouble public order. The sections might continue to meet, but without the attendance payments, which had ensured a large turnout among the radical *sans-culottes* under the Jacobins, popular interest tailed away. In part, no doubt, their decline can be attributed to the successful pursuit of the war and the repression of their leaders during the previous months. But the Thermidorians also isolated the popular movement from the decision-making process and prosecuted those radical leaders in the Convention who had been their political allies. Without a role in politics, and with Paris increasingly exposed to dearth and starvation, the *sans-culottes* found themselves powerless and paralysed. They might be driven to moments of insurrection in the Year III, at *germinal* and *prairial*, but they had ceased to count as a force in politics.[13] Paris was now treated like any large city, though it was still feared for what it represented and for the violence of which it was capable. Its role as the capital of revolution, however, was over. Or rather, its role had become largely symbolic, a beacon of revolution to inspire future generations. As Patrice Higonnet observes, from 1795 and for much of the following century, Paris continued to exert a powerful influence because of what it represented, 'a constructed memory of who the *sans-culottes* had been and what they had wanted'.[14]

The new government made clear its desire to establish a solid political order and to end the excesses of Terror. That did not mean that the polity was changed overnight. Those in power were still Jacobins, many of them yesterday's terrorists or deputies-on-mission, cleansed only of those of their number who had been closely identified with Robespierre. They felt it necessary to make a clear statement of their philosophy, and there were many questions to which Frenchmen wanted answers. Were they staunchly republican? Did they intend to restore Christian worship? What was their attitude to former Girondins, or to those émigrés who expressed a desire to return? And how would they react to the loud demands that were heard throughout France for some form of retribution to be taken against those who had promoted terror, the local clubbists and prosecutors, deputies and public officials whose policies over the previous thirteen months had resulted in the deaths of so many good citizens? France was in no mood for forgiveness, particularly in those areas which had experienced an extreme and bloody Terror, and the new government had to decide quickly whether it would stand out for the rule of law or give in to strident calls for vengeance. Here it was helped by the nature of the Ninth of Thermidor itself, by the fact that the Thermidorian regime was founded on a parliamentary coup rather than on popular violence. Unlike previous revolutionary regimes, it did not have to confront the problem, so central to the French Revolution, of the double nature of violence, or to legitimate public disorder as one of the foundation stones of the constitution. Moreover, since the uprisings of *germinal* and *prairial* were aimed against the constitution, the Thermidorians could dissociate themselves from the action of the streets and denounce popular violence – in particular Parisian violence – as being wholly criminal in intent.[15]

The tone of Thermidorian politics was set by the decision to prosecute the terrorist *comité révolutionnaire* of Nantes, a trial which, over a period of nearly two months, exposed the excesses that had been committed in the name of the Revolution in the West.[16] Hundreds of victims passed through the courtroom to give evidence – in all, 220 witnesses were heard – and though Carrier himself was not initially on trial, his was the name mentioned in every news article and pamphlet, his the head that everyone seemed to be demanding. Public opinion screamed for his arrest, insisting that the past had not been set to rest by the executions on 10 *thermidor* and that public anger had to be appeased. On the same evening as he was arrested, an angry crowd of monarchists and other *jeunes gens* stormed the Paris Jacobin Club, demanding its closure. Carrier's was, of course, a show trial whose outcome was never in doubt, an opportunity for the public to gaze on a monster who had gratuitously slaughtered so many civilians, for pamphleteers to dredge up every detail of sadism and sexual depravity, and for the regime to cleanse itself of unsavoury associations. He defended himself by claiming – as those in executive roles customarily do – that he had simply acted on the orders he had received from the Convention; his errors, if such they were, were shared by the rest of the deputies, and by putting him on trial the deputies were also judging themselves.[17] But his words made little impact, and the trial ended, as it was predestined to end, in his conviction and execution on the Place de la Révolution. Public opinion demanded nothing less, but what is more significant is that the Thermidorians allowed him to be prosecuted and threw the weight of governmental authority against him. In vain did Carrier call upon his former colleagues in the Convention to show a degree of loyalty and solidarity; he was too notorious, too widely hated, not to form the perfect scapegoat for all that had gone before. It was a landmark decision, for in sacrificing Carrier the new regime helped establish its own identity and distinguish itself from the Terror that had preceded it. During the following month, on the pretext that crowd violence was a threat to public order, the Convention ordered the closure of the Paris Jacobins, and so another part of Paris's radical identity was destroyed.

If the government increasingly gave way to demands for vengeance in Paris, for rooting out close collaborators of the Robespierrist regime, those described satirically and somewhat picturesquely as *la queue de Robespierre*,[18] what was the reaction in the rest of France? At first there was considerable confusion, as local officials waited to be informed of the exact nature of the political change they had experienced; but letters soon arrived from the capital, or commissioners were sent there to collect news, while local deputies wrote to their constituents providing their reading of events at the centre. There was soon a flurry of paper as local towns and clubs sent addresses and eulogies to Paris. Everyone, it seemed, rushed to praise the Convention for saving liberty and overthrowing tyranny – their addresses routinely rejoiced in the fate of the *buveurs de sang*, the treacherous hydra, the new Cromwell risen among us[19] – but more in hope than expectation. The majority simply wanted an end to bloodshed and the cycle of denunciation and exe-cution. But little changed, at least immediately. France was still governed under the same constitution, that voted under the Jacobins; deputies still circulated on their regular missions to the provinces (sometimes the very same men as had preached Terror three months earlier); *agents nationaux* still acted as prosecutors; and if individual judges on the Revolutionary Tribunals and military commissions were sometimes purged, their roles continued to be carried out by others. A few newspapers which had been outspoken in their support for Terror were prudently closed, but more com-monly Thermidor was greeted as a new dawn of press freedom – particu-larly for papers of an anti-Jacobin persuasion which played to the political mood of the day. In Marseille, for instance, Ferréol Beaugeard profited from the changed climate to resume publication of his *Journal de Marseille*, and through its pages to preach an unremitting campaign against the former Jacobin leadership of the city.[20] Along with the radical press, the Jacobin club movement in the provinces came under pressure. The months follow-ing Thermidor saw a gradual but relentless decline in the number of provin-cial societies and the influence which they could exert on the authorities. Some stopped all correspondence; most lost the right to petition local coun-cils; a few, like that in La Rochelle, were closed by deputies-on-mission from Paris as part of the process of normalization after the Terror.[21] Through public apathy as much as through official persecution, they drifted into insignificance. Some passed new constitutions to rid themselves of their for-mer egalitarian principles, as men who had been prosecuted under the Terror returned to resume their places. Others simply saw their membership fade away as their meetings became more and more perfunctory and bureau-cratic. Club membership, which had once been so dearly cherished, was now seen as a liability and meetings were scantly attended. At Le Havre, a club that had regularly commanded attendances of two to three hundred at the height of the Terror could claim only about twenty, six months after Robespierre fell. Provincial clubs were dying, the fall in their membership resulting in an equally serious decline in levels of income. Around 270 of them were forced to close their doors in the twelve months after Thermidor, especially, though not exclusively, in response to the closure of the Paris Jacobins.[22]

The government hoped that this process of normalization could be achieved peacefully, with a transfer of authority from the radical militants who had controlled local sections, clubs and revolutionary committees to the legally constituted local authorities. If the committees and courts were not immediately abolished, their purpose underwent a clear change. Whereas previously they had been used to pursue those who deviated from the path of virtue, now they attacked the former terrorists and their agents. Those towns where terror had been most intense during 1793 and 1794 invariably had their own scores to settle, their local Carriers to pursue. In Bordeaux, for instance, the Terror was only considered to be over once the president of the terrorist *Commission Militaire*, Jean-Baptiste Lacombe, had been arrested and tried for a string of offences dating from his months in power, from extortion and the misappropriation of public funds to abuse of trust and corruption of morals, crimes that were, in the court's words, sufficiently odious to merit the death penalty. His trial, like Carrier's, was carefully staged, its outcome never in doubt; and it provided its share of theatre for the people of Bordeaux to enjoy. Ysabeau, who had been a terrorist deputy-on-mission in the city only a few months earlier, returned to play his part in sending Lacombe to the guillotine.[23]

Trials like Lacombe's were part of the legal apparatus for ending the Terror, the last acts of a judicial system that was about to be demolished. They were regarded by the authorities as a necessary part of public expiation, symbolic moments that were intended to draw a curtain around the exceptional and often cruelly disproportionate justice of the previous months. With his execution a chapter could be closed, and the job of recreating some sort of normality could be seriously broached. Within hours, for instance, Ysabeau ordered the removal of the guillotine from the central square where it had stood, glowering menacingly at the local population, and began the task of freeing the 2,400 suspects who were still held in the city's prisons.[24] Its work, it was implied, was done. The Ninth of Thermidor had restored the rule of law: the era of factional politics was over and France could get back to the task of building a stable republican order from which all would benefit. This notion was naively optimistic, since much more was jettisoned in the search for this new order than just the excesses of the Terror. By placing such strong emphasis on legality and the stability of the political order, the Thermidorians talked a different language from their predecessors, one that omitted all reference to a republic of virtue, to human perfectibility and regeneration. If the Ninth of Thermidor marked the end of the Terror, it also spelt the end of idealism and the death of revolutionary utopia.[25] It implied an acceptance that government should be left to elected councillors and professional administrators – something that seemed incomprehensible to the idealists and political militants who had lived through the turbulence of the previous five years.

These principles were enshrined in the constitution of the Year III and the local government reforms which accompanied it, laying down the parameters of local administration during the directorial years. The constitution gave France its first bicameral legislature, consisting of a *Conseil des Anciens* of 250 members as an upper house and the larger *Conseil des Cinq-cents* as a lower house. It was designed to avoid a return to the factionalism of the Jacobin republic, to stabilize republican institutions and 'steer a course between the extremes of royalist reaction and Jacobin anarchy'.[26] But it was also highly complex and difficult for the public to understand. Who could and could not take part? To be a member of the *Conseil des Anciens*, one had to be aged forty, an elector and resident in France for at least fifteen years; to qualify for the *Cinq-cents*, one had to be at least thirty and resident for ten years. To vote, a man had to be twenty-one and pay taxes; he was also required to have lived for twelve months in the canton. Election was indirect, with electors choosing delegates from among their wealthier fellow citizens in proportion to population: they were to have one delegate for every 200 registered electors. There would be annual elections for one-third of the deputies, though in the first elections deputies were to be elected to a single legislative body, then allocated by those qualifying as *Anciens* by the drawing of lots for the upper house. To make matters even more confusing, the document that was the subject of the plebiscite of 1795 also contained two codicils, electoral decrees that further modified electors' freedom – one demanding that two-thirds of the new deputies should be chosen from among members of the outgoing Convention, the other specifically exclud- ing sixty-seven former Montagnards from standing in future. The plebiscite was approved, of course; but the confusion of the electors was reflected in low turnouts at the polls, while results unwelcome to the government could be invalidated if either royalists or neo-Jacobins posed a threat to public order.[27] In these circumstances it might seem easy to deride the directorial elections as shallow and unrepresentative, an opportunity for conservative elites to reimpose a political domination that had been broken under the Convention. In some places – especially in the cities – men who had fled during the Terror returned to resume what they saw as their rightful pos- itions on local authorities. But in other parts of France participation levels, especially in the Years IV and V, suggest a rather greater commitment to electoral politics.[28] Moreover, what the electoral lists show most clearly is less a record of apathy than the emergence of a local republican aristocracy, a new political elite that controlled the essential posts of local government. Slates of candidates began to be presented – whether conservative republi- cans, royalists or neo-Jacobins – that would seem to indicate the demise of individualism in favour of distinct groups and political identities.[29]

This was not quite what Paris had intended when it had drafted the con- stitution of 1795. It had introduced a number of reforms to local govern- ment, modifying the centralized administrative system introduced during the Terror, but still maintaining clear lines of authority. The Thermidorians had no interest in decentralization, and the Directory would retain a high level of central control. The main changes that were introduced aimed at simplicity and a degree of concentration. The largest cities, those with more than 100,000 inhabitants, were divided into cantons, in part to emasculate the power of the most powerful provincial centres where Jacobin politics had been most evident. Bordeaux, for instance, was subdivided into three – cantons of the North, South and Centre – with a single *bureau central* to coordinate municipal government and to assure the policing of the city.[30] At the other end of the scale, communes with fewer than 5,000 people lost their elected municipal councils; instead, they elected an *agent national* to ensure their representation on the new cantonal administrations. In this way, much of the authority of the old districts, which many saw as contaminated with Jacobin influence, was transferred to the cantons, which in future would provide the link in the administrative chain between the commune and the department. Under the new system, responsibility for large parts of local government and local services rested with the department, whose authority was greatly enhanced: it controlled policing and public order, finance and tax collection, public works projects and education. But the departmental council was neither widely representative of the people it served nor directly answerable to them; it consisted of five men, mostly drawn from the main towns, with one of them renewable each year. And its work was closely supervised by a *commissaire du Directoire*, appointed by the Directory, who was to be present at departmental meetings and whose views were sought before any vote was taken.[31] *Commissaires*, indeed, were a major feature of directorial local administration, and were appointed at every level of local government, in cantons and municipalities as well as in departments. They offered the guarantee that decisions would be taken in an ordered manner and reported up the line to a higher authority. They reduced the need for broad political involvement and avoided what Paris saw as the overly political outlook of many local militants. In the process they created a very hierarchical system where any vestige of dialogue between communes, cantons and departments was removed, and where the appointed *commissaires* already had some of the characteristics of Napoleonic prefects, loyal to the state, answerable to Paris and appointed and removed without reference to the local community.[32] They had to report regularly to Paris under a specified series of rubrics that left little to chance or personal initiative. Within a year it was clear that their primary responsibility lay in the field of public opinion, informing the minister of riots, disturbances and outbreaks of discontent.[33] The special laws of the Terror might have been removed, but what had replaced them remained highly centralist and often highly directed.

Disengaging from Terror at local level would turn out to be both more difficult and more violent than the politicians in Paris had imagined. For if among the electors there was a tendency to continue to support the public authorities – in Paris in the Year IV, for instance, their steadfastness was a major element in preventing the city from falling to the royalists[34] – large sections of the population at large noisily shouted their scorn for the revolutionaries, or at least for such of them as they identified with Terror in their communities. They understood Thermidor as a moment when they could properly settle accounts, and were in no mood to seek the stabilization of the republic or offer their protection for a republican settlement. And without local support for that cause, neither the Thermidorians nor the First Directory could hope to achieve their primary goal, that of leading France out of the unruliness and turmoil of revolution, away from a polity that was constantly racked by internal division. To achieve that, Paris had to persuade the provinces to forget the wrongs of the past three years and unite behind the new constitution. But here it failed. In the countryside the refractory clergy continued to haunt areas loyal to the Catholic Church, while among the more respectable, innately conservative bourgeois of the towns, royalism began to make converts. The first of the émigrés, their intolerance of republicanism hardened by their experience of exile, began to filter back across the Rhine or the Pyrenees. Kernels of opposition to the regime began to form. The result was a republic undermined and ultimately destroyed by violence, from royalist uprisings to troubles over conscription, from bread riots in the cities to full-blown insurrection in the West and South-West. The royalist rising of 18 Fructidor was particularly damaging, since the government became dependent on the army and had to sacrifice the rule of law in a crude bid to stay in office. The period after Fructidor is marked by authoritarianism, violations of the constitution, the erosion of democracy and inexorable centralization.[35] As Colin Lucas notes, this adds up to an ultimate failure.

> Whatever the successes the Directory may have had in such areas as the stabilization of the currency, the containment of militant extremism, the repression of banditry and the organization of the bureaucracy, it did not attain the fundamental political objective of the union of the nation behind the government in defence of an agreed revolutionary settlement.[36]

Much of the opposition came from the Right, especially in 1795 and again in 1797. Both in the capital and in many provincial cities young men of bourgeois and aristocratic backgrounds saw the post-Robespierrist regime as theirs. Reclaiming the streets and pavements for their own, and forming themselves into bands of *jeunesse dorée*, fashionably and even foppishly attired, they proclaimed their opposition to all that was plain and egalitarian. In particular, they resented the destruction of elegance and style, of public entertainments, theatre and any notion of fun in the name of some hateful concept of virtue. Dress was again a form of political expression, just as it had been for the sectional militants with their cockades and liberty caps. The *jeunes gens* wore ostentatious waistcoats and expensive silk cloaks to signify that the era of drab conformity was finally over. They derided the plain clothing and plaited hair of the now discredited Jacobins as extravagant fashions gave expression to a new kind of anti-revolutionary identity, the self-indulgence and flaunted luxury of the *incroyables*. Or, as Richard Wrigley has expressed it, 'actively dressing up rather than down signalled an uninhibited liberation from and non-compliance with the residual post-Thermidorian republican ethos'.[37] By showing off their style and wealth they were making a deliberate political gesture, and one which, they knew, would arouse the animosity of the popular classes and more committed republicans.

The theatre was a favoured gathering place for the *jeunes gens*, just as it had been under the *ancien régime* when the stage had flourished both in Paris and in the larger provincial cities. The fact that no national elections were held for nearly two years after the fall of Robespierre, while the government also revoked the right of association to curb the emergence of organized opposition, gave the theatre a new importance as the most significant political space available to those Frenchmen who sought to make their opinions felt.[38] Factions gathered to out-shout and out-sing one another, and for the Right this presented a particular opportunity. In theatres up and down the country, young men of the law and the professions could now enjoy one another's company in a certain style, while taking full advantage of the anonymity of the pit to participate in the entertainment on offer: cheering their preferred actresses, booing any reference to the political correctness of the day, joining in royalist refrains, and generally turning the occasion into a political morality play in which audience and actors alike were implicated. In Paris these young *muscadins* rapidly became the most visible force for political reaction, disrupting civic festivals, removing Marat from the Pantheon and creating their own anti-Jacobin fête on 2 *pluviôse* to commemorate the death of Louis XVI. As Mallet du Pan remarked, they 'henceforth formed the sovereign people; judges in all the theatres, oracles in all the cafés, orators in all the sections, in a word the magistrates of public opinion'.[39] In the eyes of royalists and moderates they were heroes, combining a rollicking lifestyle with brutal and thuggish assaults on those they saw as their enemies, and showing a healthy contempt for both the *sans-culottes* and the public morality which they associated with the Year II. Theirs was a social as well as a political movement, for just as they asserted their right to the city and the enjoyment of a conspicuous pattern of consumption, so they reclaimed the carefree, hedonistic years of adolescence that had been so rudely taken from them by the puritanism of the Jacobin movement. For the Thermidorian leadership they provided welcome, if unpredictable, allies, effervescent and uncompromising as they expressed their revulsion for everything the Jacobins had done and sought to efface the carefully controlled symbolism of the revolutionary years. Too often their political involvement did not stop with symbolic gestures, however; both in Paris and in provincial centres the *jeunes gens* sought to avenge the victims of Terror, leading to incidents of anarchic violence and murder. Their ranks included many who had little truck with the republic, including those *ultras* and committed royalists who were happy to join Fréron in his conservative crusade against the republic. They warmed to the violence of his language and his denunciation of the materialism of *philosophes* like Voltaire and d'Holbach.[40] And they followed him in baying for reprisals against the men of blood of 1794, turning their anger against anyone who seemed compromised by the Terror and launching massed attacks after *prairial* on the popular faubourgs of northern and eastern Paris.[41]

Lyon provided an ideal social and political environment for the *jeunes gens*; a city whose suffering during the previous months guaranteed that their ideas would find a willing audience. Around 2,000 people had been shot or guillotined; the city had been besieged by the forces of the Convention; and in the course of the siege some of its finest buildings, both along the quays of the Rhône and round the Place Bellecour, had been reduced to rubble or left pockmarked by artillery fire. Lyon emerged from the Republic physically diminished, with its territory reduced to eleven cantons, its economy shattered by war and emigration, and its population down by around one-fifth when compared to 1789. It counted itself among the victims of the Revolution and the egalitarian views of the Jacobin republic, since 'more than any other city in France it had suffered both in its pride and in its flesh'.[42] The *jeunes gens* knew how to turn that suffering to their advantage, playing on the indignation of local people and imposing their own form of justice on the community. Especially targeted were the men who had served the terrorist authorities or had provided them with information; in this, Lyon's *compagnie de Jésus* was aided by the timely publication in Lausanne in 1795 of a list of those who had denounced or been denounced in the Lyonnais, a publication that ran to over ninety pages, listing last known addresses and constituting a sort of directory for counter-terrorists. It was mirrored in a score of *livres rouges* throughout the Midi and helped open the way to an orgy of revenge killing throughout the region. In Lyon, with the municipal police seriously under strength and unable to enforce the law, and with the political authorities indifferent to their activities, the killers had a field day. As well as the individual execution-style killings that were the hallmark of White Terror, the region was awash with popular violence as mobs attacked prisons and massacred their inmates. At Bourg-en-Bresse six terrorists were murdered as they were being transferred to prison in Lons-le-Saunier; while in Lyon and its immediate vicinity the attacks on prisons multiplied and the death toll mounted, seemingly beyond the control of either the local authorities or the military. Forty-one were murdered at Roanne, while in Lyon itself there were massacres at three prisons, the Recluses, Saint-Joseph and Saint-Genis-Laval.[43] The killers were aided by the collusive geography of France's second city and its position on the edge of another department, the Isère, to which they often escaped; they were helped, too, by its unique topography of cramped streets between the Rhône and Saône, and mean, almost perpendicular *traboules* clinging to the slopes of the Croix-Rousse. Lyon was full of dark corners and secret spaces out of view of the authorities, while bodies could always be dumped in the fast-flowing waters of the Rhône. It made, in Richard Cobb's words, a natural capital for murder; and in Lyon after 1793 murder acquired a certain respectability. Here 'there was no frontier between private vengeance and collective vengeance, while any murder was political, or at least would at once be taken as so'.[44]

That judgment applies equally to much of the Midi after 1794, or at least to those parts of the region which retained a burning sense of hatred for the men who had brought Terror to their homes and families. For White Terror was essentially about revenge, and it could only flourish in those areas where individuals and families had suffered great hurt, and where there was a keen desire for vengeance. Revenge was the common theme of many of the murders and ambushes that punctuated the years of the Thermidorians and Directory in the South-East; only the intensity of such murders varied with the strength of policing and the national political climate. In the spring and summer of 1795, Jacobins in a broad area of the South-East were singled out for such vengeance attacks; these fell away somewhat in 1796 when the government tried to install former Jacobins in positions of public responsibility in the region, only to be revitalized in the following year against a background of ultra-conservatism and royalist plotting. But it would be a mistake to dwell too much on any conservative or counter-revolutionary organization here; a lot of the killing was individual, or the work of small groups of local men or army deserters. Colin Lucas has suggested that in the violence that characterized the region it is possible to distinguish three distinct strands which all contributed to the general lawlessness of the area and helped to pin down government forces throughout the 1790s and into the Consulate.[45] The first was peasant unrest and the sorts of brigandage that were characteristic of mountain areas, traditional violence exacerbated by the demands of recruitment and requisitioning. The second was the violence of organized bands of insurgents, often using the language of counter-revolution and the refractory Church, those who followed leaders like Saint-Christol and Lestang in the badlands of the southern Drôme. They were local men, the sons of peasants and rural artisans from local villages, following local *chefs*, and carrying out their attacks in a terrain that they knew well, always in a clearly defined perimeter.[46] The third category was more individual, communal violence in towns and villages that had suffered in the Terror and which now turned the former terrorists into victims, ambushing them in their homes, gunning them down on their way from work, spreading fear through a policy of cold-blooded assassination. These murders occurred all the way down the Rhône valley and across the southern plain; they were most common in the immediate aftermath of Thermidor when the desire for blood and revenge was most ardent and much of southern France still prey to localized anarchy.

In the Midi, family politics ran deep: this was the land of feuds and vendettas, where sons fought and murdered to save their fathers' honour and where wrongs did not go unpunished. Revenge had more to do with land and family than with revolutionary politics, though in time of revolution vendettas could often be more persuasively fought in the name of ideology. In particular, the history of federalism and of the Terror is crucial to any understanding of the politics of 1795 in the provinces. That period had created victims and counter-victims and had traced out the shape of vengeance to come; and it often produced strange bedfellows and curious local alliances. In the Gard, for instance, both the Catholic royalist elite, led by Froment, and the wealthier Protestant elite, which had controlled the department since 1790, had suffered terror at the hands of the Jacobins. They might have dramatically different ideologies, but that common experience, and the animosity it had created, meant that they now showed a degree of mutual understanding in the face of those whom they both saw as their enemy. As a result, Protestant departmental administrators would collude with Catholic murder gangs so long as their victims were former terrorists, and would prefer the banners of Louis XVIII to anything that recalled the misery they had suffered under Robespierre.[47] In doing so, they provided little effective protection or respect for the law, and condemned the region to years of murder and tit-for-tat killings.

Royalists were well aware of the opportunities which the popular thirst for vengeance provided, and in some parts of France they succeeded in infiltrating both the *jeunesse dorée* and the ranks of local government itself. Bordeaux was one city where there had been a consistent royalist challenge to the Republic, offering a choice of two royalist clubs back in 1790, a vigorous royalist press that reminded its readers of the case for counter-revolution, and, in the Jeunesse Bordelaise and the short-lived Société de Belleville, a right-wing youth movement that kept the royalist cause alive even under the Republic.[48] Here disaffected young royalists, like Brochon and Ravez, had sought to whip up support among the young of wealthy and aristocratic backgrounds, the sorts of men who would join the ranks of the *jeunesse dorée* after Thermidor in the tribunes of the *Grand Théâtre*, jeering republican actors, denouncing revolutionary plays like the anticlerical *Jean Calas*, and insisting that the cast sing the royalist anthem, the *Réveil du Peuple*, in place of the hated *Marseillaise*.[49] But they did not stop at singing royalist songs or cutting down trees of liberty, one of their favourite gestures of contempt for the revolutionary authorities. After Thermidor lax regulation allowed them to become bolder in their actions, encouraging a cult of Louis XVI in the city and marking the day of his martyrdom, 21 January, with solemn processions and wakes. The former Société de Belleville, closed during the Terror, was now resurrected under a new name, the Société du Gouvernement, presided over by Dupont-Constant, a wealthy Creole colonist from Santo-Domingo, again offering a platform to men like Ravez and Brochon. Under the Directory royalist activity throughout the South was further boosted when royalist societies became subsumed into the Institut Philanthropique, a tightly structured network of royalist clubs that maintained a clandestine presence in at least thirty-five departments;[50] it had a recognized leader in the Abbé Lacombe in Lyon, was given encouragement by the Comte d'Artois, and was linked to groups of royalist émigrés in Turin and Mainz. It remained a powerful force in the South and South-West throughout the years of the Directory, preaching counter-revolution and the need for a king, and would be responsible for fomenting rebellion in the area in 1797–1800. In parts of provincial France ideological Catholic royalism was a force with roots in the community, and Paris was right to see it as a serious threat.

The continued strength of royalism, clericalism, and that rejection of authority which is best described as 'anti-revolution', led in extreme cases to open conflict and civil war. Unsurprisingly, the influence of royalist agents and refractory priests was strongest in the West, where memories of the Vendean war and its savage repression continued to undermine the image of the Republic. Republican mayors and government *commissaires* reported increasingly frequent attacks on liberty trees on village greens and voiced particular concern around Easter, when the malign influence of nonjuring priests was deemed to be greatest. There were also sightings of known royalist agents, while peasant bands roamed the countryside, threatening life and property. Sundays were seen as days when danger threatened, as peasants gathered in wayside inns, recalling with the benefit of drink their glorious triumphs over republican forces back in 1793. By 1799 these threats had been transformed into insurrection, with a series of armed risings again plunging the region into civil war; in October the *chouans* attacked major towns in the region, including Nantes and Saint-Brieuc, La Roche-Bernard and Le Mans.[51] There was also a major outbreak of violence in Languedoc between 1797 and 1800, when insurrection swept through large areas of the Haute-Garonne and the Gers, and aroused renewed fears of an orchestrated royalist assault on the institutions of the state.[52]

But it would be a mistake to present violence as a conservative monopoly. The extreme misery of the winter of 1795 – the infamous 'Nonante-cinq', when inflation and food shortages combined with the most penetrating cold for decades to push tens of thousands of people into conditions of dire distress – aroused fear among the city poor and gave rise to urban violence born of desperation. It also provided an opportunity for the *sans-culottes* to demand greater controls and more equal distribution, and for neo-Jacobins to re-emerge from the impotent silence to which they had been reduced by the closure of the clubs. Many did so, helped by the amnesty that had accompanied the proclamation of the Directory and allowed them to return to civil society. In Paris the radicals were swayed by the journalism and oratory of Gracchus Babeuf, who stubbornly refused to accept the constitution and demanded the common ownership and equal distribution of goods, and a return to the constitution of 1793. He had little in common with the Jacobins, who continued to believe devoutly in the moral necessity of property ownership; and one of Babeuf's closest allies, Sylvain Maréchal, was close to anarchism and opposed to the centralist pretensions of the Jacobin state.[53] Babeuf's *Tribun du Peuple* sold 2,000 copies per issue in 1796; and there were those in the popular *arrondissements* who were prepared to accompany him all the way, even to plotting a popular insurrection to overthrow the Directory. The plot failed; an attempt to induce the troops to mutiny at Grenelle led to more than twenty deaths, and Babeuf and his fellow conspirators were arrested. In the provinces Babeuf could rely on a small number of dedicated supporters and sympathizers – the police conveniently obtained their names when they seized the subscription lists of the *Tribun du Peuple* – but they were not a significant movement outside the capital. For most provincials news of the conspiracy served as a reminder of the dangerous radical violence that lurked in Paris, evoking images of guillotines and a return to the bloody days of the Terror. *Babouvisme* was not a powerful force in the provinces, though Lebois' radical paper, *L'Ami du Peuple*, did have a significant readership in both Lyon and Marseille.

More common in provincial towns was the re-emergence of Jacobin cells, especially in the months following Fructidor, when government attention was focused on their royalist opponents. Indeed, it is arguable that in seeking to destroy the royalist threat, the Directory became too dependent on radical support, with the result that by 1798 Jacobins had established important bridgeheads of support in a number of centres and were in a position to pose a real electoral threat in their turn. Clubs and *cercles constitutionnels* were set up in a large number of towns, holding meetings, stimulating republican sentiment and preparing to oppose directorial deputies in the elections of the Year VI. Their views were put across by an increasingly assertive Jacobin press in towns like Marseille and Bordeaux, Grenoble and Toulouse. And through correspondence with other like-minded societies, the Jacobins became increasingly involved in national as well as local politics, seeing themselves as a bulwark against conservative reaction and looking for leadership to those who had an established record in revolutionary politics. Deputies who had been expelled from the Convention by the Thermidorians now made their way back into local politics, while collaborators of executed terrorists like Claude Javogues and Joseph Lebon were voted into power. The elections of 1798 showed, indeed, the capacity of the radical Left to organize and attract support, not just in Paris and a few large urban centres, but in over fifty towns and cities across the country, including Le Mans and Laval in the West, Pau and Tarbes in the Pyrenees, Nevers and Clamecy in the Nièvre, and a cluster of towns across the Massif Central (Tulle, Brive, Clermont, Mauriac, Saint-Affrique). Of the biggest provincial cities, the Left made dramatic gains in Marseille, Aix, Avignon, Dijon, Besançon and Bordeaux.[54] The results were greeted with wild enthusiasm in radical circles, and with an anxiety among the directorial leaders which, in time-honoured fashion, they addressed by arbitrarily suppressing elections whose outcome they found embarrassing.

The regime survived, staggering from crisis to crisis in line with the annual elections, because its enemies on both Right and Left were isolated, and a sufficient consensus in favour of stability remained. In most areas of France the Thermidorian reaction had not involved open violence, but was limited to the legal measures which the new government imposed – the liberation of suspects, the purging of municipal and district assemblies, and the arrest of those men who were designated as 'terrorists'. Similarly, in many communities there was little desire for vengeance, no rush to denounce enemies and rivals. Mouths and doors remained shut and there was limited opportunity for prosecution. Indeed, a majority of those communities which had not been subjected to brutal excesses during 1793 and 1794 showed similar restraint in 1795; terror bred terror, while moderation encouraged tolerance. This was especially true outside the Midi where the spirit of vendetta ran less deep. In the department of the Meurthe, for instance, the White Terror, like the Red, was largely bloodless; here, if there were resentments, they were directed towards the émigrés, numerous in a frontier region, and to the Revolution's religious policy.[55] But there was often another explanation, one which the Thermidorian authorities had no interest in making public. Reluctance to wreak revenge might indicate a continued sympathy with the disgraced Jacobins, or a failure by the local elites to reimpose their control. In the Toulouse area, for instance, and stretching down to the valley of the Hérault, White Terror was limited to a few isolated attacks. There was no thirst for vengeance; indeed, former Jacobin militants made common cause with those whom they had once denounced as moderates in a bid to reject the temptation of further terror. This was, of course, a fragile alliance – it brought together popular Jacobins, bourgeois radicals and republican moderates, men who in other circumstances would have been deadly rivals for power – but by rejecting political violence they strengthened the appeal of the Republic and helped resist the tide of counter-revolution in the Year V and Year VII.[56]

The dominant issues of the day remained largely unresolved – inflation, the devaluation of savings, taxation, conscription for the armies and religious worship were all matters that alienated Frenchmen from their government and made consensus difficult to establish. They contributed to the destabilization of politics and ensured that the Directory would remain largely unloved by those it administered, using its *commissaires* and, where necessary, the army to maintain control. France was divided into *divisions militaires*, and soldiers of these divisions were used to fight brigandage and maintain order; in the Midi, particularly, the region covered by the Eighth Division Militaire, they frequently had to declare a state of siege in order to impose the rule of law.[57] The Directory felt obliged to turn to the military since they no longer enjoyed the ideological hegemony or tight judicial control which the Jacobins had exercised during the Terror, and politics in the departments had become a political game whose rules everyone understood. It was to do with personality and faction, with notables of opposing persuasions battling over influence and access to power. *Commissaires* did not remain above this faction-fighting; rather they found themselves harassed and bullied by the dominant local factions, to the extent that they in their turn became 'an integral part of the game of local politics'.[58] With an imperfect understanding of the local terrain, it was a hard game for central government to play and, to the degree that they did enforce the rule of law, they did so only with the agreement and through the filter of local elites. Where their consent was not obtained, taxes went unpaid and military levies unfilled. Even in relatively law-abiding communities, unpopular measures could take a long time to enforce, as decrees became subject to negotiation between the law-enforcers and local custom and tolerance. The imposition of a forced loan on the rich in the Year IV is a good example of this process. In the Aisne, a department with no history of rebellion or federalism, the decree

was viewed with disfavour by local communities, who dallied over the com-
position of tax roles, and by republican elites, who protested that the law
discriminated against their interests. To avoid a fiasco the government agreed
to allow the tax to be modified; as a consequence it was not collected until
several months after it was due; it was not imposed in the manner laid down
by the decree; and it raised only a fraction of the money the government
required.[59] It was, in other words, manipulated by local politicians to fit
better with their priorities and those of their clientele. The Directory could
do little but accept, for, however much it might protest its belief in a centralized Republic, these were matters on which Paris no longer exercised
sufficient authority to enforce its will. The game of local politics had
changed, and with it the relationship between centre and periphery. It
would take the institution of prefects by Napoleon and the imposition of a
security state to reassert the dominance of Paris over the provinces, and to
reduce once again the degree of autonomy enjoyed by France's local elites.[60]

Notes

 1 Michael Kennedy, *The Jacobin Clubs in the French Revolution,
    1793–95* (New York, 2000), p. 114.
 2 Richard Cobb, 'Le ravitaillement des villes sous la Terreur: la question
    des arrivages, septembre 1793 – germinal an II', in *Terreur et subsis-
    tances, 1793–95* (Paris, 1965), p. 219.
 3 Alan Forrest, *The Revolution in Provincial France. Aquitaine, 1789–99*
    (Oxford, 1996), p. 311.
 4 Bronislaw Baczko, *Ending the Terror. The French Revolution after
    Robespierre* (Cambridge, 1994), pp. 10–13.
 5 Kennedy, *Jacobin Clubs*, p. 239.
 6 R. R. Palmer, *From Jacobin to Liberal. Marc-Antoine Jullien, 1775–1848*
    (Princeton, NJ, 1993), pp. 31–62.
 7 Richard Cobb, *The Police and the People. French Popular Protest,
    1789–1820* (Oxford, 1970), pp. 5–13.
 8 For a telling documentary account of the events of the days immediately
    preceding 9 *thermidor*, see Richard Bienvenu, *The Ninth of Thermidor:
    the Fall of Robespierre* (New York, 1968).
 9 Donald Sutherland, *The French Revolution and Empire. The Quest for
    a Civic Order* (Oxford, 2003), pp. 231–3.
10 Morris Slavin, *The Hébertistes to the Guillotine: Anatomy of a
    'Conspiracy' in Revolutionary France* (Baton Rouge, LA, 1994), p. 264.
11 Richard Cobb, *A Second Identity. Essays on France and French History*
    (Oxford, 1968), p. 140.
12 Georges Lefebvre, *The Thermidorians* (London, 1964), p. 9.
13 Kåre Tønnesson, *La défaite des sans-culottes. Mouvement populaire et
    réaction bourgeoise en l'an III* (Oslo and Paris, 1959), p. 377.

14 Patrice Higonnet, *Paris, Capital of the World* (Cambridge, MA, 2002), p. 56.

15 Colin Lucas, 'Les thermidoriens et les violences de l'an III', in Roger Dupuy and Marcel Morabito (eds), *1795. Pour une République sans Révolution* (Rennes, 1996), p. 42.

16 Jacques Dupâquier, 'Le procès de Carrier', in Michel Vovelle (ed.), *Le tournant de l'an III. Réaction et Terreur blanche dans la France révolutionnaire* (Paris, 1997), pp. 27–34.

17 Baczko, *Ending the Terror*, pp. 171–2.

18 The phrase was taken from the title of a satirical pamphlet by Felhémési, published in *fructidor* II, alerting its readers to the dangers posed by those of Robespierre's supporters who had been left behind after his execution. Robespierre himself was rumoured to have said, just before his death, that 'You can cut off my head but I have left you my tail'; ibid., p. 53.

19 Sutherland, *French Revolution*, p. 237.

20 René Gérard, *Un journal de province sous la Révolution: Le Journal de Marseille de Ferréol Beaugeard, 1781–97* (Paris, 1964), p. 230.

21 Philippe David, *Un port de l'océan pendant la Révolution. La Rochelle et son District, 1791–95* (La Rochelle, 1938), p. 241.

22 Michael Kennedy, *Jacobin Clubs*, pp. 263–70.

23 Pierre Bécamps, *J.-B.-M. Lacombe, Président de la Commission Militaire* (Bordeaux, 1953), pp. 355–7.

24 Forrest, *Aquitaine*, p. 316.

25 Patrice Gueniffey, *La politique de la Terreur: essai sur la violence révolutionnaire, 1789–94* (Paris, 2000), p. 344.

26 Isser Woloch, 'Republican Institutions, 1797–99', in Colin Lucas (ed.), *The French Revolution and the Creation of Modern Political Culture, vol. 2: The Political Culture of the French Revolution* (Oxford, 1988), p. 371.

27 Jacques Godechot (ed.), *Les constitutions de la France depuis 1789* (Paris, 1970), pp. 101–41; Malcolm Crook, *Elections in the French Revolution* (Cambridge, 1996), pp. 131–5.

28 A good example here is the region round Toulouse: see Georges Fournier, 'La République directoriale: une phase originale dans l'histoire électorale du Midi toulousain', in Philippe Bourdin and Bernard Gainot (eds), *La République directoriale. Actes du colloque de Clermont-Ferrand, 22–24 mai 1997* (2 vols, Paris, 1998), vol. 1, pp. 331–50.

29 Crook, *Elections*, p. 185.

30 G. Ducaunnès-Duval, 'Les municipalités de Bordeaux sous le Directoire', *Revue historique de Bordeaux* 6 (1913), pp. 150–2.

31 Martyn Lyons, *France under the Directory* (Cambridge, 1975), pp. 161–2.

32 Serge Bianchi, 'Le fonctionnement des municipalités cantonales dans le sud de l'Île-de-France sous le Directoire', in Jacques Bernet, Jean-Pierre Jessenne and Hervé Leuwers (eds), *Du Directoire au Consulat. 1: Le lien politique local dans la Grande Nation* (Lille, 1998), p. 179.

33 Bernard Gainot, 'La province au crible des rapports des commissaires départementaux du Directoire', *Annales historiques de la Révolution Française* 330 (2002), pp. 145–7.

34 Emile Ducoudray, 'L'accueil fait à la Révolution par l'électorat parisien de l'an IV', in Michel Vovelle (ed.), *L'image de la Révolution Française* (4 vols, Paris, 1989), vol. 1, pp. 83–6.

35 Howard G. Brown, 'The search for stability', in Howard G. Brown and Judith A. Miller (eds), *Taking Liberties. Problems of a New Order from the French Revolution to Napoleon* (Manchester, 2002), p. 25.

36 Colin Lucas, 'The First Directory and the Rule of Law', *French Historical Studies* 10 (1977), pp. 231–2.

37 Richard Wrigley, *The Politics of Appearances. Representations of Dress in Revolutionary France* (Oxford, 2002), p. 265.

38 Jeff Horn, 'La lutte des factions au théâtre de Troyes sous le Directoire', in Philippe Bourdin and Bernard Gainot (eds), *La République directoriale*, vol. 2, p. 679.

39 François Gendron, *La jeunesse dorée. Episodes de la Révolution Française* (Québec, 1979), pp. 53, 90.

40 Jeremy Popkin, *The Right-wing Press in France, 1792–1800* (Chapel Hill, 1980), p. 164.

41 Gendron, *La jeunesse dorée*, p. 260.

42 Renée Fuoc, *La réaction thermidorienne à Lyon, 1795* (Lyon, 1957), p. 14.

43 Ibid., p. 131.

44 Richard Cobb, *Reactions to the French Revolution* (Oxford, 1972), p. 56.

45 Colin Lucas, 'Themes in southern violence after 9 thermidor', in Gwynne Lewis and Colin Lucas (eds), *Beyond the Terror. Essays in French Regional and Social History, 1794–1815* (Cambridge, 1983), pp. 152–3.

46 Richard Maltby, 'Le brigandage dans la Drôme, 1795–1803', *Bulletin d'archéologie et de statistique de la Drôme* 79 (1973), pp. 117–34.

47 Gwynne Lewis, *The Second Vendée. The Continuity of Counter-revolution in the Department of the Gard, 1789–1815* (Oxford, 1978), pp. 78–9.

48 Pierre Bécamps (ed.), *Un Bordelais sous la Terreur: mémoires de Jean-Baptiste Brochon* (Bordeaux, 1989), *passim*.

49 Henri Lagrave, Charles Mazouer and Marc Regaldo (eds), *La vie théâtrale à Bordeaux des origines à nos jours, vol. 1 – des origines à 1799* (Paris, 1985), pp. 403–4.

50 Gustaaf Caudrillier, *L'association royaliste de l'Institut Philanthropique à Bordeaux* (Paris, 1908); for a more general study of royalist conspiracy in the provinces, see Ernest Daudet, *La conjuration de Pichegru et les complots royalistes du Midi et de l'Est, 1795–97* (Paris, 1901).

51 Jean-Clément Martin, *La Vendée et la France* (Paris, 1987), pp. 331–3.

52 For an account of this outbreak of peasant violence, see Jean Lacouture, *Le mouvement royaliste dans le Sud-ouest, 1797–1800* (Hossegor, 1932).

53 Ian Birchall, *The Spectre of Babeuf* (Basingstoke, 1997), p. 56.
54 Isser Woloch, *Jacobin Legacy. The Democratic Movement under the Directory* (Princeton, NJ, 1970), pp. 282–7.
55 Pierre Clémendot, *Le département de la Meurthe à l'époque du Directoire* (Nancy, 1966), p. 83.
56 Georges Fournier, 'Réalité et limites de la réaction thermidorienne dans l'Hérault, l'Aude et la Haute-Garonne', in Michel Vovelle (ed.), *Le tournant de l'an III. Réaction et Terreur blanche dans la France révolutionnaire* (Paris, 1997), pp. 495–6.
57 Jonathan Devlin, 'The Directory and the Politics of Military Command: the Army of the Interior in South-east France', *French History* 4 (1990), pp. 199–223.
58 Colin Lucas, 'The Rules of the Game in Local Politics under the Directory', *French Historical Studies* 16 (1989), p. 364.
59 Laurent Brassart, 'Des décisions parisiennes aux municipalités cantonales: la mise en oeuvre de la politique directoriale dans le département de l'Aisne', *Annales historiques de la Révolution Française* 330 (2002), pp. 116–20.
60 Howard G. Brown, 'From Organic Society to Security State: the War on Brigandage in France, 1797–1802', *Journal of Modern History* 69 (1997), pp. 661–95.

11

Paris and the provinces: the image of the other

For many in eighteenth-century Europe, Paris was a city of culture, elegance and sophistication, the natural heart of that *République des Lettres* to which those desiring progressive reforms and representative government increasingly looked for inspiration. Provincial cities might aspire to such culture, but they could not attain it, and provincial Frenchmen often looked on the capital with respect, sometimes tinged with envy. Of course, they complained about Parisian arrogance and aspirations to cultural hegemony, and in moments of political crisis they were wont to denounce the concentration of power in the capital. Paris, even after the King had removed his court to Versailles, was still associated with power, and at times with the abuse of power. But the identification of government with its capital city was as nothing compared to that which was created by the French Revolution, and by the increasing identification of the nation and the sovereign people with the state and the people of the capital. The experience of the Revolution changed the relationship with provincial France. The ideology of the nation state and the sovereign people, and the insistence that sovereignty was to be exercised at national level through the Assembly or Convention, produced new levels of envy and resentment in the provinces, as well as fierce criticisms of the particular revolutionary values that Parisians came to represent. One effect of the political claims and counter-claims of the 1790s was that the position of Paris was no longer uncontroversial. It had acquired an ideological character which made Paris and its people a pawn in domestic politics and a recurrent theme in the competing discourses of revolution. Whether it chose to or not, Paris was now contested as it had never previously been, a subject of controversy which political factions found it increasingly difficult to ignore.

In the summer of 1789 it all looked very different, as the initiatives of the Paris crowd repeatedly gave new impetus to the Revolution and helped steer national politics towards the wishes of the Third Estate. Paris at that moment symbolized liberty and progress. The Bastille, as we have seen, rapidly found its place in the revolutionary Pantheon, and won for the Paris crowd a special place in revolutionary folk memory. Pamphleteers vied with one another to present lurid pictures of the bloodshed and despotism that had been threatening, and which had now been banished forever by the courage and prescience of ordinary Parisians. Paris was again the city of light, its people the heroic antithesis of kings and tyrants. References to royal despotism and ministerial tyranny were legion, both in the press and in the polemical pamphlets that found a sudden vogue both in Paris and beyond. One such pamphlet made the point graphically, with despotism represented as a twelve-headed hydra, whose heads depicted royal ministers of the *ancien régime* from Richelieu to Lamoignan. All had used the Bastille to further their policies of repression, and, warned the writer, 'without the fortunate insurrection of 14 July these tormentors would have perpetuated despotism'.[1] The inference was clear. If the French people were now free, they owed that freedom to Paris and the sacrifice of its citizens. And if the Parisians had resorted to violence in pursuit of their ends, their violence paled into insignificance when compared to the greater good of the nation which their action had inspired. It had to be accepted as the product of popular panic or an impassioned crowd, as the unavoidable price of the nation's freedom. Within days, with the King's visit to Paris on 17 July and the apparent reconciliation of the monarchy with the Revolution which that symbolized, even some doubters were converted and claimed to see the end of disorder, the beginning of a new and lasting national unity created amid the turbulence of the Bastille.[2] Paris could take pride in its achievement and bask in the approval of a grateful nation.

Not all, however, were prepared to accept this rather optimistic interpretation of events. Even in July of 1789 some voiced fierce criticisms of the Parisians and insisted that mob rule was morally indefensible in any circumstances, and that it was wrong to try to defend any popular action, however bloody, on grounds of political ideology or simple convenience. Large numbers of Frenchmen remained uneasy about what had happened, especially when the attack on the Bastille gave way in the succeeding days to the lynching of Foulon and Berthier. A distinction had to be drawn between freedom-fighting and bloodlust, and many in the provinces already voiced the opinion that the people of Paris could not be trusted to exercise moderation or obey the laws of the land. Many began to express fears that the entry of the Paris crowd on to the political stage could only presage an uncontrollable spiral of violence, and with it a descent into the abyss of fear and anarchy. Those deputies in the National Assembly who placed their faith in the rule of law were often among the most spirited critics of such violence, which they saw as the very antithesis of their dream and a fundamental denial of the rights of man. For Gouy d'Arcy, for example, what Paris was witnessing had little to do with the Revolution. It was mob violence, brutish and barbarous, a 'catastrophe' that flew in the face of all the teaching of the Enlightenment, 'barbarism' that could too easily 'become habitual'.[3] Another deputy spoke for the provinces when he urged that controls should be placed on the freedom of Paris, lest the city that had been the 'cradle of liberty' should end up terrorizing the rest of France and, possibly, burying the very liberty it had helped create. 'If there were one town in the kingdom,' he argued, 'that could be subjected to a particularly close control from the central administration, then that town should surely be Paris, because it holds, one might say, in its hands the destiny of the nation; because it now contains within its boundaries both the legislature and the supreme head of the executive, which are the common treasures of the nation'.[4] In provincial France many agreed with him. Behind all the celebration that followed the fall of the Bastille, some continued to regard Paris with suspicion, some jealousy, and even an element of fear.

Of course, the Paris of the Bastille, where popular violence blended easily with patriotism, and the cause of the people with that of the Revolution, was still relatively easy to justify, and those brave enough to criticize the people's action were a small minority. But mindless violence and bloodletting were a different matter, especially where these involved blind hatred and indiscriminate slaughter. Not all the incursions of the Paris crowd on to the political stage could be held up as examples of political prescience. The prison massacres of 2 September 1792 proved especially difficult to explain away, as they were characterized by nothing more noble than panic, hysteria and a desire to kill. The massacres were first announced to the Legislative Assembly by a deputation from the Paris Commune, but even they used carefully measured tones. They described how crowds had formed outside all the major prisons of the capital, intent on breaking down the doors; they explained that Paris municipal councillors had tried to reason with them, but that the crowd was intent on vengeance and would not listen, that already a number of prisoners had been slaughtered. But they added, in mitigation, that the people of the capital had legitimate fears. 'The people are eager to march to the frontiers, but they have understandable fears about the intentions of a large number of individuals who are under arrest charged with crimes of counter-revolution'. And rather than condemn the crowd out of hand, which would have been politically sensitive, they appointed two *commissaires* to visit each of the prisons to 'speak to the people and re-establish calm'.[5] This was a rare moment of tension, when the brutality of the crowd seemed impossible to justify. Yet in the political context of the Revolution many still found it difficult to condemn Paris, or to imply that the instincts of men who had fought for freedom at the Bastille could be so dangerously flawed. Besides, Paris could never be ignored or its wishes swept aside, since the brute force that had been exerted against the Revolution's perceived enemies in the prison massacres might at any moment be used again, and turned against moderate voices in the Convention. It is instructive to note how very cautiously the deputies chose to proceed.

Even when the *commissaires* reported back on their experiences there was no rush to condemn Paris. One deputy, Dusaulx, returned that same evening to confirm that their mission had been anything but straightforward. They had struggled to reach the gates of the Abbaye, where they had tried desperately to make themselves heard above the din: 'One of us stood on a chair; but he had scarcely opened his mouth when his voice was drowned by noisy shouting'. And when a second deputy, Basire, tried to attract the attention of the crowd, they listened only momentarily, until they realized that his views were not theirs, at which point they shouted him down. Rather sheepishly Dusaulx added that they had tried to convince their neighbours that violence did not offer a solution.

> But the peaceful intentions of those who listened to us could not be communicated to a mob several thousand strong. We then withdrew, and as it was growing dark we could not see what happened next, but I would not like to offer the Assembly any assurance about the outcome of this unfortunate event. The people is overexcited to the point where they will not listen to anyone, and they are afraid of being deceived.[6]

The crowd, in other words, was now out of control, driven by panic and phobia, fearful for the safety of the city and loved ones. It became violent and murderous, butchering all before it in moments of blind rage and fear; but, representing as it did the popular will of the capital, it could not be condemned.

Only on the following day did the full horror of what had taken place become clear for all to see. One after another the prisons had been ransacked and the prisoners massacred. But to put it in these terms might itself have seemed counter-revolutionary and attracted condemnation. Tallien, in his report to the Legislative, stressed that the Paris Commune had tried to moderate the excesses of the crowd, though without success; they had rampaged from prison to prison, exacting their terrible vengeance. Yet even here there were elements of mitigation, for this was popular justice as much as it was blind passion. At the Abbaye the killing was not random: 'the people had asked the gaoler to hand over his registers; and it was those who were held for their part in the massacre of 10 August or for manufacturing false *assignats* who perished on the spot'. Tallien knew very well the effect of these words on his audience, for the massacre of republicans on 10 August – and republicans who were also Parisians – was a sore issue, one that presented a clear dichotomy of good and evil. Even as he spoke, money was being collected and offered to the Assembly to help the widows and orphans who were left behind.[7] At the Force, where the Commune had tried to intervene, he went still further in justifying the bloodletting. The *commissaires* had been unable to prevent what he called 'the just vengeance of the people', for 'we ought to make it clear that the blows fell on those who had forged *assignats* or who had been held in prison for four or five years'; 'what most excited the vengeance of the crowd was the fact that the prison contained known scoundrels'. The Assembly was repeatedly reminded that violence was also a form of justice. At the Châtelet, deputies were told, several prisoners were released amidst cries of 'Vive la Nation!' and inside the prisons the people had organized a form of kangaroo court, a tribunal composed of twelve judges who would review the charges listed in the prison registers and ask the prisoners a few cursory questions, before either ordering their release or casting them on to the pikes held by their colleagues in the crowd.[8] While this was not justice as the Assembly understood the term, at least it gave the naked violence of the massacres some hint of legitimation and helped maintain the fiction that the people were good, inspired by notions of what was just rather than by thuggery, bloodlust or a criminal desire for vengeance.

In the immediate aftermath of the massacres, indeed, the National Assembly was reluctant to condemn Paris, preferring to maintain a dignified silence or take comfort in having averted the danger of counter-revolution. Many journalists went further, openly advocating the use of violence and praising the courage of the people. Some had responded angrily to the massacre by the Swiss Guards on 10 August and had pointed to the need for perpetual vigilance. Among the more radical, Gorsas had told his readers that they should show no mercy to their enemies if they and their families were to be safe;[9] while Marat, as a matter of public safety, had called upon the Parisians to rid themselves of the 'traitors in the prisons' before they left for the front.[10] When the blood flowed they saw no reason to relent. Gorsas spoke of the massacred prisoners as men who had betrayed liberty, who were guilty of plotting against the state and who 'wish for the deaths of patriots'. It was therefore a war to the death, gloated Gorsas, of which the massacres were a necessary part. 'Let them perish!' he urged; 'for we must not hide the fact that we are now in a state of open war with the enemies of our liberty'. If the Parisians had not done so, others would have to have killed them themselves.[11] Gorsas, it should be emphasized, was not a Montagnard; already he had swung to the Girondin cause, and it is significant that many of those who would later be counted among the leaders of the Gironde – Roland, Louvet and Brissot among them – took care in September of 1792 to offer muted support to the Parisians or to pass over their actions in silence.[12] Even those Girondins who would later manipulate public anger and outrage at the massacres remained silent at the time. Some even applauded the Parisians, thanked them for saving the Revolution, or approved their patriotism.[13]

These were, however, largely Parisian reactions, those of men who lived in the capital or who, as deputies, had made their political careers there. Provincial France did not always see things in the same light, and outside Paris the September Massacres were often pointed to as being symptomatic of the anarchistic streak which, many felt, was never far from the surface of the Parisian psyche. And where apologists for the city emphasized its long-standing commitment to freedom and the revolutionary cause, there were many in the provinces who saw in the violence of the Paris crowd something more sinister, a betrayal of the republican values to which they remained committed. In most provincial centres Jacobin influence remained a minority one, and city politics were still in the hands of more moderate elements, often Girondin sympathizers. News of what had happened was received in gloomy silence, and throughout the subsequent months provincial politicians justified their continued suspicion of Paris by referring back to the blood-letting of September, which they saw as damning evidence of the unwhole-some influence of *anarchistes* and popular extremists. The local club in Lourdes expressed this eloquently in an address to the people of Bordeaux. Paris was blamed for corrupting the Republic – for the massacres themselves, for the election of Marat, that most potent symbol of violence and brutality, and for the choice of 'crooks and extortionists' to represent the city in the Convention.[14] Where Jacobins did control local politics, the Massacres could lead to emulation, particularly in Lyon, which witnessed smaller-scale massacres of its own in the wake of reports from Paris. At Roanne, for instance, the prison was attacked by an angry crowd, seven prisoners were dragged out of their cells, and two – a forger and a baker – were murdered.[15]

However, the provinces had to be careful to moderate their criticism lest bloody reprisals should follow. Governments changed too often during the revolutionary years for criticism to be welcome, and often these changes followed upon pressure from the streets of the capital. However much provincial republicans might dislike the actions of the Paris sections – and there is no doubting that many of them did – they were too far distant from government, too disparate and disorganized, to exercise a fraction of the influence that fell to their Parisian counterparts. And, as was eloquently demonstrated in the summer of 1793, Parisian anger and prejudice could be exported to the provinces, bringing violence and terror to the streets of provincial cities. So canny provincials soon learned that it was wise to respond to Paris with caution, polite words of praise, even occasional deceit. Rouen, for instance, generally reacted to change at the centre – the declaration of the Republic, the Jacobin *coup d'état*, or whatever – with a cautiously worded address, praising the wisdom of the Parisians and thanking them for their intervention. The neighbouring textile town of Elbeuf, with a similar eye to self-preservation, would follow Rouen's example several days later, when it was safe to assume that the new government was securely in place. At the same time they took care to celebrate revolutionary fêtes and mount appropriate public festivities.[16] They were wise to do so. Lyon had been terribly punished in early June when its anti-Jacobin town council, after overthrowing the Jacobin Chalier and his clique, announced their achievement to Paris only to discover that in the meantime the Jacobins had seized control in the capital. Lyon was besieged; its identity was taken away and the houses around the Place Bellecour flattened; and the reprisals that followed resulted in nearly 2,000 executions.[17] The men of Elbeuf may not have been very heroic in their approach to revolutionary ideals; but at least they all died in their beds.

Such moderation rarely survived the bitter summer of 1793, the months of the Jacobin *coup d'état* in the Convention and fratricidal battles between Girondins and Montagnards in many of the largest provincial cities.

Federalism, as we have seen, was not to be confused with anti-republicanism or regional autonomy. But if those cities which added their voice to the federalist cause had no reason to criticize republican institutions, they were relatively free with their criticisms of Paris and its inhabitants. For the Lyonnais, the problem stemmed from Paris's status as a capital city and the role which it was able to play in national politics. It had used that position to impose its values and to oppress others; Paris was a 'proud city that has for too long abused its power and its dangerous influence'.[18] On occasion this sense of resentment boiled over into an openly anti-Parisian rhetoric, most memorably, perhaps, when Henri-Maximin Isnard, the outspoken deputy for the Var, rashly declared 'in the name of the whole of France' that, if repeated Parisian violence were to undermine the authority of the Convention, then Paris would have to be razed to the ground, so that 'soon people would search the banks of the Seine to find the place where the city had stood'.[19] In provincial centres there was sometimes an added economic reason to attack Paris in that many believed that the Parisians had manipulated the Maximum to their own advantage, subsidizing their own bread while the poor of other cities had been left to starve. But more often the outbursts against the capital were born of less focused anger, a sense of resentment at the powers which the Parisians seemed determine to exercise, a desire to free themselves from the *dictature* of the capital. In Toulouse, Arbanière even urged, in a moment of creative frustration, that all the cities of the South and West should band together and sweep Paris aside, 'so that the waters of the Garonne, the Gers, the Aude, the Tarn, the Lot, the Corrèze, the Ariège, the Hérault, the Durance and the Rhône might form a huge torrent to engulf the monstrous city that is Paris'.[20]

A closer examination shows that these attacks on Paris were less likely to target the entire population than to single out the extremists whom it was believed to harbour. Everywhere, it would seem, people were convinced that Paris was being corrupted, and would eventually be destroyed, by the 'anarchists' of the popular movement, who might operate on the streets, or in the Paris Commune, or in the tribunes of the Convention itself. According to this vision of politics the Montagnards were stripped of any real authority in Paris, and were reduced to the status of helpless puppets by the onslaught of popular violence. Power lay with the Paris Commune, with men whose credibility was undermined by their advocacy of Terror, their defence of Marat, and their unashamed participation in the September Massacres. They were men of blood and the natural enemy of political stability. In the words of the Section of the Grande Côte, on the Croix-Rousse in Lyon, the Convention had become oppressed 'by the tribunes which, by their shouts and cries and jeers, reduce patriotic deputies to silence', and by the Paris Commune 'which is more powerful than the Convention and which permits itself to break a number of laws, notably those that relate to the freedom of the press'.[21] To that extent the interests of Paris were presented as being opposed to those of the nation, and the call went up for the pretensions of Paris to be curbed. 'Impose silence on those hired tribunes whose shouting can be heard even here,' demanded the department of the Eure, before asking that Paris contain its extremists within its own borders and stop contaminating the nation. Paris must finally learn, they declared, 'that it is no more than the depository of the national representation, and that the departments will never tolerate a situation where Paris either competes with the sovereign authority or blackens its reputation'.[22] As long as national government was subject to the influence of the Paris streets, it was commonly believed, it would be impossible for the nation to express itself freely, which led some federalist cities to demand the transfer of the Convention to a quieter location, to a town outside Paris that could be the location for a truly national representation, an assembly where everyone could say what they thought without fear of verbal abuse or physical violence. A number of cities proposed Bourges for this role, as providing both a central location and a calm environment where the views of all the departments could be heard, free from threats and intimidation.[23]

An alternative solution would be to purge Paris of its extremist elements and end the threat of anarchy by force. Provincial fears were exacerbated by the trial of Marat and the controversy surrounding the Commission of Twelve, both issues which suggested that the Parisian crowd was now operating in league with the more radical sections and exercising dangerous and disproportionate power to the detriment of the elected deputies.[24] For as long as the Paris authorities remained intact, provincial opinion argued, there could be no real freedom, and hence no constitutional liberty for the people. Government was undermined, in the words of the municipal council of Gray in the Haute-Saône, by Parisian extremists, 'those driven by a spirit of faction or anarchy, pillagers and embezzlers of state funds, men who despise the majesty of the nation in the person of its deputies, and who seek by their machinations to put off the moment when the constitution will be decreed'.[25] The Breton departments made the case that the Paris Commune must be immediately purged and all state subsidy to the *sans-culottes* ended. To secure this goal they asked that there be established in Paris as many communal authorities as there were judicial divisions. They wanted, in other words, the complete destruction of the *sans-culottes'* power base so that Paris could be reduced to the status of other cities, and the rest of France be freed from the tyranny of the capital.[26] By early July some federalist leaders were contemplating the use of force to achieve this goal, raising departmental armies that would march against Paris with the aim of destroying the 'anarchists' and 'liberating' their deputies. One of the leaders of the anti-Parisian movement in Marseille, Paul-Raimbaud Bussac, replied to his judges in October 1793 that he had never regarded the *force départementale* as a threat to the independence of the Convention. It had been created 'to guarantee the deliberations of the Convention'; it 'was not directed against the Convention, but against the armed force deployed by Paris which oppressed the Convention, and which in the process both destroyed representative government and insulted all the departments of France'.[27]

When Robespierre was finally overthrown at Thermidor there is no reason to doubt that many provincial towns felt an enormous sense of relief. Life could get back to what some still thought of as normal, and they rushed to thank the Convention for its part in the *coup*. Interestingly, many of their addresses went out of their way to mention Paris and its role in what was in essence a palace revolution by largely Jacobin deputies. The significance of Paris's contribution was less what the sections did than what they desisted from doing; but that did not prevent provincial towns and cities from praising the Parisians' prescience. The city council in Lille had no doubts, declaring that:

> The brave republicans who man the sections of Paris have done their duty; their conduct in no way surprises us. The Convention is saved, and it has saved France! We have just celebrated this day, this memorable victory which is worth more than winning ten battles because it has not cost the life of a single patriot![28]

The council at Maubeuge wrote in the same vein, thanking 'our brothers the Parisians', and rejoicing in the notion that together they form a single republican family.[29] And Arras, despite being Robespierre's birthplace, joined the chorus of voices denouncing him as a 'tyrant'. They addressed their thanks directly to the people of Paris. 'Brave Parisians,' they wrote, 'once more you have contributed to saving liberty. You have assisted the sublime and generous insurrection of the National Convention against a handful of ambitious tyrants who wanted to put themselves in the place of the people and usurp the terrible power to massacre the motherland and reduce a nation of free men to servitude'.[30] Their earlier distrust of the capital had all but evaporated.

If provincial addresses took care to praise the role played by Paris in the fall of Robespierre, they were quickly joined by the Parisians themselves, eager to have their part in events recognized and to distance themselves from the long months of the Terror. To achieve this they had to be persuasive. Robespierre, after all, remained closely identified with support from their more radical sections and particularly from the Paris Commune. So the tone had to be rather different, one that breathed outrage rather than virtue, lamentation instead of triumph. The Section de Bonne-Nouvelle affected horror that Robespierre should have abused Paris in this way, that the city had been chosen as the scene of fighting and bloodshed. Paris had been shamed and insulted by what had happened, they argued; 'Paris, which took up arms only to secure the happiness of the universe and which quivered with joy when the first fruits of the Revolution were directed to the unfortunate inhabitants of the countryside; and it was from Paris that the scoundrels hoped for the crime that would serve their cause!' The section could scarcely contain its indignation and rushed to condemn the whole Robespierrist conspiracy. 'The monsters,' they declaim. 'How could they forget for a single moment that the genius of liberty had kindled its sacred fire in the hearts of our children?'[31] Behind the oratory, Parisians clutched at the opportunity to remind the deputies of the particular role which Paris continued to play in the life of the nation, the unique place of Paris in the revolutionary movement.

If Parisian radicals had a view of their own importance and the degree of respect and deference which Paris should command, so, too, they had somewhat fixed ideas of the character of provincial France and the role which the provinces could be expected to play in revolutionary politics. Given the central position of Paris in their world picture, and their equation of liberty with their own efforts, that role was a predominantly passive one, one in which revolutionary activists received news and instructions from the centre, where they followed rather than led. Catherine Lacour illustrates this very persuasively in her study of the language used by Prudhomme in his radical newspaper, *Les Révolutions de Paris*, between 1789 and 1792, noting that frequently the provinces are represented either as the victim of circumstance or as the target for counter-revolutionary intrigue, roles which are used to free them from any direct moral responsibility. They are presented as being deliberately cultivated by aristocrats and refractory priests, stirred, propagandized, methodically worked over (*travaillées*) by outsiders set on spreading sedition.[32] The language used by the paper is revealing. Again and again we are told that the people of the countryside were *trompés*, often by religious enthusiasm or by royalist tracts; that provincial leaders who fell foul of government policy were *égarés*; that the countryside was continually *infecté* by the most dangerous of errors. Here the inference is clear – that in many parts of the provinces people were so cut off from Paris and national events that they could have no clear idea of what was going on, and were therefore left at the mercy of every passing rumour. Villagers had no way of checking the truth of the news they received, and much of it was being deliberately distorted by royalist pamphleteers and agents of counter-revolution. Provincials, through no fault of their own, were victims, led into error, *dupes des artifices*.[33] This lack of culpability is something which the paper underlines again and again, for it is keen to emphasize that the French people were fundamentally good, and that the Revolution was a single, united movement enveloping not just Paris, but the whole of France from the Ardennes to the Pyrenees. All had a part to play by the Parisians' side, insisted the paper, since Paris alone could not make the Revolution. Instead, Paris had been supported by the provincial cities since news of the Bastille had spread to the four corners of the land. Far from being tempted by counter-revolution, the provinces had sought to imitate the capital and would rise to defend the Parisians should Paris itself be threatened. Only the opportunity had proved lacking. As Prudhomme wrote in August 1789, 'it seemed that every town or *bourg* regretted that it did not have a head to cut off or a bastille to storm'.[34]

There is, of course, something deeply patronizing about this attitude, a belief, which the Parisians made no attempt to conceal, that only those who lived and worked in the shadow of the Convention and who shared Paris's radical vision of the Revolution could claim the credit due for advancing humanity. This was especially true of the *sans-culottes*, who brought to their politics not just the moralistic delight in unmasking traitors and moderates which so characterized the terrorist mentality, but a peculiarly Parisian outlook, born of the collected prejudices of the Paris artisan and the small shopkeeper of the *faubourgs*. It showed in his dislike of wealth and speculation, his insistence that virtue was the monopoly of the small man, the small property holder, the craftsman making his living from a small shop or *atelier*. It showed, too, in a distrust of those who did not share his background, and who for that reason could not be expected to share his values or his outlook. In an age where suspicion and conspiracy abounded, this of itself was enough to damn the merchant from Lyon or Marseille, or the Catholic peasant from the West. It also explains the disdain and mutual incomprehension which surfaced whenever the *armées révolutionnaires* left the familiarity of their Parisian backstreets to encounter men from other backgrounds, with different assumptions. They met them with an ill-disguised sense of contempt, born of their experience of life in the Paris sections, their sense that they alone could understand what the Revolution meant. They sought, as Richard Cobb has pointed out, to convert and proselytize in the provinces, to bully and cajole to get others to think in the same progressive, Parisian way – or in the language of the true revolutionary, to *révolutionner* local people, to steer events *dans le bon sens*, or to think *dans le sens de la Révolution*. Suspicious of those who did not share the same culture, they tracked down anyone who slandered the Convention, the deputies or – most significantly – the fulcrum of revolutionary ideology which was the city of Paris. In the process they were uninterested in questions of tact or popularity, and might, as Cobb points out, make themselves thoroughly obnoxious to provincial opinion, giving themselves 'the airs of a "Ph.D. in revolution" and affecting an attitude of scorn, condescension and distrust towards their "provincial brothers" '.[35]

With the growing sectarianism of revolutionary politics, that rather pedagogical view of provincial France – a willingness to forgive combined with a superior and aloof view of provincial backwardness – came under intolerable pressure, and the provinces were increasingly represented as a dangerous territory where opponents and counter-revolutionaries could find refuge while they planned new outrages against the Republic. In these circumstances the excuse of ignorance or gullibility was less likely to be accepted, until in 1793 federalism and counter-revolution were counted among the most serious of crimes, with their roots in ideology rather than political naivety. The picture which the Paris Jacobins faced by June seemed both confused and vacillating, as provincial cities sent contradictory addresses to central government, and rumours spread of violently anti-Parisian messages passing from department to department. From the information available to deputies, it was not just in Lyon, Marseille and Bordeaux that political loyalties were suspect. In the North there were alarming reports from a raft of departments across Brittany and Normandy, but also from the Jura, Aisne, Somme,

Mayenne and Saône-et-Loire; in the South there was equal cause for disquiet, especially in the Haute-Garonne, Gard, Isère and Hautes-Alpes.[36] Provincial opinion, it seemed, was volatile; once again it was easy to believe that the provinces could not be trusted.

This distrust was reflected in the language used to discuss federalism, whether by Jacobin deputies in Paris, by those of their number sent out on missions to the interior, or by Jacobins in provincial towns and cities. Though there was the usual acknowledgement that many of the poorer citizens may have been 'misled' by the federalist leadership, this merely meant that the rich and politically influential bore the brunt of the repression. The Montagnards had, indeed, a stereotyped image of the provincial cities which was every bit as unsubtle as the provincial view of the Parisians. Cities like Lyon, Marseille and Bordeaux were dominated by merchants and marked by the mentality of merchants – greed, egotism and a concern for profit which almost necessarily meant that they would put their own self-interest above the cause of the nation or that of the Republic. For the Jacobins the republic of virtue could come only with the extirpation of vice, and it was with vice that the provincial cities were increasingly equated. In Lyon the Jacobins exulted in repression and the opportunity it provided for the redistribution of property: 'they supposed it axiomatic that it was wealth that had brought about Lyon's political degradation.'[37] So in Bordeaux Marc-Antoine Jullien was in little doubt that he had a social as well as an ideological mission to carry out if the city were ever to become truly republican. The Committee of Public Safety had said as much when it accused previous deputies-on-mission of being too moderate, too prepared to listen to the local elite. Was it really politic to do so, they asked, in an environment where 'the mercantile aristocracy had plotted federalism and had for so long killed off the spirit of revolution'?[38] The sickness, in their somewhat caricatured vision, ran deep and contaminated large sections of the city's elite.

The identification of the provinces with the 'other' is well illustrated in the language used by Fréron during his mission to the South-East, where he was particularly concerned to root out the cancer of federalism which, he argued, had been spread from Marseille to Toulon and other parts of the Midi. Fréron denounced Marseille for what he called its 'spirit of egotism, of self-interest and cupidity, of federalism, isolation, a desire to dominate'.[39] These, in his view and that of many of his Jacobin colleagues, were the most salient characteristics of the city, the qualities which had driven it to forsake its role as the radical heart of the Midi and defy the Convention. These were characteristics which could only be eradicated by ruthlessness, by stripping the city of its corruption and much of its identity. The roots of Marseille's corruption were doubtless manifold: Fréron was even capable of blaming the heat of the Provençal sun for turning the heads of the inhabitants and blinding them to their true responsibilities. And of course he deplored the city's wealth, gained by turning away from its hinterland and towards the ocean and the wider world. Therein, he believed, lay a large part of the problem, since the people of Marseille were not truly French in their thoughts and loyalties. 'All Europe knows,' he wrote to the Committee of Public Safety:

> that when you ask a Marseillais if he is French, he will reply no, that he is Provençal. That naive reply describes the spirit of Marseille. That is the view they have here from birth: it is an original sin, an unerasable notion. By their nature the Marseillais see themselves as a people apart. Its geography, the mountains, the rivers which separate it from the rest of France, everything feeds this federalist view of the world. Even the best patriots here see only Marseille: Marseille is their fatherland, while France means nothing.[40]

In a letter to his colleague, Moïse Bayle from Toulon, Fréron developed his idea further, and claimed that Marseille was 'incurable for all time'. The only realistic solution to its disease would be a population transfusion, 'the deportation of all its present inhabitants and their replacement by men from the North'.[41]

If the Parisians were tempted to dismiss the federalist cities in these hackneyed terms, their real contempt was reserved for the peasant counter-revolutionaries of the West, whom local Jacobins had reviled, since the first stirrings of the revolt, as fanatical counter-revolutionaries driven by their hatred of liberty and equality to take up arms against their fellow citizens. To such people the Revolution could offer no quarter: they were 'brigands' who had chosen to live outside the law, and who were therefore to be hunted down and slaughtered like common bandits.[42] It is true that the Jacobins in Paris did make some attempt to distinguish between the leaders and the led – Turreau himself explained to the Minister of War that the northern part of the Vendée Militaire was particularly difficult terrain for the Republic because it was 'cankered (*gangrenée*) with aristocratic corruption'[43] – but at a time when republican soldiers were being killed and tortured by the rebels, any concern to distinguish between degrees of responsibility soon faded. It was the population of the West that was in a state of rebellion, men and women led into sedition by their nobles and their priests – especially by their priests in a countryside where all were assumed to be the pawns of a refractory and deeply counter-revolutionary clergy. The Vendean is not just *séditieux*; he is *fanatisé*, the dupe of the local clergy and deaf to reasoned argument. This is a theme to which Jacobins like Robespierre and Bertrand Barère repeatedly returned – the credulity and childlike faith of peasants who understood little of the Revolution and harked back to the world of the *ancien régime*. Barère, a 'reluctant terrorist' perhaps, saw in the conflict further evidence of a British fifth column which demanded an immediate and ruthless response, and he advocated a pitiless scorched-earth policy against the rebels.[44]

Once the Vendean was condemned as the 'other', as someone without moral scruples or a commitment to citizenship, it followed that he could not be considered as other men. The language of denunciation grew more violent, the representation more cruelly distorting. On the battlefield the Vendean did not conduct himself as a soldier and appeared to delight in acts

of unspeakable cruelty. To cite Turreau again, this time from a personal letter, 'They are less concerned here with fighting than with taking us by surprise and massacring us. The leaders of the rebels kidnap our soldiers and
make them die in the most indescribable torment'.[45] As the months passed,
the vitriolic tone of republican condemnation grew progressively harsher, until
the very humanity of the rebels came to be questioned. Of course they were
not rational, enlightened human beings; that was self-evident. They were
primitive peasants who belonged to what Parisians saw as an alien, super-
stitious culture, one where men sought the blessing of their priests before
battle and the promise that, should they have the honour of dying for Christ
and king, they would return from the dead after three days.[46] But was it
possible that men who committed such atrocities in cold blood and with
such apparent pleasure could retain even the palest remnants of human sen-
sibility? Were they really men at all? In the language of urban *commissaires*
and deputies-on-mission to the West it is noticeable how systematically the
terms of abuse that were heaped on the rebels sought to dehumanize them,
and to suggest that their behaviour was akin to that of wild beasts rather
than men. The same language occurred again and again in reports and memoirs, words like 'beasts', 'monsters', 'vermin', 'ferocious animals who seek to
devour the republic' – words which were used with deliberation to devalue
the lives of the enemy. They had, it was inferred, a taste for blood and a love
of killing that more properly belonged to wild animals, and, like refractory
priests and émigré nobles, their savagery was reserved for supporters of the
new political order. This impression was made more vivid when it was
observed that they lived like beasts, skulking behind hedges, leaping out
from bushes, retiring to lick their wounds in a clearing in the scrub or dragging their unfortunate victims back to their lairs (*tanières*).[47] The propaganda effect of this language was considerable, especially in the capital and
the republican strongholds of the interior, and also in the army, where soldiers soon learned that these were not honourable opponents whom they
should treat with respect. They obeyed no rules of war, nor had they any
understanding of honour in the way the revolutionary soldiers understood
it. Indeed, it was their animal instincts which best explained their successes
in engaging the republican army. As one cavalryman from the Gironde
wrote of his experience in the Vendée, 'if they had not acted like wild beasts
and sought refuge in the woods', they would surely have been wiped out.[48]

There was nothing haphazard about this representation. As in more recent
wars, the government was dehumanizing its opponents and spreading
atrocity stories with a clear awareness of the effects their propaganda would
have in angering civilian opinion and spurring their soldiers to new efforts.[49]
This was a war in which public opinion mattered and where words carried
a special weight. Once dehumanized in this way, once stripped of those
characteristics which others shared with him and depicted as a beast of the
fields, the Vendean became an easier target for vengeance. French civilians
would be less likely to shelter him, while revolutionary soldiers would have

fewer qualms about ordering him before a firing squad. It is easy to see why. Wolves and wild dogs pose an obvious threat to human beings, and no French peasant would hesitate to gun them down. Vermin must be trapped or poisoned so that others can enjoy good health; they have to be wiped out, eradicated in the interests of survival. The language that was used to revile the Vendeans went a long way to remove any lingering sense of the sanctity of human life, leaving them vulnerable to republican revenge. It is the language of extermination, the extermination of a corrupt community, an act of killing that evoked few moral qualms or repugnance, and no danger of fellow feeling.[50] It was a cleansing exercise, *épuration* in the fullest sense of the term.

What all this says, of course, is that words acquired an exceptional importance in revolutionary France, words and the images which they conveyed. It was dangerous to use them lightly, to praise the wrong values or political factions, or to show by the choice of terms a predilection for moderation or a taste for violence. The words a man chose told others so much about his politics, his ideology, his dependability in a world where fear of plots and conspiracies was so widespread and the possibility of betrayal never distant. Words were pored over and their tone closely analysed, and any inferences that they contained could return to haunt him. Like his choice of symbols or gestures, a man's words could reveal so much. Did he in his speech defer to the will of the people and recognize the authority of the Convention? Did he adhere closely to the revolutionary calendar, or use the new system of weights and measures? Did he address others as 'citoyen' and banish the social vocabulary of the *ancien régime*? Did he *tutoyer* those he met in the street or did he continue to show contempt for the *sans-culottes*? Words betrayed attitudes, and in creating a new and regenerated population it was above all attitudes that must be reformed: for many Jacobins, indeed, regeneration was the very essence of what the Revolution was about.[51] In that sense language itself had become imbued with political power at a time when different factions were intent on imposing their values on a Revolution still in the process of being defined. At different moments the good revolutionary was supposed to show by his language and demeanour respect for the person of the King; a belief in constitutional monarchy; faith in the Convention and the Republic, in the nation and the popular movement; acceptance of the Constitutional Church, dechristianization and the Supreme Being. Men must learn to change with the times, embrace new causes and recognize the general will, even at the price of self-contradiction. This was not easy, and all these ideas were fiercely contested, most commonly in words. If, as Keith Baker maintains, 'political authority is essentially a matter of linguistic authority', this was a key period in defining that authority through the creation of new discourse.[52]

In the provinces the battle of words assumed a dimension of its own, since at the heart of the republican project was the cult of unity and the nation state. This posed particular problems for local and regional identity as the opportunity for local initiatives progressively diminished. Whereas the National

Assembly had represented a conscious coming-together of deputies from the four corners of France to create a new polity, the balance of power between centre and periphery rapidly changed, to the detriment of the provinces. Thus the early encouragement of regional federations to cement loyalty to the Revolution gave way to a distrust of anything that smacked of decentralization and pluralism, until the moment was reached where even the use of regional dialects could render one suspect. By 1793 many republicans felt that the people could have only one legitimate focus for their loyalty, the 'one and indivisible nation' that was symbolized by the Convention, now purged of Girondins and moderates. And Paris lay at the core of that nation. Paris was at once the symbol of unity, the rallying point of Revolution, the head of the body politic.[53] To criticize Paris, to suggest that Parisians were too anarchic or too passionate in their pursuit of terror, or to imply that the more radical sections were dangerously autonomous, was therefore to risk the charge that one was criticizing the sovereign people and committing *lèse-nation*. It might also seem to imply criticism of the entire revolutionary project, of a 'revolution' the very name of which had come to acquire a symbolic power of its own. The identification of the word 'revolution' with ideas of virtue and morality left its critics exposed to a new vocabulary of exclusion, as 'contre-révolutionnaires' or as 'ennemis de la Révolution', powerful and damning charges in an increasingly chiliastic world that saw things in terms of black and white, good and evil.[54] It was a world where words signified moral qualities, where use of the wrong word could leave a man exposed as an enemy of the Revolution, and hence of the people. Revolutionary discourse was, from the very outset, a discourse of denunciation and accusation; Mirabeau was among the first to define denunciation as one of the main duties of the legislator, arguing that 'delation, a horrifying act under despotic rule, must be seen as the most important of the new virtues and the palladium of our nascent liberty'.[55] Not for nothing was one of the principal crimes of the Terror that of uttering 'propos inciviques', words that invoked unsound political sympathies or cast doubt on revolutionary virtue. Men were condemned for their words in 1794 just as they were condemned for their deeds. They were often what distinguished the true revolutionary from the 'other', and those critical of the capital and its citizens were well advised to weigh them with care.

Notes

1 Hans-Jürgen Lüsebrink and Rolf Reichart, *The Bastille. A History of a Symbol of Despotism and Freedom* (Durham, NC, 1997), p. 54.

2 Colin Lucas, 'Talking about urban popular violence in 1789', in Alan Forrest and Peter Jones (eds), *Reshaping France: Town, Country and Region during the French Revolution* (Manchester, 1991), p. 127.

3 Ibid., p. 125.

 4 Marcel Reinhard, *Nouvelle histoire de Paris: la Révolution* (Paris, 1971), p. 172.
 5 *Archives Parlementaires*, vol. 49, p. 216.
 6 *A.P.*, vol. 49, p. 219.
 7 *A.P.*, vol. 49, p. 236.
 8 *A.P.*, vol. 49, p. 231.
 9 Gorsas, *Courrier des Quatre-vingt-trois départements*, 18 August 1792; Leigh Whaley, *Radicals: Politics and Republicanism in the French Revolution* (Stroud, 2000), p. 82.
10 Olivier Coquard, *Jean-Paul Marat* (Paris, 1993), pp. 359–60.
11 Gorsas, *Courrier*, 3 September 1792.
12 Marcel Dorigny, 'Violence et révolution: les Girondins et les massacres de septembre', in Albert Soboul (ed.), *Actes du Colloque Girondins et Montagnards* (Paris, 1980), pp. 103–20.
13 Morris Slavin, *The Making of an Insurrection: Parisian Sections and the Gironde* (Cambridge, MA, 1986), pp. 6–7.
14 Alan Forrest, *The Revolution in Provincial France. Aquitaine, 1789–99* (Oxford, 1996), p. 205.
15 W. D. Edmonds, *Jacobinism and the Revolt of Lyon, 1789–93* (Oxford, 1990), p. 128.
16 Jeffrey Kaplow, *Elbeuf during the Revolutionary Period: History and Social Structure* (Baltimore, 1964), p. 242–3, 248.
17 Edouard Herriot, *Lyon n'est plus* (4 vols, Paris, 1939), vol. 3, 'La répression'.
18 Alan Forrest, 'Federalism', in Colin Lucas (ed.), *The French Revolution and the Creation of Modern Political Culture, ii: The Political Culture of the French Revolution* (Oxford, 1988), p. 316.
19 A. Kuscinski, *Dictionnaire des Conventionnels* (Paris, 1916), pp. 337–40.
20 Martyn Lyons, *Révolution et Terreur à Toulouse* (Toulouse, 1980), p. 67.
21 Forrest, 'Federalism', p. 318.
22 Danièle Pingué, *Les mouvements jacobins en Normandie orientale: les sociétés politiques dans l'Eure et la Seine-inférieure, 1790–95* (Paris, 2001), p. 132.
23 Alan Forrest, *Society and Politics in Revolutionary Bordeaux* (Oxford, 1975), p. 135.
24 Paul Hanson, *Provincial Politics in the French Revolution. Caen and Limoges, 1789–94* (Baton Rouge, LA, 1989), p. 88.
25 *A.P.*, vol. 65, p. 51.
26 Albert Goodwin, 'The federalist movement in Caen during the French Revolution', *Bulletin of John Rylands Library* 42 (1960), p. 340.
27 William Scott, *Terror and Repression in Revolutionary Marseilles* (London, 1973), p. 183.
28 *A.P.*, vol. 94, p. 195.
29 *A.P.*, vol. 94, p. 95.
30 *A.P.*, vol. 94, p. 72.

31 *A.P.*, vol. 94, p. 197.

32 Catherine Lacour, 'La province dans l'idéologie révolutionnaire: étude d'un discours politique' (mémoire de maîtrise, Université de Paris – I, 1988), pp. 10, 25–8.

33 Ibid., p. 36.

34 Ibid., p. 70.

35 Richard Cobb, 'Some aspects of the revolutionary mentality', in Jeffrey Kaplow (ed.), *New Perspectives on the French Revolution. Readings in Historical Sociology* (New York, 1965), pp. 308–9.

36 François Bourdillat, 'La crise fédéraliste, mai 1793–décembre 1793: l'image de la province insurgée à travers les Archives Parlementaires' (mémoire de maîtrise, Université de Paris – I, 1986), p. 146.

37 Edmonds, *Jacobinism and the Revolt of Lyon*, p. 289.

38 Pierre Bécamps, 'Girondistes et Montagnards', in François-Georges Pariset (ed.), *Bordeaux au dix-huitième siècle* (Bordeaux, 1968), p. 422.

39 Scott, *Terror and Repression,* p. 136.

40 Jacques Guilhaumou, *Marseille républicaine, 1791–93* (Paris, 1992), p. 231.

41 Scott, *Terror and Repression,* p. 138.

42 For a fuller discussion of the manner in which republicans talked of the Vendeans, see Peter Tyson, 'The Role of Republican and *Patriote* Discourse in the Insurrection of the Vendée' (MA dissertation, University of York, 1994).

43 Michel Chatry (ed.), *Turreau en Vendée: Mémoires et Correspondance* (Cholet, 1992), p. 367.

44 Leo Gershoy, *Bertrand Barère: A Reluctant Terrorist* (Princeton, NJ, 1962), p. 175.

45 Chatry (ed.), *Turreau*, p. 270.

46 Tyson, 'Republican and *Patriote* Discourse', p. 98.

47 Ibid., pp. 96–7.

48 G. Pages, 'Lettres de requis et volontaires de Coutras en Vendée et en Bretagne', *Revue historique et archéologique du Libournais* 190 (1983), p. 155.

49 See, by way of example, John Horne and Alan Kramer, *German Atrocities, 1914. A History of Denial* (New Haven, 2001).

50 Reynald Secher, *Le génocide franco-français. La Vendée-vengé* (Paris, 1986), *passim*. The idea that the Vendée is best understood as genocide is proposed in the *préface* by Jean Meyer, who compares the repression of the region with that of German Jews in the Holocaust (p. 15), and in the *avant-propos* by Pierre Chaunu, who writes that 'the sadistic imagination of Turreau's columns equals that of the SS, the gulags and the Khmers Rouges' (p. 22).

51 Mona Ozouf, *L'homme régénéré. Essais sur la Révolution Française* (Paris, 1989), p. 132.

52 Keith Michael Baker, *Inventing the French Revolution* (Cambridge, 1990), p. 5.

53 Lucien Jaume, *Le discours jacobin de la démocratie* (Paris, 1989), pp. 113–14.

54 Alain Rey, *'Révolution'. Histoire d'un mot* (Paris, 1989), p. 134.

55 Quotation from the *Chronique de Paris*, 75 (6 November 1789); see Jacques Guilhaumou, 'Fragments of a Discourse of Denunciation, 1789–94', in Keith Michael Baker (ed.), *The French Revolution and the Creation of Modern Political Culture, vol. 4: The Terror* (Oxford, 1994), p. 140.

|12|

The Revolution and the growth of regional identity

Relations between the provinces and the revolutionary state were never easy, as the Revolution's expressed hatred of privilege and hierarchy attacked vested interests, while the language of state centralism was often seen as an affront to local traditions. Of course, the threat posed by the revolutionaries was often exaggerated, and it would be wrong to regard the Revolution as wholly centralist. The municipal revolution and the federations of 1790 brought a new dynamism to the stagnating local institutions of the *ancien régime*. And even the Republic's insistence on the use of French was never comprehensively implemented in the way Grégoire or Barère would have favoured: in the Midi, for instance, the 1791 constitution was translated into several local dialects, Provençal was spoken, quite openly and flagrantly, in Jacobin club debates, and even the republican constitution of 1793 was posted on the walls of Marseille in Provençal.[1] Yet the myth that lingered into the nineteenth century – a myth forged on the Jacobin experience and perpetuated by Napoleon's administrative reforms – was of a harshly centralist polity based on nationalism and the ideal of the 'one and indivisible republic'. At the time, much of France accepted this with apparent passivity, though a sense of local identity did play some part in defining the anti-revolutionary movements in Brittany, the Vendée and other parts of the periphery. But in the course of the following century, regionalism would emerge as a major force in French provincial culture, a regionalism that was often rather vaguely focused, opposing the concentration of economic and demographic growth in the Paris Basin with the same voice as it lamented the growing authority of the French state. For some it was primarily a cultural movement, urging the use of local languages and dialects or trying to revive provincial literary traditions that were in danger of being lost for ever. For others, its main force was political – the demand for greater autonomy, greater freedom from the control of Paris. Others again turned to monarchism, seeing regionalism as a useful weapon with which to attack the

French Republic. 'All arguments were thrown in, higgledy-piggledy,' concluded Léon Dubreuil of the regionalism he knew in the early years of
the twentieth century, 'some geographic, others economic or historical'.[2]
They played to an emotionalism, an anti-rationalist spirit in parts of the
provinces which, with clever manipulation, could be mobilized against Paris
and against the tradition of the revolutionary state.

It was an emotional response born of a sense of loss and hurt. During the
1790s, provincial opinion had suffered the indignity of looking on as the
values and language of the Revolution became increasingly identified with
Paris and the people of the capital. 'Le peuple', only too often, was taken to
mean the Parisian *peuple*, just as the language of virtue and public commendation was increasingly a reflection of the wishes of the capital. 'Le peuple
s'est levé,' said Robespierre in 1792, as if that gave added authority to the
Jacobin cause. Yet the people in question were not to be found in the countryside, nor yet in any provincial city; they were, quite specifically, the Paris
crowd, a crowd instigated and led by the radical sections and the Paris
Commune. The fact that 'le peuple s'est levé' was deemed sufficient to provide legitimation not just for their immediate actions, but for the political
cause they embraced; and the people, the crowd, was now the insurrectionary people to whom others must defer. Indeed, as Jacques Guilhaumou
suggests, from that point the nature of politics changed, and the task of the
legislator became that of defining politics in terms of the *langue du peuple*,
the language of the Paris streets.[3] For many in the provinces the nineteenth
century brought repeated reminders of the special status which the Republic
accorded to the Paris crowd, as the revolutionary movement became identified with the barricades of 1830 and 1848. That identification of Paris with
the nation, with liberty and the Republic, was reborn – at least for republicans – during the siege of the city in the Franco-Prussian War. Others might
capitulate or seek a rapid armistice, but Paris held out, its volunteers and
francs-tireurs battling on valiantly against the Prussian army for the honour
of their city and of France. In the process, the capital once again became identified with the Republic and national pride, and the heroism of the Parisians
inspired a new republican myth.[4]

Regionalists argued that there is a fundamental conflict of interest
between Paris and the French regions which lies at the very heart of French
history.[5] According to this view, there is no distortion in presenting the issue
as a consistent tussle for power across the two centuries since 1789 between
Paris and the provinces, between state and regional interests. Barrès, Maurras,
Renan and a host of other writers during the Third Republic took the side
of the provinces, arguing that their culture and identity had been submerged
in the wake of nascent nationalism and state-building, to the point where
the French Republic had developed into one of the most insensitively centralized states in the modern world, with Paris starving the periphery of its
native talent and draining much of the vitality from provincial France. A
Jacobin tradition had emerged from the revolutionary decade, they claimed,

which continued to inform French bureaucracy and stunt provincial development. As recently as 1947, in a somewhat apocalyptic vision of a country where the provinces were starved to service the capital, Jean-François Gravier called upon the Fourth Republic to reverse a centuries-old tradition of centralized power, criticizing centralist policies which, he argued, would lead to the death of many hill farms and pastoral communities. He put his case clinically and polemically. 'Ignoring both decentralisation (that is, local liberties) and deconcentration (or delegating authority to the prefects),' he wrote, 'the unitary system favoured by the French concentrated all forms of authority in a capital city which emerged as the sole nervous centre of national life'.[6]

For much of the nineteenth century the ideal of the nation was muddied by political dissension, by the countermanding discourses of royalism and republicanism, Orleanism and Bonapartism. Provincial sentiment, too, was influenced by these conflicting currents of political thought, as well as by the cultural romanticism of the age. By the 1880s, much of the strength of regionalist appeal was rooted in culture. Provincialism had become infused with a sense of mission to speak regional languages, read half-forgotten literature and reinvent cultural identities which were in danger of extinction. Breton and Provençal, Catalan and Occitan all found themselves at the heart of regional revivals, while the poetry of Frédéric Mistral and the political message he held out to the young *Félibriges* of the Midi attracted new adherents to the cause of a provincial linguistic renaissance.[7] Dialects, *patois*, songs, regional languages, religious practices, folk tales and folklore, all had their place in the lives of the people, and all, regionalists insisted, must be protected against the apathy and educational reductionism of the nation state. They still tended to advance their case in a very defensive way, emphasizing the need to champion traditional ways of life against intrusions from the outside, from the ministries in Paris on the one hand, and from technology and the forces of modernity on the other. Many remained frightened by what they saw as the threat of the modern state, and the extension of the tentacles of Paris through both the advance of the railway and telegraph and the administrative machinery of the Republic. It is easy to write them off as provincial conservatives dedicated to resurrecting a cult of the past in defiance of the values of the new industrial age.

A particular focus of regionalist concern and propaganda was what they saw as the deliberate use of schooling by the politicians of the Third Republic to undermine cherished identities and inculcate loyalty to the nation. In Jules Ferry the Republic had an education minister who was not only fanatical in his belief in universal lay schooling, but who saw *civisme* as being an essentially national quality, one in which the periphery was seriously deficient. In rural France, he believed, the taste for communal life and associative enterprise was underdeveloped, and the spirit of liberty remained weak. Schools had a duty to bring peasant children into the French nation, to teach them civic responsibility and republican values.[8] In this process the primary schoolteacher had an indispensable role, with the consequence that *instituteurs* came to be portrayed by those who championed provincial identity as insensitive centralizers, men set on a 'civilizing mission' which would destroy local cultures and mould peasant children into citizens of the French Republic. They were denounced as outsiders, their loyalties to the ministry in Paris rather than to the communities they served, as colonizers as much as civilizers who, in the words of the *Dictionnaire Pédagogique* of Elie Pécaut, received children 'from the hands of nature' and set out with the express aim of civilizing them. This may indeed have reflected the tone of school manuals and the instruction offered in some teachers' training colleges. But, as Jean-François Chanet has shown, on the ground the picture was far more varied, with the vast majority of primary teachers men of rural origins who never left their native region, teaching in a succession of tiny communes and seeking advancement only to get closer to their roots and their village. They might appear as outsiders in a *France profonde* where even the next village could seem distant and hostile; and some did adopt the values of their profession and refused to tolerate anything but grammatical French. But that did not make them all dogmatic Jacobins intent on erasing every vestige of local identity, as regionalists were wont to claim. Indeed, the notion that *instituteurs* were uprooted, embittered individuals, stripped of their local ties, their souls perverted by the propaganda to which they had been exposed while at the *école normale*, is palpably untrue, and a distortion redolent of much of the regionalist propaganda of the time.[9]

Many local schoolmasters became key figures in the regionalist revival of the years after 1871, writing municipal and departmental histories, contributing to local learned societies, and exalting the supposed qualities of regional life as a central part of their patriotic discourse. They remained nationalists and republicans, but in the wake of the military disaster of 1870 they had to rethink their definition of the nation to which they were dedicated. It could no longer be reasonably presented as the most powerful in Europe, nor as the most wealthy or the most technically advanced. So they stressed the variety, the richness, the generosity of France – its landscape, its river valleys, its soil and climate – and taught their classes to appreciate their good fortune in being born in such a blessed society. Frequently they transmitted this message by talking of their local region, the *petite patrie* of which the children had a first-hand experience, using it as a template for the wider community that was the nation, a paradigm of the manifold riches that were France. They praised its culture and folklore; they stressed the character of its people; and they emphasized the part that local heroes had played in the wider history of the French nation, presenting them as paragons of the qualities which had helped shape French development. They encouraged their pupils to appreciate their own locality, to go on walks around its historical sites, and to write accounts of its past glories. And they saw no tension between an appreciation of their region and an understanding of France, a view repeated again and again in the departmental histories which were so widely used in French primary schools in the years between the two world wars. This view is well illustrated by the words of one such *manuel*, distributed in the Haute-Marne in 1928, which concludes:

> Child, now you have got to know your locality a little better. You have been able in this short book to understand how, in the image of France, it presents, both through its history and in its physical appearance and its riches, the twin qualities of *moderation* and *variety*.[10]

The authors always stressed regional character – fiery and enthusiastic in the Midi, solid and responsible in the North – as part of the wider canvas that was France.

Provincialism had undergone a sea change since the eighteenth century. What had for many in the *ancien régime* been little more than provincial difference had now resurfaced as a full-blown regionalism, which in turn developed into a political ideology in its own right, based on the belief that France was administratively over-centralized and culturally intolerant, and arguing that centralism must lead to tyranny. For some regionalists, most notably Jean Charles-Brun, founder of the Fédération Régionaliste Française in 1900, all forms of centralism were to be condemned, whether monarchist, Bonapartist or Jacobin, and he took care not to place all responsibility on the Revolution or on its republican tradition. The enemy, he believed, was an over-reliance on state bureaucracy, which killed off the energy and cultural diversity of all those who lived beyond the gates of Paris. Regionalism, he reminded his readers, was a process which allowed the various *pays* of France to regain their own organic life. It was not the same as decentralization, since that implied that political powers legitimately belonged at the centre, something which regionalists firmly denied. Nor was it just a political ideal; it was also a discipline of the mind, a way of reconciling the conflicting imperatives of individualism and unitarity. For if the regionalist was opposed to the power of the centralized state, argued Charles-Brun, he also challenged undisciplined individualism, the right of each individual to seek advancement without reference to his origins or to the interests of the natural group from which he had sprung.[11] In regionalism, he believed, lay an essential organizing principle for France, a way of unleashing the energy of the nation, a true and creative form of nationalism.

Other regionalists identified bureaucracy with the Republic and with republican institutions; and they sought salvation in monarchy. They believed that it was the First Republic which had made France the most over-bureaucratized state on earth and had created public institutions which were 'perversions of the real ideals and spirit of the nation'.[12] This is the argument first explored by the Félibriges in Provence and later identified with Charles Maurras and the Action Française, the authoritarian, right-wing voice of a more traditional, Catholic France that felt itself unrepresented in the Third Republic and which held that only the restoration of a king could offer Frenchmen an impartial system of justice and protect them from the state and bureaucratic centralism. Maurras drew a distinction between what he termed the 'real France', which commanded his loyalty and affection, and the current legal state of the country, and he insisted that republican institutions were the abnegation of the true values of the French people, a people that had its roots deep in the soil of the provinces. He was curiously sentimental in his depiction of the provinces of the *ancien régime*, emphasizing their freedom from central control, and claiming that they enjoyed cultural individuality before the Revolution imposed its terrible standardization.[13] This was a convenient fiction, but it was one that had great appeal to the cultural regionalism of Provence or Lorraine, Flanders or the Basque country, to the poets and folklorists, for instance, who clustered around Mistral and campaigned for the revival of local dialects. Maurras shared their passion for Provençal autonomy, but he believed that language and tradition were only a staging post, and that full political autonomy must follow. In 1892, indeed, he was one of the younger generation of Félibres who subscribed to a manifesto calling for the restoration of regional liberties and the dismantling of the heavily bureaucratized French state. It was a cry that came from the heart, a demand for political liberty and for sovereign assemblies in the great cultural *pays* of the South, and a challenge to the unity and authority of the Republic.

> We want to release from their departmental cages the souls of provinces whose names are still used everywhere by everyone: Gascons, Auvergnats, Limousins, Béarnais, Dauphinois, Roussillonnais, Provençaux and Languedociens. We are autonomists, we are federalists, and if somewhere in northern France a people wants to march with us, our hand is outstretched ... We want sovereign assemblies in Bordeaux, in Toulouse, in Montpellier, in either Marseille or Aix. These assemblies will run our administration, our courts, our schools, our universities, our public works.[14]

For Maurras and his kind, the appeal of regionalism was precisely that it provided an alternative to the nation state and the bureaucratic centralism of the modern world, an alternative that was reassuring in its timelessness, its linking of past and present, its trust in traditional ways of organization. It was a call to undo the administrative reforms of the French Revolution, to escape from its humanism and secularism, and to wallow in cultural difference. The cause of the French regions, as Maurras preached it, was that of reaction, a return to an imagined pre-revolutionary world, unsullied by ideas of liberty or equality, nationalism or citizenship. For him, regionalism could only be achieved by overturning the whole tradition of the Republic, and by returning to a past of kings and sovereign courts, honour and regional pride. It was a past without 1789, a world from which the French Revolution had been erased.

Notes

1 Philippe Blanchet, 'Langues et pouvoirs en France de 1780 à 1850: un problème de définition', in Roger Dupuy (ed.), *Pouvoir local et Révolution* (Rennes, 1995), p. 545.

2 Léon Dubreuil, 'Sur le régionalisme pendant la Révolution', *Annales Révolutionnaires* 9 (1917), p. 595.

3 Jacques Guilhaumou, *La langue politique et la Révolution Française. De l'évènement à la raison linguistique* (Paris, 1989), p. 20.

4 Stéphane Audoin-Rouzeau, *1870. La France dans la Guerre* (Paris, 1989), p. 257.

5 For a more cursory discussion of the place of provincialism in modern French history, see Alan Forrest, 'Paris versus the provinces: regionalism and decentralisation since 1789', in Martin Alexander (ed.), *French History since Napoleon* (London, 1999), pp. 106–26.

6 Jean-François Gravier, *Paris et le désert français* (Paris, 1947), p. 14.

7 Philippe Martel, 'Le Félibrige', in Pierre Nora (ed.), *Les lieux de mémoire*, part 3, *Les France*, vol. 2, *Traditions* (Paris, 1992), pp. 567–611.

8 Mona Ozouf, *L'école de la France: essais sur la Révolution, l'utopie et l'enseignement* (Paris, 1984), p. 411.

9 Mona Ozouf, 'Préface' to Jean-François Chanet, *L'École républicaine et les petites patries* (Paris, 1996), p. 9.

10 Anne-Marie Thiesse, *Ils apprenaient la France: l'exaltation des régions dans le discours patriotique* (Paris, 1997), p. 66.

11 Jean Charles-Brun, *Le régionalisme* (Paris, 1911), pp. 61, 69–70.

12 Sudhir Hazareesingh, *Political Traditions in Modern France* (Oxford, 1994), p. 129.

13 Maurice Bordes, 'De la Province à la Région', in *Études et Documents (Société archéologique, historique, littéraire et scientifique du Gers)*, fasc. IV, 1971, p. 7.

14 Robert Gildea, *The Past in French History* (New Haven, 1994), p. 180.

BIBLIOGRAPHY

Aberdam, S., Bianchi, S., Demeude, R., Ducoudray, E., Gainot, B., Genty, M. and Wolikow, C. (eds), *Voter, élire pendant la Révolution Française, 1789–1799* (Paris, 1999).

Ado, Anatoli, *Paysans en Révolution. Terre, pouvoir et jacquerie, 1789–94* (Paris, 1996).

Andress, David, *French Society in Revolution, 1789–99* (Manchester, 1999).

Andress, David, *Massacre at the Champ de Mars: Popular Dissent and Political Culture in the French Revolution* (London, 2000).

Annat, Jean, *Les sociétés populaires: la période révolutionnaire dans les Basses-Pyrénées* (Pau, 1940).

Arbelot, Guy and Lepetit, Bernard, *Atlas de la Révolution Française, vol. 1: Routes et communications* (Paris, 1987).

Arches, Pierre, 'Le premier projet de fédération nationale', *Annales historiques de la Révolution Française* 28 (1956).

Archives parlementaires de 1787 à 1860, première série (1787–1799), ed. M. J. Mavidal and M. E. Laurent (Paris, 1879).

Ariès, Philippe, *Histoire des populations françaises et de leurs attitudes devant la vie depuis le 18e siècle* (Paris, 1971).

Aston, Nigel, *Religion and Revolution in France, 1780–1804* (London, 2000).

Audoin-Rouzeau, Stéphane, *1870. La France dans la Guerre* (Paris, 1989).

Baczko, Bronislaw, *Ending the Terror. The French Revolution after Robespierre* (Cambridge, 1994).

Baker, Keith Michael (ed.), *The French Revolution and the Creation of Modern Political Culture, vol. 4: The Terror* (Oxford, 1994).

Baker, Keith Michael (ed.), *The Old Regime and the Revolution* (Chicago, 1987).

Baker, Keith Michael, *Inventing the French Revolution* (Cambridge, 1990).

Baratier, Edouard (ed.), *Histoire de la Provence* (Toulouse, 1990).

Bart, Jean, *La Révolution française en Bourgogne* (Paris, 1996).

Bayon, Jacqueline, 'Saint-Étienne et les Stéphanois face à la crise fédéraliste lyonnaise', *Cahiers d'histoire* 38 (1993).

Bécamps, Pierre, *J.-B.-M. Lacombe, Président de la Commission Militaire* (Bordeaux, 1953).

Bécamps, Pierre (ed.), *Un Bordelais sous la Terreur: mémoires de Jean-Baptiste Brochon* (Bordeaux, 1989).

Becker, Jean-Jacques, 'Y a-t-il une culture de guerre civile?' in *La guerre civile entre Histoire et Mémoire* (Nantes, 1995).

Bell, David A., *Lawyers and Citizens: The Making of a Political Elite in Old Regime France* (New York, 1994).

Bell, David A., *The Cult of the Nation in France. Inventing Nationalism, 1680–1800*, (Cambridge, MA, 2001).

Bellanger, Claude (ed.), *Histoire générale de la presse française* (4 vols, Paris, 1969), vol. 1.

Bellée, A. and Duchemin, V. (eds), *Cahiers des plaintes et doléances des paroisses de la province du Maine pour les États-Généraux de 1789* (Le Mans, 1881).

Bély, Lucien (ed.), *Dictionnaire de l'Ancien Régime: royaume de France, 16e–18e siècle* (Paris, 1996).

Bercé, Yves-Marie, *Histoire des Croquants. Étude des soulèvements populaires au XVIIe siècle dans le Sud-ouest de la France* (2 vols, Geneva, 1974).

Berlanstein, Lenard R., *The Barristers of Toulouse in the Eighteenth Century, 1740–93* (Baltimore, MD, 1975).

Bernard-Griffiths, Simone, Chemin, Marie-Claude and Ehrard, Jean (eds), *Révolution française et 'vandalisme révolutionnaire'. Actes du colloque international de Clermont-Ferrand, 15–17 décembre 1988* (Paris, 1992).

Bernet, Jacques, Jessenne, Jean-Pierre and Leuwers, Hervé (eds), *Du Directoire au Consulat. 1: Le lien politique local dans la Grande Nation* (Lille, 1998).

Bertaud, Jean-Paul, *Camille et Lucie Desmoulins* (Paris, 1986).

Biard, Michel, 'La mission du 9 mars 1793', in Christine Le Bozec and Eric Wauters (eds), *Pour la Révolution Française. Études en hommage à Claude Mazauric* (Rouen, 1998).

Biard, Michel, *Missionnaires de la République: les représentants du peuple en mission, 1793–95* (Paris, 2002).

Bienvenu, Richard, *The Ninth of Thermidor: the Fall of Robespierre* (New York, 1968).

Birchall, Ian, *The Spectre of Babeuf* (Basingstoke, 1997).

Blanchet, Philippe, 'Langues et pouvoirs en France de 1780 à 1850: un problème de définition', in Roger Dupuy (ed.), *Pouvoir local et Révolution* (Rennes, 1995).

Blaufarb, Rafe, 'Démocratie et professionalisme: l'avancement par l'élection dans l'armée française, 1760–1815', *Annales historiques de la Révolution Française* 310 (1997).

Bodinier, Bernard and Teyssier, Eric, *'L'événement le plus important de la Révolution': La vente des biens nationaux (1789–1867) en France et dans les territoires annexés* (Paris, 2000).

Bohanan, Donna, *Old and New Nobility in Aix-en-Provence, 1600–1695. Portrait of an Urban Elite* (Baton Rouge, LA, 1992).

Bois, Jean-Pierre, *Histoire des 14 juillet, 1789–1919* (Rennes, 1991).

Bois, Paul, *Paysans de l'Ouest* (Paris, 1971).

Bordes, Maurice, *La réforme municipale du contrôleur général Laverdy et son application, 1764–71* (Toulouse, 1963).

Bordes, Maurice, 'De la Province à la Région', in *Études et Documents (Société archéologique, historique, littéraire et scientifique du Gers)* (fasc. IV, 1971).

Bordes, Maurice, *L'administration provinciale et municipale en France au dix-huitième siècle* (Paris, 1972).

Bordes, Maurice, 'La Gascogne à la fin de l'Ancien Régime: une province?', in Christian Gras and Georges Livet (eds), *Régions et régionalisme en France du dix-huitième siècle à nos jours* (Paris, 1977).

Bossenga, Gail, *The Politics of Privilege: Old Regime and Revolution in Lille* (Cambridge, 1991).

Bourdillat, François, 'La crise fédéraliste, mai 1793–décembre 1793: l'image de la province insurgée à travers les Archives Parlementaires' (mémoire de maîtrise, Université de Paris – I, 1986).

Bourdin, Philippe and Gainot, Bernard (eds), *La République directoriale. Actes du colloque de Clermont-Ferrand, 22–24 mai 1997* (2 vols, Paris, 1998).

Bourgin, G. (ed.), *Le partage des biens communaux: documents sur la préparation de la loi du 10 juin 1793* (Paris, 1908).

Boutier, Jean, 'Jacqueries en pays croquant. Les révoltes paysannes en Aquitaine', *Annales: ESC* 34 (1979).

Boutier, Jean, *Campagnes en émoi. Révoltes et Révolution en Bas-Limousin, 1789–1800* (Paris, 1987).

Boutier, Jean and Boutry, Philippe (eds), *Atlas de la Révolution Française, vol. 6: Les sociétés politiques* (Paris, 1992).

Bouton, Cynthia, *The Flour War: Gender, Class and Community in Late Ancien Regime French Society* (University Park, PA, 1993).

Brassart, Laurent, 'Des décisions parisiennes aux municipalités cantonales: la mise en oeuvre de la politique directoriale dans le département de l'Aisne', *Annales historiques de la Révolution Française* 330 (2002).

Brown, Howard G., 'From Organic Society to Security State: the War on Brigandage in France, 1797–1802', *Journal of Modern History* 69 (1997).

Brown, Howard G., 'The search for stability', in Howard G. Brown and Judith A. Miller (eds), *Taking Liberties. Problems of a New Order from the French Revolution to Napoleon* (Manchester, 2002).

Brunet, Michel, *Le Roussillon. Une société contre l'État, 1780–1820* (Toulouse, 1986).

Butel, Yannick, 'Fêtes et divertissements en Bordelais au dix-huitième siècle' (mémoire de maîtrise, Université de Bordeaux – III, 1978).

Cameron, J. B., jun., 'The Revolution of the Sections of Marseille – Federalism in the Department of Bouches-du-Rhône in 1793' (PhD thesis, University of North Carolina at Chapel Hill, 1971).

Caron, Pierre (ed.), *Paris pendant la Terreur: rapports des agents secrets du ministre de l'intérieur* (7 vols, Paris, 1910–78).

Carrière, Charles, 'Le travail des hommes, 17e–18e siècles', in Edouard Baratier (ed.), *Histoire de Marseille* (Toulouse, 1990).

Carrot, Georges, *La garde nationale (1789–1871): une force publique ambigüe* (Paris, 2001).

Caudrillier, Gustaaf, *L'association royaliste de l'Institut Philanthropique à Bordeaux* (Paris, 1908).

Censer, Jack, *Prelude to Power. The Parisian Radical Press, 1789–91* (Baltimore, 1976).

Certeau, Michel de, Julia, Dominique and Revel, Jacques, *Une politique de la langue: la Révolution* (Paris, 1975).

Chabalier, R. de, 'Les camps de Jalès', *Revue du souvenir vendéen* 95 (1971).

Chagny, Robert (ed.), *Aux origines provinciales de la Révolution* (Grenoble, 1990).

Chagny, Robert (ed.), *La Révolution Française: idéaux, singularités, influences* (Grenoble, 2002).

Chanet, Jean-François, *L'École républicaine et les petites patries* (Paris, 1996).

Charles-Brun, Jean, *Le régionalisme* (Paris, 1911).

Chartier, Roger, 'Cultures, Lumières, doléances: les cahiers de 1789', *Revue d'histoire moderne et contemporaine* 28 (1981).

Chatry, Michel (ed.), *Turreau en Vendée: mémoires et correspondance* (Cholet, 1992).

Chaumié, Jacqueline, *Le réseau d'Antraïgues et la contre-révolution, 1791–93* (Paris, 1965).

Chaussinand-Nogaret, Guy, *Mirabeau* (Paris, 1982).

Chianéa, Gérard, 'Institutions dauphinoises, pré-révolution et identité provinciale', in Vital Chomel (ed.), *Les débuts de la Révolution Française en Dauphiné, 1788–91* (Grenoble, 1988).

Church, Clive H., *Revolution and Red Tape: The French Ministerial Bureaucracy, 1770–1850* (Oxford, 1981).

Clémendot, Pierre, *Le département de la Meurthe à l'époque du Directoire* (Nancy, 1966).

Cobb, Richard, *L'armée révolutionnaire parisienne à Lyon et dans la région lyonnaise (frimaire–prairial an II)* (Lyon, 1952).

Cobb, Richard, 'The people in the French Revolution', *Past and Present* 15 (1959).

Cobb, Richard, *Les armées révolutionnaires: instrument de la Terreur dans les départements, avril 1793–floréal an II* (2 vols, Paris, 1961–3).

Cobb, Richard, 'Some aspects of the revolutionary mentality', in Jeffrey Kaplow (ed.), *New Perspectives on the French Revolution. Readings in Historical Sociology* (New York, 1965).

Cobb, Richard, *Terreur et subsistances, 1793–95* (Paris, 1965).

Cobb, Richard, *A Second Identity. Essays on France and French History* (Oxford, 1968).

Cobb, Richard, *The Police and the People: French Popular Protest, 1789–1820* (Oxford, 1970).

Cobb, Richard, *Reactions to the French Revolution* (Oxford, 1972).

Cobb, Richard, *Paris and its Provinces, 1792–1802* (Oxford, 1975).

Cobban, Alfred, 'Local Government during the French Revolution', in *Aspects of the French Revolution* (New York, 1970).

Collectif, *Existe-t-il un fédéralisme jacobin?* (111e Congrès National des Sociétés Savantes, Poitiers, 1986).

Condorcet, *Essai sur la constitution et les fonctions des assemblées provinciales* (2 vols, Paris, 1788).

Coquard, Olivier, 'Le Paris de Marat', in Michel Vovelle (ed.), *Paris et la Révolution* (Paris, 1989).

Coquard, Olivier, *Jean-Paul Marat* (Paris, 1993).

Coquery, Natacha, *L'espace du pouvoir. De la demeure privée à l'édifice public, Paris, 1700–90* (Paris, 2000).

Corbin, Alain, 'Paris-province', in Pierre Nora (ed.), *Les lieux de mémoire*, part 3, *Les France*, vol. 1, *Conflits et partage* (Paris, 1992).

Cormack, William S., *Revolution and Political Conflict in the French Navy, 1789–94* (Cambridge, 1995).

Courteault, Paul, *La Révolution et les théâtres à Bordeaux* (Paris, 1926).

Crook, Malcolm, 'Federalism and the French Revolution: the revolt in Toulon in 1793', *History* 65 (1980).

Crook, Malcolm, *Toulon in War and Revolution. From the* ancien régime *to the Restoration* (Manchester, 1991).

Crook, Malcolm, *Elections in the French Revolution* (Cambridge, 1996).

Crook, Malcolm, 'The French Revolution and Napoleon, 1788–1814', in M. Crook (ed.), *Revolutionary France, 1788–1880* (Oxford, 2001).

Crubaugh, Anthony, *Balancing the Scales of Justice: Local Courts and Rural Society in South-west France, 1750–1800* (University Park, PA, 2001).

Cubells, Monique, *La Provence des Lumières: les parlementaires d'Aix au dix-huitième siècle* (Paris, 1984).

Cubells, Monique, *Les horizons de la liberté. Naissance de la Révolution en Provence, 1787–89* (Paris, 1987).

Czouze-Tornare, Alain-Jacques, 'Les troupes suisses à Paris', in Michel Vovelle (ed.), *Paris et la Révolution* (Paris, 1989).

Dalby, Jonathan, *Les paysans cantaliens et la Révolution française, 1789–94* (Clermont-Ferrand, 1989).

Daudet, Ernest, *La conjuration de Pichegru et les complots royalistes du Midi et de l'Est, 1795–97* (Paris, 1901).

David, Philippe, *Un port de l'océan pendant la Révolution. La Rochelle et son District, 1791–95* (La Rochelle, 1938).

Desan, Suzanne, *Reclaiming the Sacred. Lay Religion and Popular Politics in Revolutionary France* (Ithaca, NY, 1990).

Descimon, Robert, 'Milice bourgeoise et identité citadine à Paris au temps de la Ligue', *Annales: ESC*, 48 (1993).

Désert, Gabriel, *La Révolution Française en Normandie* (Toulouse, 1989).

Devlin, Jonathan, 'The Directory and the Politics of Military Command: the Army of the Interior in South-east France', *French History* 4 (1990).

Deyon, Pierre, *L'État face au pouvoir local: un autre regard sur l'histoire* (Paris, 1996).

D'Hollander, Paul and Pageot, Pierre, *La Révolution Française dans le Limousin et la Marche* (Toulouse, 1989).

Donnadieu, Jean-Pierre, '1789, motions et adresses. Le Languedoc écrit à Paris', in M. Vovelle (ed.), *L'image de la Révolution Française* (4 vols, Paris, 1989).

Dorigny, Marcel, 'Violence et révolution: les Girondins et les massacres de septembre', in Albert Soboul (ed.), *Actes du Colloque Girondins et Montagnards* (Paris, 1980).

Dorigny, Marcel, 'Crise des institutions municipales et émergence d'un parti patriote: l'exemple de la ville d'Autun, 1787–90', in Robert Chagny (ed.), *Aux origines provinciales de la Révolution* (Grenoble, 1990).

Doyle, William, 'The Parlements of Paris and the Breakdown of the Old Regime', *French Historical Studies*, 1970.

Doyle, William, *The Parlement of Bordeaux and the End of the Old Regime, 1771–1790* (London, 1974).

Doyle, William, 'Provinces', in S. F. Scott and B. Rothaus (eds), *Historical Dictionary of the French Revolution* (2 vols, Westport, CT, 1985).

Doyle, William, *The Oxford History of the French Revolution* (Oxford, 1989).

Dubreuil, Léon, 'Sur le régionalisme pendant la Révolution', *Annales Révolutionnaires* 9–11 (1917–19).

Ducaunnès-Duval, G., 'Les municipalités de Bordeaux sous le Directoire', *Revue historique de Bordeaux* 6 (1913).

Dupâquier, Jacques, 'Le procès de Carrier', in Michel Vovelle (ed.), *Le tournant de l'an III. Réaction et Terreur blanche dans la France révolutionnaire* (Paris, 1997).

Dupuy, Roger, *La Garde Nationale et les débuts de la Révolution en Ille-et-Vilaine, 1789–mars 1793* (Paris, 1972).

Dupuy, Roger, *De la Révolution à la chouannerie. Paysans en Bretagne, 1788–94* (Paris, 1988).

Dupuy, Roger (ed.), *Pouvoir local et révolution: la frontière intérieure* (Rennes, 1995).

Dziembowski, Edmond, *Un nouveau patriotisme français, 1750–70. La France face à la puissance anglaise à l'époque de la guerre de Sept Ans* (Oxford, 1998).

Echeverria, Durand, *The Maupeou Revolution: a Study in the History of Libertarianism. France, 1770–74* (Baton Rouge, LA, 1985).

Edelstein, Melvin, *La Feuille Villageoise. Communication et modernisation dans les régions rurales pendant la Révolution* (Paris, 1977).

Edelstein, Melvin, 'Electoral behaviour during the Constitutional Monarchy (1790–91): a "community" interpretation', in Renée Waldinger, Philip Dawson and Isser Woloch (eds), *The French Revolution and the Meaning of Citizenship* (Westport, CT, 1993).

Edmonds, W. D., 'Federalism and urban revolt in France in 1793', *Journal of Modern History* 55 (1983).

Edmonds, W. D., *Jacobinism and the Revolt of Lyon, 1789–93* (Oxford, 1990).

Egret, Jean, *La Révolution des Notables. Mounier et les Monarchiens, 1789* (Paris, 1950).

Egret, Jean, *The French Pre-revolution, 1787–88* (Chicago, 1977).

Ellis, Harold A., *Boulainvilliers and the French Monarchy: Aristocratic Politics in Early Eighteenth-century France* (Ithaca, NY, 1988).

Fairchilds, Cissie, 'The Production and Marketing of Populuxe Goods in Eighteenth-century Paris', in John Brewer and Roy Porter (eds), *Consumption and the World of Goods* (London, 1993).

Farge, Arlette, *La vie fragile: violence, pouvoirs et solidarités à Paris au dix-huitième siècle* (Paris, 1986).

Farge, Arlette, *Dire et mal dire. L'opinion publique au dix-huitième siècle* (Paris, 1992).

Farge, Arlette, *Subversive Words. Public Opinion in Eighteenth-century France* (Cambridge, 1994).

Farge, Arlette and Revel, Jacques, *The Vanishing Children of Paris. Rumour and Politics Before the French Revolution* (Cambridge, MA, 1991).

Félix, Joel, *Finances et politique au siècle des Lumières: le ministère L'Averdy, 1763–68* (Paris, 1999).

Fitzsimmons, Michael P., *The Remaking of France: The National Assembly and the Constitution of 1791* (Cambridge, 1994).

Fitzsimmons, Michael P., *The Night the Old Regime Ended: August 4, 1789, and the French Revolution* (University Park, PA, 2003).

Forrest, Alan, *Society and Politics in Revolutionary Bordeaux* (Oxford, 1975).

Forrest, Alan, 'Federalism' in Colin Lucas (ed.), *The French Revolution and the Creation of Modern Political Culture, ii: The Political Culture of the French Revolution* (Oxford, 1988).

Forrest, Alan, *Conscripts and Deserters. The Army and French Society during the Revolution and Empire* (New York, 1989).

Forrest, Alan, 'Le découpage administratif de la France révolutionnaire', in Centre Méridional d'Histoire, *L'espace et le temps reconstruits. La Révolution Française, une révolution des mentalités et des cultures?* (Aix-en-Provence, 1990).

Forrest, Alan, *The Soldiers of the French Revolution* (Durham, NC, 1990).

Forrest, Alan, *The Revolution in Provincial France: Aquitaine, 1789–99* (Oxford, 1996).

Forrest, Alan, 'Paris versus the provinces: regionalism and decentralisation since 1789', in Martin Alexander (ed.), *French History since Napoleon* (London, 1999).

Forrest, Alan and Jones, Peter (eds), *Reshaping France: Town, Country and Region during the French Revolution* (Manchester, 1991).

Foucault, Michel, *Discipline and Punish. The Birth of the Prison* (London, 1977).

Fournier, Georges, 'Réalité et limites de la réaction thermidorienne dans l'Hérault, l'Aude et la Haute-Garonne', in Michel Vovelle (ed.), *Le tournant de l'an III. Réaction et Terreur blanche dans la France révolutionnaire* (Paris, 1997).

Francesco, Antonino de, *Il governo senza testa. Movimento democratico e federalismo nella Francia rivoluzionaria, 1789–95* (Naples, 1992).

Frénay, Etienne (ed.), *Cahiers de doléances de la Province de Roussillon, 1789* (Perpignan, 1979).

Fuoc, Renée, *La réaction thermidorienne à Lyon, 1795* (Lyon, 1957).

Gainot, Bernard, 'La province au crible des rapports des commissaires départementaux du Directoire', *Annales historiques de la Révolution Française* 330 (2002).

Garrioch, David, *Neighbourhood and Community in Paris, 1740–1790* (Cambridge, 1986).

Garrioch, David, *The Formation of the Parisian Bourgeoisie, 1690–1830* (Cambridge, MA, 1996).

Garrioch, David, *The Making of Revolutionary Paris* (Berkeley, CA, 2002).

Gaston-Martin, *La mission de Carrier à Nantes* (Paris, 1924).

Gégot, J.-C., 'Le rôle des représentants-en-mission sous la Révolution dans l'Hérault', in *Les pratiques politiques en province à l'époque de la Révolution Française. Actes du colloque tenu à Montpellier les 18, 19 et 20 septembre 1987* (Montpellier, 1988).

Gendron, François, *La jeunesse dorée. Episodes de la Révolution Française* (Montréal, 1979).

George, Jocelyne, *Histoire des maires, 1789–1939* (Paris, 1989).

Gérard, Alain, *La Vendée, 1789–93* (Paris, 1992).

Gérard, Pierre, 'L'armée révolutionnaire de la Haute-Garonne, septembre 1793–nivôse an II', *Annales historiques de la Révolution française* 155 (1959).

Gérard, René, *Un journal de province sous la Révolution: Le Journal de Marseille de Ferréol Beaugeard, 1781–97* (Paris, 1964).

Gershoy, Leo, *Bertrand Barère, A Reluctant Terrorist* (Princeton, NJ, 1962).

Gildea, Robert, *The Past in French History* (New Haven, 1994).

Girardet, Raoul, 'La Vendée dans le légendaire national français', in Alain Gérard and Thierry Heckmann (eds), *La Vendée dans l'histoire* (Paris, 1994).

Gobry, Ivan, *Joseph le Bon: la Terreur dans le Nord de la France* (Paris, 1991).

Godechot, Jacques, *Les institutions de la France sous la Révolution et l'Empire* (Paris, 1951).

Godechot, Jacques (ed.), *Les constitutions de la France depuis 1789* (Paris, 1970).

Godechot, Jacques, *The Taking of the Bastille* (London, 1970).

Godechot, Jacques, *La Révolution Française dans le Midi Toulousain* (Toulouse, 1986).

Godineau, Dominique, *The Women of Paris and their French Revolution* (Berkeley, CA, 1998).

Goodman, Dena, *The Republic of Letters: A Cultural History of the French Enlightenment* (Ithaca, NY, 1994).

Goodwin, Albert, *The French Revolution* (London, 1953).

Goodwin, Albert, 'The federalist movement in Caen during the French Revolution', *Bulletin of the John Rylands Library* 42 (1960).

Gotlib, Roland, 'Les Gravilliers, plate-forme des enragés parisiens', in Michel Vovelle (ed.), *Paris et la Révolution* (Paris, 1989).

Goubert, Pierre, 'Sociétés rurales françaises du dix-huitième siècle: vingt paysanneries contrastées', in P. Goubert (ed.), *Clio parmi les hommes* (Paris, 1976).

Gough, Hugh, *The Newspaper Press in the French Revolution* (London, 1988).

Gourel de Saint-Pern, Thérèse, 'Particularisme et provincialisme en Provence, 1787–90' (mémoire de maîtrise, Université d'Aix-en-Provence, 1969).

Goyeneche, E., *Le Pays Basque: Soule – Labourd – Basse-Navarre* (Pau, 1979).

Gras, Christian and Livet, Georges (eds), *Régions et régionalisme en France du dix-huitième siècle à nos jours* (Paris, 1977).

Gravier, Jean-François, *Paris et le désert français* (Paris, 1947).

Greer, Donald, *The Incidence of the Terror during the French Revolution. A Statistical Interpretation* (Cambridge, MA, 1935).

Greer, Donald, *The Incidence of the Emigration during the French Revolution* (Cambridge, MA, 1951).

Gross, Jean-Pierre, *Saint-Just: sa politique et ses missions* (Paris, 1976).

Gross, Jean-Pierre, *Fair Shares for All: Jacobin Egalitarianism in Practice* (Cambridge, 1997).

Guégan, Isabelle, *Inventaire des enquêtes administratives et statistiques, 1789–95* (Paris, 1991).

Gueniffey, Patrice, *Le nombre et la raison. La Révolution Française et les élections* (Paris, 1993).

Gueniffey, Patrice, *La politique de la Terreur. Essai sur la violence révolutionnaire, 1789–94* (Paris, 2000).

Guignet, Philippe, *Le pouvoir dans la ville au dix-huitième siècle* (Paris, 1990).

Guilhaumou, Jacques, 'Fédéralisme jacobin et fédéralisme sectionnaire à Marseille en 1793: analyse de discours', *Provence historique* 36 (1987).

Guilhaumou, Jacques, *La langue politique et la Révolution Française. De l'évènement à la raison linguistique* (Paris, 1989).

Guilhaumou, Jacques, *Marseille républicaine, 1791–93* (Paris, 1992).

Guiomer, Jean-Yves, *L'idéologie nationale: nation, représentation, propriété* (Paris, 1974).

Guttwirth Madelyn, *The Twilight of the Goddesses. Women and Representation in the French Revolutionary Era* (New Brunswick, NJ, 1992).

Halévi, Ran, 'La sociabilité maçonnique et les origines de la pratique démocratique' (thèse de doctorat, EHESS, 1981).

Halévi, Ran, *Les loges maçonniques dans la France d'Ancien Régime. Aux origines de la sociabilité démocratique* (Paris, 1984).

Hanson, Paul, *Provincial Politics in the French Revolution. Caen and Limoges, 1789–94* (Baton Rouge, LA, 1989).

Hanson, Paul, *The Jacobin Republic Under Fire. The Federalist Revolt in the French Revolution* (University Park, PA, 2003).

Hardman, John (ed.), *French Revolution Documents, ii, 1792–95* (Oxford, 1973).

Hazareesingh, Sudhir, *Political Traditions in Modern France* (Oxford, 1994).

Herbert, Sydney, *The Fall of Feudalism in France* (London, 1921).

Herriot, Edouard, *Lyon n'est plus* (4 vols, Paris, 1939).

Higonnet, Patrice, *Goodness beyond Virtue. Jacobins during the French Revolution* (Cambridge, MA, 1998).

Higonnet, Patrice, *Paris, Capital of the World* (Cambridge, MA, 2002).

Hirsch, Jean-Pierre, *La nuit du 4 août* (Paris, 1978).

Horne, John and Kramer, Alan, *German Atrocities, 1914. A History of Denial* (New Haven, 2001).

Hourmat, Pierre, *Histoire de Bayonne: i – Des origines à la Révolution Française* (Bayonne, 1986).

Hufton, Olwen, *The Poor of Eighteenth-century France, 1750–1789* (Oxford, 1974).

Hufton, Olwen, 'The reconstruction of a church, 1796–1801', in Gwynne Lewis and Colin Lucas (eds), *Beyond the Terror. Essays in French Regional and Social History, 1794–1815* (Cambridge, 1983).

Hufton, Olwen, *Women and the Limits of Citizenship in the French Revolution* (Toronto, 1992).

Hunt, Lynn, 'Committees and communes: local politics and national revolution in 1789', *Comparative Studies in Society and History* 18 (1976).

Hunt, Lynn, *Revolution and Urban Politics in Provincial France. Troyes and Reims, 1786–90* (Stanford, CA, 1978).

Hyslop, Beatrice F., *A Guide to the General Cahiers of 1789* (New York, 1936).

Jaume, Lucien, *Le discours jacobin de la démocratie* (Paris, 1989).

Jessenne, Jean-Pierre, *Pouvoir au village et révolution. Artois, 1760–1848* (Lille, 1987).

Jessenne, Jean-Pierre, 'De la citoyenneté proclamée à la citoyenneté appliquée: l'exercice du droit de vote dans le district d'Arras en 1790', *Revue du Nord* 72 (1990).

Johnson, Hubert C., *The Midi in Revolution. A Study of Regional Political Diversity, 1789–93* (Princeton, NJ, 1986).

Jollet, Anne, *Terre et société en Révolution. Approche du lien social dans la région d'Amboise* (Paris, 2000).

Jones, Colin, *The Longman Companion to the French Revolution* (London, 1988).

Jones, Colin, *The Great Nation. France from Louis XV to Napoleon* (London, 2003).

Jones, Peter, *Liberty and Locality in Revolutionary France. Six Villages Compared, 1760–1820* (Cambridge, 2003).

Jones, P. M., *The Peasantry in the French Revolution* (Cambridge, 1988).

Jones, P. M., *Reform and Revolution in France: The Politics of Transition, 1774–91* (Cambridge, 1995).

Kaplan, Steven L., 'The Famine Plot Persuasion in Eighteenth-Century France', *Transactions of the American Philosophical Society* 72 (1982).

Kaplow, Jeffrey, *Elbeuf during the Revolutionary Period: History and Social Structure* (Baltimore, 1964).

Kaplow, Jeffrey, 'Sur la population flottante de Paris à la fin de l'Ancien Régime', *Annales historiques de la Révolution Française* 187 (1967).

Kaplow, Jeffrey, *Les noms des rois. Les pauvres de Paris à la veille de la Révolution* (Paris, 1974).

Kennedy, Michael L., *The Jacobin Club of Marseilles, 1790–94* (Ithaca, NY, 1973).

Kennedy, Michael L., *The Jacobin Clubs in the French Revolution. The Middle Years* (Princeton, NJ, 1988).

Kennedy, Michael L., *The Jacobin Clubs in the French Revolution, 1793–95* (New York, 2000).

Kuscinski, A., *Dictionnaire des conventionnels* (Paris, 1916).

Kwass, Michael, *Privilege and the Politics of Taxation in Eighteenth-century France* (Cambridge, 2000).

Labrosse, Claude and Rétat, Pierre, *Naissance du journal révolutionnaire, 1789* (Lyon, 1989).

Labroue, Henri, *L'esprit public en Dordogne pendant la Révolution* (Paris, 1911).

Labroue, Henri, *La mission du conventionnel Lakanal dans la Dordogne en l'an II* (Paris, 1911).

Lacour, Catherine, 'La province dans l'idéologie révolutionnaire: étude d'un discours politique' (mémoire de maîtrise, Université de Paris – I, 1988).

Lacouture, Jean, *Le mouvement royaliste dans le Sud-ouest, 1797–1800* (Hossegor, 1932).

Laffon, J.-B. and Soulet, J.-F. (eds), *Histoire de Tarbes* (Roanne, 1982).

Lagrave, Henri, Mazouer, Charles and Regaldo, Marc (eds), *La vie théâtrale à Bordeaux des origines à nos jours, vol. 1 – des origines à 1799* (Paris, 1985).

Langlois, Claude, Tackett, Timothy and Vovelle, Michel (eds), *Atlas de la Révolution Française, vol. 9: Religion* (Paris, 1996).

Lapied, Martine, *Le Comtat et la Révolution Française: naissance des options collectives* (Aix-en-Provence, 1996).

Laurent, Robert and Gavignaud, Geneviève, *La Révolution Française dans le Languedoc méditerranéen* (Toulouse, 1987).

Lavergne, Léonce de, *Les assemblées provinciales sous Louis XVI* (Paris, 1864).

Le Boterf, A., 'La vente des biens nationaux dans le District de Saint-Sever, 1791–an X' (mémoire de maîtrise, Université de Paris – I, 1971).

Le Bozec, Christine and Wauters, Eric (eds), *Pour la Révolution Française. Études en hommage à Claude Mazauric* (Rouen, 1998).

Lefebvre, Georges, *La Grande Peur de 1789* (Paris, 1932).

Lefebvre, Georges, *Les paysans du Nord pendant la Révolution Française* (Bari, 1959).

Lefebvre, Georges, *The French Revolution* (2 vols, London, 1962–4).

Lefebvre, Georges, *The Thermidorians* (London, 1964).

Le Goff, T.J.A., *Vannes and its Region. A Study of Town and Country in Eighteenth-century France* (Oxford, 1981).

Legrand-Baumier, Béatrice, 'La réforme municipale de L'Averdy 1764–65: glas de la représentation patricienne au sein des corps de ville? L'exemple de Tours', in Claude Petitfrère (ed.), *Construction, reproduction et représentation des patriciats urbains de l'Antiquité au 20e siècle* (Tours, 2000).

Leguillois, Robert, 'Étude de la population masculine de Paris en 1793 d'après les cartes de sûreté', in Michel Vovelle (ed.), *Paris et la Révolution* (Paris, 1989).

Le Marec, Yannick, *Le temps des capacités. Les diplômés nantais à la conquête du pouvoir dans la ville* (Paris, 2000).

Lemay, Edna Hindie (ed.), *Dictionnaire des Constituants, 1789–91* (2 vols, Oxford and Paris, 1991).

Lepetit, Bernard, *Les villes dans la France moderne, 1740–1840* (Paris, 1988).

Lerat, Serge, *Landes et Chalosses* (2 vols, Pau, 1983–4).

Le Roy Ladurie, Emmanuel, *Histoire de France des régions. La périphérie française, des origines à nos jours* (Paris, 2001).

Leuwers, Hervé, 'Elire les juges: l'exemple des juges des tribunaux de district du Nord et du Pas-de-Calais, 1790–1792', in Robert Chagny (ed.), *La Révolution Française: idéaux, singularités, influences* (Grenoble, 2002).

Lévêque, Roger, *Napoléon, ville de Vendée. La naissance de La Roche-sur-Yon* (La Roche-sur-Yon, 1998).

Lewis, Gwynne, *The Second Vendée: The Continuity of Counter-revolution in the Department of the Gard, 1789–1815* (Oxford, 1978).

Lewis, Gwynne and Lucas, Colin (eds), *Beyond the Terror. Essays in French Regional and Social History, 1794–1815* (Cambridge, 1983).

Lhéritier, Michel, *Liberté, 1789–90: les Girondins, Bordeaux et la Révolution Française* (Paris, 1947).

Lhéritier, Michel, *L'Intendant Tourny, 1695–1760* (2 vols, Paris, 1920).

Ligou, Daniel, *Montauban à la fin de l'Ancien Régime et aux débuts de la Révolution, 1787–94* (Paris, 1958).

Luc, Jean-Noël (ed.), *La Charente-Maritime: l'Aunis et la Saintonge des origines à nos jours* (Saint-Jean-d'Angély, 1981).

Lucas, Colin, *The Structure of the Terror. The Example of Javogues and the Loire* (Oxford, 1973).

Lucas, Colin, 'The First Directory and the Rule of Law', *French Historical Studies* 10 (1977).

Lucas, Colin, 'Themes in southern violence after 9 thermidor', in Gwynne Lewis and Colin Lucas (eds), *Beyond the Terror. Essays in French Regional and Social History, 1794–1815* (Cambridge, 1983).

Lucas, Colin (ed.), *The French Revolution and the Creation of Modern Political Culture, vol. 2: The Political Culture of the French Revolution* (Oxford, 1988).

Lucas, Colin, 'The Rules of the Game in Local Politics under the Directory', *French Historical Studies* 16 (1989).

Lucas, Colin, 'Talking about urban popular violence in 1789', in Alan Forrest and Peter Jones (eds), *Reshaping France: Town, Country and Region during the French Revolution* (Manchester, 1991).

Lucas, Colin, 'Les thermidoriens et les violences de l'an III', in Roger Dupuy and Marcel Morabito (eds), *1795. Pour une République sans Révolution* (Rennes, 1996).

Luckett, Thomas Manley, 'Hunting for Spies and Whores: A Parisian Riot on the Eve of the French Revolution', *Past and Present* 156 (1997).

Lüsebrink, Hans-Jürgen and Reichart, Rolf, *The Bastille, a History of a Symbol of Despotism and Freedom* (Durham, NC, 1997).

Luxardo, Hervé, *Histoire de la Marseillaise* (Paris, 1989).

Lyons, Martyn, *France under the Directory* (Cambridge, 1975).

Lyons, Martyn, *Révolution et Terreur à Toulouse* (Toulouse, 1980).

Lyons, Martyn, 'Politics and patois: the linguistic policy of the French Revolution', *Australian Journal of French Studies* 18 (1981).

Maciak, Jill, 'Learning to Love the Republic: Jacobin Propaganda and the Peasantry of the Haute-Garonne', *European Review of History* 6 (1999).

McLeod, Jane, 'A Social Study of Printers and Booksellers in Bordeaux from 1745 to 1810' (PhD, York University, Toronto, 1987).

McManners, John, *Church and Society in Eighteenth-century France* (2 vols, Oxford, 1998).

McPhee, Peter, *Revolution and Environment in Southern France. Peasants, Lords, and Murder in the Corbières, 1780–1830* (Oxford, 1999).

McPhee, Peter, '"The misguided greed of peasants"? Popular attitudes to the environment in the Revolution of 1789', *French Historical Studies* 24 (2001).

Maltby, Richard, 'Le brigandage dans la Drôme, 1795–1803', *Bulletin d'archéologie et de statistique de la Drôme* 79 (1973).

Mansfield, Paul, 'The Missions of Collot d'Herbois. A Study in his Political Career' (unpublished PhD thesis, Macquarie University, 1985).

Margadant, Ted W., *Urban Rivalries in the French Revolution* (Princeton, NJ, 1992).

Marion, Marcel, *Dictionnaire des institutions de la France* (Paris, 1923).

Markoff, John, *The Abolition of Feudalism: Peasants, Lords and Legislators in the French Revolution* (University Park, PA, 1996).

Markov, Walter and Soboul, Albert (eds), *Die Sansculotten von Paris. Dokumente zur Geschichte der Volksbewegung, 1793–94* (East Berlin, 1957).

Martel, Philippe, 'Le Félibrige', in Pierre Nora (ed.), *Les lieux de mémoire*, part 3, *Les France*, vol. 2, *Traditions* (Paris, 1992).

Martin, Jean-Clément, *La Vendée et la France* (Paris, 1987).

Martin, Jean-Clément, *La Vendée de la mémoire* (Paris, 1989).

Martin, Jean-Clément (ed.), *Religion et Révolution* (Paris, 1994).

Martin, Jean-Clément, *Révolution et contre-révolution. Les rouages de l'histoire* (Rennes, 1996).

Melchior, Jeanne, 'Histoire du Club National' (thèse de doctorat, Université de Bordeaux, 1951).

Merriman, John, *The Stones of Balazuc. A French Village in Time* (New York, 2002).

Métairie, Guillaume, *Le monde des juges de paix de Paris, 1790–1838* (Paris, 1994).

Meyer, Jean, *Études sur les villes en Europe occidentale, du milieu du 17e siècle à la veille de la Révolution Française*, vol. 1 – *France* (Paris, 1983).

Mitchell, Harvey, 'The Vendée and counter-revolution – a review essay', *French Historical Studies* 5 (1968).

Mitchell, Harvey, 'Resistance to the Revolution in Western France', *Past and Present* 63 (1974).

Monnier, Raymonde, 'L'image de Paris de 1789 à 1794: Paris capitale de la Révolution', in Michel Vovelle (ed.), *L'image de la Révolution Française* (4 vols, Paris, 1989), vol. 1.

Moulinas, René, *Histoire de la Révolution d'Avignon* (Avignon, 1986).

Naudin, Michel, *Structures et doléances du Tiers Etat de Moulins en 1789* (Paris, 1987).

Nicolas, Jean, *La Révolution Française dans les Alpes, Dauphiné et Savoie* (Toulouse, 1989).

Nières, Claude, 'Les obstacles provinciaux au centralisme et à l'uniformisation en France au dix-huitième siècle', in Roger Dupuy (ed.), *Pouvoir local et révolution: la frontière intérieure* (Rennes, 1995).

Nieto, Philippe, *Le centenaire de la Révolution dauphinoise. Vizille, un mythe républicain* (Grenoble, 1988).

Ozouf, Mona, *La fête révolutionnaire, 1789–99* (Paris, 1976).

Ozouf, Mona, *L'école de la France: essais sur la Révolution, l'utopie et l'enseignement* (Paris, 1984).

Ozouf, Mona, *L'homme régénéré. Essais sur la Révolution Française* (Paris, 1989).

Ozouf-Marignier, Marie-Vic, *La formation des départements. La représentation du territoire français à la fin du dix-huitième siècle* (Paris, 1989).

Pages, G., 'Lettres de requis et volontaires de Coutras en Vendée et en Bretagne', *Revue historique et archéologique du Libournais* 190 (1983).

Palmer, R. R., *From Jacobin to Liberal. Marc-Antoine Jullien, 1775–1848* (Princeton, NJ, 1993).

Pardailhé-Galabrun, Annik, *La naissance de l'intime. 3000 foyers parisiens, xviie–xviiie siècles* (Paris, 1988).

Pariset, François-Georges (ed.), *Bordeaux au dix-huitième siècle* (Bordeaux, 1968).

Patrick, Alison, *The Men of the First French Republic. Political Alignments in the National Convention of 1792* (Baltimore, 1972).

Patrick, Alison, 'French Revolutionary Local Government, 1789–92', in Colin Lucas (ed.), *The French Revolution and the Creation of Modern Political Culture, vol. 2: The Political Culture of the French Revolution* (Oxford, 1988).

Péronnet, Michel, 'Province, Provinces', in Lucien Bély (ed.), *Dictionnaire de l'Ancien Régime* (Paris, 1996).

Perrot, Jean-Claude and Woolf, Stuart, *State and Statistics in France, 1789–1815* (Chur and London, 1984).

Petitfrère, Claude, 'Un anticlérical angevin: La Révellière-Lépeaux et sa religion, 1753–1824', in Jean-Clément Martin (ed.), *Religion et Révolution* (Paris, 1994).

Peyrard, Christine, *Les Jacobins de l'Ouest. Sociabilité révolutionnaire et formes de politisation dans le Maine et la Basse-Normandie, 1789–99* (Paris, 1996).

Pierre, Roger (ed.), *240,000 Drômois aux quatre vents de la Révolution* (Valence, 1989).

Pijassou, R., 'La crise révolutionnaire', in Arlette Higounet-Nadal (ed.), *Histoire du Périgord* (Toulouse, 1983).

Pingué, Danièle, *Les mouvements jacobins en Normandie orientale: les sociétés politiques dans l'Eure et la Seine-inférieure, 1790–95* (Paris, 2001).

Poirier, Jean-Pierre, *Turgot. Laissez-faire et progrès social* (Paris, 1999).

Poitrineau, Abel, *Remues d'hommes. Les migrations montagnardes en France aux 17e et 18e siècles* (Paris, 1983).

Popkin, Jeremy D., *The Right-wing Press in France, 1792–1800* (Chapel Hill, NC, 1980).

Popkin, Jeremy D., *News and Politics in the Age of Revolution: Jean Luzac's* Gazette de Leyde (Ithaca, NY, 1989).

Popkin, Jeremy D., *Revolutionary News. The Press in France, 1789–99* (Durham, NC, 1990).

Popkin, Jeremy D. (ed.), *Panorama of Paris: Selections from* Le Tableau de Paris *by Louis-Sébastien Mercier* (University Park, PA, 1999).

Potter, David, *War and Government in the French Provinces. Picardy, 1470–1560* (Cambridge, 1993).

Poussou, Jean-Pierre, *Bordeaux et le Sud-ouest au dix-huitième siècle: croissance économique et attraction urbaine* (Paris, 1983).

Quétel, Claude, *Escape from the Bastille: The Life and Legend of Latude* (Cambridge, 1990).

Ramsay, Clay, *The Ideology of the Great Fear. The Soissonnais in 1789* (Baltimore, MD, 1992).

Rapport, Michael, *Nationality and Citizenship in Revolutionary France: the Treatment of Foreigners, 1789–99* (Oxford, 2000).

Reinhard, Marcel, *Nouvelle histoire de Paris: la Révolution* (Paris, 1971).

Rétat, Pierre, 'La légitimation du discours révolutionnaire dans le journal de 1789', in Michel Vovelle (ed.), *Aux origines provinciales de la Révolution* (Grenoble, 1990).

Rey, Alain, *'Révolution'. Histoire d'un mot* (Paris, 1989).

Richard, A., 'Les troubles agraires dans les Landes en 1791 et 1792', *Annales historiques de la Révolution Française* 4 (1927).

Riffaterre, C., *Le mouvement anti-jacobin et anti-parisien à Lyon et dans le Rhône-et-Loire* (2 vols, Lyon, 1912–28).

Roberts, J. M. and Cobb, R. C. (eds), *French Revolution Documents* (Oxford, 1966).

Robin, Florent, *Les représentants en mission dans l'Isère: chronique d'une Terreur 'douce'* (Paris, 2002).

Roche, Daniel, *Le siècle des lumières en province. Académies et académiciens provinciaux, 1680–1789* (2 vols, Paris, 1978).

Roche, Daniel, *The People of Paris. An Essay in Popular Culture in the Eighteenth Century* (Leamington Spa, 1987).

Roche, Daniel, *A History of Everyday Things. The Birth of Consumption in France, 1600–1800* (Cambridge, 2000).

Roche, Daniel (ed.), *La ville promise. Mobilité et accueil à Paris, fin 17e–début 19e siècle* (Paris, 2000).

Rose, R. B., 'The revolutionary committees of the Paris sections in 1793: a manuscript in the John Rylands Library', *Bulletin of the John Rylands Library* 35 (1952–3).

Rose, R. B., *The Enragés: Socialists of the French Revolution?* (Melbourne, 1965).

Rose, R. B., *The Making of the Sans-culottes* (Manchester, 1983).

Rudé, George, *The Crowd in the French Revolution* (Oxford, 1959).

Saint-Jacob, Pierre de, *Les paysans de la Bourgogne du Nord au dernier siècle de l'Ancien Régime* (Dijon, 1960).

Scott, William, *Terror and Repression in Revolutionary Marseilles* (London, 1973).

Secher, Reynald, *Le génocide franco-français. La Vendée-vengé* (Paris, 1986).

Shapiro, Gilbert and Markoff, John, *Revolutionary Demands: A Content Analysis of the Cahiers de Doléances of 1789* (Stanford, CA, 1998).

Shennan, J. H., *The Parlement of Paris* (London, 1968).

Sieyès, Emmanuel-Joseph, *Observations sur le rapport du Comité de Constitution concernant la nouvelle organisation de la France* (Paris, 1789).

Sieyès, Emmanuel-Jospeh, *Qu'est-ce que le Tiers Etat?* ed. Jean Tulard (Paris, 1982).

Sirich, John Black, *The Revolutionary Committees in the Departments of France, 1793–94* (Cambridge, MA, 1943).

Skinner, Jonathan, 'Republicanism and Royalism. The Conflicting Traditions of Peasant Politics in the Department of the Vaucluse, 1789–1851' (PhD thesis, University of Manchester, 1988).

Slavin, Morris, *The Making of an Insurrection: Parisian Sections and the Gironde* (Cambridge, MA, 1986).

Slavin, Morris, *The Hébertistes to the Guillotine: Anatomy of a 'Conspiracy' in Revolutionary France* (Baton Rouge, LA, 1994).

Smith, Jay M., *The Culture of Merit: Nobility, Royal Service and the Making of Absolute Monarchy in France, 1600–1789* (Ann Arbor, MI, 1996).

Soboul, Albert, *Les sans-culottes parisiens de l'an II* (Paris, 1962).

Soboul, Albert, 'De l'Ancien Régime à la Révolution: problème régional et réalités sociales', in Gras and Livet (eds), *Régions et régionalisme en France du dix-huitième siècle à nos jours* (Paris, 1977).

Soboul, Albert and Monnier, Raymonde, *Répertoire du personnel sectionnaire parisien en l'an II* (Paris, 1985).

Sonenscher, Michael, 'Journeymen, the courts and the French trades, 1781–91', *Past and Present* 114 (1987).

Sonenscher, Michael, *Work and Wages. Natural Law, Politics and the Eighteenth-century French Trades* (Cambridge, 1989).

Spagnoli, Paul G., 'The Revolution Begins: Lambesc's Charge, 12 July 1789', *French Historical Studies* 17 (1991).

Stewart, John Hall, *A Documentary Survey of the French Revolution* (New York, 1951).

Sutherland, Donald, *The Chouans. The Social Origins of Popular Counter-Revolution in Upper Brittany, 1770–96* (Oxford, 1982).

Sutherland, Donald, *The French Revolution and Empire. The Quest for a Civic Order* (Oxford, 2003).

Sydenham, Michael, 'The Republican revolt of 1793 – a plea for less localised local studies', *French Historical Studies* 12 (1981).

Sydenham, Michael, *Léonard Bourdon. The Career of a Revolutionary, 1754–1807* (Waterloo, Ontario, 1999).

Tacheva, Rossitza, 'Sur certains aspects de l'activité sociale des Jacobins parisiens, 1792–94', in Michel Vovelle (ed.), *Paris et la Révolution* (Paris, 1989).

Tackett, Timothy, *Priest and Parish in Eighteenth-century France* (Princeton, NJ, 1977).

Tackett, Timothy, 'The West in France in 1789: The Religious Factor in the Origins of Counter-revolution', *Journal of Modern History* 54 (1982).

Tackett, Timothy, *La Révolution, l'Église, la France* (Paris, 1986).

Tackett, Timothy, *Becoming a Revolutionary. The Deputies of the French National Assembly and the Emergence of a Revolutionary Culture, 1789–90* (Princeton, NJ, 1996).

Tackett, Timothy and Langlois, Claude, 'Ecclesiastical structures and clerical geography on the eve of the French Revolution', *French Historical Studies* 11 (1980).

Taillefer, François (ed.), *Les Pyrénées de la montagne à l'homme* (Toulouse, 1974).

Taylor, George V., 'Revolutionary and non-revolutionary content in the *cahiers* of 1789: an interim report', *French Historical Studies* 7 (1972).

Thiesse, Anne-Marie, *Ils apprenaient la France: l'exaltation des régions dans le discours patriotique* (Paris, 1997).

Thomas, Chantal, *The Wicked Queen. The Origins of the Myth of Marie-Antoinette* (New York, 1999).

Thompson, Eric, *Popular Sovereignty and the French Constituent Assembly, 1789–91* (Manchester, 1952).

Tilly, Charles, 'Local conflicts in the Vendée before the Rebellion of 1793', *French Historical Studies* 2 (1961).

Tønnesson, Kåre, *La défaite des sans-culottes. Mouvement populaire et réaction bourgeoise en l'an III* (Oslo and Paris, 1959).

Trénard, Louis (ed.), *Histoire de Lille* (2 vols, Toulouse, 1981).

Tulard, Jean, *Nouvelle Histoire de Paris: la Révolution* (Paris, 1989).

Turreau, Louis-Marie, *Memoirs for the History of the War of la Vendée* (London, 1796).

Tyson, Peter, 'The Role of Republican and *Patriote* Discourse in the Insurrection of the Vendée' (M.A. dissertation, University of York, 1994).

Uriu, Yoichi, 'Espace et Révolution, enquête, grande peur et fédérations', *Annales historiques de la Révolution Française* 280 (1990).

Vovelle, Michel (ed.), *La Révolution Française, images et récit* (5 vols, Paris, 1986).

Vovelle, Michel (ed.), *L'état de la France pendant la Révolution* (Paris, 1988).

Vovelle, Michel (ed.), *L'image de la Révolution Française* (4 vols, Paris, 1989).

Vovelle, Michel (ed.), *Recherches sur la Révolution* (Paris, 1991).

Vovelle, Michel, *The Revolution against the Church* (Cambridge, 1991).

Vovelle, Michel, *La découverte de la politique. Géopolitique de la Révolution Française* (Paris, 1992).

Vovelle, Michel, *Les Jacobins de Robespierre à Chevènement* (Paris, 1999).

Wahnich, Sophie, *L'impossible citoyen: l'étranger dans le discours de la Révolution Française* (Paris, 1997).

Wallon, Henri, *La Révolution du 31 mai et le fédéralisme en 1793* (2 vols, Paris, 1886).

Wauters, Eric, 'La dialectique province-Paris dans la presse des départements: entre vie politique locale et réseaux nationaux d'opinion', *Annales historiques de la Révolution française* 330 (2002).

Whaley, Leigh, *Radicals: Politics and Republicanism in the French Revolution* (Stroud, 2000).

Williams, Alan, *The Police of Paris, 1718–89* (Baton Rouge, LA, 1979).

Woloch, Isser, *Jacobin Legacy. The Democratic Movement under the Directory* (Princeton, NJ, 1970).

Woloch, Isser, *The New Regime. Transformations of the French Civic Order, 1789–1820s* (New York, 1994).

Wrigley, Richard, *The Politics of Appearances. Representations of Dress in Revolutionary France* (Oxford, 2002).

Young, Arthur, *Travels in France during the Years 1787, 1788 and 1789* (London, 1889).

Index